D1086765

OCT 2009

PUBLIC LIBRARY

"Back in the day, *everybody* in New York watched Clay Cole."
— Frankie Valli

"Clay Cole. Saturday Night. Rock 'n' Roll. New York City. Glued to the tube. I should know; I was there." *— Dion*

"Thanks for all the wonderful and warm memories. You lit up our Saturday nights and then every other night. You didn't know it, but I had a secret crush on you. (Don't tell that to the National Enquirer.)"
With admiration and affection, *Connie Francis*

"I was always jealous of that head of hair and your tall, skinny body! Otherwise, good memories of your TV show and the Brooklyn Paramount."
— Neil Sedaka

"I remember watching and loving the Clay Cole Show with my girlfriends and talking about what a cool and handsome guy he was. Today's young ladies would call him a hunk."
— Gloria Gaynor

"Clay Cole is an unsung hero far too long; He is a true friend to all of us."
—Anthony Gourdine (Little Anthony & the Imperials)

"When we came to America we were told we *should* do Ed Sullivan and Clay Cole. Trouble is we didn't know which was which. So we did Clay and then Ed came through!"
— Peter Noone (Herman's Hermits)

"What made the Clay Cole Show so special was Clay Cole. Clay was *talented, personable, professional* and *fun*! His personal interest in presenting the artist in the best possible light made it a great show to do."
— Johnny Tillotson

"Clay gave me my very first shot on TV and I will be forever grateful. Clay is a legend in music television and should be in the Rock & Roll Hall of Fame. Thank you Clay; you rock!"
— Ron Dante (Archies, Cuff Links, Detergents)

"The Clay Cole Show was so much more than a Saturday night TV dance party. It was a New York City family – a family with talent, kindness and charisma that came from our friend Clay. Linda Scott, Annette, Tony Orlando, Little Anthony and Lesley Gore were all lucky to have hits and were proud and excited to perform with the "Rock and Roll Ringmaster," Clay Cole!"

– *Lou Christie*

"My experience with Clay was always delightful; he's in my good golden memory bank. He is also a great, big talent."

– *Bob Crewe*

"Re-connecting with Clay Cole via his delightful website brought back a carload of happy memories. One of the best television rock 'n' roll hosts in the '50s & '60. Clay was loved by the press and adored by the thousands of fans that flocked to all his venues. So "let's all twist again", and bring back all the fun."

– *Ira Howard*, Editor, Cashbox Magazine (1952 -1965)

Clay Cole is about the best television personality that I ever had the pleasure of working with; still today he is one of the coolest people that I know.

– *Tommy DeVito (The Four Seasons)*

I found Clay to be one of the most talented men in the business and also one of the nicest. Talent is usually a given; being nice is an option. With Clay Cole you get the feeling it's a given. I was fortunate to be asked to appear on his TV show several times and always found him to be gracious and supportive. So what else can be said about Clay Cole? Well, what else can be said about a legend?

– *Ed Rambeau* (formerly known as Eddie Rambeau)

What I remember most about the Clay Cole show was that it was a fun show to do because of Clay. So, congratulations Clay on your 100 years in the "biz!"

– *Paul Evans*

Clay Cole is our missing link to the Sixties.

– Charles Massi

I get the biggest kick watching our old movies on TCM. I saw you just last month and started laughing with joy remembering all the good times we shared tripping around New York City like a whirlwind. I never forgot how talented and witty you were, that wry sense of humor like myself. It seems like only yesterday.

– Linda Scott

I was only five when I appeared on the Clay Cole Christmas Show – you can't help but notice that Clay was as enthusiastic when introducing new up-and-coming artists as he was introducing established stars like Simon & Garfunkel and George Carlin. I'm still very grateful; he was a champion to so many. Those shows were absolutely a highlight

– Deb Ferrara

I had always hated the "Little" in front of my name, but I remember vividly being on the Clay Cole Show, blowing out the candles on my birthday cake, celebrating 16 years – the "Little" was officially crossed out. Clay was always very sweet to me.

– Peggy March

Thank you for keeping our memories alive. I remember you as a very young handsome dude. You were so full of energy and enthusiastic who really loved the music. May God Bless you, and keep on rockin'.

– Carl Gardner (The Coasters)

"It's been said by everyone. I just wanted to add my name to the list of all the people whose careers you have launched. My days on your show at WPIX were a highlight for me. I had the most fun being with you and our little "regular cast:" the Del Satins, Angela Martin and Chuck McCann. The show was funny and creative because we had you to come up with the most unique segments."

– Tracey Dey

"I was lucky enough to be on "The Clay Cole Show" many times and we had such fun. There will never be another Clay Cole and I would love to see him get the credit he deserves for all the talent he has discovered. Clay is a living legend.

– Vicki Spencer

"Clay. Think and walk tall; you are."

– Jerry Lewis

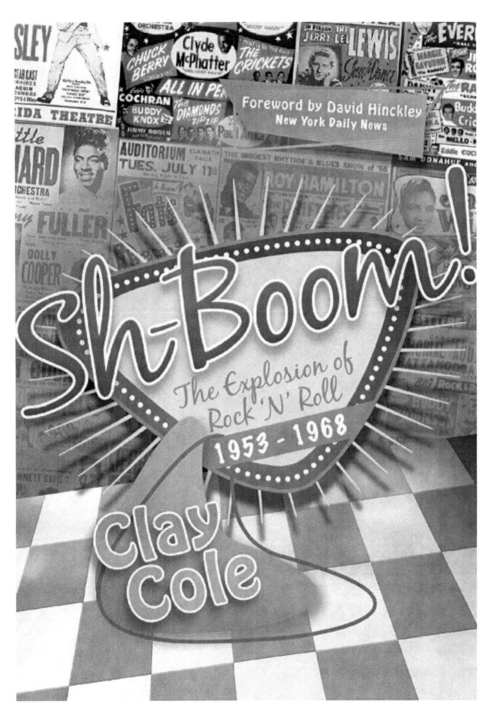

Sh-Boom!

The Explosion of Rock 'N' Roll

1953 - 1968

Foreword by David Hinckley
New York Daily News

Clay Cole

New York

SH-BOOM!
The Explosion of Rock 'N' Roll (1953-1968)

Copyright © 2009 Clay Cole. All rights reserved.

No part of this publication may be reproduced or transmitted in any form or by any means, mechanical or electronic, including photocopying and recording, or by any information storage and retrieval system, without permission in writing from the author or publisher (except by a reviewer, who may quote brief passages and/or short brief video clips in a review.)

Disclaimer: The Publisher and the Author make no representations or warranties with respect to the accuracy or completeness of the contents of this work and specifically disclaim all warranties, including without limitation warranties of fitness for a particular purpose. No warranty may be created or extended by sales or promotional materials. The advice and strategies contained herein may not be suitable for every situation. This work is sold with the understanding that the Publisher is not engaged in rendering legal, accounting, or other professional services. If professional assistance is required, the services of a competent professional person should be sought. Neither the Publisher nor the Author shall be liable for damages arising herefrom. The fact that an organization or website is referred to in this work as a citation and/or a potential source of further information does not mean that the Author or the Publisher endorses the information the organization or website may provide or recommendations it may make. Further, readers should be aware that internet websites listed in this work may have changed or disappeared between when this work was written and when it is read.

ISBN 978-1-60037-638-2 (pb)
ISBN 978-1-60037-639-9 (hc)

Library of Congress Control Number: 2009927682

Cover design: Rachel Lopez
                rachel@2cdesign.com

Morgan James Publishing, LLC
1225 Franklin Ave., STE 325
Garden City, NY 11530-1693
Toll Free 800-485-4943
www.MorganJamesPublishing.com

In an effort to support local communities, raise awareness and funds, Morgan James Publishing donates one percent of all book sales for the life of each book to Habitat for Humanity. Get involved today, visit **www.HelpHabitatForHumanity.org**.

Dedicated to Marciabird
You make all things possible

Acknowledgements

To the many special friends, some not noted in this book, which have passed through the revolving doors of my life, to inspire and inform me. Here are a few I think about often and with great affection: Charles Massi, Dennie Gordon, Caroline Wilson, Tom Ashley, Judi Jones, Arlene Gallup, Lucky Leighton, Kenny Solms, Gail Parent, Tony Loria, John Van Doorn, Blair Sabol, Mike Burrows, Mark Russell, Dick DeBartolo the 'Giz Wiz', Frank Pavlick, Tom Butrim, Don Ovens, Chance Kelly, James Karayan, Alan Newman, Ketti Frings, Mike Paccione, Phyllis Gangel, Audrey Wertheim, Robert Morton, Jim Dougherty, Art Labriola, Chita Rivera, Gregory Hines, Mickey and Ingrid Hughes, Pam and Larry Uttal, Joel Siegel, Leo Steiner, Billy Daniels, Don Luftig, Don Horan, Danny Rosen, Irv Jarvis, Dr Douglas Hiltz, Dr Robert Pearson and Dr Felix Crincoli & Matty Nielsen of the Elizabeth, NJ Elks Club.

Special thanks to Ray Reneri, Ronnie Allen, Vinny Adinolfi and the Bronx Wanderers, my "Jersey Girls" Linda Jansen, Bernadette Carroll and my special angel, Denise Ferri.

To Joel Whitburn for his essential *Billboard* reference books and to the many journalists who have influenced and inspired me over the years, some quoted herein: Paul Shansky, Murry Frymer, Dan Lewis, Ed Wallace, Richard Goldstein, Al Aronowitz Lisa Robinson, Robert Christgau, Rex Reed, Lillian Roxon, John A. Jackson, Ray D'Ariano and special thanks to David Hinckley of *The New York Daily News*, the one writer I most admire for his passion for music and his many kindnesses.

For rummaging through attics, and dusting off vintage photo albums, my gratitude goes to Janet Belleville Jones, John Cassese, Robert DuCharme, Deb Ferrara, James Glynn and Patricia Salerno for their photographs. To Shari Chertok, the photo research professional, founder of Re-Search, for her due diligence. Shari was once my production assistant and is the daughter of my friend, the late Bernie Chertok, custodian of the Grinberg Film Library in Manhattan.

To my proofreader and step-mother, Virginia Biggerstaff Rucker, who spent a lifetime as a newspaper woman. She gave me an A+ for spelling, grammar and action verbs; at 95 she's sharp as a syn-tack!

Shawn Swords, writer/producer of the film "Wages of Spin," a chronicle of the Philadelphia music scene from 1952 thru 1963, the first honest, comprehensive look at the inner workings of the music industry during that period of time.

Robert Gorman came into my life in 1985, as production assistant, right-hand man, and – after fifteen years traveling to the great destinations of America – my closest confidant. Bob is like a 45 played at 78rpm, energetic, gregarious and outgoing, a champion at darts and softball, and most importantly, he can lift heavy things. Except for our shared passion for music, we are complete opposites. Bob has tutored me in the intricacies of hard rock and heavy metal, introducing me to Pink Floyd, Queen and Journey. In turn, I schooled him in the gritty funk of Bo Diddley, Joe Cocker and Etta James. Ironically, Bob was born in 1959; the year "Rate the Records" went on the air in New York. Watching him mature, I can measure the years separating me from my glory days.

And finally, to the handful of recording stars still performing after all these years – fifty years on the bus, in the van, at the airport; 50 years of sound checks, bounced checks; hot tempers, cold food, bad sound, and good vibes… all for the love of music.

"Twist Around the Clock" © 1961, (Renewed 1989)
Four Leaf/Columbia Pictures Industries, Inc. All rights reserved
DVD available on Sony Pictures Home Entertainment (14016)

SOMEONE TO WATCH OVER ME (from "Oh, Kay")
Music and Lyrics by GEORGE GERSHWIN and IRA GERSHWIN
© 1926 (Renewed) WB MUSIC CORP
All Rights Reserved Used by permission from ALFRED PUBLISHING CO., INC

SH BOOM
Words and Music by JAMES KEYES, CARL FEASTER,
FLOYD MC RAE, CLAUDE FEASTER and JAMES EDWARDS
© 1954 (Renewed) UNICHAPPELL MUSIC INC
All Rights Reserved Used by permission from ALFRED PUBLISHING CO., INC

AS GOOD AS I ONCE WAS
Words and Music by TOBY KEITH and SCOTTY EMERICK
© 2004 Sony/ATV Songs LLC, Big Yellow Dog Music, Florida Cracker Music, Tokeco Tunes
All Rights on behalf of Sony/ATV Songs LLC, Big Yellow Dog Music and Florida Cracker Music,
administered by Sony/ATV Publishing, 8 Music Square West, Nashville TN, 37203.
All Rights Reserved Used by permission

Contents

Introduction

David Hinckley, *The New York Daily News*

Back in the 1950s, before the Beatles and even before Clay Cole, television was trying to figure out how to package and sell rock 'n' roll.

The template, partly by default, became "Bandstand," a show started by Bob Horn in Philadelphia in 1952 and brought to national prominence by Dick Clark when ABC picked it up in the summer of 1957.

A host played the hits. Guest stars came in to sing, or not sing. Kids danced.

Most major cities had their own local version of "Bandstand," and these productions spanned a wider range than Little Richard to Fabian. Some were as stilted as sixth graders holding hairbrushes to sing along with Connie Francis 45s in front of the bathroom mirror. Some were so good they were subversive, thereby feeding grownup America's worst nightmare.

Almost all of them, like Clay Cole's, remain today only in memory. Rock 'n' roll? Try to find a television station manager in the old days who'd waste a $200 reel of kinescope tape keeping that noise around.

But that doesn't mean the shows didn't leave their mark. Each one was heard by somebody, or many somebodies, who thereafter felt and approached some part of life a little differently.

A show with a $50 talent budget, barely enough to put a combo behind a local teenage singer, could still be a pebble in a pond, sending ripples into distant coves.

Clay Cole hosted a rock 'n' roll show for almost a decade in America's most important city, New York. That show was the first American television gig for the Rolling Stones.

Clay Cole was a lot more than a pebble in the American rock 'n' roll pond.

Television, like most of American culture, mostly regarded rock 'n' roll with condescending amusement during its first decade. But from the minute the ratings for Elvis Presley's first Ed Sullivan appearances rolled in, television was smart enough to put rock 'n' roll on the menu - even if, behind the cameras, all those smart executives privately assured each other it was just a matter of months before those silly teenagers moved on to the next hula hoop or started swallowing goldfish again.

Funny thing was, they didn't. So television kept working to do what it does best with popular culture -- turn it into cost-efficient programming.

Dick Clark and "American Bandstand" got most of the attention because they were seen daily on a national ABC broadcast. But in New York, Dick Clark was regarded as a sanitized and officially approved version of rock 'n' roll. Alan Freed and Jocko Henderson, that's where you went to hear the real stuff alongside the rhythm and blues with which it was so tightly interwoven.

Even in New York, though, 1950s television could never give rock 'n' roll fans one of their own as the host of a rock 'n' roll show.

That wasn't all television's fault. Most 16-year-olds were too busy with their algebra homework to host a television show. But whatever the reason, even most revered rock 'n' roll TV hosts tended to be older guys who grew up with the big bands and followed the wind to rock 'n' roll.

Enter Clay Cole.

When WNTA in New York hired Clay Cole to host its "Rate the Records" show in September 1959, he was 21 years old. That may have been slightly older than the average rock 'n' roll fan - a gap WNTA tried to narrow by billing him as 19 - but the point was that he knew the Drifters and Gene Vincent from hearing them on the radio, not from the promotion man at Atlantic or Capitol Records.

Kids, who are never as dumb as adults think, got this. They bought Cole's wise-guy remarks about the music because they knew he had the right to make them, the same way Italians get to tell Italian jokes. They sensed he wasn't just playing the music, he liked it. He could dance with a rock 'n' roll rhythm.

It's also true that by 1959, a battalion of rock 'n' roll fans would have killed for Clay Cole's WNTA gig, and every one was sure he, or she, could have done it.

But Clay Cole was the right man for the job, ironically, because he was not a single-minded rock 'n' roll fanatic. Unlike hard-core fans, he had not spent the previous six years memorizing master numbers of Cadillac's flip sides and analyzing the rhythm guitar mix on Buddy Holly's Decca recordings.

Admirable and rewarding as that kind of devotion often has been, it tends to produce tunnel vision and condescension toward those not equally immersed.

Clay Cole's path over those six years was learning to create an entertaining show within which the music could remain as authentic as possible.

Then, as now, that synthesis was a struggle. Rock 'n' roll at its best has always delivered at least the illusion of spontaneity, and television by nature looks staged.

The difficulty of reconciling those opposites goes a long way toward explaining why, two decades later, television would so eagerly embrace MTV and the world of music video.

With videos, the pressure was off, because live performance was by definition not required, or even useful. Pre-recording was a basic premise of video, which were visual entertainment that used the song as a bed.

In a way, MTV was a kind of surrender, an admission that television couldn't convey the excitement of live rock 'n' roll. Videos, for television purposes, were flashier and easier.

Clay Cole's shows on WNTA and WPIX came from an earlier age when it was still considered worth the time and effort to try and catch the lightning.

His shows also argued that having an intelligent host mattered, a lesson not universally applied then or now in a medium where the right empty smile can be a ticket to fame and fortune.

Ed Sullivan was not an empty smile - okay, he rarely smiled at all - but when he introduced a rock 'n 'roll singer, he looked as if he had just found an alien walking down Broadway. When Clay Cole introduced Jackie Wilson or Dion, you believed he could sing the first verse of "Lonely Teardrops" or "I Wonder Why."

On one level, Clay Cole had the same simple goal as a medicine show proprietor pulling his wagon onto a Tennessee fairground on a hot Saturday night in 1924. He just wanted to give the people a good show.

On another level, he was shooting for something complex. Impossible, probably. He was trying to set a stage where the Rascals could play "Good Lovin' " or the Shirelles could sing "Will You Still Love Me Tomorrow" and it wouldn't feel like the music had been processed through a camera and a TV screen.

It had been, of course, and the truth is, that was not altogether a bad thing, because that became one of the ways rock 'n' roll sneaked out of dark clubs and late-night radio and made its way to prime-time in America's nervous living rooms.

The truth is that if rock 'n' roll's pure primal inspiration hadn't met show biz and the blunt realities of cultural commerce, it never would have had anywhere near the impact it did.

That's the place Clay Cole worked, the intersection of art and commerce, and his impact on the game was magnified because he knew both sides.

He also left the game early. He was just 30 - the age over which youth in the 1960s were warned not to trust anyone - when he walked away from his WPIX show.

He had some disagreements with his bosses, not the first or last time that has happened in the rock 'n' roll television world. Mainly, the times were a-changing and he just wasn't enjoying the new ones as much as he did the old ones.

He never left music altogether, producing shows into the 21st century. But as rock 'n' roll moved from free-spirited fun into big business, from independent labels to conglomerates, from three-minute songs to 15-minute guitar solos, some of the original exhilaration faded.

The music in several ways became bigger than ever. But the new "rock" culture was different from the original rock 'n' roll culture, and contrary to later assumptions, it wasn't always or necessarily better.

It may be heresy to suggest 1961 and 1962 produced more great rock 'n' roll than 1968 and 1969, but the idea is worth a discussion.

That contrast also helps explain both Clay Cole's impact and his departure.

He didn't launch rock 'n' roll, but he helped embed it, and in the process he became part of the engine that propelled it on the long trip from 1958 to 1968.

When he left, in a sense, his work was done.

That work, by the way, involved far more heavy lifting and sheer willpower than any casual viewer of WNTA or WPIX could have imagined.

That part is Clay Cole's own story, so he'll pick it up from here.

From the living room side of the TV, let's only say that with Clay Cole, as with Rick and Ilsa in "Casablanca," the fundamental things applied.

He wasn't just young. He was good.

Overture

"Sing your song, dance your dance, tell your tale."
– *Frank McCourt, Pulitzer Prize-winning author*

There was a small sliver of time wedged between Be-bop and Hip-Hop when America's teenagers created their own music. I was one of those teenagers with a difference – I was the teenage host of my own television show, dancing to the Top Ten tunes of 1953 to 1968, the precise year's rock 'n' roll arrived, kicking and screaming onto the national charts.

Since departing my rock 'n' roll show in 1968, I have politely refused all requests for interviews – except for one chat with David Hinckley, the *New York Daily News* reporter whom I admire. I just wanted to let it rest. I don't think about the past very much at all. Like those movie starlets who gush on late-night television, "I live in the moment." I never look at old pictures, scrapbooks, home movies or tapes, and I seldom shoot-the-breeze about "the good old days." I am equally uneasy about pondering the future; I'm impulsive; a spur of the moment kind-a guy.

With the coming of the Internet, in response to a blog, "What ever happened to Clay Cole?" someone named Dave posted with great certainty, "I heard that Clay Cole died ten years ago." That could explain a note I received shortly thereafter from Dionne Warwick: "So nice to hear you are okay." Is she psychic or what? Another blogger falsely reported that I was jailed following a marijuana bust and banned from television. I was exonerated by one supportive blogger who called me "the missing link to the Sixties." I will admit I do get a kick out of all this belated attention. Was it time to poke my head out and tell my story?

I have been cajoled many times over the years by publicists, musicologists and effusive fans to set down my rock 'n' roll recollections in a book. I always expressed doubt, remembering that Mick Jagger returned his million-dollar book advance simply because he couldn't remember one single thing about the seventies.

The desire to be remembered forever – the allusion of immortality – is one of the secret fantasies of most celebrities; but with each passing generation, fame, like fads, diminish. The truth of the matter is, some of the most celebrated entertainers of the 20th Century – Bing Crosby, Kate Smith, Arthur Godfrey – are completely forgotten today. Just this week, my twenty-something barber admitted he'd never heard of James Dean! The fact that I am remembered at all – forty years later – astounds me. But that's not the point. It's what *I* remember that is relevant here and when it comes to the sixties, I remember every detail.

There would be no story had I not made the decision in 1957 at age 19, to leave Ohio and try my luck in New York City. In the process, I became a New Yorker – neither native born and raised, nor a nine to five suburban commuter, but a New Yorker by choice – New York was my final destination.

Becoming a New Yorker is a privilege not easily granted, but one that comes with years of diligence. One must be adept at Yiddish slang, Italian hand gestures, and Latin dance steps, suffer endless evenings of tedious off-Broadway plays, mind-numbing films with subtitles and decades of gut-wrenching knishes and spicy meatballs. But, the rewards are noble. New York offers self-possession as powerful as a Don Mattingly grand slam, a Rocky Marciano haymaker or a Liza Minnelli encore – plus, the natives greet you with a kiss, a most agreeable custom.

New York City was once called "the entertainment capital of the world," and Broadway was "The Great White Way," a boulevard that came with a warning: "There's a broken heart for every light on Broadway." Each year, bright, talented, witty young people came to The City to follow their dream, only to confront the nightmare of unspoken rules, unnatural rhythms and implicit rituals. They return home defeated. It's our way or the highway. But, if you can stick it out, the payoff comes with a guarantee – once a New Yorker, a New Yorker for life.

It's a city shared equally by rich and poor, bleacher bums and center court fanatics. The mogul in the glass tower may run the city, but the guy in the basement holds the keys. In New York there is a tacit respect for the workingman – the cabbie, the teamster, the stagehand. In 1959, before Fax, FedEx or the Internet, messengers ran the city; without them, all commerce would have come to a halt.

In 1959, with my new television show, I was suddenly a wanted guest at premiers, awards dinners and social events. Arriving at parties, people were happy to see me. As the new kid on the block, I was interviewed and photographed and the name Clay Cole began popping-up in the gossip columns. A billboard a half-block wide sat on top of Broadway at 50th Street, with my picture smiling down on Tin Pan Alley. Taxi drivers would honk, wave and call out "*Claycole!*"

The Way We Were

In the late Fifties, before Jell-O shots and bellybutton refills, New York City was a twenty-four hour cocktail party. A lady would never chug beer from a bottle and manly-men did not sip cocktails through a straw. No. We drank our gin martinis straight-up, inhaled unfiltered cigarettes and devoured beefsteaks. Men could smoke in elevators, but respectfully removed their hats whenever a woman entered the carriage. A lady would never smoke on the street, but she could now enter barrooms through the front door, rather than the side Lady's Entrance and the "lady" could actually drink unescorted at the bar. 'Last call' was shouted-out at four o'clock in the morning and the streets would fill with hungry drunks pouring out of saloons, bound for Reuben's or Ratner's or Rapoport's for breakfast.

Brassy blondes were the dames of choice. Women were shapely, with wide hips, clenched waists and décolletage plunging out of little black 'cocktail dresses.' Faye Emerson was the reigning First Lady of television, with her revealing low-cut Ceil Chapman gowns, requiring producers to camouflage her cleavage with swaths of gauze. On Sunday afternoons, ladies in Hattie Carnegie hats, Saks Fifth Ave gloves and Christian Dior dresses paraded their French Poodles, the dog of the decade. Weekdays, dog walking became doorman's duty. Of course, sidewalks and gutters were littered with fresh piles of doggie poop, a minor inconvenience, forcing the natives to look downward. Only tourists looked up.

Little did I realize, with my brush of celebrity and the rush of the seasons, that I was witnessing the end of an era. All that had pulled me to this great city would soon be gone, and civilization, as we knew it, for better or worse, was about to end. The great Radio City networks would be brought down by the portable transistor, 45-records, and the local deejay. Network television production, once rooted in the earthy black and white streets of New York, would soon to be transplanted to the sunset boulevards of Hollywood – "the glamour capital of the world" – where studio property was plentiful and cheap. Eddie Fisher would no longer be idealized as the perfect boy next door – crooners would give way to teen idols. Bongo-thumping Beatniks would soon be replaced by bong-tokeing Hippies. In 1959, as the "Fabulous Fifties" decade was winding down, we were about to enter "The

Swinging Sixties." Times – they were a' changing. They gave me the keys to the city, but they were about to change the locks.

The Sixties would begin with an assassination by a grassy knoll in Dallas, and end in the muddy fields of Woodstock. A decade that began with a whimper, Percy Faith's "Theme from a Summer Place" would end with a bang, Led Zeppelin's, "Whole Lotta' Love." The Sixties would bring about a sexual, social and Cultural Revolution. On campus, the inmates take over the asylum; bras and draft cards would "burn, baby, burn." Fraternities would become irrelevant, proms passé; refined culture begets the counter culture. The Strawberry Statement was "we didn't start the fire."

A musical earthquake was about to jolt Sixties America, charted by *Billboard,* the Richter Scale of Pop Music: The British Invasion, Bob Dylan, Motown and the Twist. Rock 'n' roll, rockabilly and rhythm and blues would give-way to folk-rock, protest-rock, hard-rock, acid-rock, and finally give it up to disco dancing in the 70s, heavy-metal in the 80s, punk-rock in the 90s, rapping into the Millennium.

Every word is true, as I remember it. If it's not true – I forgot.

In the words of Ken Kesey: *"To hell with facts! We need stories."*

Here is my story.

rock 'n' roll: (rk'ən-rl') a rocknroller, rock 'n' roller or rock' - and - roll'er, *noun*
A pop music genre, originating in the 1950s, a blend of black rhythm-and-blues with white country-western; rock is a generic term for the range of styles that evolved out of rock 'n' 'roll.

The Great American Songbook	Jerome Kern, Rodgers & Hart/Hammerstein, Irving Berlin, Cole Porter, Frank Loesser, Duke Ellington, "Fats" Waller, Harry Warren, Johnny Mercer, George & Ira Gershwin
1930s Delta Blues	Robert Johnson, Eddie "Son" House, Jr., Dave "Honeyboy" Edwards, Bessie Smith
Country-Western Blues	Red Foley, Carter Family, Roy Acuff, Bill Monroe, Flatt & Scruggs, Bob Wills
Bluegrass	Arthur "Guitar Boogie" Smith, Sons of the Pioneers, Hank Williams, Jimmie Rodgers
1940s Jump, boogie-woggie	Louis Jordan & the Tympany Five, Cab Callaway, Andrew Sisters, the Mills Brothers
Jive, be-bop	Coleman Hawkins, Charlie Parker, Dizzy Gillespie, Bud Powell, Ella Fitzgerald
Big Bands, swing	Glenn Miller, Lionel Hampton, Artie Shaw, Harry James, Benny Goodman Tony Pastor
Jazz	Louis Armstrong, Miles Davis, Count Basie, Modern Jazz Quartet, Dave Brubeck
Pop Singers	Frank Sinatra, Rosemary Clooney, Tony Bennett, Patti Page, Eddie Fisher, Perry Como
Gospel	Mahalia Jackson, Soul Stirrers, Clara Ward, Sister Rosetta Tharpe, the Staple Singers
Blues	Billie Holiday," Little" Walter Jacobs, Dinah Washington, Sonny Boy Williamson, B B King, Howlin' Wolf, Muddy Waters, Willie Dixon, Jimmy Reed, Junior Wells
Country	Eddy Arnold, "Tennessee" Ernie Ford, Jimmy Dean, Marty Robbins, Don Gibson
Folk-Calypso	Woody Guthrie, the Weavers, Pete Seeger, Kingston Trio, Harry Belafonte, Odetta

Rock 'n' Roll

1950s Rhythm and Blues	Johnny Otis, John Lee Hooker, George "Harmonica" Smith, Chuck Berry, Fats Domino, Little Richard, Jerry Lee Lewis, Bo Diddley, Clyde McPhatter, the Clovers, Ruth Brown
Rock-a-Billy	Elvis Presley, Buddy Holly, Everly Brothers, Kitty Wells, Gene Vincent, Charlie Gracie
Doo Wop, a cappella	The Orioles, Dells, Willows, Chords, Dion & Belmonts, Cleftones, Crests, Skyliners
Teen Idols/Pop	Paul Anka, Frankie Avalon, Fabian, Bobby Vee, Jimmy Clanton, Bobby Rydell, Dion
1960s Pop	Bobby Darin, Connie Francis, Platters, Four Seasons, Drifters, Annette, Lou Christie, Brenda Lee, Danny & the Juniors, Righteous Brothers, Vogues, Tokens, Neil Diamond
Folk-Rock	Byrds, John Denver, Judy Collins, Joni Mitchell, Richie Havens, the Band, First Edition
Protest-Rock	Bob Dylan, Joan Baez, Barry McGuire, Phil Ochs, Tom Paxton, Country Joe & the Fish
Twist	Chubby Checker, Hank Ballard & the Midnighters, Joey Dee & the Starlighters, Isley Bros

British Invasion	Beatles, Rolling Stones, Hermits, Kinks, Zombies, Animals, Yardbirds, Moody Blues, DC5
Girl Group	Chantels, Bobbettes, Shirelles, Dixie Cups, Shangri-Las, Ronettes, Bluebelles, Supremes
Boy Bands	Rascals, Lovin' Spoonful, Cyrkle, Association, Buckinghams, Blood, Sweat & Tears
Bubblegum	Archies, 1910 Fruitgum Company, Ohio Express, Cowsills, Lemonpipers, the Monkees
Motown	Miracles, Contours, Four Tops, Temptations, Mary Wells, Marvin Gaye, Stevie Wonder
Memphis	Sam & Dave, Otis Redding, Booker T. & the MGs, Carla Thomas, Wilson Pickett
Philadelphia	Patti LaBelle, the Soul Survivors, O'Jays, Harold Melvin & the Bluenotes, Jerry Butler
California	Herb Alpert & the Tijuana Brass, the Mamas & the Papas, Sonny & Cher, Beach Boys
Acid Rock	Jefferson Airplane, Grateful Dead, Jimi Hendix, New Riders of the Purple Sage, Cream 1970s Hard Rock/AC/DC, Van Halen, Alice Cooper, Aerosmith, Eric Clapton, Iron Maiden, Uriah Heap
Classic Rock	Carlos Santana, Tom Petty & the Heartbreakers, Eagles, Crosby, Stills, Nash & Young
Heavy Metal	Led Zeppelin, Black Sabbath, Deep Purple, Ozzie Osborne, Blue Oyster Cult, KISS
Arena Rock	Styx, Queen, Foreigner, Journey, Genesis, Pink Floyd, U2, Grand Funk Railroad, Who
Southern Rock	Doobie Brothers, Allman Brothers, 38 Special, Lynard Skynard, Atlanta Rhythm Section, Black Oak Arkansas, James Gang, Marshall Tucker Band, Ozark Mountain Daredevils
Male Rockers	Billy Joel, Elton John, Bryan Adams, Bob Seeger, Rod Stewart, Sting, Bruce Springsteen
Lady Rockers	Heart, Joan Jett, Pat Benatar, Madonna, Cindy Lauper, Blondie, the Pretenders, Bangles
Glam Rockers	Marc Bolan and T.Rex, Gary Glitter, Slade, David Bowie, Roxy Music, Mott the Hoople
Disco	Bee Gees, Donna Summer, Village People, Gloria Gaynor, KC & the Sunshine Band
Punk Rock	New York Dolls, Ramones, Sex Pistols, the Clash, the Patti Smith Group, Lenny Kaye
Hip Hop	Melle Mel, Afrika Bambaataa & the Soulsonic Force, Sugar Hill Gang, MC Hammer
Rap	Grandmaster Flash & the Furious Five, Run-D.M.C., Snoop Dogg, Sean "Puffy" Combs
Gangsta Rap	Ice-T, N.W.A, Beastie Boys, Ice Cube, Public Enemy, OutKast, Notorious B.I.G, Jay-Z

1) Youngstown, Ohio 1938 – 1954

"A coincidence is a small miracle,
in which God chooses to remain anonymous."

Some people are lucky enough to have been born at the exact moment in time. I was one of them, born on the cusp of rock 'n' roll and ten years before the post-war baby boom. I was a New Year's baby, born Albert Rucker, Jr. and delivered in the early morning hours of January 1, 1938. By an ironic twist of fate, it was a Saturday, a night destined to be my television time-slot in the coming two decades.

"Thanks for the Memory" was the song of the year, winning the Oscar. When Bob Hope sang it in the picture "The Big Broadcast of 1938," a long-standing Hollywood technique was abandoned. When musical numbers are filmed, the songs are prerecorded and the actors lip-synchronize the lyrics to a playback track, to accommodate all the stops and starts. Hope's rendition moved his producers to tears, so Paramount brought an entire orchestra onto the set and Bob Hope sang it *live*. My entry into television many years later would be lip-synching records. 1938 was also the year that Robert Johnson, considered to be the "Grandfather of Rock 'n' Roll," died. He was twenty-seven.

Radio delivered the top seven songs of the week from a "scientific survey" conducted by a tobacco company—the makers of Lucky Strike cigarettes. Listeners were informed that the weekly "Lucky Strike Hit Parade" survey checked the best-selling sheet music, phonograph records and the songs most played on automatic coin machines. At no time during its twenty-four-year broadcast (1935 to 1955 on radio, and 1950 to 1959 on television) was the exact procedure of this "authentic tabulation" ever revealed.

Radio was also our direct access to wartime news bulletins, miraculously broadcast—in spite of static distortions—live from London. To save money, some folks bought radio kits to assemble themselves. Soon, tabletop models were produced, beginning the golden age of network radio. Grandpa Nash purchased a two-tube, AM deluxe floor model console, as imposing as a Wurlitzer jukebox—furniture that spoke. We would sit on the carpet, in a circle, quietly listening, staring at the illuminated dials.

In the forties, our doors were seldom locked, bicycles were parked unchained, and hitchhiking was an acceptable method of getting from here to there. Our only fear was the ominous possibility of a Japanese kamikaze raid over downtown Hubbard, Ohio. Each night, a curfew signaled a blackout and our air raid warden would pound on Grandpa's front door, admonishing us to dim the lights and close the shades!

Hubbard was a town of about seven thousand, one of those Midwestern towns where everyone knew everyone and most of the men worked in the nearby mill town, at the steel factories of the Youngstown Sheet and Tube. Youngstown boasted its own symphony orchestra, art museum, and a burlesque house with "Busty" Russell grinding out four a day. The downtown centerpiece was the opulent Warner Theatre, far more lavish than a town of 240,000 deserved, a gift from four hometown boys: Albert, a soap salesman; Harry, a butcher; Sam, a carnival barker; and Jack, a deliveryman—the Warner Brothers.

Youngstown was also a mob town, a hideaway for racketeers, conveniently tucked midway between New York and Chicago, Cleveland and Pittsburgh. "The boys" controlled the unions, ran numbers and rigged car bombs; in one year, a record sixteen car bombs were triggered, a violent demolition derby. The Pick-Ohio Hotel was the mobster's gathering place, and as *Reader's Digest* reported, "In the barbershop, a sign was posted: 'We'll cut your hair and start your car for one dollar.'"

There was also a mob-controlled, illegal roadhouse, the Jungle Inn, on the outskirts of Hubbard, where a young Dean Martin worked as a dealer.

Big events in Hubbard were the annual soapbox derby down Liberty Hill, the Friday night football games, and the Memorial Day parade, when my Great Uncle proudly marched as the lone veteran of the Spanish-American War.

Jack O'Brian, the television critic for the *New York Journal-American*, once chastised me in print for opening one holiday show with "Happy Memorial Day": "that's like wishing his viewers a Happy Yom Kippur." What the smart-assed, big-city Mr. O'Brian didn't realize is that Memorial Day is a small-town thing, a parade with strutting drum majorettes, the high school band (a final march for senior class band members), the ladies' auxiliaries, and battalions of hometown veterans marching up Liberty Hill to the cemetery. The wide front porches of Hubbard were draped in red, white, and blue bunting and the Stars and Stripes fluttered from flagpoles up and down Mackey Street.

At 122 Mackey Street, a backyard picnic was part of the tradition, with aunts and uncles and cousins arriving with giant ceramic Fiesta bowls of potato salad and quivering ambrosia molds. (The colorful ceramic Fiestaware that was all the rage was created by two pottery-makers, the Laughlin brothers, in East Liverpool, Ohio, just down the road a-piece.) Meanwhile, Grandpa Nash presided over the flaming red brick grill he had assembled in our backyard. A Memorial Day picnic was just one ingredient in the secret recipe of a successful television personality.

The coming of television created a new job description, "The Personality," a person with charm but no discernable talent. If radio was a hot medium—with disc jockeys shrieking like used car salesmen, fearing that dreaded two seconds of silence—then television was a cool medium, folksy and down-home. This is the low-key television style perfected by Dave Garroway, Perry Como, Arthur Godfrey, even Edward R. Morrow—they spoke to that one viewer sitting at home alone. Sammy Davis, Jr., Jerry Lewis, and Chevy Chase may be great entertainers, but they failed as television hosts. It's that Memorial Day factor—they needed warm and fuzzy flannel under that shiny mohair suit. Andy Williams got it, Steve Lawrence ain't. Johnny Carson had his slice of "American Pie" growing up in Nebraska, and then topped it off with a dollop of New York sophistication, before becoming the urbane Hollywood host. A Midwestern Memorial Day picnic is one ingredient that prepared me to become an agreeable television host.

Dad and Mom and I shared a seven-bedroom, two-family house with her parents and two brothers, who spoiled me rotten. I was the firstborn, the first grandchild: "This kid will never have to walk!" My Uncle Bud and Uncle Sherm were still teenagers; Sherm was fourteen when I was born. It was like having two big brothers; they were my heroes. Mom's sister Louise had left the home to study nursing. Grandpa Nash purchased the family a brand-new, bright yellow Buick convertible with a rumble seat and a powerful radio ($3500 in 1940) and we would sing along to "Chattanooga Choo Choo," "Elmer's Tune," "Rum and Coca-Cola," and all the latest swing band favorites. Mom's three teenage cousins, Margaret, Bea and Ruth, who lived just across the street, introduced me to strange new music, unlike anything I had heard before—"Golden Earrings," "Nature Boy," "Mona Lisa"—

songs with poetic images that haunted my imagination. In our family, music was everywhere.

Mom always said Dad looked exactly like Errol Flynn, but I couldn't see the resemblance. I hadn't seen Flynn in anything but "Robin Hood," and I just couldn't imagine Dad swinging from the trees of Sherwood Forest—in green, wool tights. Dad had gained quite a reputation on the basketball court, playing on the many church leagues that were all the rage at that time. He once won three games on three courts in three different divisions, all in one day. He quickly converted from Baptist to Methodist to Catholic simply by changing his shirt. It was through basketball that he met Mom.

Mom (Evelyn) was thin and fragile with worry-lines permanently etched into her forehead. She could still accomplish a split, perfected as a high school cheerleader, and had the uncanny ability to pluck handfuls of four-leaf clovers from our sprawling lawns. Mom, as well as most married women, proudly identified herself as "housekeeper" on my birth certificate. In 1938 you were a nurse, a typist, or a housewife. Popular radio hosts like Art Linkletter were guaranteed a round of applause whenever they proclaimed "homemaker" as "the most important job in America!" If you happened to be a homemaker from Brooklyn, the audience went berserk. (A "Brooklyn housewife" was a double-whammy to a radio host.)

All the men in our family, and in most families, worked for one company for their entire lives. The men in the Nash family worked at Republic Rubber, where Grandpa Nash was a highly paid executive; Dad was employed at the G-F (The General Fireproofing Company), a fabricator of high-end office furniture molded from a new, lightweight metal called aluminum. The G-F was his first and only employer, starting as a teenage time clerk at forty cents an hour, eventually working his way up through the ranks to superintendent of the chair division and eventually his own factory. (This would require a move to North Carolina, to supervise the construction of the plant; his assembly-line innovations eventually saved his company millions.) At night, Dad would sit at the kitchen table practicing the Palmer Method to improve his handwriting skills; his perfect penmanship was one of the gifts he passed on to me.

On those notoriously dreary Ohio winter nights, Grandpa Nash would host a Saturday night shindig, dinner and a show, meatballs and spaghetti prepared from his secret recipe. After a few highballs, the show would begin with Uncle Sherm behind his prized mother-of-pearl drum set, providing drum rolls and rim-shots. I've been told that Uncle Sherm was such a good drummer that he considered becoming a professional, until he learned that his idol Gene Krupa was seriously addicted to drugs. He never played the drums again. The show was staged by the men under the proscenium archway leading into the kitchen, the rest of us taking our positions on the dining room floor. The men ad-libbed their way through an evening of skits, impressions and send-ups of popular radio shows. Costumes and props magically materialized—a rubber nose for Jimmy Durante, a mustache for Jerry Colonna, a cap and gown for "Professor" Kay Kyser. The grand finale was always Uncle Sherm's impression of Hitler in hilarious guttural German double-talk, and we would respond with the required "Sieg Heil!" One night, Grandma Nash, in a fit of laughter, launched a full set of dentures across the dining room. Many years later, as a student at Northwestern University (in a drama class, which included future film stars Jeffrey Hunter and Charlton Heston), Uncle Sherm was asked to perform his Hitler routine as the centerpiece of a football halftime show.

Our summertime ritual was two-weeks at Lake Erie in one of those rustic beach cottages, with its musty-damp smell, mix-and-match furniture, lumpy beds, and screened-in porch. To this day, whenever I hear a screen door slam, I am snapped back to those nostalgic summers at the Lake.

Family life revolved around the Baptist Church, where Grandpa Nash and my Great (Spanish American War) Uncle were deacons. At thirteen I was baptized – immersed into the water tank conveniently tucked under the choir loft behind the altar. I was president of the B.Y.P.U. (Baptist Young Peoples Union), and sang in the choir. The congregation is still reeling from my top-of-the-pops, boy-soprano rendering of "I Believe" – the Frankie Laine version. For a brief moment, I aspired to become a man of the cloth; a preacher or an interior decorator, I wasn't sure.

The good times ended on December 7, 1941 when America entered the war. Uncle Bud and Uncle Sherm joined the Army, while Aunt Louise (Mom's older sister) married and became a nurse. Dad was deferred from the draft because he held an essential job, supervising the making of fighter planes for the war depart-ment. In wartime, aluminum was the material of choice for the Army Air Force, a lightweight but sturdy component of the Thunderbolt, a war department favorite. Overnight, the G-F factory was converted to war production, working round the clock, in three eight-hour shifts. I seldom saw my father, except on payday; he would take mom and me into Youngstown for broiled scallops at the Nimrod Inn. There was tension in the air between my mother and father. I was too young to understand what was happening in our home, but I sensed unhappiness.

One unforgettable day, I came home from kindergarten to find my mother in tears, sobbing much more than usual. She rushed upstairs and threw herself across the bed. I scampered up the steps after her, to comfort her.

"Some day," she wailed, "some day, you and your father will come home and find me gone. Then maybe you'll appreciate me."

Psychiatrists will tell you, a child's worst fear is abandonment from parents. Fifteen years later, my "shrink" had a field day with that one. He reasoned, "Why didn't your mother simply say, 'someday your father will come home to find us both gone'? Why was she so willing to abandon you and leave you alone with your father?" I had a distant relationship with my father. He just never tossed me the ball.

From that moment on, I conspired never to leave the house. I had to keep an eye on Mom, for fear she might run away. I devised all sorts of schemes to be sent home from school. I feigned stomach aches and the flu. When I ran low on illnesses and diseases, I would go to the boy's room and rip the seam at the seat of my pants or pee in my underwear, anything to be sent home, to keep an eye on Mom. I once pretended to faint and lay motionless in spite of a prolonged tickling from the school nurse. Although I am extremely ticklish, I didn't stir; my first understanding that the mind is more powerful than the physical body. I also developed unprovoked nose bleeds – bright red drops would suddenly splatter on my school desk, sending me straightaway to the nurse for a home pass. I couldn't explain that one. Was my brain in cahoots with my body to get me home to Mom? It was beyond me.

I became the target of the school bully, a mean-spirited classmate named Raymond Nadjim whose father was an eye doctor and maintained his practice in his home, which was halfway between my house and school. In his window, Dr. Nadjim displayed one ominous oversized eyeball, which seemed to say to me: "I've got my eye on you boy." I walked three blocks out of my way every school day to avoid his wrath and ridicule.

So, without playmates and with a tenuous mother, I kept company with Grandma Nash, as she stood vigil, peering out between the slats of her Venetian blinds, as if she might see her boys coming home from overseas. As all war mothers had done, she proudly placed a banner with two stars in her window, signaling to passerby's that she had two sons in service. Grandma Nash was my secret source of pocket money for all the essentials in life, like marbles, a Klondike bar or hand puppets. She purchased all the correct breakfast cereals so that we could mail box tops off to that exotic sounding Battle Creek, Michigan and then patiently wait for the postman to deliver my "secret decoder ring" or my Little Beaver headband. Grandma sent so much money to Battle Creek that surely somewhere up in Michigan, there must be a Helen Nash Highway.

Grandma Nash also bankrolled my many trips uptown to the Palace Theatre, where the movies were double bills that changed three times a week. It was here, sitting alone in the dark, that my notions of Manhattan were formed. It seemed that every New Yorker lived in an all-white apartment, with shiny-shiny floors, and a wraparound terrace overlooking the 59th Street Bridge. In Manhattan, a man's wardrobe consisted entirely of tuxedoes, smoking jackets and broad-shouldered bathrobes. "One day," I thought, "I too will own an ascot."

The first movie I remember was "Bambi," a film that so traumatized me that Mom and Dad had to drag me kicking and screaming from under my seat and out and into the street. When Bambi loses his mother in the forest fire and starts crying, "Mother! Mother," I lost it. Not losing my own mother had become my life-mission.

Mickey Rooney devised a life-saving solution to all of Judy Garland's problems, "I know! We'll put on a show!" That became the solution to my problems as well. The movies inspired me to create my own little backyard productions – puppet shows, Wild West pageants and vaudeville shows. I would write the script, stage direct my little cast of troopers *and* provide the costumes. I was six when my brother Jim was born, and we briefly moved into Youngstown to be closer to Dad's factory, in a townhouse owned by the G-F. Dad could walk the half-block to the main gate. I quickly found a whole new gang of troopers for my backyard shows.

Jim and I shared a bedroom and we were often rambunctious, as young boys are supposed to be. When Dad's patience gave out, he would come bounding up the stairs, take off his belt and come to my bed pretending to thrash me good, but only hitting the mattress. Then he would turn to my brother's bed and spank poor little Jimmy, bringing him to tears. It wasn't until years later, when Jim and I compared notes; I learned that Dad never actually spanked him either. To dad it was probably an act of kindness, but to me it registered as "he cares so little, he won't even discipline me."

When I entered the sixth grade, I was chosen to play the Pumpkin in the annual Thanksgiving pageant, wrapped in orange crepe paper. A brief notice in the local paper caught my attention; the Youngstown Playhouse was auditioning boys for a theatre production of "The Indian Captive." Saying nothing, I boarded a bus after school that would take me to the far south side of Youngstown to audition for the part. The thrill of being in a real theatre for the first time, with its musky smell of paint and glue was intoxicating. The Playhouse was a well-respected regional theatre, and has produced its share of well-known actors, Ed O'Neil, Joe Flynn,

Austin Pendelton, Ray "Boom-Boom" Mancini and Elizabeth Hartman, who was a Best Actress Oscar nominee for "A Patch of Blue,"(1965) before killing herself.[1]

My performance in the children's theatre production so impressed the director that I was asked to play a role in the main theatre, a two week run of Eugene O'Neill's "Ah, Wilderness." In the Second Act, the on-stage family gathers around the dinner table for a typical New England lobster dinner. The prop men served up bite-sized chunks of white bread, soaked in milk, stuffed into foul-smelling, weeks-old lobster shells. To this day, I cannot eat lobster.

In the audience during one of the performances of "Ah, Wilderness" was Elaine Carroll, a popular radio broadcaster, who produced a live radio show called the "Enchanted Forest." Each afternoon, Tommy and Nancy would enter the forest for an adventure with the Fairy Princess, the Woodsman, Gruffy the Bear and a cast of English-speaking animals. Elaine scripted each adventure, directed the show and played the Fairy Princess; she cast me as "Tommy." We had a regular group of radio actors who played all the character parts and a sound effects man for wind, rain, crashes, door slams and galloping hoof beats. Gerri Myers played Nancy, my first leading lady. Gerri was the daughter of a wealthy, social family up on Fifth Avenue. On my one visit to their home, I was greeted by a butler. I fell instantly and madly in love with her.

"The Enchanted Forest" resonated with my own life as it was at the age of eleven. For a half hour each afternoon, I could leave my confusing life at home and enter an enchanted world. My life suddenly fell into a routine; attending Grade Six during the day, then after school taking the bus to the WKBN radio studios in the YMCA building in downtown Youngstown. We would rehearse each day's script, followed by a full run-through with music and effects, and then go on the air live at five o'clock. I was now a full-fledged actor with a Social Security number and paycheck to prove it. I became "the boy" whom radio producers called upon when casting local dramatic productions, like "Survival Under Atomic Attack" This was hardly the typical agenda of other Ohio schoolboys. I had few buddies; my new friends were grownup theatre eccentrics.

Theatre gypsies seemed so exotic to me, smoking, drinking and cursing like pirates. There is no bias or bigotry in the theatre – blacks, homosexuals, Jews are all

---

1   In 1966, Elizabeth Hartman won the Golden Globe as New Star of the Year and an Academy Award nomination for Best Actress. In 1987, Hartman fell to her death from a fifth-floor window in Pittsburgh, in what was believed to be a suicide. Also from Youngstown, DJ Alan Freed, Maureen McGovern ("The Morning After"), the Edsels ("Rama Lama Ding Dong"), Robert and Ronald Bell of Kool & the Gang, Tiny Bradshaw (bandleader), Chris Columbus (Film director of two Harry Potter films and "Home Alone"), and two Hubbard High School graduates, Paula Wagner, one-time producing partner of Tom Cruise (Cruise/Wagner Productions*)* and Albert Stratton, a well-known daytime drama star

mocked with equal disdain. They also taught me a whole new language of oxymorons: pancake makeup, asbestos curtains, spirit gum. I observed that theatre folk don't laugh at something witty; they simply announce, "Oh, *that's* funny." I had to learn to keep from laughing. But – with sandals and all – I later came to realized they were just a bunch of early fifties Beatniks.

Like actors everywhere, they had their favorite funky bar, where the beer was cheap and the piano was in tune. I would sit back in the dark, sipping a Shirley Temple through a haze of cigarette smoke and drift into the world of Cole Porter, Rogers & Hart, and the Gershwin's. It was here I discovered my soul song, a melody and lyric that would remain the theme of my life: "Someone to Watch Over Me" with the verse tagline, *Tell me, where is the shepherd for this lost lamb?* George and his brother Ira wrote "Someone to Watch Over Me" in 1926, as a wistful ballad for their Broadway show, "Oh, Kay!" The *Herald Tribune* critic wrote of the song: "Someone to Watch Over Me" wrung the withers of even the most hardhearted of those present."

Dad's steady rise into the upper ranks of G-F management afforded us the luxury of a television console, offering a few hours of programs each night from just three networks, CBS, NBC and Dumont. We were the first in our neighborhood to see "Mr. Television" Milton Berle in his Tuesday night "Texaco Star Theater," and 'The Great One' Jackie Gleason's "Honeymooners." My favorites were the variety shows, the "Colgate Comedy Hour" and the "Admiral All-Star Revue" with Jimmy Durante, Martin & Lewis and Abbott & Costello. Then there were the fifteen-minute, early-evening pop music shows – Eddie Fisher hosted the prophetic "Coke Time," Dinah Shore had her Chevy show and Perry Como with the Fontane Sisters sang the virtues of Chesterfield's cigarettes.

In the early years of live, black and white television, a single sponsor – Texaco, Colgate Coca-Cola – owned and produced the shows, so the networks, in order to wrest more control, created spot sales. In the intervening years, viewers have become so numbed by commercial clutter, they unconsciously tune out. Soon, we shall see the return of the single-sponsored show, resulting in better quality programming, and, finally put a lid on "Billy Mays."

In the afternoons, Brother Jim and I would race home from school and sit in front of the set, waiting for NBC to sign-on with "The Howdy Doody Show" – in fact so many youngsters sat mesmerized by the tone and test-pattern that NBC replaced the Indian Chief at the center bulls-eye with a picture of Howdy Doody. I was babysitting on a snowy Saturday night watching CBS when Mom checked-in by telephone; "Quick," she said, "tune into NBC." I ran to the television to discover a completely bizarre new kind of comedy – satire. I sat there slack-jawed as Sid Caesar, Imogene Coca, Carl Reiner and Howard Morris performed the most outrageous sketches, send-ups of movies, plays, politicians, singers and songs. I had stumbled onto "The Admiral Broadway Revue (later, "Your Show of Shows,") a ninety minute musical comedy show, produced *live* by Max Liebman, featuring the Billy Williams Quartet ("I'm Gonna Sit Right Down And Write Myself A Letter," 1957.) Along with millions of others, I was hooked for the next four years. (Years later, when co-hosting the former Mike Douglas show in Cleveland, Imogene Coca taught me their "shoe salesman" pantomime – I was Sid Caesar, the shoe salesman, Imogene was the vain customer who demanded small-sized shoes. What a thrill.)

As if on cue, another six years passed, and Brother Rick was born; I was twelve, Jim was six and Dad was now enjoying the starring role in his own version of "My Three Sons." We returned to Hubbard, once again into the arms of Grandma Nash, this time, with my heady resume as an actor.

I made a conscious effort to become just a normal kid. I subscribed to *Boy's Life*, and joined the Boy Scouts, banging out a swath of merit badges, and went to the YMCA every Saturday to hone my athletic skills and swim. I tried to please Dad by trying out for the basketball team, but I was a complete failure on the court, on the diamond and on the track; I wouldn't go near a football field. By the time I was fourteen I had broken my left arm five times. The first time, Lillian Shook pushed me off her chicken coop, the rest were fractured in gym class, tumbling in track, and skidding across the shower room floor dancing the Gleason Glide, ("and *away* we go.") When my bones didn't heal properly, the doctors had to surgically break my arm and wrist – I had brittle bones that would snap, not bend. So I spent puberty in a plaster cast; my tonsils were clipped and judging by the ugly scar I have to this day, the doctors removed my appendix with a can opener.

I was no longer a "youngster." Social scientists, economists and newspaper reporters placed us in an entirely new fiscal category, labeling us "Teenagers." It seemed we were the first generation with pocket money and panache. Before World War II, Americans went from childhood to adulthood in short order; children were considered fit for work and marriage once puberty was complete. But with the great surge of prosperity after the war, most middleclass teens did not need to work. According to the Gallup polls, we had more leisure time and more money to spend.

Girls no longer wished to dress like their mothers, as young ladies had done for decades. At home, moms wore a uniform, marketed as "house dresses." The modern Teenage Girl created her own personal style – angora sweaters with neck scarves, skirts tailored mid-calf, with waist-cinchers and flats. Drug stores began selling lipstick and makeup for girls, right next to the Evening In Paris fragrances for mom. "Maybelline" flew off the shelves. Boys adopted the 'Ivy League Look' inspired by their university brothers – letter sweaters, plaid shirts and chinos. White bucks were meant to be scruffy, but a powder sack would dust them up nicely. Gym shoes were for gym, tennis shoes were for tennis. Some of the town toughs preferred the menacing, cinematic look of Marlon Brando and James Dean – motorcycle boots, white undershirts and Levis. This created a fashion outrage, and after several emergency meetings, Hubbard High School banned the wearing of blue jeans. The toughs also favored a Brylcreem pompadour with a ducktail cut, while the rest of us preferred the crew cut, as deference to our town's GI's. As a freshman entering high school, I created a tough new character for myself. I slouched at my desk. I sauntered with an attitude. I was a bad-assed rebel without a cause.

In High School, I found a soul mate, Patti Webb, who became Imogene Coca to my Sid Caesar in a series of pantomime skits and we excelled at the Charleston, which was having a passing revival in the early Fifties. I played the leading man in school plays and appeared as the ringmaster – the center of attention – at a circus-themed Senior Prom. To solidify my power base, I began writing a teenage gossip column for the local paper, *The Hubbard News,* as the feared Walter Winchell of Hubbard High School, naming names and taking no prisoners.

Who was that college boy seen necking with Eileen Zetterquist last Friday night at the Liberty Confectionary?

What rowdy behavior is going on at the Saturday night Polka Parties upstairs at The Odd Fellows Hall?

Orchids to the gang at the Blue and White Room at Hayman's Drug Store; their jukebox picks are groovy, especially Johnnie Ray.

New Late night hangout: Giraffe Hill – go there for a good long neck.

My editor and writing mentor, Mike Varveris recalled: "It was 1951 when this pudgy 13-year-old youngster approached me and said he wanted to write about Hubbard kids and you don't have to pay me; what did I have to lose, so I said okay. One subscriber told me, It's the first time since I subscribed to your paper that my kid wanted to read it first when it arrived in the mail."

I soon became a staff Feature Writer, then promoted to Associate Editor. I asked Mike to explain the difference, "an Associate Editor," he said, "is the only one on the paper who would associate with an editor."

I also wrote a show-biz column, The Spice of Life:
"Thursday night will not be a good night for bald-headed men to watch NBC.
They have scheduled three hours of hair-raising mysteries…"

In the summer of 1953, *The Hubbard News* sponsored a charity show to benefit polio victims and Mike nudged me into performing a skit. Most of the girls in town were taking obligatory contortion classes (the ability to execute a backbend and pick up a handkerchief with your teeth was an essential ability at the time) and boys with talent mostly played the accordion. I recruited four of the cutest girls in the school (for the record, they were: Janice Belleville, Carole Doughton, Jackie Ennis and Marilyn Smelko) and devised a record-pantomime act called Al Rucker and the Baby Sitters. We lip-synched to the Modernaires recording of "Juke Box Saturday Night," a medley that contained impressions of the top singers of the day, Don Cornell, Les Paul and Mary Ford, the Four Aces and Johnnie Ray. As an encore, we found a Rusty Draper record with female backup singers called "No Help Wanted."

Well, we were a hit. A big hit! So much so that we were invited to perform on a local television show. Timing is everything, for it was just that year, 1953, that television came to Youngstown. WKBN-TV, home to the "Enchanted Forest," had now built ultra-modern studios and signed on as a CBS/DuMont television affiliate with Ted Niemi, a dapper, old-time radio actor, hosting his own fifteen-minute variety show each night at 6:45. Al Rucker and the Baby Sitters became regular guests and when Ted took a one-week vacation, we were invited to fill the spot, with me as host. After our Wednesday night show, the program director Don Brice phoned to offer us a half-hour Saturday night time slot, to be pitched to a teenage audience. Saturday night, as it turned out, would be my domain for the next fifteen years.

In the 1950's it was a popular idea to remodel your basement and convert it into a party room, usually wrapped in knotty pine with a bar, a billiard or ping-pong table, couches and a Hi-Fi record player – it was called a rumpus room. I decided that Rumpus Room would resonate with Ohio teens as a gathering place to play records and dance – and "Rucker's Rumpus Room" had a nice alliteration. I found myself producing, staging and writing a weekly half-hour program, the emcee's responsibility during the early days of television. I was fifteen years old.

Eventually, I was able to coerce a few high school boys onto the show, to join us in our rousing production numbers and to lip-synch all the popular new male vocal groups, the Hilltoppers, the Four Freshmen and the Hi-Lo's. The four squeaky-clean boys were named the Collegians.

The show shaped up to be a Hit Parade with our cast lip-synching the actual hit records rather than a Dorothy Collins - Snooky Lanson recreation. The Rumpus Room grew progressively more ambitious, which excited the WKBN crew who were eager to experiment with stage sets, creative lighting and special effects, flying on a magic carpet, sleigh riding in a blizzard, dancing on clouds or singing in the rain. We developed seasonal theme shows, the senior prom, the football game, the beach party, and our Christmas shows went on for weeks with my cousin Suzie and brothers Jim and Rick forced to sit under the tree in their 'jammies," bribed with the promise of an Isaly's ice cream skyscraper after the show.

It was during my fourteen months at WKBN-TV that a miraculous transformation took place in Dad's relationship towards me. A glossy in-house magazine published by the G-F featured a two-page picture story, lavishly praising Al Rucker Sr.'s teenaged son, the fifteen-year-old television star. The article was an eye-opener to Dad, who reaped a lot of attention and backslaps from his co-workers. I think Dad realized for the first time that perhaps I had found my place in life. He had witnessed firsthand all the effort it took to research, write, produce, stage and em-cee a highly-ambitious, half-hour *live* television show each week, and just maybe, all those backyard shows had a purpose. Television might just catch on and offer a rewarding career opportunity. For the rest of his life, there was nothing Dad would not do for me. He purchased an expensive Hi-Fi unit for our Rumpus Room rehearsals and played chauffer, prop man and off-stage engineer for our personal appearances. Dad paid for private acting classes, elocution lessons and vocal training. I went to dance school to learn the soft shoe and perfected a mean double-shuffle time-step. I took piano lessons and practiced at home on a cardboard keyboard – buying a piano was beyond Dad's financial reach. Ukuleles were hot, thanks to Arthur Godfrey, and we all had one, thanks to Dad. Dad purchased my prized Davy Crockett hat with an authentic, detachable coonskin tail. On business trips to Chicago, Dad returned with magic tricks and stage props from National Magic Co, located in the mezzanine of the Palmer House or at one of the four other magic stores crammed within a three block area of the Loop – Abbott's Joe Berg's, the Treasure Chest, and the Ireland Magic Co. Sadly, one is hard-pressed to find a single magic store in and around the Loop nowadays, or in all of Chicago for that matter.

Friday night high school football is the major pastime in Ohio, so always looking for a hook, I created a radio show with hit tunes and sports scores called the Varsity. It aired on WKBN throughout the 1954 gridiron season, my first stint as a radio deejay.

(It is also worth noting that ten years earlier, Alan Freed from Salem High School, just a few miles from Youngstown, also began his broadcast career at WKBN, as a sportscaster.) It was on my radio show, I played my very first rock 'n' roll record, the wildly infectious "Sh-Boom" by the Crew-Cuts. I had no idea at the time that this clean-cut white group covered the original "Sh-Boom" by a black rhythm-and-blues group, the Chords. In Youngstown we were isolated from race music, as R&B was called in the fifties. Dan Ryan, the town's top deejay, preferred the vanilla versions, spinning the sanitized "Earth Angel" by the Crew Cuts, rather than the gritty original by the Penguins. His sponsor, the Record Rendezvous, probably preferred it that way.

Except for a brief sponsorship by a local storm window shop, "Rucker's Rumpus Room" was sustaining, a broadcasting term meaning no sponsor, which also meant that for the past forty-six weeks we were working without a talent fee. Our December 28th 1954 show on WKBN-TV was our last, and ironically it was our New Years' show, complete with "Auld Lang Syne," a surprise birthday cake, and our final goodbyes.

<u>Theme: Top Six Songs of 1954</u>

6-	"Teach Me Tonight"	(De Castro Sisters)
5-	"Bell Bottom Blues"	(Teresa Brewer)
4-	"If I Give My Heart To You"	(Kitty Kallen)
3-	"Mister Sandman"	(The Chordettes)
2-	"Hernando's Hideaway"	(Four Lads)
1-	"Let Me Go, Lover"	(Joan Weber)
	"Auld Lang Syne"	Happy New Year 1955

The very next day, we were scheduled to perform at the Youngstown Rotary Club Christmas party at the Pick-Ohio Hotel and after the show, Dad and I were approached by the promotions director of an aggressive local food store, Century markets, who brokered a deal for us to meet the very next day with the sales manager of the local NBC affiliate, WFMJ-TV. They offered to pay us $50 a week, with a $20 costume budget and the promise of future sponsorship. So on January 8th, 1955, without missing a beat, the Rumpus Room rolled onto WFMJ-TV. I was now a senior in high school and with Dad and Mom solidly behind me, our show really took off. Our shows became more ambitious, the productions more challenging and we each had a few bucks in our pocket.

We would often lip-synch the original cast recordings of Broadway shows or the soundtracks from movies. When the national road company of "South Pacific" came to Youngstown, we performed a half-hour of highlights from the original. We recreated "Damn Yankees," "The Pajama Game" and "Guys and Dolls." Dad built a ranch house and a surrey with the fringe on top for our half-hour "Oklahoma." We received 300 postcards requesting the Collegians repeat the "Sobbin' Women" number from "Seven Brides for Seven Brothers." We staged minstrel shows, without the blackface, Wild West shows, a circus, and our first remote, live on-location at Idora Park, Youngstown's 'Million Dollar Playground.' (I wrote "Rock 'n' Roller Coaster," my very first song, inspired by the click-click-click of Idora Park's old-fashioned, wooden coaster, the Wildcat, a frightening, rickety ride.)

We rushed to the Warner Theatre to see Elvis Presley in his first film, "Love Me Tender," disappointed seeing him off in the distance plowing the fields. We really got all shook-up seeing "Blackboard Jungle." When "Rock Around the Clock" blasted off the screen, the audience went ballistic, stunned by a brand new sound from Bill Haley & His Comets. Bill Haley made rock 'n' roll an international phenomenon. Haley may have been an oddball choice as rock star – he was over thirty, overweight and over his forehead, a spit-curl – and his band were all middle-aged musicians pandering to the kids – the sax man on the floor on his back honking, the stand-up bass pitched high into the air, the guitar man on his knees – theatrics that were an embarrassment even to teenage onlookers, better left to lounge acts like the Treniers, Freddie Bell & the Bellboys, or Sam Butera and the Witnesses with Louis Prima and Keely Smith. Nonetheless, Bill Haley & His Comets inspired thousands of young musicians abroad and introduced rock 'n' roll to the world across the ocean. Here at home, Billy Haley's music further reinforced a perceived link between rock 'n' roll and juvenile delinquency, attached significantly to the soundtrack of "Blackboard Jungle." In the 1950s, the Gallup organization reported, "Americans were very concerned about the factors contributing to teen crime; the U.S. Senate even assigned a subcommittee to study the problem."

The preliminary report from the 1954 Senate Investigation of Juvenile Delinquency in the United States, reads: "The child today in the process of growing up is constantly exposed to sights and sounds of a kind and quality undreamed of in previous generations." A 1954 Gallup report on teenage crime revealed that seventy percent of Americans placed blame on comic books, television and radio, with one in four saying a *great deal* of blame was in order. Ground zero of rock 'n' roll corruption was the record hop. Preachers, politicians and "concerned citizens" pointed to record hops as the breeding ground of rapidly escalating juvenile crime. Rock 'n' roll was, after all, raw sexuality, and dancing was really sex with music. Radio disc jockeys discovered they could take advantage of their local popularity, and augment their income, by moonlighting as record hop hosts.

Guidelines were quickly set, published in *The Youngstown Vindicator*:

> "An 11:00pm curfew will be established; all teens must carry parental permission slips. Shorts, T-shirts, pedal pushers and jeans were banned. Record hops were limited to those between the ages of fourteen and eighteen; sock hops were restricted to those under fourteen. All record hops must be sponsored and supervised by a church or school organization."

Radio disc jockeys were now working for "the man."

2) Chicago/Cumberland Gap – 1954

"Will the real Clay Cole stand up please?"

I had seen enough movies to know that when a rich uncle suddenly appears at your door, the plot is about to thicken.

So it was, in the summer of 1954, that a brand new Cadillac pulled into the driveway of 122 Mackey Street and Edna and Clay Cole came a-calling. Edna was a long-lost cousin of my Dad, displaced in a childhood shuffle of divorce and desertion. She was now the happily married wife of a Chicago millionaire on a summer quest to find her roots and retrace her footsteps; the path lead to our front door.

Clay Cole – his business card read Gilbert Clay Cole, but he was known as, and preferred Clay Cole – was the Executive Vice President of Worldwide Sales for the Encyclopedia Britannica, beginning as a youthful door-to-door salesman, growing a moustache and sporting horn-rimmed glasses to appear older and more intellectual. He was a born salesman, becoming Britannica's top bookseller, earning him a corner office at the world headquarters in Chicago. Clay was understated, old-school formal, but sharp as a tack; He played George Burns to Edna's Gracie Allen. Edna was a blonde version of Marjorie Main, plain and straightforward, but terribly well groomed. Her scatterbrain routine was a sham, perfected for the amusement of her doting husband.

Naturally, I won them over, becoming "Aunt" Edna and "Uncle" Clay, and they immediately took me under their wing. Rumpus Room was on a one-month summer hiatus, so Dad had planned to drive our family on a vacation trip to seek out his own long-lost father in Tennessee, then continuing south to Florida. The trip was still two weeks away, so the Cole's kidnapped me for an unexpected holiday in Chicago, with

Dad, Mom, Jim and Rick to reclaim me in two weeks. Off I went, engulfed in that fresh-car sensation of 'Uncle Clay's' Cadillac, inhaling that sweet smell of success.

Apartments had always fascinated me – a fantasy castle in the sky – an image embedded from dozens of Hollywood movies, and the Cole's apartment was straight out of a Cedric Gibbons film-set. Edna and Clay lived in a sprawling penthouse on Chicago's Lake Shore Drive filled with antiques and paintings, crated and shipped home from their many trips around the world. The master bathroom was Tuscan marble with gold filigrees and His and Hers toilets, hers a French bidet resembling a wicker throne.

Edna proudly showed-off her couture collection of suits and dresses from The House of Chanel, Balenciaga and Givenchy, delicately preserved on padded silk hangers wrapped in tissue paper. She was as proud and excited as a kid revealing rare baseball cards, fondling her precious wardrobe as fine works of art. "Uncle" Clay's wardrobe was much simpler, but equally well thought-out. Clay wore the exact same blue suit, blue shirt and Sulka tie each day, but one of a dozen, neatly hanging in his wardrobe closet. Clay's one concession to individuality was his cufflinks, ornate antique buttons, culled from the world's junk shops. He presented me with a set of rare Napoleon army uniform buttons, the "N" crest protruding from a glazed background of deep-blue, red, white, indicating the rank of the officer, which were fashioned into cufflinks. I cherished these unique, antique gifts and was heartbroken many years later when they disappeared from my dressing room at The Apollo Theatre.

Uncle Clay gave me his gallery tour, displaying Monet street scenes and his Bernard Buffet. (My first investment in art was a signed Buffet print, purchased in 1965 at The Wildenstein Gallery on 57th Street.) A massive Japanese screen dominated the living room, darkened by thick green velvet drapes, shutting out the neighborhood. They preferred casual dining on an oversized ebony coffee table, usually Chinese take-out, while listening to Billy Daniels records. We seldom ate in; the Cole's were on a mission, to turn this small-town country bumpkin into a refined, cultured gentleman.

Uncle Clay laid down the ground rules, "You must try new things and if there was anything you don't like, it's okay move on, but come away with an opinion." We dined our way through the finest restaurants in Chicago with Uncle Clay enlightening me on how to interact with the maitre' d and his staff, and how, and how much, to tip.

(Gentlemen never make a splashy show when tipping; rather discretely fold the currency and palm it in a handshake.) One never gets too clubby with the help.

The lady never makes direct contact with the waiter; the gentleman always orders for the lady. They taught me the proper silverware to accommodate each course and how to butter a dinner roll – a tip that separates gentlemen from boys. Table manners may seem arcane in today's fast-food universe, where folks order dinner with their car double-parked, but they sure make an impression on the ladies. My favorite first-date restaurant was the romantic Forum of the Twelve Caesars, once on 48th Street in Manhattan, where I could finesse my table manners with a maitre d', captain, waiter and sommelier. Orson Wells understood, when he said: "If there hadn't been women we'd still be squatting in caves eating raw meat, because we made civilization in order to impress our girlfriends."

Clay introduced me to the arbiter of Chicago style, columnist Irv Kupcinet, who arranged for me to observe WBKB-TV's Jim Lounsbury "Record Hop" and the early morning ABC radio broadcast of Don McNeill's "Breakfast Club." At the regal Blackstone Theatre we saw the stage play, "Time Out For Ginger," the first "generation-gap" comedy, starring Melvin Douglas, and playing Ginger's high school beau was a spunky unknown actor named Steve McQueen. At The Chicago Theatre, I was enthralled by a spectacular stage show starring "that new Sepia sex-kitten" Eartha Kitt, with boy baritone Tommy Leonetti and an off-the-wall new comic named Dick Shawn. I sat ringside for dinner and an ice show at The Conrad Hilton, reeking of Noxzema, meant to sooth my lobster-red sunburn from an extended afternoon at the beach.

Mom and Dad's arrival couldn't have been timelier, and I bid farewell, but not good-bye to the high-life, to Chicago and the Cole's, promising to return. This was a particularly uncomfortable ride for me, still on-fire from my killer sunburn, to the delight of my backslapping brothers, Jim and Rick. The Rucker family station wagon headed south to Tennessee for an all-new adventure, reuniting Dad with his biological father who deserted him when he was a child. Dad had only vague memories of him and this was to be a healing of old wounds; reconciliation as adult men.

Dad found Frank Rucker's farmhouse, just off the back roads of Cumberland Gap, complete with a pack of hound dogs, a litter of country cousins and a playground – a tire roped to a tree limb. Frank Rucker had remarried, settled-in as a tobacco farmer and state game warden, engendering a large family of Rucker kinfolk. In just two weeks, I had discovered a new Grandfather and six cousins in Tennessee, who were actually my aunts and uncles, and an all new "Uncle" and "Aunt" in Chicago, who were actually my second cousins.

The Tennessee Rucker clan was church going, hard working and fun. Great country meals were served picnic-style, with baskets of hush puppies, cornbread, grits and butter, red coleslaw, sweet potato salad, black-eyed peas, a salty country ham and rabbit. I had no idea what fork to use. We stayed several days in their big, rambling homestead, fishing in a nearby creek, playing double-dare on a busy freight-train trestle, and climbing the Kentucky-Tennessee-Virginia Mountains. I was on a social see-saw, bouncing from penthouse to outhouse. Let me put this as delicately as possible, or as they say in Tennessee, "Let's get the cow over the bucket." The bathroom was out back; nary a bidet for miles.

One night at a rollicking prayer meeting, Dad became the target of an aggressive young preacher man who singled him out to come forward and be "saved." That was the night we packed our bags and high-tailed it out yonder. The old wooden church house was rockin' with a guitar-thumping preacher man who was pretty certain that "Jesus is in the room with us tonight." Apparently the congregation felt it too, they started shaking and stomping and jumping in the air, gyrating on the floor, culminating into a whirling dervish frenzy. The preacher-man smashed his guitar like a lumberjack attacking a redwood, grunting *Jee-zus, Jee-zus* with each powerful stroke. The preacher man then produced the biggest-baddest snake I'd ever seen, holding it with two hands high above his head, spinning. Then, as if dumbstruck by a dizzying blackout, he fell faint to the floor, hurling the slimy creature at the congregation. The Rucker station wagon roared off into the night, all elbows and tail lights.

I did come away from Cumberland Gap with some startling new information – I was part Cherokee. (That might explain why, as a youngster at the Saturday movie matinees, I always rooted for the Indians.) It seems Frank Rucker's father was a full-blooded Cherokee, and his wife a half-breed. That makes my bloodline three times removed. Somehow, this news gave me great comfort; my roots were solid, more defined than any vague connection to our Welsh-English-German-Irish family genealogy.

We edged our way towards Miami, sleeping in those motor court cabins with the cobalt-blue night lights casting an eerie glow across the swimming pool, and at last, palm trees and pelicans, a sure sign we were in Florida. My summer adventure in Chicago had given me a taste of civility and my Cumberland Gap episode reinforced my middleclass manner, but – mosquito bites aside – there was nothing memorable about Florida. Oh yes; our motel had a cocktail lounge called The Rumpus Room.

When the family returned to Hubbard, a deluxe thirty-two volume set of The Encyclopedia Britannica had arrived, shipped as a gift from Edna and Clay Cole.

3) Ohio to NYC, 1955 – 1957

"Don't step on my blue suede shoes" wasn't a threat.
It simply meant, "Don't hurt me."

1955. Still a virgin and about to lose it!

I was seventeen, a senior in high school, enjoying a new recognition of respect; boys no longer flicked my ear, slapped books from my arms or goosed me. I was evolving from an awkward juvenile stage and radio actor into a full-grown host-producer of my own Saturday night television show. I was becoming a more confident on-camera personality. As "Rucker's Rumpus Room" entered its third season in 1955, I had already witnessed three distinct popular music trends – Big Bands, the emergence of the Pop Singer and, now, Rock 'n' Roll.

The Big Band era officially ended in 1947, and as if by coincidence, 1947 also marked the beginning of the Baby Boom. Couples just stopped dancing and started copulating. "The Hokey Pokey" was also introduced in 1947, a wartime favorite brought home by our GI's stationed in Great Britain. "You put your whole self in, you put your whole self out, you put your whole self in and you shake it all about." Hmmm; maybe the *Hokey Pokey* is what the baby boom's all about.

It was the *Washington Post* in a January 1947 story that first published the idiom 'baby boom,' noting the dramatic rise in childbirth. "Three and a half million babies were born," the Post reported; "a trend that wouldn't last." In the next twenty years, 78-million diapers were changed!

Another event occurred in 1947 that passed unnoticed. Tenor sax man, "Wild Bill" Moore wrote and recorded, "We're Gonna Rock, We're Gonna Roll," for the Savoy label. It was our first allusion to rock 'n' roll.

I was just nine years old in 1947, but I vividly recall uncles and cousins spinning their 78rpm vinyl records, and blasting their AM car radios non-stop throughout the Forties. But, Big Bands, barnstorming in a bus, stalled with the wartime gas rationing, and war-weary GI's, seeking tranquility, returned home, married bob-bysoxers and settled into the quiet of the countryside. Big-city hotels closed down their ballrooms, adapting them to the rush of post-war wedding receptions; dance pavilions dismantled their bandstands, converting into roller rinks with the mighty Wurlitzer now piping the music.

In the early Fifties, Big Band vocalists stepped out, recording solo for one of four major labels (RCA Victor, Capitol, Decca, Columbia); Rosemary Clooney from Tony Pastor's band; Peggy Lee from Benny Goodman; Doris Day from Les Brown and most notably, Frank Sinatra from Jimmy Dorsey. The emerging popularity of the singer as solo star then fashioned Eddie Fisher, Patti Page, Johnnie Ray and Tony Bennett.

1947 also marked the appearance of the radio disc jockey. The FCC allowed for more radio frequencies, which resulted in a rush of new local broadcast stations and the least-expensive programming was an announcer with a stack of records. It was the powerful wartime columnist Walter Winchell who first coined the phrase "disc jockey" to describe the on-air duties of Martin Block on WNEW's "Make Believe Ballroom." In 1947, Alan Freed signed on at WAKR in Akron, Ohio, his first effort as a deejay. Al Jarvis at KFWB in Los Angeles set the standard and Arthur Godfrey at WFBR in Baltimore set the style – chatty, intimate and breezy. Radio announcers were no longer just anonymous narrators; for the very first time were permitted – encouraged – to identify themselves, to develop a following, and become personalities.

It was about this time that Top 40 radio hit the airwaves. The story behind the creation of the Top 40 radio format is legend in the music-biz. Broadcast pioneer Todd Storz was in an Omaha diner and noticed that the teenage waitress played the same tunes over and over on the jukebox – there were 40 slots on the early Wurlitzer jukeboxes. This concept, of a radio station playing only the 40 best-selling singles, transformed radio. When, in 1954, the transitor was introduced, the small, portable radio became a symbol of teenage independence and the catalyst for the biggest music upheaval in history. Rock 'n' roll music on Top 40 AM radio pushed the sale of transitor radios over the brink.

Rock 'n' roll snuck up on me, through a dark backdoor marked Rhythm & Blues, with "race music" inscribed on the doormat. I could only listen to authentic R&B on far off frequencies, my transistor lighting up my darkened bedroom with dangerous, taboo sounds. It was a shadowy, double life I lived – illicit girlie-magazines under my mattress, the devil's music on my bedside radio and the forbidden ritual of masturbation, followed by prayers of redemption. A mighty fortress was the bedroom bunker of a Fifties boy, a fallout shelter of self-abuse and jungle music.

The Crows' oh-oh-oh-"Gee" was the first black R&B song I can remember being played on the radio to a white teenage audience. A close second was the Willows' recording of "Church Bells May Ring" (with the catchy bass-line "hello, hello again" and with an unknown sixteen year old Neil Sedaka on chimes). Most mainstream disc jockeys were feeding us "cover records." White boys, the Diamonds, covered "Church Bells May Ring" –thankfully, it's the Willows' record we all remember. We were getting our first taste of musical soul-food in easily-digestible platters served up by pleasant white singers, copied from the black man and handed down through the generations, like a favored family recipe. All the main ingredients were there, but it lacked the spice, the heat, those stick-to-the-bones secret ingredients – soul and inspiration. I actually saw the Clovers' green station wagon drive through Hubbard, Ohio one afternoon, but they were just passing through, which is what most black artists did in mid-Fifties America.

Pat Boone and Elvis Presley were the most popular male singers of the Fifties, as opposite as white bucks and blue suede shoes; each found success as cover artists. "Hound Dog" was a twelve-bar blues wailer, written by Jerry Leiber and Mike Stoller and originally recorded in 1952 by Willa Mae "Big Mama" Thornton, as a grinding blues lament. Then, three years later, Freddie Bell and the Bellboys, a popular lounge combo, adapted the lyrics to appeal to a broader audience. "Snoopin' round my door" was replaced with "cryin' all the time," and "You can wag your tail, but I ain't gonna feed you no more" was replaced by "You ain't never caught a rabbit, and you ain't no friend of mine." This new version of "Hound Dog" became the centerpiece of the Bellboy's act in the Silver Queen Bar at the Las Vegas Sands Hotel. Elvis visited the Sands to take in their show and flipped over their reworking of "Hound Dog." He quickly added the song to his own show at the New Frontier Hotel, then recorded the song as a frenetic, up-tempo ditty, supported by the Jordanaires' wop-doo-wop back vocals, a novelty tune masking as rock 'n' roll. Elvis Presley's "Hound Dog" spent a record eleven weeks at No.1 on the national charts. His next No. 1 was "Love Me Tender," a century-old, sentimental Civil War melody, "Aura Lee" first published in 1861, a popular polecat of barbershop quartets, college glee clubs, and sung at West Point. "Hound Dog" and "Love Me Tender" rewarded Elvis Presley with sixteen consecutive weeks at No.1, longer than any other artist of the rock 'n' roll era.

His outrageous hip-swiveling and "racy" lyrics produced an army of Elvis detractors – Elvis became the devil personified. Undeterred, Elvis' personal manager Colonel Tom Parker quickly capitalized on the anti-Elvis uprising by ordering five million "I Hate Elvis" button-pins, selling them at $1 each and splitting the profits 50-50 with Elvis." It's my duty," said the crafty huckster, "to keep Elvis in the 90% tax-bracket."

Pat Boone, on the other hand, was a much more blatant plagiarizer, cutting clean-cut, note-for-note versions of down-and-dirty-ditties by Little Richard, Fats Domino and Ivory Joe Hunter.

Bandleader Johnny Otis, famous for "Willie and the Hand Jive," recorded an answer song to Hank Ballard and the Midnighters' ambiguous and sexually suggestive novelty song, "Work with Me Annie." "Her nibs," Miss Georgia Gibbs cleaned-up the lyrics to mask the sexual overtures of the original, and responded with "Dance with Me Henry," a top of the charts smash hit. Georgia Gibbs then made a career covering the note-for-note arrangements of LaVern Baker, beating her onto the national charts, and then Dorothy Collins would further whitewash the songs on "Your Hit Parade." The feisty Miss Baker felt so violated that she took a $125,000 accident insurance policy naming Miss Gibbs as the sole beneficiary. In a letter to Georgia Gibbs, LaVern wrote "this policy is to provide for you in the event of my untimely death, of the opportunity of copying my songs and arrangements in the future." LaVern signed the letter, "Tra La La and Twiddle Dee Dee, LaVern Baker."

The wholesome harmonies of the McGuire Sisters were ideal recordings for my television Baby Sitters to lip-synch, and believe me, they performed them all on "Rucker's Rumpus Room." But, who knew that their greatest hits were R&B knockoffs? "Goodnight, Sweetheart, Goodnight" was a Spaniels' recording, "It May Sound Silly" was from Ivory Joe Hunter; and "He" was an Al Hibbler tune. The McGuire Sisters biggest hit, "Sincerely," was first recorded by the Moonglows – and we never saw the Moonglows on Ed Sullivan!

While R&B was being scrubbed-up into palatable rock 'n' roll for white kids, small independent labels were stepping up to the plate, scoring homeruns with raw, ground-breaking hits by Chuck Berry, Jerry Lee Lewis, and Clyde McPhatter. Atlantic, Vee Jay, Sun and Chess may have been minor league players, but according to the *Billboard* scoreboard, the playing field was leveling. By 1955, specialty record stores began selling oldies of the Clovers, the Ravens and the Moonglows, and *a cappella* groups (four-part harmony without musical accompaniment.)

One of the giant ballads of 1955, the haunting "Pledging My Love," by Memphis-born blues singer Johnny Ace, was released posthumously in 1955, after his tragic death. On Christmas Eve 1954, drunk on vodka backstage at a "Negro Christmas Party" at the City Auditorium in Houston Texas, he shot himself. There are conflicting stories about his end game. Playing Russian roulette, he placed a .45 caliber revolver to his temple and pulled the trigger, ending his life. Big Mama Thornton, a witness to the shooting, said in a written statement that "Ace had been playing with the gun, but not playing Russian roulette." "Pledging My Love," (Duke Records), his biggest hit ever, was released weeks after his death, and is now a rock 'n' roll classic.

When RCA Victor bought out Elvis' contract from Sun Records in the mid-Fifties, Columbia Records wanted a rock 'n' roll idol of their own; their star Johnnie Ray was, by 1955, a Johnny-come-lately. Columbia turned to Tony Bennett, attempting to market their pop crooner as a rock 'n' roll singer. Bennett actually appeared in one of Alan Freed's Big Beat stage shows, bursting a blood vessel in his throat trying to sing over the clamor. "It was chaos," Tony remembered. "They can't sit still. They'd jump around and dance and scream. It scared the hell out of me." It wasn't until 1963 that Dion joined Columbia Records, becoming their first rock 'n' roll solo artist.

It was emblematic of the times that RCA's two biggest selling recording artists were Elvis Presley, the rockabilly baritone and Mario Lanza, the pseudo-operatic tenor. Presley often said that Mario Lanza was his favorite singer, and each had similar careers; both were former truck drivers, recorded for RCA, starred in custom-made MGM musicals, struggled with obesity and died early, under mysterious circumstances.

The appearance of Elvis, Pat Boone, and the Platters on the pop music charts signaled a shift for "Rucker's Rumpus Room." Soon, the Everly Brothers, Chuck Berry and Little Richard slipped onto our top-tunes play-list. I lip-synched "Blueberry Hill," with Fats Domino's distinctive 'N'Orleans' drawl rolling off my pearly-white lips. I was, without fully-becoming aware, now hosting a rock 'n' roll show. I had never heard music so unique, so irreverent, and as instinctively appealing as rock 'n' roll. And besides, you could dance to it, and I *loved* to dance. I fell in love with rock 'n' roll music, little knowing that rock 'n' roll music would one day define my life. I needed to jump onto this rockin'- rollin' bandwagon in a bigger way.

Recalling Jim Lounsbury's 1954 TV record hop in Chicago, I immediately sold the WFMJ-TV brass on the idea – we needed to produce our own studio dance party! So, each Saturday afternoon, in addition to our 7pm Rumpus Room, I began hosting "One O'clock Jump," dancing with a studio audience of high school rabble-rousers.

My musical jargon up to that point was limited to Baptist church hymns, high school glee club anthems, and Broadway show tunes – the Great American Songbook of Berlin, Porter and the Gershwin's. None of today's young people will believe this, but my high school chums actually played Broadway show tunes at our weekend house parties. We knew all the words, and sang along to "The Pajama Game" and "Damn Yankees." Some parents were able to afford holiday trips to New York to see the latest shows, and would return with armfuls of Original Cast Recordings. The Fifties were also the Golden Age of the Hollywood Musical and soundtrack recordings were suddenly available on a single 331/3 Unbreakable Long Playing vinyl album – The LP.

At that exact moment in time, while my Ohio gang was going gaga over "Can-Can" and "The Song from Moulin Rouge," over in England, at 20 Forthlin Road in Allerton, Liverpool, thirteen-year old Paul McCartney was captivated by British music hall songs, and at fourteen, composed his own vaudeville-styled ditty, "When I'm 64," as a birthday present to his dad. The Beatles later recorded the tune on their landmark "Sgt. Pepper" album, with a co-credit to Lennon. "I would never even dream of writing a song like that," Lennon said of the song, "Paul wrote it in our Cavern days. We just stuck a few more words on it like 'grandchildren on your knee'. This was one that was quite a hit with us." But with the new exported Broadway show LP's, Paul became infatuated with musical comedies, most particularly Meredith Willson's brilliant pastiche of cornball Americana, "The Music Man." One of Paul's very first angelic recordings was the show's love ballad, "Till There Was You."

Meanwhile, over at 3260 Coney Island Avenue in Brooklyn, in the Brighton Beach apartment of the Sedaka family, show tunes were beguiling a budding songwriter Neil Sedaka, who directed a production of "Carousel" at Lincoln High School and "Annie Get Your Gun," at a Lake George summer camp. His neighborhood buddy, a tone-deaf poet named Howie Greenfield, preferred the sophisticated lyrics of Lorenz Hart ("Where or When"), Richard Rodger's first writing partner. Although Greenfield hated rock 'n' roll, his first hit collaboration with Neil would be the Connie Francis rocker, "Stupid Cupid." But many of their early collaborations echoed Broadway: "Calendar Girl" was patterned after Cole Porter's idiosyncratic laundry-list tunes, ("You're The Top" or "Let's Do It"), and "Where the Boys

Are" was like an epic, soaring show tune. A generation's DNA is forever imprinted with the incidental music of its youth – nursery rhymes, radio jingles, campfire songs, Steven Foster, John Philip Sousa, and Irving Berlin: "White Christmas," "Easter Parade" and "God Bless America." It's a start.

The power of television to the benefit of the record industry was hammered home in a big way on the CBS anthology series Studio One. When the producers were planning an hour-long drama about the music business, they turned to Mitch Miller at Columbia Records to come up with an original song for the program's soundtrack. Miller recorded "Let Me Go, Lover," sung by the unknown Joan Weber, and then, with great foresight, shipped it to record stores, where it sat on the shelf, with little demand, until the night of the telecast, November 15, 1954. The next morning, 500,000 copies of "that song I heard last night on television" were sold, becoming the biggest-selling record of 1955. It wasn't until January of 1957, when Tommy Sands appeared in an Elvis-like role on a Kraft Television Theatre drama, "Teenage Idol," singing "Teen-age Crush," that literally overnight Sands himself became a "teenage idol," a million seller. Of course, there were some misdirected misfires, most memorable James Brown singing "The White Buffalo" on Rin Tin Tin.

Pop-rock music also became the subject and ridicule of the nation's television comics, fresh new territory for parody. On "Your Show of Shows," Sid Caesar, Howard Morris, and Carl Reiner took a satiric swipe at the Crew-Cuts, dressed as the Three Haircuts in white dinner jackets and string bowties, singing "You Are So Rare to Me," a skit that became a minor hit recording. Milton Berle couldn't wait to slap on black sideburns, a pompadour wig, strap himself into a guitar and swivel his hips as Elvis Pretzel, amid a stage full of yapping hound dogs.

Steve Allen on the Tonight show took a more somber approach, reciting the lyrics of "Sh-Boom" as poetry, respectfully enunciating each syllable, as Skitch Henderson set the appropriate reverential mood, accompanying on the organ:

Hey nonny ding dong, alang alang alang
Boom ba-doh, ba-doo ba-doodle-ay
Oh, life could be a dream (sh-boom)
If I could take you up in paradise up above (sh-boom)
If you would tell me I'm the only one that you love
Life could be a dream, sweetheart
(Hello, hello again, sh-boom and hopin' we'll meet again)
Sh-boom sh-boom Ya-da-da Da-da-da Da-da-da Da
Sh-boom sh-boom Ya-da-da Da-da-da Da-da-da Da
Sh-boom sh-boom Ya-da-da Da-da-da Da-da-da Da, sh-boom!

A two-page story in the national edition of *TV Radio Mirror* (December, 1955) profiled "Rucker's Rumpus Room" with a photo spread, typical of fan magazines at the time, of the Rucker family at home. "Al points to Steve Allen as his greatest inspiration," they reported with gushing quotes from me about "wishing to warm his seat when he is old and gray." That bit of adulation prompted an invitation from Tom Naud, a Tonight show producer, for me to sit on the aisle at The Hudson Theatre for a brief, "spontaneous" chat with Steve Allen. Steve, sauntering up the aisle with his hand-mike, got this-close, and then the clock ran out.

My network debut was destined to be on the "Today" show. I awoke early the next morning to rush over to the RCA Victor showrooms in Radio City where NBC broadcast the show with Dave Garroway, *live* each morning at 7am. When the cameras panned through the windows to the sidewalk spectators, there I was. I was also up on the monitors in the WFMJ-TV control room back in Youngstown. "Hey. There's Al Rucker!" They were not amused. I was supposed to be home, sick in bed. I was caught red handed in black and white.

Trips to New York City to see "the shows" became more frequent; my aspirations still remained in the theatre, as a song-and-dance man. The G-F sent Dad to inspect their furniture aboard The S. S. United States, the world's fastest ocean liner, now berthed along the West Side piers, and I tagged along. Dad allotted me twenty-dollars to see Johnnie Ray at the late-show at The Latin Quarter – I had a steak and a Coke, well-pampered by a kind, grandfatherly waiter. Mom and Dad also treated me to a Manhattan weekend to see the McGuire Sisters, my first visit to The Copacabana. Kids back home weren't the least daunted by the singing sisters; they were more impressed that a Coca-Cola in New York cost a dollar!

My television sponsor, Century Foods ran a sweepstakes, a Grand Prize all-expense-paid Weekend at The Waldorf, and Mom's brother, Uncle Bud won. We joined the party on a Capital Airlines flight to New York City where Bud and his wife Gwen were VIP guests in an elaborate suite at The Waldorf-Astoria. Mom and Dad and I stayed in lackluster rooms at The Taft, appropriately named for our least-memorable President.

Vic Damone was the star attraction at The Waldorf's Empire Room, while over at The Taft, Charlie Drew was spewing bawdy "songs mother never taught you" in the Tap Room. "Oh, that Charlie Drew!" ads appeared in the *New Yorker* for decades. Uncle Bud took us to Toots Shor's, Jack Dempsey's and The Brass Rail for a "Kosher Corned-Beef Sandwich on Rye." We sampled strange new breakfast treats, bagel and lox at The Carnegie Deli ("Which is the bagel and which is the lox?"), a prune Danish at Schrafft's, and an English muffin at ColBee's, the CBS coffee shop at that magic address, 485 Madison Avenue. We discovered Manhattan's best hamburger at Arthur Maisel's Californian on Broadway and something called cheese cake at Lindy's.

Soon, I was brazen enough to demand New York weekends on my own to catch the latest musical comedies. I mail-ordered my tickets through McBride's Ticket brokers, and always got front-row seats for a Friday night show with a matinee and evening show on Saturday. My favorites were "The Most Happy Fellow," "L'il Abner" and "Ankles Aweigh," with Betty & Jane Kean and the longest, leggiest line of chorus girls I had ever seen. I was becoming infatuated by an all-new fantasy – one that could only be realized on that magical island of Manhattan.

To capitalize on my January 1st birthday, I created a televised clockwatching party on New Year's Eve, hosting the show in a nightclub setting with a live studio audience dancing, and the Baby Sitters and the Collegians lip-synching the top tunes of 1955, before joining NBC in Times Square at 11:55. The songs we performed reflect the conflicts and contradictions of the schizophrenic music scene of 1955 – pop, novelties, marches, show tunes, R&B covers, and the official coming of rock 'n' roll:

"Somethin's Gotta' Give"	(McGuire Sisters) *from the film, "Daddy Longlegs"*
"Moments to Remember"	(The Four Lads)
"Love and Marriage"	(Frank Sinatra) *from the TV musical special, "Our Town"*
"Seventeen"	(The Fontane Sisters)
"Honey Babe"	(Art Mooney) *march from the film "Battle Cry"*
"Rock Around the Clock"	(Bill Haley & the Comets) *from the film "Blackboard Jungle"*
"Mister Sandman"	(The Chordettes)
"The Yellow Rose of Texas"	(Mitch Miller) *march from the film, "Yellow Rose of Texas"*
"Dance With Me Henry"	(Georgia Gibbs) *a cover of Etta James' "Roll With Me Henry"*
"Heart"	(The Four Aces) *from the Broadway musical "Damn Yankees"*

It was also on that show that I performed Buddy Hackett's classic Chinese waiter routine ("One from Column A, Two from Column B"), actually lip-synching his spoken-word recording. I also mastered Jerry Lewis' frenetic, "I'm A Little Busybody," a song with twenty-five-words-or-less per second, and the tenor's aria from "Il Trovatore" – in Italian! By this time lip-synching had become a challenge and I was willing to take impossibly difficult records and master the lip synchronization. I was delighted to learn later that Dick Van Dyke, Steve Martin, James Kirkwood,

Mitzi Welch; even Jerry Lewis entered show business with a record pantomime act. Debbie Reynolds won a teenage talent contest (and a movie contract) lip-synching Betty Hutton records, and in her first film, "Three Little Words," Debbie lip-synched Helen Kane's famous 'boop-boop-bee-doo' recording of "I Want To Be Loved By You." Lip-synching is currently enjoying a major reawakening on MySpace by those Pampered Millennium babies, flapping their lips, shaking their hips, dancing around their bedrooms in their tighty-whities, posturing for their webcams.

I was one of the lucky few in my high school; I actually knew what I wanted to do when I grew up. I had taken advantage of every opportunity that small-town Ohio had to offer, I had produced and hosted a unique and successful television show for four years and it was time to move on. I was itching to get out of Dodge. The itch was in my groin.

Annette was waiting for me at the appointed spot on the beach. I was watching her every move from the deck, high above the dunes of Malibu Beach. Her breasts bounced as she danced across the sand, stretching against her white cotton T-shirt. She turned, looked up and waved, removing her shirt, revealing her bronzed body. My frosted tumbler of Pina Colada, freshly blended, numbed my fingers, and the hot sand, stung my toes. I hop- scotched towards her across the beach. She ran to me and fell into my arms with a big welcoming kiss.

Annette, of course, was my boyhood fantasy. Annette was the fantasy girl of every teenaged boy in the 1950's. We preferred watching "The Mickey Mouse Club" alone and in the dark. My hormones were raging, a cause for religious damnation! Like teenage zits, guilt and shame were breaking-out all over my face, blemishes brought about by secretly-held erotic fantasies, taboo in the sexually subdued Fifties. S-e-x was unspoken, revealed only in nasty magazines sequestered under-the-counter and purchased with a wink and a nod. Oh, I prayed, "God, please forgive me…I'll never do it again"…and, of course I did, and I was sure that each time I did it, the whole town knew it. In Ohio, folks could not only read your thoughts, they relished in it. Rumor is the principle commodity of small town life. Rumor would spread as fast and furious as one of Ohio's notorious winter blizzards. One flake sticks, packs, gathers power, and rolls thundering downhill, accumulating strength and girth until it overwhelms the town – a town where everyone owns a snowplow. Nobody bothered to tell me: *"You can't get arrested for your fantasies."*

I had no one to turn to for advice. Mom, designated to tell me about "the birds and the bees," totally confused me with vague biblical metaphors, and clinical references to "planting the seed." For years, I looked for the seed, to no avail. Mom had enough burdens on her shoulders; I couldn't weigh her down with my millstones. How do you tell your Mom you're a pervert? ("Lord, please forgive me … and by the way, where's my seed!")

I was incapable of sharing confidences with Dad; our static relationship did not include intimate chats. I was still stinging from the shame I felt when, a few years earlier, Dad walked into the little shed behind our garage to discover me *au natural*, playing "Doctor" with two neighborhood sisters. "I was just following the instruction of my nurses." My buddies were spilling over with sexual misinformation as well, although many claimed to have actually "done it." My early sexual thoughts manifested into twenty-four hour fantasies; theirs went down at sunup.

My actual *first time* finally arrived one moonless summer night, an awkward few minutes with Mary Lou, an overripe teenaged virgin, on the rock-strewn beach of the Cuyahoga River. A few nights later, in search of a Justice of the Peace, Mary Lou and I eloped to Illinois, a state that permitted children to marry without drawing blood. Over a basket of fried clams at an all-night Howard Johnson's, sanity prevailed and we limped home, never to see one another again. As my "Uncle" Clay had advised me, "try everything," so that's how I found myself singing "Well, Hello Mary Lou" while drawing blood on the minefield shores of the Cuyahoga River, a body of water so polluted it actually caught fire. Our brief romance did not.

Never mind. I was growing comfortable in my ever-widening circle of older friends, especially one person at the station, a continuity writer and former CIA operative, Raysa Bonow. Raysa introduced me to Chinese cuisine, the Weavers, Hebrew Seder hymns, jazz and the joys of smoking. Raysa was a two-pack a day smoker, abstaining years later, but not before teaching me how to light, hold, puff and exhale a Camel, back when it was cool and sophisticated to smoke. I have been a lifelong smoker ever since.

Raysa once asked me how much I smoked.

"That's the one thing I never discuss," I told her.

"Oh, okay. Then tell me about your sex life."

When Raysa took off for Manhattan in the summer of 1957, I was right on her heels. I had two escape routes out of Paranoia, Ohio – a firm offer as a deejay at a new radio station in Buffalo, or I take my chances as a song and dance man in New York City.

I did *not* shuffle off to Buffalo.

4) NBC to Channel 13, 1957 – 1959

"If man can live in Manhattan, he can live anywhere."
– *Arthur C. Clarke*

July 10, 1957, Dad deposited me at the Sloane House YMCA, totally unaware that the 34th Street Y was notorious in the gay underground as the "Homo Hilton." Dad was obviously drawn to the Christian aspects in its name, blind to the "Young Men's – Association." The rates were low, about $15 weekly for a room overlooking an airshaft, welcome relief to the heat of that sizzling Manhattan summer.

I landed a $29 a week job as a Page at NBC and high-tailed it out of the Y, invited into a rambling, three-bedroom apartment down in the West Village on Hudson Street, shared with seven other pageboys. Imagine my good fortune; my first job in New York at 30 Rock, that historic Art Deco masterpiece, with its vaulted Main Hall, distinctive Diego Rivera murals, and brass-accented elevator banks, staffed by uniformed starters. To me, Rockefeller Center seemed to be the center of the universe. On payday, we Pages raced downstairs to Hurley's, an old-time sawdust saloon, tucked into the 49th Street corner of the towering Rockefeller Center. During the Depression, Mr. Hurley refused to sell his property to Mr. Rockefeller, so his four-story building still stands; they just built the mighty RCA Building around him.

Being an NBC Page was a highly desirable position to a young man wishing to climb the ladder of the booming new television industry. NBC patterned their prized Page division after the military, with uniforms, rank and a morning line-up for fingernail, facial-hair and shoe inspection. We worked out of the NBC wing of the RCA Building, from which we were dispatched to the various NBC theatres and studios around town, working the daytime game shows of Bill Cullen and Hugh Downs and the primetime variety shows of Steve Allen and Perry Como.

The NBC Guest Relations Department carefully screened the 1957 Page staff, eager young WASP's with solid-sounding American names like, Simpson, Hopkins and Boone, with not a female or black among us. Our token Jew was Larry Cohen. Women were admitted to the guide staff, (Eva Marie Saint had recently departed) shuttling herds of bewildered tourists through the maze of empty radio and television studios of NBC.

Among my buddies on the 1957 page staff were several who shared my showbiz ambitions: Doug Lewellen carved out a long-running career as the on-camera reporter on Judge Wapner's "People's Court," and Joey Rogers, (as Joey Powers) sang his way onto the 1963 Top 10 with his hit, "Midnight Mary." Harv Moore became a radio star in Buffalo, co-hosting a memorable morning show, Taylor & Moore, 'your breakfast flakes.' Al Onorato created the Universal Studios Tour in Hollywood, Warren Robertson distinguished himself as one of New York's most innovative drama teachers with his breakthrough "acting as therapy" technique, and Gary Geld and Peter Udell became an award-winning Broadway team, writing the book and score to "Purlie" and "Shenandoah," among others. They also wrote and produced pop tunes for Connie Francis, Jackie Wilson, Gene Pitney, and most notably Brian Hyland's 1962 classic "Sealed with a Kiss."

The day crew fought for a spot on "Treasure Hunt," a morning game show hosted by comedy star Jan Murray, who generously provided urns of coffee, Danish and bagels for his staff, production crew and us poor, starving pages. One morning Jonathan Winters suddenly appeared in the "Treasure Hunt" theatre lobby assuming the role of a German Gestapo Officer, breaking-up our little coffee clutch, and ordering us in line and at attention. Eager to play along with the wacky comedy star and more than willingly to accept his abuse, we snapped to attention, as he paced up and down the lineup, barking expletives. Except for the giggles, it was very much like the morning locker room inspections by our own Gestapo, Page Supervisor Jim Anderson.

Jack Barry hosted a daily game show, "Tic-Tac-Dough," in Studio 6-B, a "Hollywood Squares" without the laughs. A half-hour before airtime, Jack fell ill and his stand-by, Jay Jackson was overjoyed at the news. However, Mr. Jackson's hairpiece was in the repair shop for its 3,000-mile check up, so I was recruited to run the fifteen blocks to his wig maker and return to the studios before airtime. I made it back in a hairsbreadth, with five minutes to spare; enough time for the glue to dry.

Working studio 6-B one afternoon, Milton Berle's rehearsal for a Tab Hunter ice spectacular was suddenly halted by Uncle Miltie's piercing police whistle, and a gush of foul four-letter words. Uncle Miltie was using the "F" word! My Uncle Miltie! I soon discovered that all trendy New Yorkers embrace the "F" word. Raysa used it as often as possible. Wishing to be among the smart-set, I was now smoking, drinking and evoking the "F" word. I quickly learned colorful Jewish and Italian endearments like *"schmuck"* and *"va fongool,"* essential skills in becoming a subscriber to *The New Yorker.*

I devised a ten-year plan: make it in New York or call it quits and return home, writing for my hometown newspaper. I had been in New York for just a few months when I received a phone call from Dad. "Sit down," he said, "I've got news for you. Your mother is expecting a baby."

Oh my gawd, I thought, I've only been gone two months and they've replacing me already. Mom was 43, at an age when delivery might be difficult, and besides, what happened to that six-year rule? Rick, Jim and I were each born exactly six years apart.

Tammy Rucker arrived the next year, without complication. Throughout her adolescence she was haunted by that Debbie Reynolds' tune "Tammy," so in the Sixties, she insisted we call her Tama, befitting her new Birkenstock flower-child persona. Tama it is.

Mom and Dad and Jim and Rick came to visit as often as possible and I became a hero to my brothers when I got them into the peanut gallery of "The Howdy Doody Show" with Buffalo Bob Smith. Even up close, they didn't realize that Bob Smith was a ventriloquist, providing the voice for Mr. Doody and his gang of marionettes. Peanut gallery kiddies were required to sing-a-long the sponsor's jingle:

Brush your teeth with Colgate, Colgate Dental Cream

It cleans your breath, while it cleans your teeth.

Trouble is, moms at home were using just any old toothpaste, not the red and white Colgate tube, thinking they could fool their unsuspecting tykes. Bob Smith himself solved the dilemma, rewriting the jingle:
Brush your teeth with Colgate, Colgate Dental Cream
You'll know its right, *if it's red and white.*

When Buffalo Bob signed off the show, NBC Pages had just two minutes to hustle the kiddies out of the peanut gallery and into the next-door studio to be on "Pinky" Lee.

NBC Pages were allowed all-access to studio theatres, and there were three primetime music-variety shows from New York that season, Perry Como, Steve Allen and Polly Bergen with the Peter Gennaro Dancers. My favorite was The Kraft Music Hall starring Perry Como, the classiest music-variety show ever produced, televised from the celebrated Ziegfeld Theatre on Sixth Avenue.

The line on the super-cool, relaxed Mr. Como went like this:
"Did you see Perry Como last night?"
"No. I fell asleep."
"So did he."

I never missed a rehearsal, watching Perry, the Ray Charles Singers (not *that* Ray Charles) and producer Gary Smith at work. Ray Charles was the stand-in for Perry during rehearsals, when the notoriously tranquil 'Mr. C' sauntered on stage, dressed in his trademark cardigan sweater, for a flawless final dress rehearsal.

Steve Allen was now starring in a one-hour comedy revue, scheduled by NBC to go head-to-head with the long-running CBS "Ed Sullivan Show" at eight o'clock on Sunday night. Steve's new format borrowed a page from Dave Garroway's "Wide Wide World" program, staging elaborate musical spots *live* on location, with guest stars singing on rooftops along Broadway or dancing around fountains at The Fontainebleau in Miami. It took an appearance by Jerry Lee Lewis to spike the ratings, the only time Steve Allen's hour topped the mighty Ed Sullivan. (To mark the occasion, Jerry Lee Lewis named his newborn son, Steve Allen Lewis.) In spite of Steve's big-name guest stars, his infusion of jazz, and his merry "Man On The Street," it was Ed Sullivan who had "the really big show."

In July of 1957, it was the summer replacement shows that really excited me. In the early days of television, before videotape, primetime network stars like Garry Moore, Jackie Gleason, and Perry Como took a thirteen week hiatus, and the networks filled their timeslots with low-budget music shows, hosted by big-name record stars. Right here in NBC Studio 8-H, Manhattan's largest television studio (constructed in the radio days especially for Arturo Toscanini and the NBC Symphony Orchestra, and decades later as home-base for "Saturday Night Live"), were all the great singing stars of the early Fifties, whose records were staples of my lip-synching Rumpus Room gang.

From the secluded balcony, I could look down starry-eyed as Georgia Gibbs, Tony Bennett, Patti Page, Guy Mitchell, Teresa Brewer, and vocal fours like the Four Aces, the Four Lads, the Four Freshmen, the Hilltoppers and the Ames Brothers rolled out their greatest hits. Pat Boone, Ricky Nelson and Elvis were considered mainstream enough for network television, but other late 50s rock stars were still off-limits.

One mismatched occasion was Elvis Presley's six appearances on "Stage Show," a summer series replacing Jackie Gleason on CBS, which paired Mr. Swivel-Hips with the Forties' Big Bands of Tommy and Jimmy Dorsey. (Jimmy Dorsey actually had one of the hottest recordings of 1957, "So Rare," sounding very much like a Johnnie Ray track without the vocals.)

During the summer of 1957, the ABC network attempted to bring rock and roll to a nationwide audience by giving Alan Freed a shot. Alan's talent lineup included top R&B stars like Chuck Berry, Bo Diddley, and Clyde McPhatter. Frankie Lymon received a wildly enthusiastic reception from the studio audience singing his current hit "Goody Goody," and swept away by all excitement, plucked a white teenage girl from the audience for an impromptu Lindy-hop. ABC's affiliates went ballistic, particularly the Southern stations, and within two weeks the show was abruptly cancelled.

Also that summer, and without fanfare, ABC quietly patched into their Philadelphia affiliate to broadcast a new teenage dance party, hosted by a former radio deejay named Dick Clark; the show was called "American Bandstand."

I was enjoying the noontime sun in Rockefeller Plaza, browsing *Cue Magazine*, when I read the announcement that NBC was reviving the "Tonight" show in an all-new format, tailored to the talents of Jack Paar. I remember thinking that this was a terrible idea and besides, who could replace the inimitable Steve Allen. After all, Jack Paar had failed as emcee of four daytime game shows and as host of a morning show that CBS had programmed against NBC's popular "Today" show. Jack Paar's new one hour-forty-five minute show would be broadcast 'live' from The Hudson Theatre in Times Square, which meant the page division had to create a late-night crew. I was chosen to work the first and every "Tonight" show for most of the first season.

Jack Paar was a puzzling personality, an enigma. "What is Jack Paar really like?" became the prevailing question across America. I recall that he was extremely tall and a snappy-dresser, very cordial to me, very calm and quiet off-stage.

"Good evening, son," he would say to me backstage, as he descended the spiral staircase that led from his second floor dressing room.

"Good evening, Mr. Paar," was about the extent of our banter.

But, on-camera Mr. Paar's high jinks are legendary. His take-no-prisoners feuds with Walter Winchell and Dorothy Kilgallen, his tear-filled walk-off, his triumphant return and his kooky regulars made Jack Paar the most talked-about man in America. NBC would soon reward his popularity, re-naming it "The Jack Paar Show."

Rather than the comedy-driven "Tonight" perfected by Steve Allen, Jack Paar brought chat to television, a format perfectly suited to the leisurely, late-night time slot, the intimate close-up camera and a responsive studio audience. Paar was drawn to the more colorful guests, glib raconteurs like Oscar Levant, Peter Ustinov and Judy Garland, rather than big stars with sizzle but no substance. Many important Hollywood film stars simply would not appear on television and most Broadway performers enjoyed limited recognition to Jack's middle-America audience.

Zsa Zsa Gabor was the perfect Paar foil, and was scheduled one evening as an unannounced guest to surprise the actor, Jean Pierre Aurmont (who, by the way, reeked of French perfume). It was my job to greet Ms. Gabor at a rear door and escort her through the maze of tunnels and boiler rooms in the cellars of the ancient Hudson Theatre, then take her up to a secure area backstage.

Zsa Zsa stepped out of her limousine shimmering, wrapped in white mink with diamonds cascading over her low-cut white evening dress. She was the most beautiful woman I had ever seen. She was so dazzling that she had to be dusted down to soften the sheen.

"Take my hand *dah-link*," she giggled, as we descended into the musty underbelly of the theatre, prompting me to adlib my best Claude Rains' "Phantom of The Opera," descending into the sewers of The Paris Opera House with his leading lady. We were hysterical laughing and Zsa Zsa could not have been nicer, amused at our secret adventure together. This was the first, but not my last with Ms. Gabor. Over the next three decades, I witnessed her sheen tarnish, her wit sour, until a cranky old cartoon remained.

It was Jack Paar's handpicked little basket of fruits and nuts that kept his audience coming back for seconds. Jack gathered a wacky gang of eccentrics whom he could count on for outrageous and thus, hysterical chatter as they walked the tight rope with him each night, coast-to-coast, without a net. Most memorable were the crusty author Alexander King, the social matron Elsa Maxwell, and the beloved Stage Deli proprietor Max Asnas.

Jack ignited a switch under fading old-timers, bringing new light to actors Hermione Gingold, Hans Conried, and Cliff Arquette as 'Charlie Weaver' and brought good-fortune to a batch of newcomers, the scatterbrained actress Dody Goodman, chanteuse Genevieve, and Jose' Melis, his Cuban-born band leader. Repeated weekly appearances with Jack made each a household name, and their personal fortunes skyrocketed, along with Paar's ratings.

Raysa Bonow and I became inseparable, racing from film to film, with our movie timetable in hand, sometimes seeing five in a day. We sat enthralled by the new wave films of Truffaut, Bergman, and Fellini and the droll British manner of Alastair Sim, Alec Guinness and Margaret Rutherford. We trolled the cellar dives to witness the emergence of Mike Nichols & Elaine May, Mort Sahl and Phyllis Diller or the intimate little Eastside clubs to see Mabel Mercer, Sylvia Syms and Bobby Cole, where we made a startling discovery – songs with verses. I diligently memorized the Sunday *New York Times* and became expert at uncovering Al Hirschfeld's concealed "Ninas." I was able to offhandedly quote the Marx Brothers and H.L. Mencken, while balancing a highball, a Camel and a plate of Swedish meatballs. I would regularly sneak into The Winter Garden with the intermission audience of "West Side Story" to see the brilliantly staged Act II opening, "Officer Krupke," hoping to see the whole piece before those feisty Irish ushers shooed me out onto the street. My Broadway hangout became Jim Downey's, an Eighth Avenue bar popular with chorus kids, stagehands and show-biz wannabes.

Raysa and I shared affection for Sid Caesar & Imogene Coca, and Raysa dated Sid Caesar's stand-in, the oddball comic Milt Kamen. Imogene Coca was a dancer before winning fame as a comedienne, inspiring me to take-up with a tiny, teen-aged ballerina, Carol Sue Sher, a member of the *corps de ballet* at Radio City Music Hall across the street from NBC.

I entered my dance period. I emceed the World Dance Festival at Columbia University and enrolled in a movement-for-actors class, under the direction of Peter Gennaro. "You move well for an actor," he told me, which was high praise from the celebrated choreographer. I was also accepted as a pupil of Colin Romoff, the dictatorial vocal coach, a tall, elegant, imposing man with a Van Dyke-goatee, which he fondled when stressed, like worry beads. I was inspired to hit the high notes by Julie Newmar, another pupil, who would languish on his divan, looking on, amused. Colin met his wife Judy Tyler at The Copacabaña, he a musician, she a dancing "Copa Girl." She appeared as "Princess Summer-Fall Winter-Spring" each day on Howdy Doody, and her big break came in 1957, co-starring with Elvis Presley in "Jailhouse Rock," his best movie. When shooting wrapped, while driving back home to Manhattan, she was killed instantly in a road accident in the middle of the desert.

All these classes were made possible by cash from Dad, stashed in his weekly CARE Package of canned goods, Spanish peanuts and Mom's freshly baked Toll-house cookies. I sent dad a Father's Day card nominating him for an Oscar – in the Best *Supporting* Role.

Tom Pyle, another from our NBC Page crew, aspired to be the next David Merrick, the exceedingly successful but highly unpopular Broadway impresario. To hone his producer skills, Tom promoted charity shows in the wards of Bel-leview Hospital so our star-struck staff could entertain their impoverished patients with songs and shtick. Larry Cohen was developing a standup comedy routine, but even the sick and infirm couldn't muster a smile. His routines were painful. Larry, however, got the last laugh. He soon became one of Hollywood's most popu-lar maverick filmmakers, writing screenplays and directing inventive low-budget fright-films, sci-fi flicks and the Blaxploitation films of the 1970s. While a Page at NBC, Larry slipped into the darkened stages of the dramatic shows of Reginald Rose, Paddy Chayefsky, and Rod Serling, broadcast *live* during that celebrated "Golden Age of Television." Larry was inspired to write several teleplays of his own, which were produced during 1958–1961, featuring performances by Peter Falk, Keir Dullea, Jack Warden and Henny Youngman. Most recently, Larry's screenplay for "Phone Booth" earned him a reported $750,000.

Tom Pyle was continually fascinated by my many stories as host of the Rumpus Room back in Ohio, so he shopped around the idea and to my surprise, found a buyer. Seymour Horowitz, program director of a wide-reaching New England sta-tion, WJAR-TV in Providence, RI agreed to clear an early Saturday time-slot, if we could package and produce the half-hour show. Although I didn't realize the prospective results, this connection is what directly led to my contract with New York's Channel 13. At heart, I owe my entire career in New York to Tom Pyle.

I called on Raysa, who was now producing shows at NBC, for input, for ad-vice and for her credit card. We quickly auditioned and signed-on four girls and three boys, attractive, young actors eager to get some television experience, will-ing to rehearse three nights a week, and travel the parkways to Providence each weekend. Tom, Raysa and I formed Parkway Productions and titled our new show, "Al Rucker and the Seven Teens." We rehearsed in various Manhattan apartments during the week, and each Saturday we'd gather at the crack of dawn, travel north to Providence, with camera rehearsals all afternoon, on-the-air *live* at 7:30 in the evening, and then fall exhausted into our rental car for the seemingly endless drive home to Manhattan.

The very first performer to sign-on was a robust NBC page, Bob DuCharme, with ambitions as a stage actor; Bob was a student at the American Academy of Dramatic Arts, alongside Robert Redford. Raysa found us a leading man, Tony Michaels, an incredibly handsome Adelphi College freshman to lip-synch the Johnny Mathis "make-out songs" that were suddenly dominating the pop charts, and Elliott James, an agreeable Jewish "nebbish" from Queens. I took the comedy cut-up role, singing "Black Leather Jacket and Motorcycle Boots" (a Leiber & Stoller song, recorded by the Cheers, dressed in leather drag on a bad-looking Harley) or Stan Freberg's take on "Banana Boat (Day-O)," making whoopee of the current Belafonte-Kingston Trio calypso craze.

Our little band of gypsies also included Sharon Farrell ("The Reivers" with Steve McQueen), and Andrew Prine ("The Miracle Worker" with Anne Bancroft), two young actors who were briefly married and became well-known in the film and television dramas of the Sixties, Alison Van Dyke, who's father was film curator at MoMA, her mom, a popular drama teacher, and Carey Porter-Moss, the most sophisticated, but hardly a teenager, hired for her wardrobe of exotic evening gowns and cocktail dresses. But, when we held a "win a date with..." contest, the boys of Providence chose Lynn Raymond, a blonde spitfire by way of Carnegie-Tech. (Lynn and Carey appear briefly, in a 1958 clip from the show, posted on YouTube.)

There is safety in numbers, and my number that year was seven. I found comfort under the security blanket of my new television gang, sharing my angst with seven others suffering their own dramatic dilemmas. At a weekend bacchanal at Tom Pyle's home on the well-heeled Fisher's Island, a drunken, sobbing Tom Pyle marched into the crashing waves, announcing, "I'm walking into the Ocean to commit suicide. Will some one please hold my watch?" (How *very* Norman Maine!)

I first met Lynn Raymond in the offices of the 1950s quiz-show sensations, Jack Barry and Dan Enright; Lynn was their switchboard operator. I left NBC and signed-on as a production assistant in the Madison Avenue offices of Barry-Enright, who were riding-high with the top-rated, primetime NBC quiz show "Twenty-One," plus several daytime game shows. It was my job to pre-screen ordinary citizens, initiating a long vetting process to weed-out the dim-witted and uncover sparkling, animated contestants that would appear with host Jack Barry on the show. On Tuesday evenings I would return to NBC Studio 6-A for the nine o'clock *live* broadcast, working backstage. As close as I was to the action, I had no idea that the whole show was rigged and was about to erupt into a sensational nation-wide scandal, retold in the 1994 Robert Redford film, "Quiz Show." In an attempt to pump-up the ratings, and bump an unpopular contestant, Herb Stempel, the Barry-Enright producers gave the players in the soundproof isolation booth all the answers in advance. Barry-Enright folded, shady as a Times Square three-card-Monty game.

So began a long list of menial, low-paying jobs; I plugged away as a stockroom boy at Bloomingdale's, as host at The Brass Rail, a soda jerk at Walgreen's and as an usher at Lowe's Lexington movie theatre. My leanest times are the most laughable now. While waiting for my $19.00 Friday paycheck at Lowe's, I was literally starving, pillaging the aisles, devouring half-eaten boxes of popcorn. Lowe's once gave me thirty-cent bus fare to deliver a heavy stack of marquee letters over to Lowe's Capital Theatre on Broadway. Instead, I decided to hoof-it over to Broadway, drop off my load, and spend the thirty cents on a hotdog, orange drink and a donut at Nedicks, eating on the fly.

My on-again, off-again 'blue funks' became a nine-month blue streak, as a runner for Colony Music, shuttling records from their satellite store, Tin Pan Alley Records, at 50th and Broadway, a shop specializing in hard-to-get oldies. The best way I can describe the feelings of depression is a sense of hopelessness. I awoke each morning in a funk and I went to bed in a funk. I wandered through the days, listless as a zombie, with one overriding emotion: sadness. I lost my appetite, couldn't eat and dropped an enormous amount of weight. I found a soul mate in the company of Alison Van Dyke, who seemed to be fighting off some hidden demons of her own. We never discussed it.

WJAR-TV in Providence was celebrating its tenth anniversary with an all-star block party, to be televised *live* from an outdoor stage mid-town, and they invited me to emcee the three-hour telecast. With a lot of cash to throw at talent, the biggest-selling recording artists of 1959 descended on Providence that day, among the line-up were Connie Francis, the Four Lads, Lou Monte (the Italian balladeer), Jerry Vale (a hometown favorite), Jack Scott, Carl Dobkins Jr., the Tradewinds and the Mystics (who were No. 1 with "Hush-a-Bye.") An unexpected crowd of over 50,000 people spilled onto the street, surging towards the stage, breaking down police barriers, an emotional frenzy that was becoming increasingly dangerous. Sensing disaster, the fire, police and station officials stopped the show, and we continued upstairs in the Outlet Company department store studios, with George

Hamilton IV ("A Rose and a Baby Ruth") setting a more mellow tone. *Billboard* reported it as "Rucker's Clambake" – but it was no picnic; I was scared. It was my first brush with the power of demonstrative teenagers.

It was at this point that Monte Bruce came into my life. Monte was a well-connected music business promoter, founder of Bruce Records, a small independent label that scored minor success with the Harptones, ("A Sunday Kind of Love"); his wife Toni was (conveniently) Alan Freed's step-daughter, from a second marriage by her mother.

Monte was managing Jim Gallant, a clean-cut blonde deejay, who was hosting "Connecticut Bandstand," a daily dance show in New Haven. I had known Jim in Youngstown when he was a staff announcer and newsman at WKBN (Jim had lip-synched "Muskrat Ramble," dressed in a roaring-twenties raccoon coat, on my Rumpus Room show), and as one of the actors at the Youngstown Playhouse, appearing in "Johnny Belinda;" I worked sound and lights backstage. Fate almost awarded Jim Gallant ABC's "American Bandstand." The story goes that Dick Clark was offered to host a local Bandstand show in his choice of cities, Philadelphia or New Haven (both ABC affiliates and owned by Triangle Communications). Dick decided on Philadelphia, leaving the "Connecticut Bandstand" to Jim Gallant.

The fact is, Dick Clark's father Richard Clark was a radio executive, and found a place for his son at a small-market television station in Utica, New York. Not wishing it to be known that he glided into broadcasting on his father's coattails, Clark chose the stage name "Dick Clay" and presided over a country-western music show as "Cactus Dick and the Santa Fe Riders." (As Jack Paar would say, *"I kid you not."*)

After a year, "Cactus Dick" told his father he was ready to move on to a bigger market, and the elder Mr. Clark once again contacted a colleague at a television station in Philadelphia,[2] the country's forth-largest market. Clark quickly established himself as a persuasive commercial pitchman, earning extra money as a spokesman for sponsors as diverse as Tootsie Rolls and Schaefer's Beer. "I was a great pitchman," he said. "I did one hell of a beer spot." It was here that Clark's path crossed with another commercial huckster, Ed McMahon, little knowing that their future efforts would be irrevocably entwined. In 1952, a local Philadelphia "Bandstand" show had segued from radio to WFIL-TV (now WPVI-Ch 6). The program was hosted by a well-liked, good-looking disc jockey Bob Horn until the summer of 1956, when Horn was dismissed for drunk driving and allegations of hanky-panky

---

2   WFIL-TV was then part of Walter Annenberg's Triangle Communications, publishers of *The Philadelphia Inquirer, The Daily Racing Form, TV Guide* and *Seventeen* magazine.

with an underage girl. Clark stepped-in and quickly began badgering the network to take the show national. The show was picked up by ABC, and renamed "American Bandstand" on August 5, 1957.

Managing Jim Gallant merely required Monte Bruce to promote their lucrative record hops around New Haven, splitting the profits. Monte had been closely watching the rising ratings of my Providence show and was curious as to what the fuss was all about.

Monte learned that Channel 13 in New York was searching for a host for their weekday "Rate the Records" show, to replace Hy Lit, who had been commuting each weekday from Philadelphia, and arranged for me to meet with the Channel 13 producers. With my scrapbook and press clippings – there was no such thing as videotape then – I met with the station executives and *bang,* got the job without an on-air audition.

The day I got the go-ahead call from Channel 13, I had exactly one dime in my pocket, enough money to spread the good news, a call to Monte Bruce and a collect call home to Mom and Dad. I was about to earn the unbelievable sum of $250 a week. Monte had a better idea. Rather than take a manager's commission, he suggested we follow in the path of Alan Freed and become involved in publishing, song writing, artist management, a record label and producing company, all things that I was ill-equipped to deal with – I was not qualified, I had no experience. What did I know about the record *business?*

"Never mind the details," said Monte.

He assured me that he would handle all the business details; I would front the company. He would take responsibility for the ancillary activities of our partnership, attaching my name as writer to new songs, supervising our publishing and record companies, managing other artists and negotiating the deals. My job was to make the television show a success. Shake. Rather than being my personal manager, Monte was now my partner, 50 – 50, which also meant 50% of my talent fee.

My debut as host of "Rate the Records" was three weeks away, enough for the Channel 13 publicity department to create a little buzz, with new photos, bios and a new name. This came about almost immediately.

"We don't like Al Rucker." was the flat-out pronouncement of the programming brass. The long knives came out, slicing and dicing my good name, in a closed-door meeting upstairs at 1481 Broadway.

"Al Rucker…well, Rucker rhymes with too many offensive words…"

"Yes, nasty connotations…"

"Don't invite mockery …"

"And, 'Al' is too similar to Alan Freed…"

"Yes, confusing!"

Alan Freed would soon be my on-air rival. But, I reasoned, "Al Rucker *had* worked for me on the air four years in Youngstown and one year in Providence, and …"

"This is New York. We need something short and catchy, something that would fit well into *TV Guide* and on marquees. But hurry; all the publicity is on hold until you come up with a new name."

Talk about pressure. Hurry and come up with a new name, one that I would carry with me for the rest of my life. This began one of the most bizarre forty-eight hours in my life, coming up with an all-new stage name. It became an exasperating – and sometimes hysterically funny – exercise. Maybe I should be called Joe Black and dress only in black. Or Joe White dressed in white. Everything in sight suddenly suggested a name.

Al Salt. Al Pepper. Burt Sugar. Bob Coffee. O.J?

How about my hometown? Bob Hubbard, or my street Bob Mackey? Nah. I couldn't sleep, the pressure to find a new name was nerve-racking, and besides, how would I break it to my dad, Al Rucker, Sr.? As the final hours approached, it hit me: Clay Cole, the "Uncle" from Chicago. What a great name, Clay had a cowboy reference and Cole was a solid American name. It was short and sweet, easy to remember, impossible to misspell and it would fit nicely on a marquee and in *TV Guide*.

The Clay Cole Show had a nice ring to it.

Doug Rogers, the program director who had signed me on, approved.

"I like it!" he said, giving the go-ahead.

Trouble is, I hadn't cleared it with the real Clay Cole. On Doug's desk phone, I phoned the Encyclopedia Britannica offices in Chicago and was connected to Clay Cole, Vice-President of Worldwide Sales.

Clay Cole was charmed, but cautiously warned: "Just use it well. Don't do anything to embarrass the family, especially Edna." He was very protective of his adorable wife. I think he was amused by the whole thing, little knowing that his published listing in the phone book would inspire many-a late-night phone calls from my future female fans.

No need to change my name legally," lawyers advised. "Just don't use the new name to defraud." So, I was officially Clay Cole, and at twenty-one, the youngest host on television. My official Ch 13 bio listed me as 19; OK by me. By 1959, one-in-ten households owned TV sets, and New York City, with seven channel selections, was the No.1 television market in America. For the first time in my career, I was no longer 'a big fish in a little pond' – I was now in televisions biggest aquarium, swimming with the sharks, Jackie Gleason, Steve Allen, Garry Moore, and all my boyhood heroes. I was determined to become the Catch of the Day.

A few days before my first broadcast, Alan Freed invited me to his all-star Fifth Anniversary stage show, a ten-day Labor Day marathon at Brooklyn's Fabian Fox theatre, with a staggering line-up of stars: Lloyd Price, Dion & the Belmonts, Johnny Maestro & the Crests, the Skyliners, the Mystics, the Tempos, Bo Diddley, JoAnn Campbell, Valerie Carr, Bobby Lewis, Ronnie Hawkins and a parade of teen-idols, Jimmy Clanton, Johnny Restivo, Johnny October, and Gerry Granahan. I had an unexpected backstage reunion with the five Mystics, who made me feel most welcome; we became lifelong friends.

Alan Freed invited me out on to the stage and introduced me as "the next big television star," and I took a bow to a very friendly reception, with Alan reminding his fans to "watch for Clay Cole on Rate the Records." This was a very generous gesture by a very powerful man. Alan Freed had mined gold in his holiday shows, assembling a mix of pop and R&B artists with a killer orchestra featuring Sam "The Man" Taylor, Earl Warren, Earl Bostic, King Curtis, "Big Al" Sears, all-star studio musicians. With the power of his radio and television shows, and his ability to program – and break – new record releases, Freed held the upper hand when purchasing acts for his stage shows. Artists were beholden to the "King of Rock and Roll" and were happy to be among the chosen, working for peanuts. Others, like the Mystics, remembering me from that anniversary broadcast in Rhode Island, would have *paid* to be a part of Freed's ten-day extravaganza. Where else could their Brooklyn friends and relatives witness 4,000 fans swooning over their a cappella harmonies and their well-oiled pompadours?

Also scattered out there in the dark were a handful of would-be songwriters, starry-eyed kids from Brooklyn's Erasmus Hall, Abraham Lincoln and James Madison High School – Howard Greenfield, Carole King, Gerry Goffin, Barry Mann, Jeff Barry, Tony Orlando and Neil Diamond – who would, in the coming decade, write the songs the whole world sing.

5) Channel 13, NYC – 1959

"There is no better time than the first time because
you can never have the first time again."

1959 was to be the beginning of a whirlwind time of firsts: my first big-time television show, an all-star stage show, recordings and a Hollywood film. I was young and eager, raring to go. After two long years of struggling, I was about to harvest the rewards. My lean-times had served a purpose; I had slimmed down from a pudgy 190 to a trim 160. I had five years of television under my belt and I was just twenty-one. Opportunity comes when talent and luck collide; I got lucky.

"Rate the Records" went on the air at 6:30pm on September 10th 1959, with two popular guest stars, Teddy Randazzo and JoAnn Campbell, so good-looking they could have been sent from Central Casting as idealized teen idols. There was also a subliminal message in their appearance – both were closely identified with Alan Freed, my on-air rival. With Teddy and Jo Ann as imprimaturs, we laid down the gauntlet: Look out New York, there's a new kid on the block…a new force to be reckoned with! Alan Freed may have nicknamed JoAnn, "the blond bombshell," but she was *my* blond bombshell now!

"Uncle" Clay and Edna Cole were in New York, watching excitedly from their suite at The Pierre Hotel. Edna gave me a good piece of advice, no doubt speaking as the mouthpiece of super-salesman, "Uncle" Clay – "you've got to sell your name," she said. "If anyone tunes in late, they have no idea who you are. Sell your name." From that day on, I always closed the show: "This is Clay Cole, thanking you very much and saying – good-night."

I wasn't aware of it at the time, but, in spite of my on-again, off-again blue funks, my next two years on Channel 13 would be the happiest time of my life. Channel 13 was much like I imagined the old-Hollywood studio system, one big happy family, super-charged, creative and loyal. Everyone, from Chairman Eli Landau to Marty, my stage manager, treated me with great respect, something I cannot say of any other studio before or since.

Mike Wallace, Barry Gray and I shared a single desk in our cramped Times Square offices, which the fastidious Mr. Gray found "much too messy." Mike, our news anchor, also hosted a late-night, half-hour interview show. A lone guest would sit in the hot-seat, sweating under a pin-spot, nakedly exposed by a close-up camera that would slowly push-in tighter and tighter veiled in smoke from Mike's cigarettes. It was riveting television. Faye Emerson (another boyhood crush) hosted one of the many afternoon talk shows in an adjoining studio, and Faye would tip-toe into my studio, glide onto the dance floor, tap me on the shoulder cutting in; there I was, dancing with "Miss Plunging Neckline" herself!

I was further blessed with the perfect producer, a former hoofer named Ken Whelan, a witty Irish leprechaun, who met his wife Cy while dancing on Broadway as chorus kids in "Oklahoma!" What could be more appealing to a dancer than music with a beat? Ken was a real upper, time-stepping around the studio keeping everyone on their toes. Kenny did have his dark side, a longtime member of AA; he nonetheless walked the twelve steps with me around the corner to the White Rose, a shot-and-a-beer gin-mill near 41st Street, for a pre-show happy-hour. Kenny and I hit it off instantly.

Kenny and Monte [Monte Bruce, my manager] on the other hand did not get along at all. Monte considered Kenny a threat to his propriety over me, thinking Ken wielded too much influence, and Kenny was suspicious of Monte's under-handed deal-making, his clandestine closed-door meetings and his endless tele-phone hustle. Monte was a wheeler-dealer. Kenny always said, "If Monte ever put all that energy into a legitimate deal he would be the biggest man in the record business," but Monte liked to hustle in the style of old-school jukebox hucksters, not in the buttoned-down manner of broadcasters. Monte's hush-hush phone calls prompted Kenny to improvise a hilarious impression of Monte on the phone, with hand cupped over his lips and the mouthpiece, eyes suspiciously shifting around the room, checking the desk drawers for an invisible "bug," and whispering into the phone, until he finally crawls under his desk, seeking shelter. Monte would laugh, but was not amused.

Alan Freed offered us one of his three Manhattan apartments, "until we get settled," so Monte, his wife Toni and I moved into a plush avocado-green and blue penthouse at Number Two Fifth Avenue, overlooking Washington Square Park in Greenwich Village. Toni's mother, Betty Lou Bean, was Alan's first wife; Alan was Toni's step-father by a previous marriage. Alan was currently married to wife number three, Inga, a statuesque, blonde, would-be singer. A few years earlier, Alan and wife number two, Jackie Freed, acquired Grey Cliffe, their big sprawling house in Stamford; so now the scattered families cozily united under one roof. It was one big happy (but confusing) family.

In 1951, Alan Freed had signed-on as "Moondog," a late-night, DJ shift on WJW radio in Cleveland, sponsored by Fred Mintz, whose "rhythm and blues" record store had a primarily African-American clientele. Deferring to his sponsor, "The Moondog House Party," played rhythm and blues, music he christened "rock'n'roll." Alan played it, but I don't really believe he liked it – he grew to like it. When it became the Alan Freed cash cow, he grew to love it! Now, with a primetime shift on New York City's powerful 50,000-watt WABC-AM and his "Big Beat" television show on WNEW-TV Ch 5, Alan was now the most powerful broadcaster in America.

Toni Bruce remained sunny, as opposed to Monte's sour-puss. Monte seemed to carry the weight of the world on his shoulders; his big, sad hound-dog eyes only sparkled when a deal was imminent. Once we settled in, Monte busied himself setting up our future enterprises that, he promised "will generate more money than I could ever imagine," while selling Harptones' records out of the trunk of his Cadillac. For comfort and advice, it was Toni I turned to, not Monte, my manager. Toni was fun and funny, often taking me on drives up to Stamford to visit Alan and Jackie.

On our many long, leisurely walks around the village, Toni would encourage me to talk about my mood swings, most particularly my depression. This was the first time anyone ever labeled my funky periods as depression. I didn't like to talk about it, assuming it was inherited, as deep-rooted as perfect pitch or natural rhythm. Toni persisted, "Talking about it sometimes eases the problem – had I ever considered therapy?" Therapy! Amusing a shrink for an hour? I get paid to talk; he should pay me!

As usual, I was *all* talk and I agreed to meet with Toni's cousin, Hannah Weiner, a psychologist, an equally engaging and bright young lady who charmed me and took me into her confidence. Hannah conducted psychodrama workshops (group therapy) with great success and although I really trusted Toni and Hannah, I was turned-off by the group aspect of Hannah's role-playing therapy. Being on television, I was gun-shy about exposing myself to an intimate circle of strangers. Private Sessions with a psychiatrist seemed more appealing, after all, "seeing a shrink" in the Fifties was the all the rage, like cha cha lessons and Tupperware parties. So, Hannah made arrangements for me to become the patient of Dr. Izadore Cohen, a well-respected East Side Freudian psychoanalyst, three mornings a week at $25.00 a pop.

Dr. Cohen immediately laid down the Freudian ground rules: I was to tell him my dreams and fantasies and reveal my ongoing feelings toward him. Dr. Freud's signature contribution was "the talking cure," but, guesses who did all the talking? The slate was blank; my job was to fill it in. So, as I stretched out, chattering away, Dr. Cohen remained stoic, occasionally managing an "hmmm." I could have told him I secretly f--- chickens, without so much as a "yuck!" from the good doctor. His prognosis: I was the requisite Fifties neurotic with "confliction anxiety and maturational variations, complicated by acute depression and an identity crisis, accompanied by compensatory delusions of grandeur and a declining ability to cope."

In other words – I was a cuckoo-bird!

My apprehension about all this psychobabble was dispelled during my first appointment, when the Broadway comic Jack Carter stormed through the waiting room; his session was immediately before mine. "If a big star like Jack Carter got up that early in the morning, this stuff must work!"

Psychiatrists and biochemists now dismiss Dr. Freud's theories of repressed dreams and the unconscious. Says one doctor: "Psychiatry is not where the action is." Today, therapy is pretty much replaced by psychiatric pharmaceuticals. Pop a pill and be normal: "Better Living Through Chemistry." NPR jumped right on it, concluding: "We should dump Dr. Freud on the trash heap of expired ideas." – Sure now! Where were they when I was tossing $75 a week into the dumpster? Do you know how many chickens I could have plucked for $75?

Americans have a repressed desire to "just be normal." The one thing that therapy taught me is, "there is no normal." Normal is a cycle on the washing machine. We should not only celebrate our differences, we should cherish them.

In the course of persuading me to seek counseling, both Toni and Hannah told me a remarkable story: Alan Freed's erotic fantasy was sex with a fully-clothed, soaking wet woman, a role he sometimes assumed himself. His particular peccadillo was to get soaking wet while in drag, under water. What amazes me is that Freed found not one, but possibly three wives willing to play swan queen to his rubber ducky. Hannah diagnosed this as an episode repeated over and over in his childhood, when his mother dressed him in frilly pinafores and soaked him in a bassinette.

What really amused Toni and Hannah was the infamous swimming pool episode. The story goes like this: Alan Freed acquired Grey Cliffe at the peak of his popularity, at a time when money bags were delivered daily from his radio/television shows, recording royalties, stage shows and motion pictures. Freed's ability to spin new record releases on his shows rewarded him great power within the music industry. Alan showed his appreciation by throwing a spectacular music-biz bash in the gardens of his new estate in September of 1957, with an orchestra, an open bar and a lavish catered buffet

No one would dare refuse an invitation and offend Alan Freed, so the highest-level executives from all the record companies and their wives accepted, dressed to the nines in furs and diamonds – including Sam Clark of ABC-Paramount, Bob Thiele of Coral records, Morris Levy and Joe Kolsky from Roulette and Jerry Wexler and Ahmet Ertegun from Atlantic. Alan was known to consume a bottle of Scotch during his three-hour nightly radio show, so he was probably feeling no pain as the party moved out to the pool area for some dancing under the stars.

Well, imagine Alan's reaction when one slightly woozy dame dumped herself, clothes and all into the pool. This was heaven – a totally soaked, elegantly dressed woman in his pool. The delight in Alan Freed's eyes was so palpable that, not to be outdone, another executive pushed his wife into the pool, then another and another, until all the women were in the pool. Diamonds dropped to the bottom, furs floated to the top, as Alan and his cronies roared with laughter. What a joke! Little did they know that this Felliniesque blending of reality and fantasy was actually Alan Freed's own private wet dream?

My daily routine settled into a pattern:
    9:00   Dr. Izadore Cohen
    9:45   Breakfast at Kauffman's Drug Store on Lexington
    10:00 Vic Tanney's Gym at the Shelton Towers Hotel
    Noon   Office / Studio

After a workout, shower and a shave, I'd go down to the pool to gossip with Georgia Winters, who as Gloria Staves was a former fashion model now in a second career as editor of *16* magazine. (More about Georgia to come.) At noon I would head over to the studio at 42nd and Broadway to put together a show with Kenny, run through commercials in the studio, then hit the gin mill for Happy Hour. Kenny wanted me out of view when the high school dancers began arriving, so I would walk up to The Astor Hotel for a shoeshine (for the obligatory dancing feet shot and my double-shuffle time-step) for Kenny's close-up cameras. This little escape gave me a chance to clear my head and remind myself that I was the luckiest guy in New York. Kenny would give me this most incredibly inflated build-up and I made my entrance, like Mickey Mantle taking the field at Yankee Stadium. This was all so unreal.

Our studio audiences were all high school age, fourteen and above, dressed in their Sunday best. The boys seemed terrified, but assumed the required so-cool attitude in sports jackets and dad's tie, probably knotted by their mothers. The girls preferred full skirts with crinolines that flared when they twirled, balancing their swelling training bras and Toni home permanents. There is no disputing the fact that dancing is a very erotic ritual, and we are a nation of voyeurs. There is something sexually compelling about watching folks dance, especially virginal, hormonal-rich teenagers. Television executives quickly realized that dance shows were a cost-effective formula for ratings success. Let's face it – dancing is just sex with your clothes on.

Fifties teenagers suffered a bad rap; "dancing to the devil's music" was considered the gateway drug to hard-core juvenile delinquency. But the truth of the matter is that dancing to rock 'n' roll separated partners, keeping the boys and girls at arms length. The twist, the slop, mashed potatoes, stroll, cha cha, and all the popular new dances were structured in such a way that partners did not touch; they fed off each other's energy through eye contact. Our grandparents' waltz was more sensual, and when performed by Fred & Ginger, downright naughty. It was the teenage love ballad, the gentle, slow-grinding while in a boy-girl embrace that produced intimate arousal. With the exception of the hustle and the bump, all rock 'n' roll dancing straight through the disco decades were spontaneous, no-contact, individual expressions.

One of those kids was Peter Salerno, a blonde, blue-eyed Sicilian-American, whose loyalty to Alan Freed was solidified one afternoon when Freed offered him a lift in his limousine, to his tenement down on Delancey Street, near his Seward Park High School. At the same time, when the school day ended at New Dorp High, a young, redheaded chatterbox, Pat Passa, was boarding the Staten Island Ferry to our studios in Manhattan. Over the course of the next few weeks, Pat & Pete won every dance contest with their attention-grabbing Lindy-hop, amassing a collection of record albums, bowling balls, frozen pizzas, teddy bears, charm bracelets and trinkets. They received fan mail, and won so many dance contests that we took them out of competition, making them judges. We rolled out a surprise cake when they announced their engagement on our show, Pete on his knees presenting a ring, and they married, producing two redheads, a boy and girl.

We had many memorable regulars, Terry, the Old Gold cigarette dancing matchbook, Jovanna, a dancer at the Times Square club, The Wagon Wheel, a sweet adorable couple, Tommy and Maria, who we later discovered were brother and sister, and Geri Miller, who became – well, Geri Miller, the Andy Warhol Factory player, who Tab Hunter describes as "the groupie girl with the silicone tits." Geri Miller would later gain notoriety by bursting naked out of a birthday cake for Mick Jagger. I came to realize that I was reclaiming my own lost teenage years, a decade when I was too busy with theatre, radio and television, acting, singing and dance classes, to engage in normal teenage pursuits. At 21, I was relating to my teenaged audience as equals, as high-school colleagues. Each season, a fresh crop of teens would arrive at the studio, a recurring audience that never grew older.

> "Clay Cole has an ingratiating eager-beaver type personality.
> He also has considerable more talent than the average TV jock;
> he dances and mugs with a solid sense of showmanship and timing."
> *Billboard* magazine, September 1959

It was my dancing that set me apart from all other dance party hosts. Since I was still very young, I cut-in and danced with the high school girls, executing a mean bop or swaying cheek-to-cheek with the ladies, both white and black. It was my fully-integrated studio audience that made the show notable. Dancing cheek-to-cheek with young "colored girls" did not seem remarkable to me; it was unfussy and anticipated. Dancing with the host guaranteed a close-up, and status back in the school yard. Kenny would dim the lights in the studio for a romantic slow dance, (maybe the Flamingo's "I Only Have Eyes For You") or quick-cut the cameras for a frenetic dance contest (to Sandy Nelson's pulsating drums on "Teen Beat.") Prizes were awarded, usually 45's or LP's. The most popular dance of the moment was "the slop," a trademark movement of James Brown. I created "slop powder," an oversized can of ordinary baby powder, and would sprinkle the dance floor in an elaborate ritual of preparation. The studio audience went wild every time I pulled out that can, because it meant "Slop-Time!" – usually to Baby Washington's "Baby Work Out" or Barrett Strong's "Money, the first national hit for Berry Gordy on his own label, Tamla. Gordy, a Korean War veteran, record shop owner, songwriter and auto assembly line worker, borrowed $800 to start-up his own independent record label for a company he brazenly called Hitsville, U.S.A.

On "Rate the Records," we would play four new releases and our two high school panels would, well ... *rate the records*. The record companies loved it because it gave instant exposure to their new releases and the teenage panels played it safe, never really knocking a record. But, how many different ways can a sixteen-year-old express a colorful opinion? "I like the words, I like the beat. I can dance to it," became the cliché.

We tried a post card write-in contest for our home viewers, playing a mystery record, and offering prizes: "I'm going to play a record and if you recognize the voice, drop me a card. The first 50 correct cards received win an LP, the next 100, single records." Channel 13 received over 11, 000 cards within two days.

I had a very short attention span, which served me well in television; when I felt a show was growing stale; the audience probably felt that way too. I begged the station to change the format, to get rid of that rigid rate-the-record gimmick. Based on our instant success, they were agreeable, allowing me to put my own personal imprint on the show, and to create a unique New York spin. Our new freewheeling show was called "The Record Wagon," which began attracting all the big names, Bobby Darin, Steve Lawrence, Connie Francis, Connie Stevens and the Queen herself, Dinah Washington. The three Isley Brothers invited me to join them in their show-stopping "Shout," and the Drifters, Skyliners and Dion & the Belmonts became recurring guests.

It was a long and winding road that led us to rock 'n' roll, an unlikely blend of gospel, country-western, the blues, and a blend of 50s be-bop, with the emphasis on saxophone and piano. Simply put, "rhythm and blues knocked-up country-western and the bastard child was called "rock 'n' roll." Can you imagine my re-action, as a teenager, hearing, "Hey nonny ding dong, alang alang alang, Boom ba-doh, ba-doo ba-doodle-day" comin' out of the radio? '" Awopbopaloobopalop-bamboom! – Hey, they were speaking my language. Multiply that by 78 million sh-boomers and you've got yourself a revolution.

Everyone agrees that rock began with gospel and blues – chanting vocals with twelve-bar chord progressions, to the rhythms of the guitar and sometimes a make-shift drum. The Isley Brothers "Shout" is pure call and response gospel. "Stand by Me," the song written and recorded by Ben E. King, Jerry Leiber and Mike Stoller in 1961, is inspired by a traditional gospel song of the same name, originally com-posed 1905. The song uses a version of the common chord progression now called "the 50s progression," also called "the Stand by Me" changes, so named after the song became a pop classic.

"Rock 'n' roll morphed from Delta blues," according to David "Honeyboy" Edwards, the last living blues artist to play with the legendary Robert Johnson, a legacy that almost no living musician can match. In 2008, at age ninety-three, as the last bluesman still standing, "Honeyboy" summed up his take on rock 'n' roll; "You can play low-down dirty blues slow and lonesome and you can take that same blues, make it up-tempo–a shuffle blues. That's what rock 'n' roll did with it. So blues ain't going nowhere. Ain't goin' nowhere."

Robert Johnson, in his time, was known as the "King of the Delta Blues Singers," but is now acknowledged as *the* major influence on modern-day rock 'n'roll. The Blues historian Elijah Wald has made the controversial appraisal that "as far as the evolution of *black music* goes, Robert Johnson was a minor figure; Johnson's major influence is on *rock music.*" When Keith Richards of the Rolling Stones was first introduced to Johnson's music by his band mate Brian Jones, he replied, "Who is the other guy playing with him?" not realizing it was Johnson also playing on one guitar.

Robert Plant of Led Zeppelin said, "It is Robert Johnson to whom we all owe our existence."

Eric Clapton described Johnson's music as "the most powerful cry that I think you can find in the human voice." Clapton admits he "did not take to Robert Johnson immediately; He frightened me."

Eddie James "Son" House, Jr., the blues-singing guitar man and an important influence on Muddy Waters and Robert Johnson, said, "When Robert Johnson got through playing, all our mouths was open. He sold his soul to the devil to get to play like that."

The story goes that, "Robert Johnson met the Devil at the Crossroads of highway 41 and 69 near Clarksville, Mississippi and sold his soul to be the greatest bluesman of all time." This fantastic legend has been passed down through the generations and celebrated in story, song, and festivals. If there is any truth to this greatest of all blues myths is inconsequential; there is no denying the influence of Robert Johnson, not only on the blues, but modern music today." In his brief career, Johnson recorded just 29 songs and died at the age of twenty-seven, in 1938.

Parishioners swooned over Sam Cooke, an early star on the African-American gospel circuit, as the lead singer with the Soul Stirrers. With that voice and that face, he was a natural for secular stardom; a "move over to the other side" that was viewed as sacrilege, as a defector turning his back on the church. The great Mahalia Jackson set the standard; she wouldn't "cross over." But Sam took the risk, and recorded "You Send Me," a traditional church anthem with altered lyrics, turning the love of Jesus into the love of his life. Once Sam Cooke led the way, Carla Thomas, Al Green, Solomon Burke, Dionne Warwick and the almighty Aretha Franklin followed. At the same time, groups like the Dominos and the Clovers were breathing new life into the smooth vocal harmony style of the Ink Spots ("If I Didn't Care"), with the frenetic flash of the Treniers ("Rockin' Is Our Bizness," featuring dancing, singing identical twins Cliff and Claude Trenier.) The seeds of rhythmic blues were blossoming.

It was a New York-born, Jewish, jazz-buff, Jerry Wexler, fresh out of the Navy after WWII, who coined the phrase "rhythm and blues" to distinguish "race music." At the time, Wexler was employed as a writer at *Billboard* magazine. Then in 1953, he joined the upstart blues label Atlantic Records and introduced Southern blues (R&B) to mainstream audiences, producing records with Aretha Franklin, Ray Charles, Sam and Dave, Wilson Pickett, Solomon Burke, Roberta Flack, Clyde McPhatter, Ruth Brown, the Drifters and dozens more, enriching Atlantic Records, and positioning the company as a powerhouse, the single most important independent label, rivaled only by Motown a decade later.

Jerry Wexler also helped Atlantic forge partnerships with the Memphis-based Stax Records – the home to Otis Redding, Sam & Dave and Booker T. & the MG's – and the FAME studios in Muscle Shoals, Alabama and Criteria Studios in Miami. David Ritz, co-author of Wexler's autobiography "Rhythm and the Blues: A Life in American Music," remembered him as "the last of the old school record business guys who had to kick and scream and fight to get his records made, but remained a New York intellectual as well."

We welcomed a remarkable lineup of up-and-coming R&B artists to our shows – the dreamy balladeers, Jimmy Charles, Johnny Nash, Sammy Turner, Tommy Hunt, Lenny Welsh, Adam Wade, and electrifying rhythm singers like Lloyd Price, Wilbert Harrison, Bobby Freeman, Gary U.S. Bonds, Chuck Jackson, Jimmy Jones, Johnny Thunder and Bobby Lewis ("Tossing and Turning," soon to be the Number One song of 1961.)

At that exact moment in time, something was brewing with the so-called "country-western" cowboy bands. In 1951, Bill Haley & His Saddlemen spent 18-months performing at The Twin Bar in Gloucester City, New Jersey, playing Western Swing. It was during this period that Haley fused country-western with rhythm and blues, crafting "rockabilly." Haley recognized his new sound as meteoric and renamed the band, "Billy Haley and His Comets." (In 2007, the Twin Bar unveiled a historic marker commemorated Bill Haley legacy. What is equally astonishing, The Twin Bar is still operating 55 years later.)

In 1933, the very year that the legendary country singer Jimmy Rodgers passed on, James Frederick Rodgers, the *other* Jimmie Rodgers, came into the world in the great state of Washington. His names are often incorrectly spelled as Jimmy or Rogers, or bring to mind Jimmy Rogers, the late-great blues singer, guitarist and harmonica player known for his work as a member of Muddy Waters' band of the 1950s. But it was our Jimmie Rodgers, spelled out on the Roulette records label, that defined 50s folk-pop-rock. In 1957, while serving in the U.S. Air Force, Jimmie recorded "Honeycomb," a huge national hit, on the top of the charts for four weeks. His follow-up songs also hit the charts, "Kisses Sweeter than Wine," "Oh-Oh, I'm Falling in Love Again," "Secretly," and "Are You Really Mine." In 1959 he hosted his own music-variety show on NBC, becoming an immensely popular mainstream television star.

In 1967, he had his last top-100 single, "Child of Clay." On December 20, 1967, while preparing to do a film for 20th Century Fox, he was the victim of an assault, after allegedly being pulled over by an off-duty LAPD officer, receiving a severe beating, leading to a fractured skull. The reason for the assault has never been established; all that Jimmie could recall were bright lights, presumably from the car of his attacker.

To make matters worse, Jimmie's wife Colleen died of a fatal blood clot shortly after the 1967 beating, leaving him to care for their two children, Michelle and Michael. Jimmie's career as an entertainer abruptly ended; for over forty years he suffered severe headaches and the accompanying nausea of a steel plate in his head.

Then forty years later, in 2007, surgery was performed to remove the steel plate. Here is the miraculous story as told to me by his son Michael:
"About four minutes after beginning surgery, the doctors pulled back the scalp to reveal the plate. When they did, the plate literally lifted up and jumped up away from his head. The doctors, five in all, a surgeon, two plastic surgeons, two stem-cell specialists and the rest of the team began to clean the plate and lift it away from the head. It released itself and came away clean. On the video tape of the surgery we could hear the surgeon say 'Oh my God, look at that. How did that get there?' Under the plate was revealed a complete and intact skull bone where three months ago there was none. The entire hole in the bone which was an eight inch by six inch oval had grown completely closed with a new skull bone which was smooth and shaped to match the existing skull. It was perfect in every way and was the same

thickness as the other bone. The doctors said that in 35 years of surgery they had never seen anything like it."

"They did not need to recreate a new skull bone at all. Dad was completely healed and made whole again after 40 years. The entire procedure took about 28 minutes; after one hour in recovery, Dad walked 'on his own,' much to the dismay of the nursing staff. He spent one night in the hospital and we went directly to a nearby Olive Garden for lunch. He is now bass fishing and playing golf."

Most of us have long-forgotten the rockabilly phase; it seemed to have crashed and burned in 1959 along with Buddy Holly, Ritchie Valens and the Big Bopper. Next came word, in April 1960, that 21-year-old Minnesota rockabilly star, Eddie Cochran ("Summertime Blues") died in a taxi cab crash while on tour in the UK. Songwriter Sharon Sheeley (Cochran's fiancée) and singer Gene Vincent ("Be-Bop-A-Lula") survived. Earlier, in 1955, Vincent was involved in a severe motorcycle accident that shattered his left leg. He refused to have it amputated; the leg was saved, but left him with a permanent limp and considerable chronic pain for the rest of his life.

Dion backs me up when he said, "Sometimes I get the feeling people look at this era of early rock as light. It was anything but. Most of these guys were street punks from all over the country, playin' Strats, Telecasters, Gretsches, Martins and Gibsons, kickin' ass, rockin' out. These giants of early guitar rock are my heroes."

There was a time when every record company came forth with a new young rebel announced as "the next Elvis" and every major city had its own rockabilly star: Jack Scott ("My True Love") was from Detroit; Ral Donner ("You Don't Know What You've Got, Until You Lose It)," from Chicago; and Charlie Gracie ("Butterfly") was from Philadelphia. Troy Shondell ("This Time") recorded in a style that has been labeled "Louisiana Swamp Rock," although Troy is from Fort Wayne, Indiana. An unknown Tommy James met Troy (his birth name is Gary Shelton) at a nightclub in Niles, Michigan (Tommy's home town), and named his "Hanky Panky" group "The Shondells" after Troy.

I was privileged to meet and introduce many of the "protopunk rockers" Conway Twitty, Billy "Crash" Craddock, Bob Luman, Gary Stites, Buddy Knox, Jimmy Bowen, Carl Dopkins Jr., Del Shannon, Ray Peterson, and the greatly revered 'Rock 'n' Roll Trio' – the Burnette brothers, Johnny and Dorsey and Paul Burlison. Who could forget those crazy cousins from Arkansas, Ronnie and Dale Hawkins ("Suzie-Q")? Many of these boys were doomed to be forever labeled "one hit wonders," a pitiless and poignant fate. I was brokenhearted when, looking out a taxi cab window, I spotted the handsome, well-mannered Ralph De Marco working as a postman, delivering mail along Eighth Avenue. It was sobering to imagine that he had his taste of adulation with "Old Shep," and then had it all taken away. His fifteen-minutes were over.

On the brighter side, there is now a shrine to all those boys, a Rockabilly Hall of Fame headquartered in a Burns, Tennessee recording studio, south of Nashville. The first inductee was the posthumous certification of Gene Vincent and the Blue-caps (named as a reference to the enlisted sailors of the U.S. Navy).

Naturally, the greater New York area offered-up its own charismatic rockers: Bobby Comstock, Gerry Granahan, Stan Vincent, Ersel Hickey, Gene Pitney and great-looking white boys Vic Dana, Frank Gari, Kenny Dino, Dick Caruso and all the Johnnies – Jon Corey and Johnny Saber (same person), Johnny Aladdin, Johnny Cymbal, Johnny October (born Johnny Ottobre) and Johnny Restivo. (A beefcake photo on the sleeve of his RCA 45, "The Shape I'm In," pictured Restivo in nothing but a skimpy bikini – pretty racy stuff for 1959.) Johnny Rivers (John Ramistella) was born in New York ("Poor Side of Town"), but we lost him to the West Coast, where he famously rocked and recorded *live* at The Whisky a Go Go in Hollywood ("Secret Agent Man").

Then there is also Santo & Johnny ("Sleepwalk"), who invited me up to their tenement rooftop to show off their prized pigeons – the Brothers Farina's passion was raising flocks of homing pigeons in caged coops. They didn't sing or even talk all that much – (in later years they didn't even speak to each other) – but their electric steel guitar spoke for them, rewarding them a now-classic No. 1 instrumental (which they composed). The steel guitar did not produce a mainstream pop sound; rather one more associated with the Hawaiian Islands, Country-Western bands and Alvino Rey (1940s "Wizard of the Steel Pedal Guitar"). Johnny sustained his monopoly on the steel guitar and forged a lifetime career.

I became a champion to talented newcomers, relentless in my promotion of naive, starry-eyed believers, the long-shot underdogs and the one-hit wonders. No one rooted for them more fervently than me. My personal passion was to introduce new talent to my television audience, defuse their nerves by making them feel safe and comfortable, and then support their records with airplay. For example, Jay & the Americans (Sandy Yaguda. and Kenny Vance) first came to our show in 1959 as the Harbor Lites (they lived in Belle Harbor, NY). Tom and Jerry became Simon & Farfunkel. The Tokens, four teenagers from Brooklyn's Abraham Lincoln High School – Jay Siegel, Hank Medress and Brothers Phil and Mitch Margo – performed on Record Wagon as Daryll & the Oxfords. ("Picture in my Wallet") Their appearance in 1959 produced a bond; when they returned as the Tokens, they introduced "The Lion Sleeps Tonight," one of the most-played records in history, and a No. 1 hit on all the charts.

Jay, Hank and the Margo Brothers would each have long careers as writers/ singers on scores of popular, familiar television commercial jingles and as writers/studio producers for the Chiffons, the Happenings and Randy & the Rainbows. Naturally, they sent all their artists to our show first – you reap what you sow. The Chiffons, four teenage girls from The Bronx, had three Top Ten hits, "He's So Fine," "One Fine Day" and "Sweet Talkin' Guy," and the Happenings' appearance in 1966, in the middle of Beatlemania, defied all logic. The four clean-cut boys from Paterson, NJ were reminiscent of a traditional Fifties' foursome, the Hilltoppers, but they had giant hits: "See You in September," "Go Away Little Girl" and astonishingly, the 1930s Gershwin standard, "I Got Rhythm." The producing partners were also responsible for revitalizing the second career of Tony Orlando (with Dawn) in the Seventies, producing multiple hits, including "Tie a Yellow Ribbon."

Paul Anka's star-power with teen girls was brought home to me when he appeared, singing "Put Your Head On My Shoulder," directly into the tear-stained faces of the least-attractive girls in our audience. Kenny's close-up cameras caught the drama, trembling schoolgirls, unaccustomed to romantic attention, placing their sobbing heads on Paul's welcoming shoulders. Paul Anka knew exactly what he was doing. At the time, photographs of Anka and Annette began appearing in the fan magazines, and it was said that he wrote "Puppy Love" with her in mind, suggesting a secret romance. Fuel to the fire was Annette's own No.1 record hit, "Tall Paul," (1959) and an LP "Annette Sings Anka," sparking more rumors. There's nothing to it," the pocket-sized Paul told me. "She's short. I just like standing next to her."

Neil Sedaka was RCA's answer to Paul Anka, a singer-songwriter of enormous versatility, the first of Brooklyn's legendary Brill Building writers to team up with Don Kirchner. I got to know Neil, his writing partner Howard Greenfield, his mom and dad, and later his wife Leba, and was their guest the night Neil debuted his adult nightclub act at Brooklyn's Palm Shore Club. Neil was a piano prodigy, trained in classical piano at Julliard, dazzling his audience with highbrow piano concertos and his lowbrow rock 'n' roll originals.

Channel 13 purchased a block-wide Broadway billboard promoting our new show with a massive picture of me, looking down on Tin Pan Alley Records at 49th Street, the very same record shop I had worked in the dark days of my nine-month funk. There was a sudden flourish of newspaper feature stories and picture spreads and my first magazine cover, the front of the January issue of *Hit Parader,* alongside

Pat Boone and Sandra Dee. Could that "lean, handsome boy" they were writing about be *me?*

"Clay Cole is being groomed as the next Dick Clark."
Dorothy Kilgallen, New York Journal-American

I was blessed with thick, black hair, picture-perfect teeth, six-foot-one, a trim 160 pounds, and a perfect size 34. I was not handsome, but had that wholesome, clean-cut, all-American, boy-next-door look. My WASP-look was non-threatening, so that I could get away with outrageous behavior, which was one of my tricks, a leading man who could take a pratfall (a gimmick that also worked much later for Chevy Chase.) I was embraced as the class clown, the older brother. The music journalist Doug McClelland made note of my dual persona, writing: "Considering Clay Cole's frequently falling-down, teen-pleaser image he affects on his show, he is surprisingly sedate and sophisticated."

In an attempt to tap into the psyche of New York teenagers, I attended full day of classes at The Bronx High School of Science (Bobby Darin's alma mater), fully expecting a highly charged, out-of-control recreation of "Blackboard Jungle," filled with hoodlums and a cowering teaching staff. Instead, I found teachers as earnest as Glenn Ford's "Mr. Dadier" and well-mannered students, awestruck that I was actually interested in their seemingly mundane routine. In reality, my day at school was just good public relations masquerading as research; but I did learn a valuable lesson that day. Young people everywhere are basically the same. The excitement of learning separates youth from old age. As long as you're learning you're not old.

From the very beginning I introduced wacky comedy elements to the show, like my very serious interviews with a "musicologist," who was actually Al Kelly, the world's greatest double-talk comedian.

Clay: What's your opinion of rock 'n' roll music?
Al: Rock 'n' roll is a mere metaphor for krine, the bly of every boy and girl.
Clay: I see. Is there a future here for this new music?
Al: Sure. Every kranitz has creen in the long-term future of melodic bilge.

Then we'd take questions from the studio audience.

Bob Crewe was the first true music man I ever met, a former model, interior decorator, antique connoisseur, painter of abstract art – a Fifties renaissance man. When I first met Bob he was preparing for a gallery showing of his colossal collages. Bob was tall and thin, blond and pale, so gaunt you could almost see through him. As a songwriter and producer, his resume speaks for itself; he is responsible for the accelerated careers of the Four Seasons, Freddie Cannon, Mitch Ryder, Diane Renay, Eddie Rambeau, the Toys, Leslie Gore and many, many more.

He wandered in and out of my life in sporadic intervals, not often, but as predictable as the total eclipse of the sun. In the late Fifties, Bob and his writing partner Frank Slay wrote and produced "Silhouettes" (a hit by the Rays), "La Dee Dah" (Billy and Lillie) and "Tallahassee Lassie" (Freddie Cannon.) After a cool period, Bob Crewe and Frank Slay split, and Bob emerged as a solo artist, performing the "Whiffenpoof Song," ye 'ole Yale drinking song, orchestrated with wailing brass modulations, a style then-associated with Bobby Darin ("Artificial Flowers"). It is ironic that Crewe produced the last Motown session for Bobby shortly before Darin's untimely death. In the Seventies, Bob (with Kenny Nolan) wrote "Lady Marmalade" (*Voulez-vous coucher avec mo, ce soir?*) for Labelle, featuring Patti La-Belle, Nona Hendryx and Sarah Dash.

Bob Crewe once volunteered to decorate the Upper East Side apartment of Howie Greenfield, Neil's writing partner, now enjoying his first flush of success with songs recorded by Connie Francis. This was Howie's first Manhattan pad, a luxury he could now afford, far and away from his childhood flat in Brighton Beach, Brooklyn, the modest middle-class building shared by the Greenfield and Sedaka families. Howie was now enjoying wealth and success and needed gallery walls to display his newly acquired gold records. Raysa and I dropped in to check the progress, and Bob Crew was full at it, gutting the traditional whitewalls, exposing the bare, bohemian red brick. Raysa went into cardiac arrest: "There was money everywhere, all over his apartment, piles of royalty checks, some unopened, and cash stacked on tables, falling out of open drawers, it was unbelievable." ("Stupid Cupid" money, no doubt.)

I quickly discovered I had "a good ear;" I could predict a hit, listening to just the first few bars. I could never have predicted, or even imagined the bonus Channel 13 was about to hand me:

> "Favorable audience reaction to Clay Cole called for a vote of confidence in the form of a 60-minute Saturday night show in less than two months."
> – *Howard Colson, The New York Journal-American*

The first Saturday night "Clay Cole Show" was an all-star blockbuster: Jackie "Mr. Excitement" Wilson, Tab Hunter, Dorothy Collins, the Skyliners, Joanie

Sommers, the Mystics, Little Anthony & the Imperials, the Shepherd Sisters ("Alone"), and when Charlie Rich didn't show, I lip-synched, in his place, "Lonely Weekends."

Around that time, Johnny O'Keefe, Australia's biggest rock star, performed on our Saturday show and I liked him a lot. Johnny was like a funny, feisty, bulldog – his fans nicknamed him "The Wild Thing." For the next few weeks, he would arrive each day and hang out at our studios, soaking it all in. When he returned to Australia, he immediately went on television, hosting his own long-running rock 'n' roll program – "The Six O' Clock Show" – Saturday nights at six.

Our Saturday night show was a dress-up show; our guest stars wore gowns, party dresses or tuxedoes, and I had amassed a colorful collection of elegant dinner jackets for our black-and-white telecast. Ken Whelan continued the "important" theme, by creating an all-new look, an in-the-round environment with ramps rising off into infinity as entry points for our singing stars. Our studio audience, dance contest winners from the daily show, was seated in circular bleachers, so that no matter where I stood, teenagers surrounded me. Ken had created a mini-circus, with me as ringmaster in the center ring. It was very stark and cost peanuts to construct. Performing a full-hour, all-star musical-variety show "live" each Saturday night was intoxicating.

It was after one of these exhilarating shows that I stepped out onto Times Square feeling euphoric, with a sensation of belonging. No longer the outsider, I was embraced and respected. I remember this moment in every detail…the smell, the chill, the heady feeling of elation, of being on top of the world.

It was one of those breathtaking 'Autumn in New York' evenings when Daylight Savings Time ends, and a late afternoon darkness stuns in a most agreeable way. I felt a snap of wind, the sound of rustling leaves brushing along the gutters and cabbies honking a fanfare, as if sensing the euphoria in the air. Manhattan is always a fast-moving town, but in autumn the pace quickens. Laughing couples, bundled together to hug off the chill, were bustling about, anticipating a night on the town, perhaps a dinner and a show. Damn, it was great to be alive. Just a few short months ago, I walked these same sidewalks, penniless and dejected, sustained by hope. Feeling unusually buoyant, rather than hail a cab downtown, I decided to walk up Broadway to savor the feeling. My stroll bounced into a swagger, as I passed the Hotel Astor, where George, the ageless shoeshine 'boy' greeted me each day, "Here comes Mr. Cool." Although Thom Mc Ann was my television sponsor, off-camera I wore the new ankle boot preferred by Sammy Davis Jr. from Lefcourts on Madison Avenue.

Here was The Paramount, where Frank Sinatra brought fame to bobbysoxers, in another time, another day. I paused to check my reflection in the polished brass façade of The Brill Building, pleased at my $15 haircut from Perry Como's barber and my $125 suit from Johnny Tillotson's tailor. Inside the Turf Restaurant, pinky-ringed song-pluggers, fresh from the racetrack, sat hyping one another over coffee and the "Turf's world-famous cheesecake." I strutted uptown, passing Fred Leighton's, where Perry and I purchased our pastel, puff-sleeved cardigans, and next to the Stage Deli was Lew Magram, "shirt maker to the stars," where I would regularly pick out a half-dozen lace-front tuxedo shirts. Each season, Mr. Magram would publish a catalogue, listing from A-to-Z all the entertainers who preferred his shirts, and there I was, between Nat 'King' and Cozy Cole.

The Latin Quarter was still standing, the last of the legendary showrooms along The Great White Way, where as a teenager I sat alone at a table far back, mesmerized by Johnny Ray and the near-naked showgirls; Barbara Walter's dad, Lou Walter's had presided here for over two decades, entertaining Time Square tourists. Across the street, The Metropole was still going strong with Lionel Hampton on stage behind the bar, mesmerizing passerby's. Morris Levy's cellar club, Birdland offered bleacher seats where jazz-buffs could roost, watching Count Basie for a buck-eighty and the Palladium satisfied Broadway's craving for Latin jazz, where Tito Puente and 'Killer Joe' Piro introduced that hot, new dance The Cha Cha Cha. Across the way, "Mack the Knife" blasted from the sidewalk speakers of Colony Records. It was on this glorious night that, at last, I felt like a true New Yorker.

I was welcomed into a new circle of friends – young performers who orbited around JoAnn Campbell and Bobby Darin. Our hangout was the swanky Harwyn Club, at 112 E. 52nd St, a supper club with dinner and dancing, operated by Ed Wynn, a former maitre d' at the Stork Club. Ed encouraged the patronage of young celebrities by tossing parties and tearing up the check, to the delight of his sweet, sixteen-year-old daughter Joanie. It was at the Harwyn Club we toasted JoAnn Campbell flashing a dazzling diamond ring, announcing her engagement to Bobby Darin. Darin, as well as Duane Eddy, Bobby Vee, the actor Nick Adams, even Dick Clark, was among the many gentlemen who unfolded the Castro Convertible in the Sutton Place pad JoAnn shared with her roommate Loretta Martin. The scuttlebutt had been that Dick Clark was secretly romancing JoAnn, but to our surprise, it was Loretta Martin, her roommate, who became the second Mrs. Dick Clark. Bobby Darin was also rumored to be engaged to Connie Francis and Peggy Lee, but in spite of grandiose diamonds, neither JoAnn nor Connie nor Peg ever became Bobby's 'lawfully-wedded-wife' – he married Sandra Dee.

There were once three high-flying birds that have been shamefully overlooked by rock 'n' roll ornithologists – Georgia Winters, Connie De Nave and Roz Ross – responsible for the sales, marketing and promotion of pop music stars. They fought the battles, led the charge, nursed the wounds, and held a powerful influence over me, and most of the young performers in the early years. If you want to understand the Sixties, you've got to meet these three thirtysomething ladies.

Georgia Winters was the editor of *16*, the most popular "teenage crush" magazine, intended for pubescent girls, with a prominence of pompadour-styled pin-up boys, and a minimum of actual music news. Dion laughingly remembers "16 magazine back then was asking, "Do you wear pajamas?"

Formerly a fashion model (as Gloria Stavers), Georgia Winters was tall and svelte, with creamy skin under a soft layer of peach fuzz, and perfect teeth, which she flossed endlessly. "These choppers set me back a few bucks, so I'm protecting my investment," she'd laugh. Georgia had a slight Dixie drawl, camouflaged by layers of elocution lessons, so that she sounded kind-a highbrow. Her store-bought blue jeans were sent off to a seamstress to be tapered to accentuate her butt, years before French-cut jeans hit America. Her Hi-Fi wafted the blues, her favorites, the Staple Singers "Will the Circle Be Unbroken."

Georgia had a colorful, diverse "unbroken circle" of friends, that included beat comic Lenny Bruce, Betty Spiegel, the jet-setting wife of movie producer Sam Spiegel, ("Bridge On The River Kwai") and Rona Jaffe, whose trashy novel, "The Best of Everything," chronicled the romantic adventures of young people in 1950s Manhattan, which later became a trashy motion picture, starring a young, unknown Robert Evans.

Georgia kept bottles of champagne chilling in the fridge of her Sutton Place flat, and was known to have an eye on the boys, who willingly popped her cork with an eye on a *16* cover shot. It was a cozy arrangement, but so many teen idols were "interviewed" in her apartment that she cleverly created a cover format that would accommodate up to six to eight boys. She would cut the faces out of photos and a graphics artist would create colorful cartoon bodies, and assemble them into a theme, like a beach party or a hayride, a clever design choice that distinguished *16* from all other teen magazines.

Georgia had the knack of plucking fresh, unpaid talent to labor up in her cramped little *16* offices on Fifth Avenue, overlooking Central Park. One was a chubby little teen with a bulbous nose, a terribly-shy thirteen-year-old President of The Eddie Fisher Fan Club, Rona Berstein. (Steve Lawrence was her high school prom date.) She would have gone unnoticed had it not been for her steel-trap mind and her amazing ability to grasp the inner workings of show business, the facts, fiction and trivia. Years later she would emerge as the glamorous Hollywood reporter Rona Barrett.

Georgia's assistant, Steve Brandt, a slight, pockmarked, intensely nervous young man, mysteriously lived in an expensive suite at the Beverly Hotel on Lexington Avenue. We could only assume that his parents, wishing to keep Steve at arms length, were supporting him. He would eventually surface in Hollywood as the well-connected gossip columnist for *Photoplay* and other popular, but fading, film fan magazines.

Connie De Nave was our publicist, a tough-talking New Yorker with a honking baritone voice, so low that she was often mistaken as Mister De Nave over the phone, which was permanently attached to her ear. She was famous for her ability to insert the F-word, not only in mid-sentence, but fracturing words as well: "Christ it's hot! It must be 100-de-F-------grees in here!" Among her clients were the Bandstand Boys, Fabian, Frankie Avalon and Bobby Rydell, as well as Jimmy Clanton, Mitch Ryder, Dion, Timi Yuro, Bobby Vee, Paul Anka, JoAnn Campbell and one hitless newcomer named Wayne Newton. She cranked out puffed-up press releases, invented colorful bios and pummeled her clients into the tabloids and onto glossy magazine covers. Connie organized fan clubs and engaged legions of teenage 'screamers,' at five-dollars a pop, to stage major riots at airports and hotels, offering a cash bonus for a hank of hair or a ripped shirt from one of her teen idol clients.

Her ink-stained staff, fueled by 'black beauties' and Pepsi-Cola, worked 'round the clock in three shifts at mimeograph machines, spitting out reams of urgent press releases. Nola Leone, Eileen Bradley, and Ray Reneri are among the few who survived those heady early days. Nola Leone surrendered her long-time crush on Mitch Ryder and moved on to Hollywood for a lifetime engagement with Curb Records, as girl Friday to Mike Curb. Eileen Bradley also moved west to become a top-notch television talent booker, her Rolodex overflowing with the private home numbers of A-List celebrities, from Nancy Reagan to Peewee Herman.

A fan club division was formed, with Bob Levine supervising a rag-tag staff of unpaid assistants, starry-eyed teens who were now in "show business." For a one-dollar membership into The Bobby Vee Fan Club, his admirer would be rewarded with an autographed picture, a membership card and a "I Love Bobby" lapel pin – interchangeable for Bobby Vee, Bobby Rydell, Bobby Darin and one other Connie favorite, Bobby Kennedy. Money by the truckload came pouring in each morning, and Levine and Ray Reneri were charged with the endless task of sorting the avalanche of dollar bills. The staff was so overwhelmed by the sheer volume of mail that hundreds of envelopes were never opened.

Bob Levine eventually packed up his Bobby pins, hooked up with Jimi Hendrix' band of Gypsies and vanished into a purple haze. Ray Reneri became a Tour Manager; the rock 'n' roll 'king of the road'. Ray has now been on the road more than many long-haul truckers, crisscrossing the country with busloads of colored girls, pretty white boys, blues cats, mop-top Brits, and disco divas. At fourteen, Ray entered show-biz organizing a Four Aces fan club from his mother's kitchen table, becoming a backstage gofer to Alan Freed, and a rack jobber for Sam Goody, stocking record bins with the latest 45's, eventually stumbling into Connie De Nave's rock 'n' roll claque. Ray always had the best gossip, like the hot and heavy romance of newcomers Tom Jones and Mary Wilson of the Supremes. Thanks to the extravagant gift-swapping of these two lovebirds, jewelers and furriers all across Europe scored big-time. So did Mr. Jones!

On my first meeting with Roz Ross, she looked me over and said, "we've gotta do something about that nose." I could fib about my age, even adopt a new name – but the nose stays! Without the benefit of a manager to guide me, I was elated to receive a phone call from Roz Ross, an agent at GAC, one of the top three booking agencies in America, the others being the might MCA (Music Corporation of America) and the Avis of Agencies, the No. 2 William Morris. "The Big Three" dismissed the emerging crop of rock 'n' roll stars, considering them not worthy to be included on a talent roster that boasted such heavyweights as Peggy Lee and the Mills Brothers. Agents sign the Artist to an exclusive contract, and then rent them out for the evening, collecting a 10% commission – the world's second oldest profession.

Roz Ross was an agent in the Variety Department at GAC, toiling away booking Steve & Eydie, and comic Betty ("Hello, Ceil") Walker, itching to get down-and-dirty in the rock 'n' roll arena. Sensing that this new "teeny-bopper music" was more than a passing musical fad, she persevered to bring rock 'n' roll artists onto the main stages of show-biz, relentlessly badgering Buddy Howe, President of GAC and a former vaudevillian, into allowing her to create a rock 'n' roll division, a little fiefdom within the kingdom of GAC. Roz was a tough cookie. Although newly svelte, she kept a 'before' picture in her bottom right-hand drawer, a chubby image I teasingly dubbed Kate Smith. Roz also had a taste for kitsch, most notably her collection of artwork by Keane[3], a trendy painter of sad, doe-eyed juveniles, and her novelty desktop cigarette lighters. She was the first to introduce me to marijuana, popping a joint in my mouth in a darkened doorway along Sixth Avenue, with Moondog, the blind Viking panhandler, keeping an eye out.

---

3   Keane portraits of wide-eyed waifs are now valued in the millions. At first signed by the flamboyant San Francisco artist Walter Keane, he was discredited in court when a 1986 lawsuit came to a climax; his second wife Margaret proved to be the real artist. Walter Keane died in 2001 at 85.

6) Payola Scandal – 1959

"Roll over Beethoven and tell Tchaikovsky the news."
– *Chuck Berry*

Everyone saw it coming, except the invincible Alan Freed himself. Ever since the quiz show scandals, Congress was not about to be caught with their pants down on further corruption over the nation's airwaves; a payola investigation targeting disc jockeys had been an ongoing front-page story. It became more an indictment of rock 'n' roll than the lynching of Alan Freed.

Payola, the old-timers agreed, that's what the trouble was: "Slip a disc jockey a few bucks and you had a hit record." Eliminating payola, they thought, would "effectively finish-off this decadent teenage music once and for all."

Frank Sinatra declared that rock 'n' roll was "the martial music of every juvenile delinquent in America…sung by cretinous goons."

Jimmy Durante chimed in, "Rock 'n' roll is just three notes and two of them are rotten." The much-acclaimed, mid-Century songwriter Johnny Mercer added, "I could eat alphabet soup and shit better lyrics."

"Popular music in this country has been sinking for some years," groused The News' Ben Gross. "Now it has reached its lowest depths."

Traditional record executives proclaimed, "Rock 'n' roll is music by the inept for the untutored." What was not understood is that, rock 'n' roll was music made *by* teenagers *for* teenagers. Paul Anka was fifteen when he wrote and recorded his No. 1 hit, "Diana;" Brenda Lee was fourteen when "Dynamite" hit the charts; the

Bobbettes were eleven to fifteen when the group wrote and recorded "Mr. Lee;" Bobby Freeman was in high school when "Do You Wanna Dance" hit. For the very first time, an entire generation of young people were creating and embracing their own music.

Alan Freed had already lost his nighttime radio show and on Friday, November 27, 1959 "the pied-piper of rock 'n' roll" signed-off his "Big Beat" television show. According to Freed biographer, John A. Jackson, "Freed planned to squeeze the last drop of emotion from his final "Big Beat" telecast that Friday evening. Freed remained in his dressing room until seconds before the show begun, at which time, clad in his familiar gold-buttoned plaid sport jacket, he made a dramatic entrance. Head bowed, Freed walked on camera to chants of "We want Alan! We want Alan!" Many of his teenage fans in the studio audience wept openly, as Freed moved among them, visibly sobbing told his studio audience to keep calm and to shed no tears."

My friend Charlie Massi, once my cameraman, sent me an audiotape of that last broadcast, as Freed says: "Thank you all for your loyalty. I'm not going any-where, I'll be back." A half-hour later, the hallways of my Time Square studios of were jammed with Alan's studio audience, clamoring for tickets to our show. In the time it had taken to wipe away the tears and dash from Alan Freed's East 67th Street studios to West 42nd Street, their allegiance to Alan Freed was forgotten.

Alan Freed's bad fortune became a stroke of luck to me; the payola scandal so frightened broadcasters they effectively slammed the door on any further compe-tition. I had clear reign on NY television. The "Big Beat Show" with pop-singer Richard Hayes faded in three months, and later, Channel 5 tried toppling our show with a Soupy Sales rock 'n' roll show, but that failed as well; nothing could stop the steamrolling '*Claycole.*' I was spotless as my Thom McAnn shoes; I was never offered, nor would I accept payola. I had been on the air less than two months.

Since back in the 1940s, it was standing operating procedure for recording art-ists to venture out into the heartlands to glad-hand the disc jockeys – in those days, it was the radio disc jockey who selected the records played on his air. The coming of television changed the game. In the mid-Fifties, Bandstand-type shows began popping-up in major markets of America: Milt Grant in Washington; Buddy Deane in Baltimore; Jim Lounsbury in Chicago; Jim Gallant on Connecticut Bandstand. Actually, the very first teen dance show was "Soupy Sales' Soda Shop," on the air in 1950 in Cincinnati, Ohio. The Philadelphia version went on the air in 1952. Now, when an artist dropped into town, it became more than an "on-the-air" interview; now the artist lip-synched his latest record in a full-blown performance. But here is where the local TV deejays upped the ante. Artists were expected to perform on the television show in the afternoon and then appear at a deejay-sponsored record hop at night. Record hops became a massive money machine for the deejays, reaping a windfall of fresh "tax-free" cash, rewards far exceeding the meager chump change they earned back at the station. Their TV shows simply became the engine to drive the machine.

Alan Freed claimed that he was paid as a "record consultant" to the music business, but in truth, he was simply capitalizing on a long-stand industry tradition of disc-jockey pay-offs. There was no federal charge against payola until 1960; so technically, payoffs weren't illegal. But, he did conduct his business surrounded by a rough crowd. "He was a flawed man who claimed songwriting credits that weren't his, paid performers very little and associated with questionable individuals."

George Goldner, owner of Gee, End and Rama Records and one of Freed's closest friends, is said to have invented payola; it was called "the $50 handshake." But, there were more subtle payoffs. Consider a songwriter copyright: Alan Freed shared writing credits on a number of records including Chuck Berry, "Maybelline," and with Harvey Fuqua, "Sincerely," (of the Moonglows), but it's suspected he contributed little or nothing to the songs and the credits were given to ensure airplay.

Dick Clark sailed through the payola scandal unscathed, appearing before the powerful and antagonistic Congressional hearings accompanied by lawyers with ties to the FCC. Clark's squeaky-clean image was simply angelic compared to the demonic, gravel-faced Freed. Clark admitted to having his finger in publishing, management contracts and an interest in Cameo-Parkway Records.

It was disclosed in fact, that Clark had partial copyrights to one hundred and fifty songs, many of them played on Bandstand, and thirty three related businesses, including record labels, pressing plants, distribution, publishing and artists' management companies. Clark's holding were so veiled that even Duane Eddy, a frequent Bandstand guest, did not know that Clark had a piece of his management company. In spite of the hoop-dee-doo, even after Eddy concluded that Clark had shortchanged him, they remained lifelong friends. Clark named his second son Duane.

Clark pleaded to the committee that, tradition be damned, he would immediately dissociate himself from all of his sheltered interests. Clark admitted to accepting a fur stole and expensive jewelry for his wife from a record company executive and was admonished only for that single transgression. Committee Chairman Oren Hatch called Clark "a fine young man." Alan Freed was sent to the gallows.

John A. Jackson,[4] who has written the most profound and meticulously researched biographies of both Alan Freed and Dick Clark, writes: "Clark was a shrewd businessman who had little in common with the bland boy-next-door persona he projected over the air. Dick Clark masked a cunning business mind and a well of ambition deep even by the standards of the entertainment industry."

Bernie Lowe was a Julliard-trained pianist, conducting the orchestra on "The Paul Whiteman TV Teen Club" (ABC, 1949 - 1954), and Dick Clark was the show's announcer, delivering *live* Tootsie Rolls commercials. The two became friends, and later business associates. The "TV Teen Club" welcomed talented youngsters, and Bobby Rydell, Charlie Gracie and Frankie Avalon, then a 12-year-old trumpet prodigy, made frequent appearances.

At the end of 1956, with a $2000 dollar investment, Bernie Lowe founded Cameo Records (later to become Cameo-Parkway), with an old friend, Kal Mann. Lowe and Mann got into the record business as songwriters for Hill & Range in New York, writing "Teddy Bear" for Elvis Presley (recorded in January 1957.) But, they were having little success with their Cameo label, and Lowe was now looking for his own Elvis.

The teenaged Charlie Gracie was becoming a well-known local Philadelphia rocker who, beginning in 1953, had appeared many times on WFIL's local afternoon Bandstand show, without the benefit of a hit record. "Bernie was looking for a tall, sexy Elvis type," Charlie Gracie remembers, "but he couldn't find anybody and wound up with 5' 4" me. He came to the house one day – I'll never forget it, because he had a cold. My mom gave him some tissues and hot, chicken soup."

"We went into the studio in December 1956, maybe two days before Christmas. We cut two songs written by Lowe and Kal Mann; (though the writing credits went to "Anthony September," their joint pseudonym); one was "Butterfly" and one was "99 Ways." By March of 1957, we had a No. 1 hit, selling well over two million." Monday, August 5th 1957, Dick Clark's "American Bandstand" began broadcasting coast-to-coast on the ABC network.

---

4   "Big Beat Heat, Alan Freed and the Early Years of Rock and Roll" (Schirmer Books, 1991) and "American Bandstand and the Making of a Rock 'n' Roll Empire" (Oxford University Press, 1999) both by John A. Jackson; a former Long Island high school gym teacher.

Gracie's follow-up, "Fabulous" also made top-20. Lowe's company quickly became the biggest and most influential independent label in the United States (this was before Motown) by marketing their product strictly to teenagers. Gracie gave the company its focus, its first hits, and opened the door for future Cameo-Parkway hit-makers, Dee Dee Sharp, Orlons, Dovells, Tymes, Bobby Rydell and Chubby Checker.

But, the unraveling came quickly. Gracie may have been a kid, but he was street-smart enough to realize that he was not getting royalty money proportionate to his million-selling hit records. Cameo gave him just enough money to keep him in flashy cars and snazzy suits. Charlie sued the record company, not knowing that Dick Clark was one of Cameo-Parkway's owners. "I was expendable," Gracie said. "I was the first one to get screwed by Cameo. I sued for my royalties, settled for $40,000 and left, but I never got on Bandstand again. Dick Clark, a silent partner at Cameo-Parkway, was none too pleased. Clark was part of this little conglomeration. I was told, 'you will never have another hit as long as you live.' You know what? They were right. They figured this guy Gracie is stirring up the pot. If everybody does what he does, we'll be in trouble, so we have to get rid of him. So the playing of my records gets diminished. I never got it all from 'Butterfly.' I got a hunk of it. It sold over two million records, man. I thought I was being cheated." Gracie, now in his 70s is still performing, especially in Great Brittan and Europe, where he is revered as a rock legend. He and Bill Haley were the first American rockers to be embraced overseas.

Kenny Dino, another no-nonsense, street-smart rocker, shares another side of the cash payoffs. "I was on Dot, and Randy Wood set up an appearance on Bandstand, and I didn't even have a record – that's the kind of power Dot and Randy had. We did the show and Dick Clark had all the checks signed back to him. That was the payola bullshit. My manager, Al Dankoff says, "My boy sings and gets paid for it!"

"Dick's producer Tony Mammarella started yelling and screaming, "This is the way it is, this is the way Dick Clark does things." So Dick comes into the office and I hear Dick yelling, "That f--- kid will never be on this f--- show again!" and ba-boom, ba-boom. My manager didn't care; he didn't give in, at least, not as far as I know. Clark was pretty pissed, but we ended up doing Bandstand once again with, "Your Ma Said You Cried in Your Sleep Last Night," so I was not blackballed." (Mammarella was later implicated in the payola scandals and insiders maintain that he took the fall for Dick Clark.)

Then there's the story of Danny and the Juniors. Formed in 1957 as the Juvenairs, the Philadelphia quartet, fronted by singer Danny Rapp signed with Artie Singer's Singular Records. Artie Singer and Dave White co-wrote a song for the group, "Do the Bop," to accommodate a new dance 'The Bop' that was popular on Dick Clark's Bandstand, and changed the name of their group to Danny & the Juniors. Their song came to the attention of Dick Clark, who suggested that they rename it "At the Hop."

In the 2009 documentary film "Wages of Spin," Artie Singer recalled, "Harry Rosen was my [Singular Records] distributor, and comes to me and says, 'Artie, you're not gonna believe this. Dick Clark won't play the record unless you give him 50% of the publishing. 'The record will not go on the air unless you give me 50% of the publishing' – wouldn't play the record on the air!'" Now fifty years later, Artie Singer admits, "I was part of this whole scene. I saw the whole crummy situation developing, everybody with their hands out, 50% of the publishing, writer's fees, and artists getting screwed..." He gave Clark the 50%.[5]

Joe Terry, an original member of the Juniors disagrees: "We were never advised of any 'pay for play' deal and we were told at that time that Dick Clark actually changed the title and premise of the song from 'Do the Bop' to 'At the Hop'. Due to the fact that there were already three writers on the song, he [Dick Clark] was given a portion of the publishing rights for his efforts."

But "At the Hop" was not initially a success; it was only after the daily exposure on Dick's ABC Bandstand that it was picked up by ABC-Paramount Records and on top of the charts for seven weeks. It went on to sell over two million copies worldwide, and a 1958 follow-up, "Rock 'n' Roll Is Here To Stay" made it into the Top 20. Then in 1960, Danny and the Juniors signed-on to Dick Clark's Swan Records label, releasing "Twistin' USA," which made it into the Top 40, and became their final hit. In 1983, the Juniors' Danny Rapp was found dead in an Arizona hotel room – a suicide. After 52 years, Joe Terry says, "We have the utmost respect and affection for Dick Clark."

It is a widely-held judgment within the music-biz that Dick Clark has very deep pockets and built his empire on the backs of starry-eyed teenagers. His grueling cross-country bus tours exploited new young artists, paying them peanuts.

---

5   Song copyrights produce the most lucrative financial rewards, offering an annuity, royalty checks from music clearing houses ASCAP and BMI (American Society of Composers, Authors and Publishers, and Broadcast Music Inc), founded on the idea that all songwriters, composers and publishers have the right to be paid for the use of their work. They collect royalty fees on behalf of artists for the public performance of copyrighted works. Singers who are also songwriters – Neil Sedaka, Neil Diamond, and Carol King – reap greater rewards, in perpetuity.

But, you know –nobody cares. Ask any artist who ever stepped onto a Dick Clark tour bus, or sang into a Bandstand camera and they'll tell you it was greatest time of their lives. They would happily be short-changed again for the chance to re-live those happy days just one more time. "Nobody gets paid; good-guys finish last, so shut-up and sing. Those are the rules, so get used to it … and, by the way, we're doing an extra matinee today!"

The House Committee decided to look into deejays who took gifts from record companies in return for playing records. Fearing the worst, record companies stepped foreword to announce they had given money to specific deejays. In all, twenty-five deejays and program directors were caught in the scandal, including Murray "The K" and Peter Tripp, (New York), Joe Niagara, (Philadelphia), Tom Clay, (Detroit) and Stan Richards, (Boston.) Each had neglected to report their cash windfall to the IRS, an oversight that also brought down Al Capone in 1931, for which he served 11 years in prison. The probe quickly focused on the two top deejays in the country, Clark and Freed. Freed refused to sign an ABC waiver, and his broadcast alliances quickly deserted him; Freed was fired from both WABC radio and WNEW-TV Ch 5. ABC television demanded that Clark divest himself from all related industry holdings – a move that cost Clark millions. Using the power of his daily television show, he went about the business of rebuilding his holdings, this time into a far more successful television production empire.

Just as Alan Fredricks, Jocko, Alan Freed, and other New York dance show hosts had, I welcomed guests on the "records promotion" cuff, and did not pay performers. When the Alan Freed explosion sent shockwaves throughout the industry and I was the last man standing, all was about to change. New rules were set.

I was called on the carpet by my union, AFTRA (American Federation of Television and Radio Artists). Irving Lewis, their chief legal council, a feisty old-timer who I really admired, grilled me relentlessly about any hidden affiliations I might have in publishing, record companies, management or organized crime. I had none, but my management partnership with Monte Bruce was based on his intention to involve me in all those activities and that infuriated Mr. Lewis. Irving admonished me not to proceed with any scurrilous behavior that would compromise my good standing with Channel 13.

Irving Lewis grilled me about Monte Bruce, and I could honestly say that Monte never asked me to "sit on" a record that would benefit George Goldner, Morris Levy or any of his powerful record industry friends. Monte was taking half of my television talent fee, but the new payola restrictions effectively froze any nefarious activities he might have planned for our partnership.

Over the course of several meetings with Irving Lewis, AFTRA initiated an acceptable compromise to accommodate both the artists and our minuscule show budget constraints. We could never have continued on the air if forced to pay union scale to the many groups, musician or performer we showcased. It would also have a devastating fiscal impact on the record industry as well. Record companies depended on shows like mine to promote their artists and new releases. The law states that everyone is entitled to one free union job before having to be a union member, but recording studios were also part of AFTRA's jurisdiction, and so an artist's recording session is considered their free ride, a TV appearance then requires AFTRA membership.

Billboard magazine explained the new policy:

> The lip-sync spots are priced $108 per artist on the hour-long show. Payments are made directly to AFTRA, the station taking care of the pension & welfare payments, and then the union sends payment checks to the artist. At sign-off, a disclaimer appears on the credit roll.

The record companies would shell out $108 to Channel 13 for the appearance, the station would reimburse AFTRA $108, plus the proper P&W. AFTRA would then send a check to the member artist (who would usually endorse it right back to the record company.) It was all a paper game. We simply called it "check swapping." Being on the air six nights a week, we introduced so many new recording artists and groups that AFTRA assigned a full-time field agent, Stan Seidenberg to cover our show. Stan set up shop in my dressing room, and signed-on more new members than any other agent; our show becoming a lucrative cash cow for AFTRA.

My brief partnership with Monte Bruce ended at AFTRA's insistence, but not before one last event. Monte promoted an all-star show at the Long Island Arena, a "Welcome Clay Cole" celebration and my very first stage appearance as Clay Cole. Pete Bennett, a drummer and well-connected promotions man, assembled a big band, The Clay Cole Orchestra and Monte booked a hot line-up of R&B groups and pop singers for me to introduce. The morning of the show, we awoke to storm warnings, an oncoming blizzard, freezing temperatures with icy roadways. Hell is an empty arena. Our hopes were dashed, until Monte's Cadillac crept into Commack and the police chief told us that 4500 fans were waiting inside. Monte and I split a sack-full of dollar bills and our partnership.

7) Copacabana

"Do not go gently into that good night;
Rock, rock against the dying of the light."
– *Dylan Thomas*

The Golden Age of Television did much to advance the assimilation of the newly-arriving, post-war immigrants streaming into the Port of New York. Viewers learned that New York City was simply a maze of small ethnic villages, each block with the population of an average Midwestern town (Hubbard, Ohio was typical, with about 7,000 residents.)

Television invited us into the raucous Jewish-Bronx apartment of "Molly Goldberg" and the unflappable parlor of the Norwegian Hansen family in "I Remember Mama." "Life with Luigi" chronicled Italian immigrants struggling to adapt to the American culture (Luigi was played by J. Carroll Naish, an Irish-American actor) and Desi Arnaz single-handedly soothed our suspicions of the surge of newly-arriving Cubans, Dominicans and Puerto Ricans. Many of these television episodes took place at citizenship classes, mingling immigrants of all nationalities, which made these programs so endearing.

So, Manhattan in the 1950s was a maze of ethnic neighborhoods, each like a dime store ring in a Tiffany box. Chinatown, Little Italy, and the Jewish Lower East Side flowed together like an uninterrupted river of immigrants across the southern tip of Manhattan. Three harmonious groups, African-Americans, Italian-Americans and newly arriving Spanish-Americans shared Harlem; the Irish had long since staked claim to Hell's Kitchen, Chelsea and the far Upper East Side of James Cagney.

I settled into Yorkville on the fringes of Germantown, home of sauerbraten and strudel, bratwurst and beer gardens, where each block wafted the distinct pungent aromas from street vendors, bakeries and the local breweries. German hausfraus not only swept their front door, stoop and gutters, but swept their entire block each day.

"Why," I asked one industrious old lady with a broom.

"I like see clean," was her straightforward reply.

Raysa found me a cozy apartment on the East River at 78th Street, nicely furnished by the populist designer Paul McCobb with Herman Miller furniture and framed Brueghel prints of dancing peasants (very *apropos*).

On York Avenue, even my local Deli-man Isidore Steinblatt used a "stage name" – "Louie." Louie would cash my checks and allow me to charge; in return, I'd oblige with autographed pictures for his sons. Today, one of his sons, Jim Steinblatt is a long-term music executive at ASCAP. I remember "Louie-Louie" with great affection.

Before the invasion of plastic-forked fast foods, New York was a mom-and-pop metropolis, a city without supermarkets, gas stations or posted speed limits – in Manhattan you accelerated at your own speed. For fifteen-cents, one could arrive in a $200,000 Grumman with a uniformed driver that stops on every other corner and offers a transfer. Limousines could be rented for about $60 a night plus tip, so I became one of the indulged elite, mollycoddled in plush backseats, chauffeured in air-cooled luxury. When Mom came to visit, I afforded her limousine treatment to The Stork Club, where owner Sherman Billingsley made a big fuss, showering her with cosmetics, candy, a Stork Club apron and souvenirs. "Uncle" Clay and Edna took Mom and me to The Colony, where Mom made several unnecessary trips to the ladies room so that she could pass the front room table of Frank Sinatra, holding court with Joan Crawford and a large party of familiar Hollywood faces.

The Café Chambord proudly advertised itself as "New York's most expensive restaurant," and it was there that I was the victim of a waterlogged prank. The fine crystal water goblets were etched with the Café crest, "CC" – for Café Chambord. Since they were also now my initials, I insisted to Edna and Clay that I must have one. Edna agreed to slip the goblet into her purse if I could empty the glass. Naturally, the service was superior, and each time I gulped down a glass of water, the waiter was there with a refill. After several unsuccessful attempts at refills, the waiter and Edna and Clay erupted in laughter. It was an impossible task to empty the glass. "Uncle" Clay made arrangements with the maitre d' to add the goblet to the check, and I proudly walked away, sloshing out to the street with my crystal grail.

I became a student to the acting guru Wynne Handman, along with classmates Penny Fuller ("Applause"), Gloria Lambert ("Sing-Along-With-Mitch") and Fran Jeffries ("The Pink Panther") – all of who would witness my table manners at the dimly lit banquettes of The Forum of The Twelve Caesars, my favorite romantic rendezvous.

I was invited to be a presenter at the second annual Grammy Awards, as an arranged escort to Miss Grammy 1960. Jimmy Dean, once the prince of country-pop long before he became the king of breakfast sausage, introduced me. My line was: "Jimmy and I made a pact. I won't call him a hillbilly singer; he won't call me a disc jockey."

I respect radio disc jockey's unique talent, the ability to sit alone in a window-less room with just a stack of records, jingles and sound effects and make believe that a wild party is in progress. Radio DJ? I couldn't do it, so I preferred to be called "television personality." This became a minor dilemma when asked to fill out bureaucratic forms that called for "Occupation." I found "television personality" too audacious. Declare yourself "actor" and you are presumed to be gay. "Producer" conjured up images of a flimflam man with a casting couch. I settled on an all-encompassing occupation, "TV" – and no, ma'am, I can't check your tubes.

It was a sober awakening the morning I realized that I could earn more money in one night than my Dad earned in a year. I knew Dad was proud of my success, but I could never flaunt my financial windfall; Dads must be allowed to maintain their personal dignity. As a member of The G-F Management Team, Dad was also aggressively anti-union, having endured his share of arm-wrestling with the labor goons of Youngstown. I never told him I was a card-carrying member of five federations: AFTRA (TV), AGVA (Stage), SAG (Film), Equity (Theatre) and The Writers Guild- East, and that I contracted all my musicians through AFM (American Federation of Musicians).

Mad magazine had difficulty defining me as well, satirizing my occupation in a full-page, six-panel cartoon.

> Panel 1: Who do you wanna be when you grow up?
> Panel 2: I wanna be just like Frankie Avalon!
> Panel 3: Who do you wanna be when you grow up?

Panel 4: I wanna be just like Fabian!
Panel 5: And, who do you wanna be?
Panel 6: I wanna be just like Clay Cole
If I can just figure out what it is he does.

Two sweetly-shy, 14-year-olds, had figured it out. Marcia Habib and Norma Lindenberg approached Raysa seeking permission to form The Claymates, a Clay Cole fan club. Marcia and Norma put forth all the effort, we supplied the official membership card, autographed photos and paid the postage; my fans would be free members. It was humbling to realize that so many young viewers singled me out as their hero. Much more significantly, Marcia made an impact on my life, a bond that has endured to this day.

For Christmas, I splurged at Bonwits, gifted Raysa with a magenta silk blouse and a matching sequined top, all very glamorous. I'd call her up and say "put on your sparkly top, we're going out tonight." I'd put on my tuxedo and we'd stroll into some swanky joint, pretending to be grownups, maybe The Little Club, telling Billy Reed we just came from a *fabulous* party and we are *famished*.

Our big, dress-up occasions were opening nights at The Copacabaña, "the hottest spot north of Havana." The Copacabaña was a celebrated supper club in the cellar of a second-rate hotel, where the unwritten rules of nightlife were abandoned; (1.) never go downstairs for dinner, and (2.) never eat dinner in a nightclub. The Copacabaña attracted all the right players, the high rollers and big spenders from Miami, Las Vegas and Hollywood – hoteliers, tycoons, industry czars, movie stars, music moguls, gossip columnists, television bookers and gentlemen of the press, the all-important reviewers. Performers appeared at The Copa for the reviews, not the money. A good review would mean good money on the road.

The canopied entranceway at 10 East 60th Street offered a choice, to the right, The Copa Lounge, an oversized oval bar, attracting husky men with thick knuckles, peeling hundred dollar bills from tightly rolled wads wrapped in rubber bands, elbow-to-elbow with tourists on a budget nursing warm beer. To the left, a mirrored staircase cascaded down into a tropical forest of white, plaster Art Deco palm trees. When Jules Podell first took occupancy in 1940, the prevailing winds were wafting from South Americans, floating the fascinating rhythms of the samba. "Copacabaña," he thought, "had the right ring to it." Jules Podell is legendary in the whispered stories of show business, but in the dozens of nights I visited The Copa, I never met, nor saw Jules Podell. He preferred to hover in the background, barking orders, scarfing bourbon.

There were no dressing rooms at The Copa, the ladies of the chorus, the house musicians, the samba band, the production singers, the opening act and the star changed in rooms above in the Hotel Fourteen, ascending to the cellar in the service elevator. The doors would open into Podell's steaming kitchens – one American, one Chinese – and with the assistance of waiters and captains, the performers made their way through the darkened audience onto the tiny dance floor in front of the bandstand. At this time there were 275 employees, armies of waiters and sub-waiters, wine stewards, Mandarin chefs, a Kosher rabbi, scantily-clad ladies in fishnet stockings, strapped into trays of cigars and cigarettes, a souvenir photographer offering the first one-hour photo service and an exotic Gypsy lady who would read your palm for a sawbuck.

The "world-famous" Copa Girls were an attraction in themselves, the most beautiful showgirls in New York, and the most fashionable. For generations, ladies of the chorus were dressed in feathers and plumes or silly satin drum majorette suits. Don Loper was brought in to design a stylish wardrobe, with hats and long gloves, and hairstylist Larry Matthews became their personal coiffure, creating an elegance that defined The Copa Girl. According to an old Copa press release, "44 Copa Girls have gone to Hollywood from The Copa stage, among them June Allyson, Carroll Baker, Janice Rule, Joanne Dru, Lucille Bremmer, Olga San Juan and Martha Stewart." (Not *that* Martha Stewart!)

There was a game that Carmine and the maitre d' staff would play at a table on the second tier, one partially blocked by a column, a highly undesirable table, but one that generated a bounty in tips. Hayseeds, out for a night on the town, would be seated there until a gratuity was flashed, then they would be instantly moved to "a more desirable table." At each show, dozens of couples would be propelled from behind the pillar to a proper seat, at the flash of a ten-dollar bill.

The Copa also increased the capacity of the audience, especially when last-minute VIP guests arrived, with waiters moving through the dark, tables and chairs high over their heads, circling the ringside ever tighter and tighter. Often The Copa Girls were so close they seemed to be offering lap dances. Andy Williams, opening for Joey Bishop, became the victim of cramped quarters and ill-manners. A late-arriving Pat Boone was seated ringside at Andy's left elbow, then proceeded to order dinner. Midway through the performance, as Andy sang his delicate, a cappella version of "Danny Boy," waiters arrived with steaming platters of food. Folding a napkin under his chin, Pat dove in, scoffing down forkfuls of chicken chow mien, never looking up at poor old Andy. At this point, no one was watching poor old Andy Williams; all eyes were riveted on Pat Boone addressing his dinner.

Dean Martin & Jerry Lewis satisfied The Copa's preference for Italian singers and Jewish comics, a double-whammy by two bigger-than-life performers, who created pandemonium in an unprecedented 13-week engagement. Their final performance together was at The Copa, July 24, 1956, exactly ten-years to the day that they first appeared as a team at Skinny D'Amato's 500 Club in Atlantic City. From this, Copa legend is born. Sammy Davis Jr. augmented Michael Durso's orchestra with an entire string section that sat quietly in the dark for a full hour, waiting to fiddle for just one song. Now that's a *star*.

Sam Cooke's 1959 appearance was a disaster and a major setback to future performances by young rockers. At age 24, with just one hit ("You Send Me") and little stage experience other than with his Soul Stirrers gospel group, Sam "laid a golden egg," according to the black-owned *Amsterdam News*. Six years later, a savvy Sam Cooke, with a string of platinum hits and Alan Klein as his manager, returned to The Copa a big winner. Alan Klein was a heretofore little-known accountant who stepped in to renegotiate Sam's contract with RCA, resulting in an unprecedented million-dollar advance. Klein heralded Cooke's return to The Copa with a block-long billboard in Times Square as "The biggest Cooke in town." (Alan Klein's growing number of detractors secretly disparaged him as "the biggest *crook* in town.")

In 1960, Paul Anka at just nineteen was the youngest performer to appear at The Copa and the first teen idol who aspired to perform for adult audiences, opening for Sophie Tucker at The Sahara in Las Vegas and headlining Miami's Fontainebleau Hotel. Paul was unique among teen idols; born in Canada, with extensive stage training as a child actor, and now a prolific songwriter. Paul became a naturalized US citizen in 1990. He also had an aggressive personal manager in Irving Feld, who operated a chain of record stores and formed Super Enterprises to promote his "Show of Stars" rock 'n' roll road shows. Feld eventually purchased The Ringling Brother's circus, transforming it from a tent show into an enduring arena attraction. Paul wrote "My Way" in 1967, providing lyrics to an obscure French melody. "When my record company caught wind of it," Paul admitted, "they were very pissed that I didn't keep it for myself. I said, 'Hey, I can write it, but I'm not the guy to sing it.'" When Elvis Presley first sang "My Way" in his stage shows, Elvis told Paul, "This is a Sinatra song." "It *was* for Frank, and no one else," Paul said. Indeed, it became Sinatra's signature song. In addition, "My Way" has been named the No. 1 most-performed song at weddings.

The biggest opening night I ever witnessed was Wayne Newton at The Copa. Without the benefit of a hit record, Wayne had worked unnoticed, upstairs in The Copa Lounge, a booking slightly better than Siberia. In those days, Wayne was a fresh-faced blonde, a very tall country bumpkin who, in his tuxedo, "looked like Doris Day in drag." Newton somehow convinced Podell to allow him to open for Myron Cohen, the low-key dialect comedian known as a long-winded story teller. Wayne pulled out all the stops, singing and dancing, banging on the piano and drums, playing the trumpet and banjo, all with an eager-to-please boyish exuberance. Wayne's forty-five minute set totally destroyed the hard-to-please Copa regulars – the audience was on it's feet cheering. The hubbub was so disruptive that Myron Cohen could not, would not, appear; from that moment on, Myron Cohen opened for Wayne Newton. A star, as they say, was born.

Bobby Rydell's opening night also produced bedlam. I took Marci and Norma, founders of The Claymates (Marcia reminded me that Chubby was in attendance, as well.) Bobby had an upbeat act, most of his hits were swingers; he danced, played drums and scored laughs with his silly but dead-on comic impressions, most notably Red Skelton's "Clem Kadiddlehopper." After the first show, the room was a-buzz with the news – Jules Podell was so thrilled with Rydell's performance he marched right up to his dressing room and signed him on-the-spot to a ten-year contract. For some strange reason, Bobby Rydell never appeared at The Copa again.

Connie Francis, with her repertoire of Italian tearjerkers and bouncy pop ditties, was the perfect Copa star, selling out the room to capacity crowds. In spite of her success, Connie was almost thrown out on her ear. Her father was a pain in the ass, and an accordion player; redundant to be sure. A gentleman is a man who can play the accordion but doesn't. "Get him out of here," Podell screamed to her manager George Scheck, "or I'll throw him *and* his accordion *and* Connie Francis out-a' here!" Her father left without a squawk. Play the accordion, go to jail. That's the law!

For one brief moment, George Scheck managed both Connie Francis and Bobby Darin, but Connie's father demanded that George release Bobby Darin from their management agreement. His ultimatum was "either Connie or Bobby. Not both!" Scheck reluctantly dropped Darin. Connie's father also broke up her romance with Bobby Darin. When Bobby and Connie planned to elope, Francis' father chased after him with a gun telling him to never see his daughter again. Bobby and Connie broke up.

"Who's Sorry Now?" After four marriages, Connie now says that "not marrying Darin was the biggest mistake of my life." Beneath Connie's sunny façade, there loomed an ominous darkness. I always felt she was unhappy with her life. Frankie Valli, Connie and I were seated ringside to see Trini Lopez at Basin Street East and

Connie seemed unusually despondent. Frankie leaned over to me and whispered, "All she needs is one good *schtup*. That'll straighten her right out." Unfortunately, it was her brutal sexual assault while appearing at The Westbury Music Fair that set Connie off her axis forever.

Frankie Valli and Connie have been friends since childhood and no one was more shaken by the news than Frankie himself.

George Scheck, Connie's long-time manager, scooped-up the teenage vocalist when she was performing on "Star Time Kids," a local New York television program he produced. Scheck guided her career to MGM records, and with Connie's meteoric rise as our Number One female recording star, George's fortunes grew as well. George moved his family from Queens to a more idyllic life on Long Island, but in 1959, the Scheck family was shattered when their beautiful new home caught fire, killing their seven-year-old daughter. His ten-year old son Barry grew up to became a lawyer, and gained national attention as part of the dream team that defended O.J. Simpson. In 1992, Barry Scheck co-founded the Innocence Project dedicated to the utilization of DNA evidence as a means to exculpate individuals of crimes for which they were wrongfully convicted. By 2006, more than 180 inmates had been freed from incarceration, credited to Barry Scheck's perceptive grasp of the liberating powers of DNA.

The final week of May, 1960 was a busy week for me, socially: Jackie Wilson was headlining a week at The Apollo, Annette was opening at Radio City Music Hall, and Bobby Darin was making a June 2nd debut at The Copa. Annette was my date, ringside for Bobby Darin – and Bobby was brilliant. Darin's shows were always high-energy; his up-tempo hits with the horn modulations, were designed to trigger excitement. But, surprisingly, Bobby's show was a riot; Bobby decided to speak his between songs patter in the voice of W. C. Fields – "go away little girl … you bother me, yeah." He was hilarious.

When Bobby signed with Roz Ross at GAC, she was booking the bus tours for Dick Clark, but Bobby wanted to make the transition from teen-idol to being a nightclub singer. He wanted to get booked into the Copa.

Roz Ross told Bobby, "Jules Podell won't book rock 'n' roll; he doesn't understand songs like "Splish Splash" and "Queen of the Hop." He doesn't get it. You have to give me a demo, something for me to show Julie to get you into the Copa."

Bobby initially had recorded and paid for the session for "Mack the Knife" and three other songs for an EP – (Extended Play 45-record with four songs) – at the Fulton Studios on West 40th Street on December 19, 1958, with Tom Dowd engineering. So, Bobby told Ahmet Ertegen at Atco Records that he could never get into the Copa unless they released the EP. He pleaded with him, saying he'd give up his royalties on "Splish Splash" and "Dream Lover." He took a gamble.

Ahmet released the EP, and when "Mack the Knife" went through the roof Atlantic/Atco released it as a single. In 1959, Darin's 'Mack the Knife' reached No. 1 on *Billboard's* Hot 100 and earned Bobby a Grammy Award for "Record of the Year." "Mack the Knife" became the biggest record of his career and his signature song. Bobby loved to tell the story that it was Dick Clark who advised him not to record the song because it wouldn't appeal to a teenage rock 'n' roll audience.

Annette was in town for an extended period, appearing with singer Dick Roman four times a day in the new stage show at Radio City Music Hall (along with the film "Pollyanna") We were all gathering at the Harwyn Club when a call rang out from The Copacabana – Bobby Darin was incapacitated, unable to perform. "Are you kidding," Annette screeched, in a gag-reflex laugh. "Me replace Bobby? Get my coat!" Annette, Dick and I raced over to The Copa, and went on with Louis Prima and Keely Smith, introduced by Walter Winchell. These were exciting times.

In the early stages of my career, I idolized two stars that transcended their teen idol reputation – Bobby Darin and Jackie Wilson. I am alone in my conviction that they were the same person, or by some trick of nature, identical twins. They did not possess God-gifted voices and they lacked technique and training, but they were simply amazing entertainers, bigger than life performers, with cockiness beyond confidence and a compulsive drive to succeed. They also shared similar onstage quirks: each walked with a swagger, danced a distinctive glide, and curled the corner of their upper-left lip in a devilish sneer. Both used their entire body to emphasize a brass riff or to punctuate a drum accent, pumping their shoulders, popping their knees, and punching imaginary balloons with one finger. Each had one idiosyncratic move that set them apart – Bobby's finger-poppin' and Jackie's dramatic drop to his knees.

"Jackie Wilson at the Copa," recorded during his April 1962 appearance, is Jackie's only live performance album, offering just a hint of Jackie's dynamic charisma. Unfortunately, an album can't convey his epic showmanship; like Bobby Darin, he was bigger than the room, igniting a party atmosphere with infinitely more style and showmanship than any other teen idol. In 1975, Jackie suffered a massive heart attack on stage at The Latin Casino and never uttered another word, remaining in a coma for eight and a half years. At a quiet birthday celebration in 1977, when the fallen star was vegetating in an out-of-the-way New Jersey nursing home, Charlie Thomas of the Drifters kneeled at his wheelchair, tears welling up, unable to connect with his friend. "It's impossible to believe," he whispered. Charlie, Beverly Lee of the Shirelles, Bobby Lewis and I were the only performers to visit the severely brain-damaged star, who died at age 49. Bobby Darin died from a heart attack following a heart valve operation in 1973 at age 37. I miss them both. Each man carries within him the soul of a poet who died too young.

GAC became my connection to show biz, a destination to schmooze with Roz Ross, get a shoeshine and star gaze – Jane Mansfield, Phyllis Diller, Peg Leg Bates – you never knew who would be passing through. One afternoon, as I was walking down the corridor, GAC agent Vic Jarmel called out to me, "Clay, c'mere. Someone wants to meet you." In his office were Mickey Mantle and Roger Maris. Can you imagine? And, they wanted to meet *me*! We were all just star-struck. Roz always had the inside scoop on all the hot gossip – Chuck Berry was doing time in Leavenworth … Don and Phil Everly don't speak … Dion's gonna split with the Belmonts …Bandleader Johnny Otis ("Willie and The Hand Jive") is white … Bobby Darin's older sister is really his mother … Little Richard quit showbiz to become an evangelist … Bo Diddley is gonna be on Ed Sullivan!

A dashingly handsome junior agent, Jerry Brandt serviced Roz – professionally and personally we all assumed, as her right hand man. Jerry immediately took me aside to make a hush-hush deal for me to appear at a Brooklyn high school record hop, for a quick $150. I remember singing endless choruses of the Wilbert Harrison's "Kansas City," which prompted screams of approval from the girls. I was overwhelmed by the reception, so much so that I didn't want the song to end, nor did I much care that I was getting paid $150 to sing it. Backstage, I insisted we split the money, giving Jerry $75. Years later, it occurred to me that he probably charged the school $300 for my appearance, pocketing half. Add my $75 to the mix, and Jerry took home $225 to my $75. In the agency business it's called a "buy and sell," a practice of the agent selling the artist to the buyer for one fee, then paying the artist a lower fee and pocketing the difference, plus the ten-percent commission. It is a practice that is still prevalent today, so much so that the artists know and accept the whole hoop-dee-doo, grateful to get their share.

Roz Ross was on a roll; top-notch clubs were making big bucks offers for her roster of teen idols. The Twin Rivers Inn in Syracuse, Palumbo's in Philadelphia and the Twin Coaches near Pittsburgh were among the clubs rolling out the welcome mat, offering weeklong engagements. Trouble is, most of her new, young recording stars offered a marquee name, but lacked the stage experience necessary to engage a more sophisticated audience. Fabian, one of the first "teen idols," never had another chart hit after 1960, and at just 17, retreated to Hollywood as a film star, with John Wayne in "North to Alaska" The rest of us were fitted into dinner jackets and rolled out on the road to Clubland.

At age 20, Frankie Avalon was already a veteran entertainer, able to smoothly segue from sock hops to supper clubs, the first of the teen idols to step on stage to an adult audience. Allentown disc jockey (WAEB), Gene Kaye picked me up in a limo as his guest at Frankie's opening at the Latin Casino, a massive supper club near Philadelphia, Frankie's hometown. Avalon charmed the packed house, crooning puppy-love ballads in his mellow baritone voice, and then blew them away with his trumpet virtuosity. He even spoofed himself by pinching his nose while singing "De-De-Dinah" mocking the tinny, nasal sound on his Chancellor record.

Frankie Avalon had been entertaining since he was ten. As a child, he was a trumpet virtuoso, tutored by his father, practicing four to five hours a day. Avalon made a name for himself playing in local theaters and clubs, and at ten, winning first prize on "Paul Whiteman's TV Teen Club" show, where he might have first met Dick Clark, the show's announcer. At twelve, he was invited to appear on "The Jackie Gleason Show" on CBS. More television appearances followed and in 1954, Avalon made a record with a small label called X-Vik Records. His first records were Italiano trumpet instrumentals, "Trumpet Sorrento" and "Trumpet Tarantella." Avalon continued playing the trumpet and joined a local band called "Rocco and the Saints," with another TV Teen Club boy, drummer Robert Ridarelli, soon to call himself Bobby Rydell. The combo played shows at the Sons of Italy Hall, weekend sock hops, teen clubs and summers at the vacation resorts, Wildwood and Somers Point, in New Jersey. It was not until 1959 that Avalon was famously discovered by Bob Marcucci and his songs "Venus" and "Why" sailed to No. 1 on the Billboard Hot 100. In all, Avalon had 31 charted singles during his career as a teen heartthrob and film star, no longer "the young man with a horn."

Gene Pitney, Johnny Tillotson, Chubby Checker, Jimmy Clanton, most of the new kids, lacked the showmanship to sustain two basically different forty-five-minute shows that the grown-up clubs demanded. They had hits, but didn't have an act. To avert a freshman fiasco, like Sam Cooke's ill-fated 1959 Copa appearance, Roz Ross initiated a talent development partnership with Noel Sherman and Lou Spencer, who created and staged complete acts, for a hefty fee, for most all of her young stars.

"Mr. Cole Won't Rock and Roll," a whimsical piece of special material, was the centerpiece of Nat "King" Cole's club act, funny, with a point of view, an attitude. It was so delicious that every performer in town wanted material just like that. That's where Noel and Lou came in; writing and producing an act, tailored to the personality of the performer, an assembly-line formula that worked for years. Their recipe didn't impress everyone; some thought that Noel and Lou were simply manufacturing cookie cutter crooners. I was in such awe of their reputation that I simply shook all over during my vocal audition for them, my knees knocking, and my palms sweating, with uncontrollable honks pouring out of my larynx.

Lou Spencer staged the shows, adding movement, the between song patter, the *shtick*. Noel Sherman was a composer and lyricist who crafted original songs, arranged medleys and wrote special material, like Dion's "I'm the Last of the First Name Singers," a musical laundry-list of all the great one-named singers, from Liberace to Fabian. Dion sang it, but hated it, eventually playing The Copa, and sang it to great response.

After many weeks of rehearsal into the mirrored walls of the Dance Players Studios on Sixth Avenue, Dion's new act would break-in at the Casino Royal in Washington, D.C., with Lou, Noel and arranger Joe Zito on-board, taking notes. Then Roz would send Dion out alone ("Lonely Teenager") on that now-familiar, well-worn path leading to the Copa: eleven days at Three Rivers Inn in Syracuse, a week at Sciolla's in Philadelphia; and then a three-week run at Jack Silverman's International on Broadway.

Dion eventually rebelled against the slick, superficial supper club routine. Shortly after a November '63 appearance on my show (introducing "Drip, Drop"), Dion set fire to his arrangements and special material. "I'm The Last of the First Name Singers" and $25,000 worth of Joe Zito's orchestrations went up in flames, never to be performed again.

Paul Anka and I shared an admiration for Johnnie Ray and Paul invited Johnnie, his long-time manager Bernie Lang and me for lunch at La Fontana Restaurant on West 57th Street. We were enjoying a leisurely, Italian lunch when Johnnie Ray, without forewarning, simply collapsed face down into a plate of *pasta e fajoele*. Bernie was both embarrassed and alarmed, "it's Johnnie's medication," he explained. Waiters rushed to the rescue with warm towels. Bernie swooped up the lifeless singer, excusing himself, saying, "allow me get him home to bed; he'll be fine." Paul and I sat at the suddenly deserted table, speechless.

Aside from Johnnie's lifelong near-deaf hearing problem (he wore a cumbersome, oversized hearing-aid), none of us were aware he was suffering multiple medical problems. It was tragic for us to witness such a dramatic performer, now at a low-point in his once brilliant career, so vulnerable. We were all secretly grateful to Dorothy Kilgallen, the powerful columnist and "What's My Line" star-panelist, for taking him by the arm as her companion, giving him renewed self-esteem. Johnnie introduced me to Miss Kilgallen at Bobby Rydell's opening night at The Copa.

"Is it proper to thank you for all the nice things you've been writing about me," I asked.

"Yes," she snapped, and that was that.

Months later, I learned that she detested Dick Clark; they had been feuding, so her malice toward Dick was satisfied by her kindness towards me.

I later dropped in on Johnnie Ray to pay my respects. He lived splendidly in a tastefully decorated all-white apartment, dominated by a shiny-white Steinway grand piano, on which he played, beautifully. Framed platinum records lined the wall, visually charting his brief but meteoric career, the two-million selling "Cry" (1952) to his last, "Just Walking In The Rain" (1956). Johnnie Ray died of liver failure in 1990, at age 63.

My link to the record business was the promotions men, a randy collection of charmers who would drop by my office each week to hype their latest releases. When old-timers get together to talk about "the good old days," these are the guys they talk about. The oral history of rock 'n' roll has elevated these characters to mythic status, but they are legends nonetheless: "Juggy" Gayles, Red Schwartz, Steve Harris, Sammy Vargas, Pete Bennett and Jerry Moss (the "M" in A & M Records; Jerry is the music mogul partner of the "A," Herb Alpert.) Pete Bennett, a one-time drummer, is now a powerhouse manager, rewarded for his many years as a trusted confidant to both the Beatles and the Rolling Stones. Then there was Mickey Eichner and Rick Picone who became my very best buddies during my first few seasons on television. Mickey held a secret daydream of becoming a radio disc-jockey and I always pictured Mickey down in his cellar, with a stack of 45s and a fake microphone, counting down the top ten songs of the week – all from his Jubilee Records Company and Cosnat, his wholesale distributor. Mickey would call me on the telephone and address me in that uncious, nasal tone preferred by small-market radio jocks. Alas, an on-air shift was not in the cards for Mickey; he would enjoy an eighteen-year career as senior vice-president and head of A&R at Columbia Records (Sony Music). Rick Picone was dashing – a dapper dresser with killer good-looks – a former paratrooper and visual-arts alumnus of New York's Parsons School of Design. Rick would later explore the world as Tour Manager for Peter & Gordon, Paul Anka, and two international pop stars managed by Gordon Mills – Tom Jones and most notably Engelbert Humperdinck. It is ironic that Humperdinck's greatest hit, the Grammy-nominated ballad, "After the Lovin" in 1976, was recorded for Epic Records, a Mickey Eichner subsidiary at Columbia.

Mick and Rick took me under their wing and I was happy to soak up their Brooklyn smarts, their Broadway savvy, and the intricacies of the record business. The two were inseparable and would drop by in Mickey's sleek, white Oldsmobile Starfire convertible with it's silver leather interior, the top-down and the radio blasting, and we'd sail along the Brooklyn-Queens Expressway, singing at the top of our lungs, giddy as three sailors on shore leave, on our way to exotic places like Nathan's Coney Island or Lundy's Sheepshead Bay. We were young, high-spirited and our lives revolved around the pop music of the late Fifties, 'the Three Muske-teers of rock 'n' roll.'

It was on one of those outings that we first heard "There Goes My Baby" by the Drifters (with lead singer Ben E. King), a Jerry Leiber-Mike Stoller produc-tion with tympani kettle drums (BOOM-bee-boom), cellos and violins with bows slicing violently across the strings, a dramatic avalanche of sound, never-before heard on a rock 'n' roll recording. It was a revelation, like, as a kid, turning cerebral cartwheels hearing "Sh-Boom" for the first time. Mickey pulled the car into a rest area so we could relish the full impact of what we were hearing over the airwaves; it was a musical milestone. We are all now semi-retired, but active: Mickey and his two sons share a production office in Northern New Jersey and Rick stages events at the Thomas & Mack Center in Las Vegas. Both told me that our moment in time together was "the greatest time of their lives," a cry shouted out by each of the players from those irreplaceable early years that I traced down for this memoir.

It is little wonder that the Drifters have remained a class act with their lineage of remarkable singers – Clyde McPhatter, "Brother" Rudy Lewis, Johnny Moore, Ben E. King, Bill Pinkney and Charlie Thomas – first rate gentlemen all. I once reunited Clyde Mc Phatter with the Drifters for a Christmas show to recreate their finger-popping version of "White Christmas" with Clyde's surprising second chorus appearance, "I-I-I-I'm dreamin' of a white Chris-masss." Backstage, Clyde gave me a bear hug and said, "Clay, I never prayed for a white man before, but I'm praying for you tonight." Clyde was a gentle-man, a great-looking guy, with a sly, sexy stage persona and an impeccably tailored stage wardrobe. Clyde taught me, "never, ever wear your stage shoes or suits off-stage…they should be well-pressed, and wrinkle free." You learn from the best.

When Clyde signed a solo contact with Atlantic Records, he personally rehearsed Jackie Wilson as his replacement as the new member of the Dominos. Jackie, a former Golden Gloves boxer, always credited Clyde for teaching him the tricks of the stage. Clyde became a huge star on the "chitlin' circuit" but sadly deprived of star status to white kids, like Sam Cooke, Brooke Benton or Jerry Butler, perhaps because he lost momentum joining the Army and away from the scene during those crucial early years.

Ben E. King (Benjamin Nelson) came from the same mold, understated, respected and a natty dresser. The Drifters name was owned by George Treadwell, (ex-husband of Sarah Vaughan) and his "Drifters" were paid a paltry weekly salary, with George pocketing the royalties. This created much dissention among group members throughout the years. Ben E. King stepped away, writing and recording "Stand By Me," becoming an international solo star. Charlie Thomas, an original member of the Crowns, developed into the latter-day lead, carrying the Drifter's dignity into the 21st Century.

The freewheeling format of "The Record Wagon," allowing our studio audience to select the dance play list, helped define our show's uniquely New York flair. A controversy erupted over a highly unlikely double-sided recording of two old standards, "Where Or When," the Richard Rodgers & Lorenz Hart torch-song written in 1936 for the musical "Babes In Arms" and "That's My Desire," the signature tune and big hit record for Frankie Laine. The two sides were the latest (and last) release of Dion & the Belmonts and, while the nation's disc jockeys were playing "Where or When," our audience demanded we flip the record to the more dramatic, a cappella sounding, "That's My Desire." I milked the disagreement, making a big deal out of it every day, challenging the kids in our studio to vote, shouting out their preference. The hoopla was ongoing, and I pounded away on the controversy, and "That's My Desire" became an East Coast hit.

Several weeks later, I was rehearsing with the band Orchid over at Morris Levy's Roundtable club when Dion appeared in the doorway. I learned later that he had spent a good part of the day tracking me down. "I just came by to thank you," he said. "My mom told me what you did for me while I was away and I am grateful." You could have knocked me for a loop. Dion & the Belmonts had been frequent guests on my show and of all the artists, Dion was the most distant. I could not connect with him.

Just a few months earlier, in February 1959, Dion had escaped death by declining to fly in the Beechcraft air charter that crashed, killing Buddy Holly, Richie

Valens and The Big Bopper – the infamous "Day The Music Died." Dion was offered a seat, but said, "I decided I couldn't afford the $36 cost to the next stop on our [Winter Dance Party] tour." But to me, Dion's aloof attitude was more than apathy; something deeper was troubling him. I later learned that Dion had gone away for "the cure," (as Rehab was called back then) and while he was gone, I had kept his name alive at home, where it counted the most to him. He was clean, clear-eyed and grateful; an all-new Dion. I was very moved by his gesture.

That night I had a dream about Dion, which I unraveled the next morning in my session with Dr. Cohen. I had dreamed that a robot had four small Scrabble-sized chips placed in the fold of its arm, a square slot at the vein favored by heroin mainliners. The chips had plus and minus symbols on them. But as I lay down on the couch, I suddenly blurted out the meaning of the dream, I said "There was this big clay robot – woops, I had said Clay, and in my dreams the robot was mummy-like, appearing in a smooth plaster cast, made of clay. Of course – the "clay" robot was me. I wanted to change *my* minus chips into plus clips, to be rehabilitated just like Dion. I too wanted to be "a good person," as Dion had now become. This was a positive break-though for me, as it had been for Dion, an intensely creative and kindhearted friend throughout all the years we interacted professionally. He had found inner peace.

Later, Dion went solo with the guidance of his manager Sal Bonafede, signing a Columbia Records deal and recording "Ruby Baby" and "Donna The Prima Donna" (Backed in the studio by the Del Satins), creating, as Bobby Darin once told him "Bronx Blues," a whole new urban sound. Dion immediately purchased an eight room house in White Plains for his parents and two teenaged sisters. Dion's contract with Columbia Records was a major news event, after all, Dion was the first rock 'n' roll artist signed to the prestigious label – it's what was called a "Get PoPsie Moment."

William "PoPsie" Randolph was the unofficial photographer of the music industry, a former band-boy with the Benny Goodman orchestra, PoPsie was available on a moments notice, came cheap, and owned his own camera and darkroom. The "moment" must be captured, immortalized for posterity, published in Cash Box, framed and displayed on an office wall – until the next management team moves in.

Portraits – now that's another matter. Artists hitting the big-time must have publicity photos, Eight-By-Tens bearing the distinctive mark of James Kreigsmann, Maurice Seymour or Bruno of Hollywood. Kreigsmann was the most revered – *the* photographer of choice since the jazz age. Giant black and white blowups of Sinatra, the Andrews Sisters, Paul Anka, and the Ladies of Burlesque lined his gallery walls. Michael Ochs (brother of the late folk singer/songwriter Phil Ochs), the caretaker of the largest private collection of rock 'n' roll photographs on the planet, purchased the Kreigsmann archives. "When I first entered Kriegsmann's studio, it was as if I died and went to heaven," he wrote. " The studio itself – entered via a broad spiral staircase that winds down from a street-level reception area – was like the robbers cave in the story of Ali Baba and the forty thieves." In 2007, Michael Ochs' massive archives were acquired by Getty Images.

Each of these three photographers planted their distinctive logo on the bottom corner of each picture, like fine artists signing their paintings, signaling the prestige attached to the portrait. I have been photographed by all three, but preferred Bruno of Hollywood for the cache' attached to the name and his atmospheric studios in the lofts high above Carnegie Hall. Each year I would visit those musty rooms to pose for a brand new batch of Eight-By-Tens bearing the stamp of "Bruno of Hollywood."

I was once invited to be the opening night performer at a brand new club in New Jersey and I sent them a packet of my new publicity photos, with the Bruno of Hollywood logo slugged at the bottom. When I pulled up to the club, their huge marquee emblazoned: "Opening Tonight. In Person. Bruno of Hollywood."

8) Palisades Amusement Park – 1960

♪ Palisades Amusement Park, Swings all day and after dark.
Ride the coaster, Get cool, In the waves in the pool.
You'll have fun, so, Come on over! ♪

In 1960, my summer place became Palisades Amusement Park, an old-fashioned cotton candy wonderland, overlooking upper Manhattan from atop the New Jersey palisades. From early spring and into the fall, Channel 13 broadcast "The Clay Cole Summer Show," six nights a week from the casino band shell, next to "the world's largest outdoor saltwater pool," a sandy beach with an artificial wave-making machine. The band shell provided the perfect set-up: a stage, dance floor, and best of all – a cocktail bar.

Irving Rosenthal, a pint-sized ex-carnival man, the owner-operator, would arrive promptly at noon, in a chauffeured limousine, from his opulent Fifth Avenue apartment. He often extended an invitation for me to join him and midway across the George Washington Bridge, he would pull himself up by the straps to take a peek at his Cyclone and Ferris wheel teetering on the edge of the New Jersey cliffs. It was a ritual that brought him great joy, seeing his empire at such distance for the first time each day. Irving got his start at Coney Island, selling sand pails for a nickel, knowing a parent would rather part with five pennies than deal with a crestfallen child. Irving bought Palisades Park from moviemaker Nicholas Schenck in 1936, promoting it to the millions on the other side of the George Washington Bridge – New York City.

Irving's flamboyant wife was also a charmer, an ideal match, she tall and thin, and he short and squat. Gladys Shelley was a svelte bottle blond with a Chihuahua permanently folded in her arms, lost amid dangling gold charm-bracelets and glossy enameled nails. Gladys was a well-known lyricist, writing film songs for Fred Astaire, and the memorable "How Did He Look," recorded by Eydie Gorme. However, Gladys will forever be remembered for a simple jingle, played millions of times on the radio and imprinted into the psyche of every East Coast sh-boomer: *"Palisades has the rides, Palisades has the fun, come on over,"* as sung by Steve Clayton

Irving ran an immaculately clean, family-friendly playground, with games of chance, gypsy palm readers, a classic antique merry-go-round, and a grand old-fashioned wooden roller coaster. Elegantly dressed in his pinstripe suit, Irving would patrol the midway, stopping to pick up a candy wrapper or reward a kewpie-doll to a weeping ball-toss loser, or sample the custard, caramel corn, and the park's famous French-fries, triple fried and laced with salt and malt vinegar. Irving could accurately gage a good day's receipts simply by inspecting the garbage hampers. For years, free admission was available through a well-known hole in the fence; Irving ordered his men not to fix it.

Irving and Gladys held court at Table Number One in The Circus Restaurant, ravenously cutting his Angus beefsteak and spewing coleslaw, while extolling his latest "gag" – carnival talk, meaning promotional idea. I was invited to sit at the esteemed Table Number One, where for the next eight years; I was never presented a check. Table Number One's windows overlooked the "Free-Act Stage" where Irving presented first-rate circus performers, four times a day. (I once witnessed a trapeze artist fall to a thud on the wooden stage, where she laid motionless before a hushed crowd, comforted by her husband, awaiting the ambulance). Each weekend was the famous, free rock 'n' roll show with deejay "Cousin" Bruce Morrow prancing the stage in his leopard-skin suit. Every artist who ever stepped into a recording studio appeared on that stage, a "gag" that brought fame to the artist, and a fortune to Irving. The Free-Act Stage had a double meaning, acts performed for no payment, and audience paid no admission. In return, Irving offered the artists a week of promotion, hiring squads of paperhangers to strike in the middle of the night, plastering giant three-sheet posters all over Manhattan, announcing each week's headliners. My picture on those posters made me a household name, to households that would never consider watching a rock 'n' roll television show. As if to illustrate my drinking days, I was literally plastered all over town.

"The Clay Cole Summer Show" at Palisades Park seemed to be the center of the music universe, as teen idols, one-hit wonders, rockabilly duos, giggly girl groups, and tuxedoed a cappella boys scampered around the park, followed by gaggles of groupies, press agents and hangers-on. It was heady, but, *we* had the bar.

Irving's "gag" for me that summer was the Miss America Teenager pageant, with preliminaries every Sunday, culminating with the finals, televised at the end of the season on Channel 13. So, every Sunday afternoon, I returned to the park to emcee the eliminations, a seven day a week employee. If you seek publicity, simply crown a pageant winner; my picture was printed in every newspaper in America crowning bathing beauties.

Televising our show six nights, next to the "world's largest outdoor saltwater pool," proved too great a temptation to visiting groups and guest stars who took great delight in tossing me into the water, fully-clothed in my blue, green, yellow or Palm Beach white dinner jackets. Irving provided me with a little cottage as a dressing room/office, discreetly tucked away off the midway. After one Saturday night dunking, my tux was wringing wet and I hung my pants, shirt, bowtie and jacket on a clothesline to dry. I returned to the cabin on Monday to find my entire wardrobe dry-cleaned, on-hangers, perfectly restored, with a note from an anonymous teenage fan.

When northern New Jersey was hit by a tornado and we were knocked off the air, Kenny and the crew cooked up a gag to amuse the boys back at master control. We pretended to go on the air, but with a profanity-riddled opening monologue. We just wanted to confuse and amuse the tech-boys. Afterwards, over steaks at The Circus Restaurant, Kenny turned white, "what if master control actually received our transmission and switched us on-the-air?" Our careers would have ended with just the flip of a switch.

Neil Sedaka drove himself from Brooklyn to the park in his newly-purchased pride-and joy, a 1960 ice-blue Thunderbird convertible, placing his brand new 45 on the dashboard. By the time Neil pulled up and into the parking lot, the record had simply melted in the August heat. Arriving at The Casino stage absolutely dejected, Neil offered up his record, looking like a licorice doily – 'by the Dashboard Light!' Neil's rippled record was "Run Sampson Run," a song that barely made a ripple on the charts. So, the show went on with Neil repeating "Oh, Carol!" and "The Diary."

Neil told me he originally wrote "The Diary" for Little Anthony & the Imperials, but their recording was never released. So, RCA agreed to allow Neil to record it, and he quickly rounded up about ten of his Brighton Beach buddies, coached them in the background vocals and cut the record. "I guess their raw, natural sound did the trick," he says, "for Diary sold over a million copies."

Connie De Nave and Ray Reneri arrived one afternoon with television's newest western star, a 6' 4" cowboy named Clint Eastwood, promoting a new album and a CBS western series, "Rawhide." Clint Eastwood, like Jack Lemmon and Dudley Moore, was a naturally gifted jazz piano player, but was positioning himself as a singing teenage idol.

Seventeen-year-old Fabian's appearance at the park on Saturday, September 9th, 1960, attracted the biggest crowd of the summer with gaggles of star-struck, screeching teeny-boppers running amuck, followed by packs of news photographers. Fabian's arrival was uneventful, but once in the park, after a chorus of "Tiger," his summer hit, (also his biggest-ever chart hit) and "Turn Me Loose," he became a prisoner of Palisades. There was no exit gate close enough for a hasty safe retreat; Irving Rosenthal to the rescue. In minutes, a helicopter swooped down on the park, blades whirring, kicking up dust, slicing a safety zone and simply whisked the terrified Fabian up, up and away. Irving turned to the gathered press photographers and mumbled. "Did you get that? *One sweet gag.*"

My loyal buddies Mick & Rick never missed a show, arranging an endless parade of first-rate acts, artists on promotional tours. Donnie Brooks had a big breaking hit, "Mission Bells," and Rick had booked him on the show. I was very excited, the song was a favorite sing-along tune of Mickey, Rick and me; we knew all the words. But, as show time neared, Donnie Brooks had not arrived for rehearsals and we were starting to panic, since I had heavily promoted his appearance. What to do? "Wait a minute," I said to Rick. "Do you know what Donnie Brooks looks like?" Rick shrugged, no "Well no one else does, either!" You are gonna be Donnie Brooks!"

Our theme song for the summer show was the catchy rondelle, "Summertime, Summertime" by the Jamies (led by brother-sister, Tom and Serena Jameson), but the really big songs of the summer came from Brian Hyland and Chubby Checker. Brian Hyland became the ideal symbol for our summer show, a bashful, blonde, fifteen-year-old, with the perfect beach record, "Itzy Bitsy Teeny Weenie Yellow Polka Dot Bikini," an innocent novelty written by Paul Vance and Lee Pockriss. Better still, he was a New Yorker, born in Queens, living with his parents in Levittown. Brian was our romantic leading man that summer and he and his faithful manager Sam Gordon became my good buddies. Brian appeared regularly as we watched his song climb to No.1 in July '60 on the Billboard Hot 100. As it turned out, Brian Hyland proved to be more than just a pretty face or a one hit wonder; his future hits would include "Gypsy Woman," "The Joker Went Wild" and "Sealed With A Kiss."

Legend has it that Chubby Checker was a former "chicken plucker," but to be precise, he plucked his chickens from the icy display cases at Farm Fresh Poultry, whose owner sent him to Kal Mann (Parkway Records) and into the Dick Clark fold, becoming one of "the Bandstand Boys." Chubby Checker was a frequent guest on "The Record Wagon," his first effort was "The Class," impersonating Elvis, the Coasters, the Chipmunks and Fats Domino, and later a duet with Bobby Rydell on "Jingle Bell Rock." It was Dick Clark's Bandstand producer, Tony Mammarella, who changed his name from Ernest Evans to Chubby Checker, as a twist on Fats Domino. He *was* chubby in those days, but fifty years of on-stage twisting has slimmed him considerably. As a young man, Chubby was charming, with a wide-eyed curiosity and a mischievous sense of humor. During one of his frequent appearances on our show, Chubby arrived in his Cadillac – ("all black men drive Caddy's," was his running gag) – and rushed onto the stage in wide-eyed astonishment. "You'll never guess what I just saw!"

"What, Chubby? What?

"A black man driving a station wagon!" Then he'd double up in laughter.

One time in Hollywood, as we were being driven back to our hotel, he begged our driver to pass by Wallach's Music City, at Sunset & Vine; the record store was featuring a huge Chubby Checker window display. At the moment in music history, Chubby was probably the biggest star on the planet and somehow seeing Wallach's window tribute confirmed his success, made it real to him. Chubby had an unrestrained child-like quality, not the least bit self-conscious about expressing excitement or glee.

Chubby, then 19-years-old, came to us with a new tune, a song that inspired and excited Kenny Whelan, who could shoot Ferris wheels, wheels-of-fortune, tilt-a-whirl, anything spinning, round and round to the beat. We also asked Chubby to perform a second song, so we flipped his 45 to the B-side, "The Twist," written a year earlier by Hank Ballard, and recorded with his group, the Midnighters, then quickly forgotten. This was the first time Chubby Checker's "Twist" was seen, heard and demonstrated on television. Chubby claims never to have seen Hank & the Midnighters perform the Twist, so he just made-up appropriate twisting movements. Sh-Boomers began twisting.

Chubby Checker has never been properly acknowledged for one major contribution to pop culture – Chubby and "The Twist" got *adults* out and onto the dance floor for the very first time. Before the Twist phenomenon, grownups did not dance to teenage music. In addition, his recording of "Let's Twist Again (Like

We Did Last Summer)" rewarded Chubby with the 1961 Grammy Award as "best rock 'n' roll single." "The Twist" went on to become the only single to top the *Billboard* Hot 100 twice, in two separate chart runs, 1960 and again in 1962. (Bing Crosby's classic "White Christmas" had done so earlier.) Most recently, *Billboard* ranked "The Twist" as the Top Song of the Hot 100 era; of all the No. 1 songs in the 50 years of that chart, Chubby Checker's "The Twist" ranks No. 1 as the most popular single *ever*. Elvis and the Beatles didn't even make the top five. "The Twist" was also named by the Rock and Roll Hall of Fame and Museum as one of the 500 songs that shaped rock 'n' roll. Is Chubby Checker in The Rock and Roll Hall of Fame? Look it up!

It was a twist of fate that brought Frankie Valli's group the Four Lovers, together with Danny & the Juniors ("At the Hop"), and the Royal Teens ("Short Shorts") on our Palisades Park show, an appearance that set the future of the Four Seasons into motion. Frankie Valli was having no luck promoting the Four Lovers, his quartet of Jersey Boys with an RCA recording contract, but little success. "We were a working-man's group," Frankie remembers, "a blue-collar group; we appealed to that guy who was struggling a bit." Producer Bob Crewe kept them busy as session musicians and background singers on recordings of Bobby Darin, Freddy Cannon and others.

Jerry Blavat, who would later become Philadelphia's most important radio deejay, "the Geeter with the Heater," was then road manager for Danny & the Juniors and recalls this story: "It was during an appearance of the Four Lovers on Clay's show at Palisades Park that Bob Crewe and Frankie Valli met Bronx-born Bob Gaudio, appearing as a member of the Royal Teens. Frankie suggested to his bandmate Tommy DeVito that perhaps they should talk to Gaudio and incorporate the two groups into one."

Impressed by Valli's unique vocal sound and their mutual admiration for R&B, Blavat, Valli, Gaudio and Crewe bonded. "When we did the Clay Cole Show at Palisades Park [it was apparent] Frankie was an incredibly talented guy," Blavat remembered.

It was Blavat who was instrumental in convincing a black record label, Vee Jay, to sign them, "the first white group ever on a label that was owned by black record company people." The Four Seasons' "Sherry," "Big Girls Don't Cry," and "Walk Like a Man" became three consecutive No. 1 hits. Bob Crewe's collaboration with Bob Gaudio produced his longest string of chart-topping hits, songs tailored to the trademark falsetto of Frankie Valli. The Four Seasons (with Valli, Gaudio, Tommy DeVito and Nick Massi – replaced later by Charles Calello, then Joe Long) became the most successful of all East Coast groups; a rags-to-riches story with all the makings of a big, fat Broadway hit.

For the record, the four violin concertos of Vivaldi, or the stylish Manhattan restaurant did not inspire the name change to The Four Seasons; Frankie borrowed the name from The Four Seasons Bowling Alley in Union, NJ. *Go figure.* I venerated Frankie Valli, both as a friend and as a performer with an incomparable sound – simply one of the great voices of pop music. Once, on a stage appearance together, Frankie invited me to sing along with the Four Seasons, just as the Drifters and the Isley Brothers had done. I was so intimidated by their perfect harmonies, I simply mouthed the words and snapped my fingers – to their great relief, I'm sure. But I can still boast, I once sang with the Four Seasons. Reminiscing with Frankie recently about the early days, he smiled wistfully and expressed what all of us old timers feel, "It was like family back then."

In the summer of 1960 a presidential election was heating-up; the country was about to elect its first rock 'n' roll Commander-In-Chief, 43-year-old John Fitzgerald Kennedy. We staged our own political rallies, an on-going gag, inspired by an upbeat, novelty song, "Teenager For President," recorded by Tony Cosmo, a charismatic, young stud from Italian Harlem. We staged parades down the midway, red-white-and-blues bands, flags, banners and political placards, with teenagers dancing around Cosmo, singing atop an open convertible. Tony's political thriller was produced by Teddy Vann who set about to convince me to allow him to produce a record with me. It didn't take much persuasion; I was itching to record.

One mid-Summer midnight, with my pals, the Mystics, the Passions and Jay Traynor (the original Jay of Jay & the Americans) singing background vocals, we recorded "Here, There, Everywhere" at Regent Sound Studios on West 66th Street. I kept the whole session a secret not knowing the outcome, but it was immediately picked-up by Morris Levy's Roulette Records. Kenny Whelan planned an elaborate production for our August 20th show, inviting "Cousin Brucie" to introduce me lip-synching the novelty d-d-d-d-ditty for the first time. It was a silly tune, basically describing a stalker. Since Brucie and I held an unspoken rivalry, Kenny staged the climax of the song, as a cinematic duel, with Bruce Morrow and me sword-fighting up and down ramps, like Errol Flynn and Basil Rathbone.

Cash Box reviewed "Here, There, Everywhere" as a Best Bet, "a sensational wax debut (B+)" and it became a minor regional hit. Georgia Winters created a two-page gossip column, "Here There Everywhere with Clay Cole" as a regular monthly feature for her *16* magazine. Although the column appeared for years, I did not write a single word; Georgia wrote every word of it. What was truly astonishingly about Georgia Winters is that she wrote every word on every page of *16* magazine and took most of the photos with a simple flash camera. If Gloria wasn't the first pop culture journalist, she was surely the first female rock 'n' roll writer to tap into the psyche of lovesick teenage girls. By the summer of 1960, *16* magazine enjoyed a circulation of a quarter-million, and was passed around to millions more.

Surprisingly, I was invited by a Cleveland radio station to perform "Here There Everywhere," at Euclid Beach, a popular old amusement park, on an all-star line-up that included everyone from Fabian to Bill Haley & His Comets to Larry Verne, who was enjoying success with his comedy hit, "Please Mister Custer." While watching Dee Clark ("Raindrops") perform original, new twist moves on stage, I copied his arched-back knee-raise, a step I later perfected to great benefit throughout my career. JoAnn Campbell and I made a day of it, riding the roller coasters, devouring vinegar French Fries, and posing for snapshots from Dad's new Kodak.

Bobby Darin invited me to perform with him at The Mosque Theatre in Newark, finally obliged to showoff my double-shuffle time step. Backstage, Bobby was a bundle of energy, tap-dancing, pounding the piano and twirling his cowboy six-shooters, drawn from double holsters hugging the hips of his jumpsuit. (I immediately went out shopping for jumpsuits, one in every color.)

As the "special guest attraction" at the Jones Beach Aquarama, I found myself center stage, singing over a water-tank to an unseen audience in bleachers a half-mile away, me singing the bridge and the Vincent Lopez Orchestra playing the chorus, fifty yards above and behind me. I wanted to cannonball into the tank along with the Diving Aquamaniacs and take Vincent and his tinkling piano with me. At Johnny M's Safari Club, seeking vertical space on his tiny stage, I leaped into Johnny M's newly installed foam ceiling, showering his ringside guests with a snowfall of plaster foam. A diving disaster, then a disaster in a dive, I decided it was time to hang it up, for a while anyway.

I found escape in a second summer place, Asbury Park, a surprisingly old-fashioned, landscaped beach resort on the "Jersey Shore," and the closest to Manhattan. I was invited to join a panel of judges to select Miss New Jersey at The Asbury Park Convention Center and we 'dignitaries' and the bathing-beauties were guests of the brand new Empress Motel, offering uniformed waiters serving champagne and fresh strawberries at the outdoor pool. The Empress, owned by a local judge Carl Kline, became my weekend destination for the next several summers. After my Saturday night show, I would simply phone Judge Kline and drive down with no reservations. Bobby Rydell, Dion, and his manager Sal Bonafede joined me one weekend and I invited my NBC page buddy Joey Rogers to tag along. At the pool, Bobby and Joey were a riot, executing explosive cannonballs and Dion dazzled us all with his perfectly accomplished swan dives off the high-board. *Who knew?* Sal dazzled me as well with a persuasive offer to take me on as manager, which I reluctantly refused.

In the summer of 1960, I discovered the one disadvantage of *live* television – I was robbed. A clever thief, knowing that I would be absent from my apartment at show time, conveniently took advantage of that information. I returned to my apartment to find it cleaned-out; the contents tossed into my shower curtain, bound together by my telephone cord, and hauled away over his shoulder like a Santa Claus with second thoughts. Just before my big Saturday night show, NYPD detectives asked me to drop by the precinct to identify my belongings, but withheld all details; and yes, several items were mine, including un-cashed checks. That night, with a wink and a smile, I dedicated my show to the diligent flatfoots of the NYPD, and then took off to Asbury Park for an overnighter. When I returned to Manhattan, the *Sunday Daily News* told the whole story in a gripping account of an Eastside Cat Burglar who, with heavily-weighted stolen coins in his pockets, plunged to his death trying to leap from a fire escape into an open window.

I don't know how I did it, chalk it up to youth, but in the midst of six *live* hour-long television shows and my Sunday afternoons with Miss Teenage America, I accepted an offer to appear in a summer theatre production of the Rogers & Hammerstein musical comedy, "Flower Drum Song." Joyce Selznick, of the Hollywood-Selznick dynasty, was New York casting director for Columbia Pictures, credited with discovering Faye Dunaway and Tony Curtis. Joyce had a vision of converting Long Island's Gateway Playhouse into a summer training camp for Columbia's stable of young contract players. James Darren had appeared last season and this summer, in need of a marquee name, she approached me, not promising, but implying that she would use her clout to open the doors to film offers from Hollywood.

"Flower Drum Song" required a commitment of four weeks. I was cast as Sammy Fong, a wisecracking, Chinese-American nightclub owner. Sammy had some wonderful songs, as did my leading lady, a delicious blond dancer, Sherry Kaye. I traveled the four-hour, round-trip daily out to Bellport, then back to Palisades Park in time for our live show at 6:00pm. Our Saturday night show was televised an hour later, to capture the nighttime dazzle and brilliant lights of the park. Saturday proved a dilemma. The Bellport curtain went-up promptly at 8:30; Irving Rosenthal to the rescue! As I signed-off at 7:30, I would dash to Irving's waiting limousine and with a Cliffside Park police escort, would motor down to the Hudson River, where a waiting seaplane would fly me up the coast of Long Island and deposit me at the harbor at Bellport. The trip took approximately 20-minutes, plenty of time to apply the necessary almond-shaped Oriental eyes. The gang at the theatre had arranged a welcoming party – the cast, crew and half the citizens of Bellport with a band, placards and balloons, greeted my splashdown at Bellport Harbor. I now know how Lindbergh must have felt arriving in Paris back in 1927. Martha Scott Phipps wrote in the Gateway guest book: "I grew up in Bellport. I remember the time Clay Cole arrived down at the bay. My best friend Gail and I ran down there and even managed to snag his autograph. Those were big doings for little Bellport!"

I must admit I worked very hard on the songs and dances, wanting to make an impact and to impress Joyce Selznick. She had originally hired me for my box office value, not knowing that I had theatre experience, music and dance training. She was overjoyed to find that I could actually sing, dance and perform comedy. She became my biggest booster. One of the joys of the summer was working with Sherry Kaye, another in a long line of blonde dancers I admired. One performance was particularly rewarding (and hysterical); Sherry lost her voice and I performed all her songs, including "I Enjoy Being A Girl." I belted the song, Sherry mouthed the words and the audience loved it!

For four uneventful Saturday nights, I chartered the same seaplane to Bellport, on time and without a hitch. It just so happened on the fifth Saturday, I was booked for another all-star stage show at The Long Island Arena in Commack, so, I decided once again to charter the seaplane, and made arrangements for a limousine to meet me at a designated harbor, then drive me to the arena. As I signed-off, I raced over to Irving's waiting car, the chauffer roared off to the river, and a seaplane was waiting in the water. It was not the exact same plane, but I recognized the pilot, my good-buddy from previous weekends. I removed my tuxedo jacket, settled into my seat, and prepared for our take-off across the water. As we were making our way south around the battery and east along the Long Island coastline, the pilot turned and asked if I noticed we were in a new craft. I had. Had I read the news? He handed me a copy of the *Daily News* with a horrific story: A sea-plane, attempting to ascend from the water, clipped the cabin of a private yacht, decapitating the captain and killing several members of his family. It was my Bellport plane.

My new plane was descending into new waters, our first-ever attempt to land in the harbor near Commack. As we circled, I could see my limousine parked, the livery driver waiting near the beach, next to an elegant-looking restaurant with windows overlooking the scene. My pilot discovered that the water was much to shallow for us to navigate close to the beach, we would have to wade to shore; he devised a plan. Picture this if you will from the point-of-view of the astonished diners in the restaurant, who were watching this scene unfold in front of their eyes: The pilot stepped into the waist-deep water, and I mounted his shoulders, full piggyback, in my tuxedo, clutching my attaché case. He then carried me 100-feet to shore, handed me over to my chauffer, who relieved me of my briefcase and escorted me across the sand to the limousine. This was unbelievable; all those people in the restaurant. How they must have hated me.

"Who the hell *is* this rich son-of-a-bitch?"

I just had to laugh at the absurdity.

"This guy is so rich he doesn't even have to walk."

9) Twist – 1961

"Let's Twist Again, (Like We Did Last Summer)"

It began as a lark. Late-night slumming on Manhattan's Westside brought "Cholly Knickerbocker" and a gay party of socialites to the Peppermint Lounge, a seedy sailor's bar over on West 45th Street, launching one of the most infamous discoveries in pop culture history.

Manhattan's Café Society claimed never to venture west, except to go to Europe, meaning the luxury ocean liners that once embarked from the Hudson River piers. Wealthy, emaciated tone-deaf matrons might cross-town to hear the fat lady sing at the Met, but quickly retreated back to the safety zones of Fifth or Park Avenue, Sutton or Beekman Place. But when "Cholly Knickerbocker" crossed the line and ventured west, the wagons circled; "Cholly's" indiscretions must not only be overlooked, but noted."

"Cholly's" social status was enhanced by his brother, the fashion designer Oleg Cassini, a favorite of First Lady Jackie Kennedy. The Cassini brothers were the two hot tickets in the Sixties society sweepstakes. Igor Cassini had embraced "café society" as subject matter for his daily column in the *New York Journal-American,* using the non de plume "Cholly Knickerbocker" (although the column was later ghostwritten by a little-known Texan named Liz Smith.)

In the dog days of summer 1961, Sh-Boomers were entering their second year of twisting, but to "Cholly" and his Knickerbockers, this was a jaw-dropping experience, as if they had fallen into Dante's hellhole and uncovered a strange new perverted world of whirling dervishes. They were witnessing a collection of hipsters, whores, drag queens, merchant marines, bus boys and bus drivers, shop girls and strippers gyrating on a postage stamp-sized dance floor. The soaking-wet, dog-tired dancers were recharged by cold blasts from massive air vents above the dance floor, forcing the bands to pump up the volume to compete with the roaring coolers. Judged against the steamy-hot sidewalks of Times Square, this was definitely the cool place to be. "Cholly" thought so, as well. "Cholly's" full-column report in the *Journal-American*, extolling the sinful virtues of this new dance ritual at The Peppermint Lounge, ignited a fireball. Flashbulbs began popping. A crush of cars appeared on 45th Street. It was impossible to left-turn from Times Square onto the block. Cadillac's, Rolls-Royces and motorcycles parked bumper to bumper, chrome to chrome, two, three-deep. Long lines formed, snaking up and around the block, VIPs gathered, begging, proclaiming influence, $20 bills jumped from mitt to mitt. Six NYPD patrol cars were on duty, keeping order; fire marshals were permanently assigned. One former cop told me: "Me and my partner were just rookies then, and we were good for a grand a week." The doofy doorman, Pinkus, dressed in an oversized military-style topcoat with "Doorman" etched on his cap, earned a small mint pocketing "sweeteners." Ethel Merman, Tennessee Williams, even Chubby Checker were given the "Pinkus pink-slip" and turned away at the door; Pinkus didn't recognize them. Marilyn Monroe, Greta Garbo, Judy Garland were among the fortunate who passed the Pinkus test and were admitted. A select few knew the secret: "The Pep" was on the street level of a hotel (By another twist of fate) called The Knickerbocker and a lobby doorway lead directly into the club's showroom. I would just glide up to the secret door and be ushered to one of the tiny tables ringing the dance floor. The management at The Peppermint Lounge usually assigned a bouncer to watch over my table, to keep autograph seekers at bay. One night, a new fellow, an amateur boxer I was told, was assigned to watch over me. Totally committed, he followed me to the Men's Room, and, confronted by a long line in front of the one and only urinal, he simply took me by the elbow and marched me to the front of the line. Naturally, I couldn't pee, but neither could any of the other gents, who were totally pissed-off at my arrogance. These things really happen, but no one believes it. I never like to sit in a public Men's Room, but on one occasion at The Wagon Wheel, sitting, a fan passed paper and pen under the door pleading for an autograph. What could I say? I wasn't going anywhere.

The Peppermint Lounge was limited to 200 patrons, but that capacity was reached at the bar alone to the frustration of fire marshals. The bar was long, maybe 50-feet, packed four-deep, leading straight back into the small L-shaped show-room, with an elevated stage and dance floor with VIP tables. The small stage was the arena for two continuous live bands; the most energy-fueled was Joey Dee & The Starlighters with a visually-exciting, choreographed show, so explosive that the diminutive, five-foot-four Joey Dee was literally propelled into the low-hanging ceiling. Waitresses in angora sweaters and pedal pushers, balancing trays of drinks over their heads, would leap upon the wrought iron railings and wobble like trembling high-wire artists. Men in white tie and tails danced side-by-side with duck-tailed hotrod boys; women dripping in diamonds danced bottom to bottom with girls dripping in sweat.

The Twist is a dance perfect for a person with no rhythm. If you could flail your arms and bend your knees you could twist. The secret of the twist is that you never have to move your feet. This was an advantage for twisters on a packed dance floor, twisting toe-to-toe, shoulder-to-shoulder; you simply stake your territory, plant your feet and twist. This was also just the thing for surfers, sun bunnies and beach bums, who could dance on sand, inspiring dozens of bikini beach party films. In spite of the simplicity of the dance, instruction manuals appeared by the truckload; Arthur Murray Dance Studios were offering twist classes and an LP with illustrated movements. Chubby had two simple tips: move your foot as if extinguishing a cigarette, and move your arms as if you had an imaginary bath towel, drying your butt.

My picture appeared dancing off the cover of *Twist* magazine, a special publication rushed to the newsstands, and Vicki Spencer and I were photographed in a six-page spread, demonstrating various twist moves; Dell produced a comic book illustrating a fictional Peppermint Lounge.

The Twist frenzy was far-greater than the Studio 54 disco phenomenon that swallowed up the city in the seventies; the Twist became a worldwide craze and the first international rock and roll dance. In Latin America, particularly in Mexico, the Twist was sparked by Bill Haley & His Comets recording of "Spanish Twist." The Mexicans even produced a quickie film, "To the Beat of the Twist," with Los Crazy Boys, preserving the same gritty cinematic style of a Sam Katzman Poverty Row exploitation film.

Everyone got in on the action. The once sedate citadels of Café Society were suddenly offering twist nights – The Stork Club, Billy Reed's Little Club, The Harwyn – only The El Morocco was a hold-out; banishing Janet Leigh caught twisting in her stocking feet. It was scandalous. The foremost society orchestras of Lester Lanin, Meyer Davis and Irving Fields all pressed twister albums. The Shirelles rush recorded "Mr. Twister;" the Marvelettes "Twistin' Postman;" Sam Cooke "Twistin' the Night Away;" and the Isley Brothers recorded their enduring "Twist and Shout," later covered by the Beatles. Late-night recording sessions were hastily arranged for Joey Dee and Chubby and their LPs flew off the shelves. Twist albums from Ray Charles, Dwayne Eddie, Bobby Darin, the Ventures, the Bill Black Combo and Bo Diddley appeared. Rod McKuen, later to become the poet laureate of the 1960s, surfaced on my show as "Mr. Oliver Twist." My television sponsor, Thom McAnn introduced new footwear, The Twister, and hired our dance champs Pat & Pete Salerno to twist with Chubby Checker in three television commercials. Pat & Pete became pros, with an AFTRA card, earning big bucks. *Life* magazine wired them with tiny lights for a stop-motion photo shoot, illustrating the movements of the twist.

Bob Hope, hosting a big-shot, black tie dinner at The Waldorf-Astoria, attended by Cardinal Spellman, General Douglas Mac Arthur and President Kennedy, joked, "I have never seen so many cop cars or celebrities outside. What is this, The Peppermint Lounge?" (President Kennedy actually made a reservation, a visit he reluctantly cancelled at the last minute.) Phil Silvers visited "The Pep" and immediately incorporated the twist into his Broadway comedy "Do Re Me." James Stewart took the dance to the silver screen, twisting with Maureen O'Hara in "Mr. Hobbs Takes a Vacation." Several television shows, from "The Flintstones," to "Leave It to Beaver" and the "Dick Van Dyke Show" all parodied the dance. Jack Paar ranted for a full six full minutes on the "Tonight" show about The Peppermint Lounge, coast-to-coast publicity that only added polish to the luster.

Naturally, whenever a cultural phenomenon occurs, out come the social anthropologists: "For me," said one leading expert on human behavior," it is a violent expression of today's youth in a world full of trouble."

"It seems people are twisting to dance themselves away from reality," claimed psychologist Dr. Albert Ellis, "but there is sex implied in it, No doubt about that."

Joey Dee & The Starlighters, (his frontline singer/dancers David Brigati and Larry Vernieri) were supported by one of the very first integrated backline bands, at one point featuring Jimi Hendrix on bass and Joe Pesci on guitar. David's brother, Eddie Brigati came aboard, as well as Felix Cavaliere and Gene Cornish, who would later regroup with drummer Dino Danelli to form the Young Rascals. Joey Dee had a string of hits for Roulette records ("Peppermint Twist"), starred in a two films for Paramount pictures and was earning top dollar. His "Peppermint Twist" was No. 1on the charts for three weeks in January 1962. Joey bought himself a Cadillac and split for the greener pastures of private parties and big-ticket venues. Joey and the Starlighters had simply become too big to be contained in a lounge. The new show at "The Pep" included three dancing girls, with beehive hair, Cleopatra eyes and shimmy dresses, sisters Ronnie and Estelle Bennett and Cousin Nedra Tally, soon to become the Ronettes. As for the Cassini Brothers: five years later, Igor and Oleg would create the ultimate dance club, the exclusive, Le Club, Manhattan's first discotheque.

The New York World-Telegram and the Sun assigned staff writer Ed Wallace to set the record straight in a multi-part series on The Twist. In Part 1, in the October 24, 1961 edition, he wrote:

"The current Twist began on a sweltering afternoon in July, 1960 at Palisades Amusement Park when a chubby young man in a checkered jacket sang and twisted on a teenage television show presided over by a handsome young man named Clay Cole. Then, as now, this is a rock and roll program on Channel 13 which plays discs for dancing and the guest performers stand in a spotlight and move their lips when their recordings are played. "Chubby Checker, the artist of this fateful afternoon, only approximated his lip movement, but his twisting was real and this was the first time the Twist was seen on television. It was not until Mr. Checker's definitive performance on Clay Cole's show that the Twist took a turn for the better."

In early November 1961, as I paused for a commercial break on the Saturday night Clay Cole Show, my stage manager rushed up to me with an urgent message from the control room: "call your agent immediately after the show." I found Roz Ross at home Saturday night and she simply said: "Are you sitting down? You are going to Hollywood to make a movie at Columbia Pictures." When the room stopped spinning, I pieced together the details. Producer Sam Katzman was in town to sign-up talent for "Twist Around the Clock" and had stumbled upon my show on the television set in his suite at The Sherry-Netherlands. He dialed Columbia's New York casting agent, Joyce Selznick, who phoned Roz Ross at home. A deal was struck over the phone while I was on the air. I was to fly to Hollywood on Thanksgiving week for two weeks of filming at Columbia Pictures studios.

Chubby Checker, the king of the twist, was on Roz Ross' GAC talent roster, as was Dion and Vicki Spencer (the sixteen-year-old singer, daughter of Lou Spencer) and the Marcels ("Blue Moon") who recorded for Columbia Pictures' record division Colpix, also came aboard. With channel 13's blessing, I was off to Hollywood.

Lou Spencer greeted me at the gate at Idlewild Airport, handing over his blossoming, beautiful daughter Vicki to me for safekeeping. There was no screenplay, the script was still being written, so we were told to bring a complete wardrobe. Jerry Brandt arranged a trade deal with a Brooklyn buddy who owned a Kings Highway men's store. I made a Saturday afternoon appearance in the showroom in exchange for a complete new wardrobe. Since Jerry and I were pretty much the same size in those days, Jerry took his 10% in "anything black." I packed eight suitcases – tennis shorts, parkas, my Perry Como cardigans, my lacey Lew Magram shirts, my King's Highway loot, and all my dinner jackets – just in case. Upon arriving in Los Angeles, while searching for our studio car, my entire wardrobe baggage disappeared from the curbside. Welcome to Hollywood!

Columbia put me up in a suite at The Hollywood-Roosevelt, across the street from Grauman's Chinese Theatre's famous footprint courtyard on Hollywood Boulevard. Bright and early, over at "Gower Gulch," was my first-time meeting with Sam Katzman, director Oscar Rudolph and music director Fred Karger. Sam had a script, and some good news. My luggage had been swept up by an airport bus driver and was placed in error on his bus, soon to be delivered to the Roosevelt. As relieved as I was, my interest was seeing a script, not my wardrobe. I was playing a singing bandleader named Clay Cole who invents a new dance, the twist. Bummer. The true story would have made a much more interesting picture with Chubby as the central character. My only bit of acting advice came from Sam Katzman, himself, leading me by the arm, out the door, whispering, "stuff a sock in your drawers; the girls will love it!" That was *it*?

The first day of filming, the studio car dropped me promptly at 5:30am at the Gower Street entrance for my appointment at the studio barbershop and make-up room. I found a trailer with my name on the door; my wardrobe cleaned, pressed and hanging neatly inside. I learned that studio fairies descend on the trailers each night to steam and press my entire wardrobe. What luxury. I was shocked to walk onto the set and see so many uniformed doctors and nurses in attendance; this must be very dangerous duty. As it turns out, this was the cast of "The Interns" filming in the studio next door – Cliff Robertson, Stephanie Powers, Nick Adams, James Mac Arthur and New Yorkers Kaye Stevens and Mickey Callan (from the Broadway cast of "West Side Story."

I was now in the hands of Fred Karger, the music director, who was in need of more twist tune for the dance sequences. We huddled in the Columbia Café, the studio coffee shop, and set down a half-dozen soundtrack tunes. With Fred conducting, I recorded the soundtrack songs at the Todd-AO studios with a roomful of L.A.'s most prominent jazzmen, names I had scrutinized over and over from liner notes on my LP's. Fred Karger and I hit it off instantly; he was fastidiously groomed, the son of a prominent, old-money Pasadena family, well-known in Los Angeles social circles as party pianist and orchestra leader. I learned much later, in reading the many Marilyn Monroe biographies that Fred was her singing coach and she fell madly in love with him, and yearned to marry him. His old-money Pasadena family would not hear of it.

Fred was now married and since it was Thanksgiving weekend and I was alone in Hollywood, he invited me to dinner with his wife Jane. I had no idea that Jane was a superstar silver screen legend. But, when Fred and I entered Chason's Restaurant, perched cross-legged on a barstool waiting our arrival was Jane Wyman! Academy-award-winner Jane Wyman! The former Mrs. Ronald Regan, Jane Wyman! The magnificent obsession – Jane Wyman! Imagine! Pepe the bartender stirred-up a round of perfectly dry martinis, and we settled into a plush, red leather booth in the small wood-paneled dining room. Jane Wyman was a blast, as unpretentious as Chason's itself and as warm as a bowl of their famous chili. This was going to be fun. Word soon spread around the room that a twister was in the house. Barbara Stanwyck, tugging at my lapels, implored me to tell her about the Peppermint Lounge. Here's Barbara Stanwyck toying with me in her familiar no-nonsense mode. "Details," she insisted, "I want details!" Jack Benny, Jack Lemmon, wife Felicia Farr and film-director Richard Quine gathered closer, enthralled, waiting for me to spill the beans. I was the center of attention; they all wanted bulletins from the frontlines, first person war stories about that sleazy little bar on 45th Street, now the most famous nightclub in the world. Maude and Dave Chason invited us into their backroom office for a cozy nightcap, where Jane made me an offer. In two weeks she was hosting a charity event to be held in the grand International Ballroom of the Beverly Hilton Hotel. Fred was in charge of the music and therefore, Jane needed an escort. Would I be her date for the event? Can you believe this, a date with Jane Wyman?

Jane and Freddy took me to the Beverly Hills Friars Club for a special performance by Billy Daniels, and to the Slate Brothers nightclub over on La Cienega to see Don Rickles, who, mistaking me for George Hamilton, abused Jane unmercifully. I once told George Hamilton that many people tell me I look just like him. "That's funny," George shot back, "people tell me I look just like Clay Cole."

We had a company of about 40 young professional dancers working in the film; among them was Elaine Joyce, another of my blond-dancer fantasy ladies. Elaine had it all, beauty, wit, a perfect dancer's body, with great long legs, and she accepted my invitation for dinner; we became bosom-buddies. Elaine and I hosted a cocktail party in my suite, and invited the chorus kids from the film and some of my west coast buddies, including Jan & Dean. We twisted at The Whiskey a Go Go and cha cha cha'd at The Coconut Grove. Elaine was not yet a star, just a kid in the chorus, but oh, what was ahead for her. Later in life she starred on Broadway in "Sugar," the musical version of "Some Like It Hot," playing the Marilyn Monroe role. Following the early death of Elaine's husband, the MGM dance star Bobby Van, Elaine was wooed by the reclusive, 80-year-old author J.D. Salinger ("Catcher in the Rye"), who sent her mash notes after seeing her on the 80's sitcom, "Mr. Merlin." Elaine eventually married playwright Neil Simon, then 72-year-old.

On the evening of my date with Jane Wyman, I rushed to my dressing room trailer to change into my tuxedo and meet Jane at The Beverly Hilton. The cocktail hour was like an Oscar Party – the giant screen star Marlon Brando appeared slightly less than three feet tall, Esther Williams appeared to be three feet around, and Jack Lemmon was three sheets to the wind.

Fred had devised a plan for me to appear in the show as a surprise guest, singing "Twist Around the Clock" with the Freddy Martin Orchestra and twenty studio dancers. The evening's entertainment included singing stars Jaye P. Morgan and husband and wife Dick Haymes and Fran Jeffries; I was to close the show. It was a disaster; a cold-sweat nightmare. Freddy Martin's dance band played my arrangement in a listless drone, reminiscent of a New Orleans' jazzman's funeral

"Mister Martin! Ix-nay on the dirge … I'm dying out here!"

I was struggling to kick the band into high gear, wishing to snap a popper under Freddy Martin's high-and-mighty nose. Martin wanted to distance himself from this trendy twist crap and surrendered, disappearing into the wings. Fred Karger leaped onto the bandstand to conduct, to accelerate the tempo and accentuate the beat. The musicians responded, the dancing couples exploded down the aisles and Jane bounded up on stage to rescue me. Twisting together, she and I finally got everyone up and twisting on the dance floor. The audience responded as if the whole effort was a planned gag; and rewarded me with approval. I returned to Table No. 1 still shaking from the whole ordeal, and Jane, trying to calm me, asked me to join her in a dance. I immediately turned her down and then I suddenly flashed, "Are you crazy! You just turned down a dance with Jane Wyman." Yes I said, and with arms enfolding the legendary star, we swayed to the romantic, danceable music of Freddy Martin.

No commanding occurrence is greater than to be in Hollywood actually making a film; your stature and desirability is enhanced immeasurably if you are working. Columbia urged me to remain in Hollywood to be available for film and television opportunities, but I had a contract with Channel 13 to fulfill and I was loyal to my benevolent bosses back in NYC.

"Twist Around the Clock" opened in New York in January 1962, just six weeks after completing filming. *The New York Times* review was happily upbeat: "The picture is painless and surprisingly perky…mass demonstrations of the twist are lively, buoyant and limber…the whole thing has a crisp air about it…a casual taste-ful little movie. Dorothy Kilgallen reported in her *Journal-American* column that "Twist Around The Clock" had earned a staggering $10-million domestically." The picture cost a half-million to make and a half-million to promote, an enormous box-office hit. I have no idea what the picture grossed in South America or Europe, but it was financial bonanza for Producer Sam Katzman.

Two other twist exploitation films were released about the same time, Joey Dee & the Starlighters in Paramount's "Hey, Let's Twist," with Teddy Randazzo, JoAnne Campbell, Joe Pesci (his first film), and Hope Hampton wearing a half-million dollars of chinchilla and diamonds – chump-change to the screwball socialite. The other film was "The Continental Twist," featuring Louis Prima with Sam Butera & the Witnesses, and the busty British starlet June Wilkinson, a feeble attempt to prop up Prima's twist LP, "Doin' The Twist with Louis Prima."

I recorded a single of "Twist Around the Clock" (backed by the Capris) and I was bowled over by an invitation to perform the song on "Bob Clayton's Boston Ballroom," telecast on WHDH. I was greeted by an uproar of approval from his studio audience, and was flabbergasted when Clayton announced that my song was No. 1 in Boston. (Personal note to that Internet blogger who wrote: "Whoever told Clay Cole he could sing?" My answer is, "the good people of Boston.")

I was invited to talk about my Hollywood adventure at a press luncheon at The Tavern on the Green restaurant in Central Park, arranged by Columbia's affable promotion veepee Charlie Powell. Columbia Pictures was not finished with me yet. Charlie conveyed an offer from Abe Schneider, the headman of the studio in New York. Abe would like me to appear at Columbia's annual staff Christmas party in their elegant 711 Fifth Avenue headquarters and in addition, make a theatre tour to promote the film. He offered me $8,000 for the tour, plus the $4,000 for my participation in the picture. Definitely. Count me in.

Abe Schneider, President of Columbia-Screen Gems waltzed me around the holiday party with his arm around my shoulder, embracing me like a proud father. His own son, Bert Schneider would later run Colpix Records, co-creating NBC's "The Monkees," abetted by Colpix record hits, and briefly out-selling even the Beatles.

"Twist Around The Clock," in a second go-round was to appear on a dou-ble bill with a new Columbia feature, "The Three Stooges Meet Hercules" on the RKO-Theatre circuit. Moe Howard, Larry Fine and Joe DeRita as "Curly Joe" and I climbed aboard our tour bus, on a three day, thirty theatre whirlwind personal appearance tour around the five boroughs of Manhattan. To enhance the Stooges shtick, an eight-foot giant in a loin cloth was hired as their on-stage Hercules. It was strange cargo. I imagined this was going to be a barrel of laughs. Zero. Off-stage, the three Stooges hardly spoke to one another, let alone make with the gags. They sat on the bus in separate seats, stoic, alone in their thoughts. There is a long tradition of show-biz teams just shutting down, turning off.

Sam & Dave were famous for having a tumultuous partnership during their 21 years together. According to Sam Moore, they did not speak to each other offstage for almost 13 years. When the Everly Brothers split in 1973, Don and Phil would not speak to each other for the next ten years, getting together only once in 1975 for their father's funeral. In the 90s, I witnessed Hall & Oates arrive in separate charter jets, drive away in twin limousines, sleep in far-distant wings of their hotel, and then appear on stage as cozy as Donny & Marie. Off stage, their rivalry was terse as Tom & Jerry; they never spoke. Perhaps, like Martin & Lewis, or Rowan & Martin, they had nothing left to say.

10) Apollo

*"If you miss the 'A' Train, you'll find
you missed the quickest way to Harlem"*

– Billy Strayhorn / Duke Ellington

Times Square: "what a dump!" Our studios were at the corner of 42nd Street and Broadway, "the crossroads of the world." It is said, if you stand on the corner long enough, you will eventually meet up with someone you know. This may be true if you happen to know hustlers, grifters, street-corner preachers, con-men or bag ladies wheeling life's garbage in baby carriages. Cranky old Jewish cabbies – night-shift hackies with their off-duty flags up – litter the all-night cafeteria, sharing a single tea bag. Seated at a safe distance, sipping coffee from lipstick-stained mugs are the aging ladies of the follies, rouged, powdered and long-forgotten Florodora girls exhaling exhausted sighs. This was the extent of *live* entertainment along "Forty-Duce" in the early 60s, with the exception of a cellar flea-circus and freak-show, grandiosely named Hubert's Museum.

The crumbling show palaces along "Forty-Deuce" had been converted into all-night movie houses, where homeless drifters could seek shelter, watch a double feature and get a good nights sleep for a dollar. In the stillness of The Victoria Theatre, during a showing of "A Summer Place," an angry voice cried out from the balcony, "You're sorry? You piss on my shoe and you're sorry!"

The time had come for Channel 13 to move out of the gutters of these infamous crossroads and into the urban pastures of downtown Newark. Channel 13 had transformed the huge second floor ballroom of New Jersey's Mosque Theatre into a television studio, the new home for the Saturday night Clay Cole Show. Downstairs was the grand concert hall, where Raysa and I once sat mesmerized by Johnny Mathis, and where I shared the stage with the magnanimous Bobby Darin.

Ted Cott and the Channel 13 program staff had all new plans for me for the new season, the fall of 1960. I was about to be on-the-air *live*, with three different programs, seven days a week. M-F they created a half-hour, after-school game show, "Teen Quiz," a Sunday afternoon amateur hour "Talent Teens" and my Saturday night musical-variety hour "The Clay Cole Show." Seven days a week, I journeyed over to Pennsylvania Station to catch the first train westbound, first stop Newark.

"Teen Quiz" required our home viewers to send us their phone number on a post card that I could pluck from a huge drum, then telephone to play rock 'n' roll trivia A sudden abundance of cards arrived from our home viewers seeking the prize pink Zenith clock radios, powder-blue portable stereos whose speakers swung out on hinges, bowling balls, super-warm fuzzies, or beauty product kits; it was pretty-much a freewheeling show.

I once called the local coffee shop and ordered an elaborate take-out to be delivered to our second-floor studios. Hector, our befuddled delivery boy arrived in his white paper hat and, thinking he was interrupting an informal rehearsal, tried to sort out the delivery ("who gets the tuna melt with fries?") on *live* television. Hector's honest, innocent appearance was sidesplitting; I rewarded him with a $20 tip.

"Talent Teens" was *live* every Sunday afternoon at 4:00, a nickel-and-dime version of "American Idol." (There is nothing new under the sun; it's all in the packaging.) Teenage amateurs performed and our three-member panel would rate their presentation. Our celebrity panel included the comic Buddy Hackett, (no Simon Cowell; Buddy gushed over each trembling teen.) and former model and charm school coach Candy Jones. Hackett would stroll-in straight from the golf course, still wearing his plus-fours, while Miss Jones would dress couture-style, as if on "What's My Line." Candy married Long John Nebel and became co-host of his popular all-night WMCA radio talk show, focusing on the paranormal, UFOs, and conspiracy theories. Candy added to the bizarre agenda by claiming to be the victim of a secret mind control program. *You get the picture?* Our "distinguished panel" would also pass-along show-biz advice to our teenage tap teams, buglers, ventriloquists, tone-deaf a cappella boys in matching sweaters and girl singers pushing puberty, singing the blues. No accordion players!

It was during this period, Raysa and I drove a daily round trip between Newark and the Catskill Mountains, for three mid-week appearances in the cavernous lounge of the Concord Hotel with Dion, Linda Scott ("I Told Every Little Star") and a band, the first rock 'n' roll show to ever play "the mountains." This engagement must have been especially poignant for Dion, arriving as a star at the very place his father and uncle had toiled for so many years with an unappreciated comedy-puppet act. The "Jewish Alps" provided a captive audience, one growing tired of Myron Cohen and the Barry Sisters. The Concord audience could not have been more receptive; families with young children for the early show and singles and adult couples for the late-late show. The Catskills took a giant leap, from "Marjorie Morningstar" to "Dirty Dancing" in four short days. Our success did not escape the attention of GAC President Buddy Howe, whose own wife, Jean Carroll was a comedy favorite on the Borscht Belt, nor Phil Greenwald, the popular talent booker for The Concord, who helped spread the word. Soon promoters from all over the country were now turning to Roz Ross for the fresh blood and new faces needed to invigorate their theatres and nightclubs.

My appearance at The Concord Hotel almost landed me on Broadway, a move that would have certainly changed the course of my career from the 'pied piper of rock 'n' roll to my lifelong fantasy as musical-comedy song and dance man. Charles Strouse, the composer of "Bye, Bye Birdie," still a huge hit on Broadway, was in the audience and came backstage with a backhanded compliment, "I didn't know you could carry a tune." Dick Van Dyke was about to leave 'Birdie' after a long run and Strouse invited me to audition for director Gower Champion.

The "Birdie" joke at the time involved Christine Jorgensen, the American sailor who returned from Denmark as a woman, the first infamous transsexual: The Christine Jorgensen Story became "Bye Bye Birdie." The Jorgensen joke took on a whole new life, when in 1964, Buddy Hackett starred on Broadway in the show, "I Had a Ball."

My audition for "Bye, Bye Birdie" went well, me belting out "Singing in the Rain," – just as Colin Romoff had relentlessly pounded out of me – but the role eventually went to NBC's "Match Game" host, Gene Rayburn.

The Saturday night Clay Cole Show was my first meeting with my boyhood hero, Jerry Lewis, who later became somewhat of a mentor to me. "If you want to impress an audience, continue to wear a tuxedo on your Saturday show," Jerry advised me. "It not only makes *you* feel important, it makes the audience feel they are about to see something important." I lived in a tuxedo for the next decade. I was also impressed by Jerry's attention to detail. He possessed the first of those miniature cameras and tape recorders, taking photos, and audio taping the proceedings, making notes of everyone's duties. All this, he said, would go into his personal archives, an accurate history of events.

Karen Kupcinet (daughter of Irv, the celebrated Chicago columnist) arrived with a new singing star, a natty-haired young red-head with dirty fingernails and badly soiled clothing. Between her fingers, she held an RCA recording, with Ann-Margret on the label. You could have fooled me. Who would have thought that within a few years, Ann-Margret would emerge in Hollywood, co-starring with Bobby Rydell in "Bye Bye Birdie," Elvis Presley in "Viva, Las Vegas," and on the cover of *Life* magazine as "America's superstar sex-goddess?"

My fantasy sex goddess was still Annette, another bouncy, first-name beauty. She appeared with us on Saturday night introducing "Pineapple Princess" and I invited her out to dinner with the Forum of the Twelve Caesars in mind. She accepted, but her mother had other ideas; it was dinner for three in their hotel dining room.

Epic Records had found a new singing star and his first-ever television appearance was to be the "Clay Cole Show." Full-page teaser ads appeared in *Billboard* and all the trade magazines for a full month, with Tony Orlando shown only in silhouette. I of course, joined the hype, announcing three-more weeks, two-more weeks, until finally the night of the show. Tony was going to introduce his first recording "Halfway to Paradise" on our show, and to build the suspense, we held him to the very last guest on the show. As it happened, in our control room, two technical misfires sabotaged his appearance; the audio engineer mistakenly cued-up the B-Side of Tony's record and the assistant director miss-timed the show. So, when Tony stepped out on stage, the wrong song was played and the closing credits began rolling over Tony's bewildered close-up. Quick fade to black, and that was Tony Orlando's ten-second introduction to the world.

Only a mafia don could have executed a more perfect hit. Tony took it much better than me; I was embarrassed, then angry, and finally went ballistic. I felt badly for Tony's large family sitting at home awaiting his television debut, and for the Epic Record brass that were assembled backstage. Naturally, Tony returned the next week, the first guest on the show – I was taking no chances. Tony appeared dozens of times, and we became lifelong friends, one of a handful of stars blessed with a good heart and a pure soul. Tony has championed many charitable causes, and has touched many people personally over the years. Not to mention, he blessed us with "Tie a Yellow Ribbon 'Round the Old Oak Tree," practically our second national anthem, which conveyed hope and strength to so many for so many years.

And, I might add – with the exception of Miss Phyllis George – nobody works a room better than Tony Orlando.

Dr. Pepper, that cherry-flavored soda pop, had been the drink of choice of Texas cheerleaders, Georgia peaches, demolition derby drivers, rodeo bull-riders, tar heels and rednecks, but had somehow escaped the attention of East Coast Sh-Boomers. The folks at Dr. Pepper decided to launch their product in New York with the "Clay Cole Show" as its advertising vehicle. A large shiny Dr. Pepper machine was installed in our studios, so as a promotional gimmick, I would reach into my pocket and furnish a dime to our biggest guest star, say Johnny Tillotson, who would walk over to the dispenser, deposit the dime, retrieve the bottle, pop it open, taste a slug and smile pleasantly for the cameras. Then came the Saturday night when it was Dion's turn. After his performance and a brief interview, I gave Dion the dime, and he walked to the dispenser, pressed the button and – nothing. The Dr. Pepper bottle did not drop. Dion, a no-nonsense, street-wise guy from the Bronx, looked left, right, as if to see if anyone was looking, then kicked the machine. Nothing. He then banged the machine with his hand. Nothing. He punched. Nothing. He pounded. Nothing. The studio audience was in fits of hysteria, and the laughs were just beginning to grow. Finally, he grabbed the machine with both hands, as if to pick it up in the air, and started shaking the machine. Nothing. Next, he just beat the shit out of the stubborn dispenser and wham-o! – a Dr. Pepper dropped. As cool as an ice cube, Dion opened the bottle, took a sip, and to thunderous applause from the studio audience and our stagehands, smiled contentedly for the camera. It was his water-cooler moment; not since Betty Furness failed to open her Westinghouse fridge has TV seen a finer, funnier spontaneous moment. Ah, *live* television.

Taking full advantage of my new celebrity, Raysa and I became regulars at the Saturday midnight show at The Apollo, always the hippest show of the week. Our favorites were the Coasters with their hilarious "story songs," choreographed into mini-skits. For one moment in time, no one could come close to the Coasters for sheer lunacy with "Charley Brown," "Along Came Jones," "Searchin'," and "Little Egypt." A close second was a five-man group out of L.A. called the Vibrations, a funny, rough and tumble dancing act. ("Stranded In the Jungle," "The Watusi" and "Peanut Butter") We saw comedy legends like "Pigmeat" Markham ("Heah come de Judge"), and that toothless flirt, "Moms" Mabley, in her sack dress and bedroom slippers. The Apollo audience was an awesome sight to behold, thrusting themselves forward in their seats in a literal wave of laughter.

The Apollo was the crown jewel of Harlem, standing proudly on 125th Street alongside Frank's Restaurant, where you could spot the power lunch regulars, Adam

Clayton Powell, Percy Sutton, and Ralph Bunch served by white waiters, and next door The Baby Grand club, where Nipsey Russell, Red Foxx and Dinah Washington entertained. The Hotel Theresa was on the corner, the home away from home for touring performers, and later the Cuban compound of Fidel Castro when the dictator visited New York City in 1960.

The Apollo was operated by Frank Shiffman, admired for his high-standards and willingness to dole-out cash advances. As The Palace Theatre on Broadway was to white vaudevillians, The Apollo represented the summit to generations of black entertainers, the last stop on the "Chitlin' Circuit," that included The Regal in Chicago, The Howard in D.C. and The Royal in Baltimore. Frank's son, Bobby Shiffman was pretty much in charge of the talent bookings and production, and he offered us an open invitation. Raysa and I would sweep-in 'round midnight, greeted by Slide, the front door-manager, and ushered to a side box, palming neatly folded $20 bills along the way, to witness the most rousing show in town.

Since 1953, when Sonny Til & the Orioles ("Crying in the Chapel") became Apollo favorites, rock 'n' roll shows were added to the Apollo menu, wedged between full-week gospel jubilees, jazz jams, blues shows and the semi-annual appearance of The Jewel Box Revue, a popular female impersonator extravaganza. The Orioles are generally acknowledged as R&B's first highly-influential vocal group who established the basic pattern for the doo wop sound. Unlike the Mills Brothers or the Ink Spots, the five Baltimore natives (named after Maryland's state bird, the oriole), sang pure vocals without orchestration, accompanied only by the solo guitar of Tommy Gaither. The Orioles also initiated the bird-group trend (The Cardinals, Crows, Flamingos, Larks, Penguins, Ravens, Robins, Wrens, etc.).

My friend Dante Drowty (Dante & the Evergreens) phoned me up one afternoon, imploring me to meet him at The Apollo to see "a mind-blowing new act." I raced up to 125th Street for a matinee performance of "Soul Brother Number One," James Brown & the Famous Flames. The skinny little screamer, once the opening act for Little Willie John was soon to become the legendary "hardest working man in show business." Brown had his shtick down, baby, his swiveling feet, deep-knee drops, and that one-legged shimmy. Brown performed an extended encore of "Please, Please, Please," falling exhausted to his knees, the Flames would drape him in a cape, only to see him rebound for one more chorus. As unique as Brown was, I loved watching his band "The J. B.'s," a rag-tag gathering of street musicians, without uniforms or music stands, dancing the mashed-potatoes with swaying saxes, twirling trumpets, and strutting guitars. Sam & Dave, Otis Reading, Wilson Pickett and Ray Charles were among the artists swept on stage by their dancing orchestras – the Memphis Horns, the Packers, Booker T and the MG's, and the Mar-Keys with Steve Cropper – a glorious, funky, down-and-dirty sight to behold.

When I first saw the raw Ray Charles, still in his "What'd I Say" (1959) period, with his fleshy, wailing Raeletts, he carried with him one of those soulful, funky dancing bands. A year later, after his classy "Georgia On My Mind" (1960) raced to No. 1 on the charts, I returned to The Apollo to see a slick, newly defined "The Genius of Ray Charles," with a new set of stylish Raeletts. His orchestra was now seated, in crisp, white dinner jackets, behind shiny-white music stands, emblazoned with the initials RC. Mr. Charles glided on stage, seated behind a white piano, propelled by a hydraulic device – so smooth, so refined, and so sorrowfully downtown.

Ray Charles had taken the middle road. James Brown became a disoriented fat cat, Sam & Dave split, and Otis Reading passed on, as did all those fabulous funky dancing bands. Years later, I saw a puffy James Brown, now "The Godfather of Soul" in concert, bursting out of a too-tight, spangled jumpsuit, swilling in sweat, apparently so stoned he performed "This Is A Man's World" twice. Never mind, James Brown became a millionaire, several times over, thanks to financial maneuvering of his life-long agent Ben Bart, and later, son Jack Bart at Universal Attractions.

Other big Apollo headliners at the time were LaVern Baker, Jerry Butler, Clyde McPhatter, Brook Benton, Sam Cooke, Chuck Jackson, Etta James, the Miracles, all the early Motown stars and that macho heartbreaker, Jackie Wilson, who was earning as much as $25,000.for seven days of sold-out performances. I witnessed Nancy Wilson annihilate the Apollo audience singing Murray Grand's heartrending classic, "Guess Who I Saw Today; and "Maxine Brown accepting seven curtain calls after singing her hit "It's All In My Mind." "There was something about that Apollo stage that was magic," Maxine said. "I have never had the thrill of my life on anybody's stage as I have had at that Apollo Theatre."

Maxine was one of the many stars who experienced the largeness protection of the Schiffman family. Brown's one-time manager-husband Mal Williams found himself in financial entanglements with some unsavory characters. He owed them money, and they leaned on Maxine, pocketing her personal appearance fees to pay-off his debt. Each time she played a nightclub, they swooped down to take her money. Bobby Schiffman at The Apollo sympathized, issuing a fake contract with a low fee, allowing Maxine to walk away with her money, quietly paid under the table.

It struck me like a thunderbolt the day that Bobby Schiffman phoned, inviting me to appear at the Apollo, another dream come true. On October 6, 1960 I began a week-long ride, presenting a show headlining the incomparable Fats Domino & His Orchestra, on a bill featuring Tarheel Slim & Little Ann, comics Cornbread & Biscuit and Mickey & Sylvia ("Love Is Strange").

Mickey & Sylvia were strikingly attractive, Mickey in elegant dinner jackets and Sylvia in shimmering, clinging evening gowns, strapped into guitars, pacing the stage like jungle cats in a seduction ritual. Their guitar riffs and electronic rim-shots accentuated the lyrical teasing "Oh, Mickey? *Yes, Sylvia?*" Their "talking guitars" made love; the sexual tension was electric, one of the most sensual stage acts I have ever witnessed. Mickey was an in-demand session musicians at Atlantic Records, working with the Coasters, Ray Charles and Ruth Brown; Sylvia was his guitar pupil when they married. With "Love Is Strange," Mickey & Sylvia created a new dance based on a popular Latin rhythm, a modified cha-cha with a calypso beat. Sh-Boomers called it the chalypso, a beat further popularized by Paul Anka on his first hit "Diana." When Mickey "Guitar" Baker and Sylvia Vanderpool split in 1961, a superstar duo disintegrated. In 1961, Mickey relocated to Paris; Sylvia married Jim Robinson, recorded a sultry solo hit "Pillow Talk" (No. 3 in 1970), and then formed Sugar Hill Records, first of the hip-hop labels.

Fats Domino held court from his second floor star dressing room, greeting clusters of local friends arriving at the stage door with giant crocks of gumbo, jambalaya, and racks of syrupy ribs, shrimps, sweet icy cakes and fried chicken of every description, cooked in the style peculiar to all the regional enclaves of black America.

Fats was equally generous in return. If Fats took a'liking to you, he was known to present you with that diamond-horseshoe stickpin he always wore, a signature trademark, akin to his sparkling diamond pinky rings. Fats liked me, I knew. From his piano stool, he'd laugh uproariously over my finale dance, giving me a big, grinning high-five on my way into the wings. I was shocked and excited when, before our last show together, Fats sent his valet to my dressing room, summoning me to a one-on-one meeting. The star suite had two rooms, a front room to entertain guests, a private changing room in the rear and Fats was waiting for me in the front room. "Cleee," he said, (he always pronounced Clay as Cleee) "I want's to thank you…it's been a pleasure to work'n with you…and I have a little somethin' for yaw." Here it comes. That damned diamond horseshoe. I couldn't believe it. His valet appeared from behind the curtained back room with a beautifully gift-wrapped bottle of Scotch.

My week with Fats was the first of three week-long Apollo launches. I could hardly sleep on Thursday nights, anticipating the early-morning Friday rehearsals in the dank basement under the stage, with production director Honi Coles inventing some creative staging and Reuben Phillips and the Apollo Orchestra rehearsing all those wailing, soulful arrangements. Working the Apollo was the most thrilling experience I have ever had in my career, a theatre reeking with tradition, churning out a new production every week for decades. The echoes of Cab Calloway, Billie Holiday, the Mills Brothers, the Ink Spots, Sarah Vaughan, the Nicholas Brothers, Ella, King-Cole, the Count and the Duke rang out. Honi Coles himself had been an Apollo star, appearing in the 1934 opening with his partner, Cholly Atkins in top hat, white-tie and tails. Atkins & Coles were a dance duo whose soft-shoe routine "Taking a Chance on Love" defined "class act." Atkins & Coles each found a second, rewarding career late in life. Cholly Atkins was recruited by Berry Gordy to choreograph and stage his roster of Motown stars, the moves of the Temptations, the Four Tops, and the Supremes are all pure Cholly Atkins. When The Apollo shuttered, Honi Coles became a Broadway star, appearing in "Bubbling Brown Sugar," several shows with Gregory Hines and at age 72, winning Broadway's highest honor, a Tony for his performance in the 1983 Gershwin musical, "My One and Only," co-starring with Tommy Tune and Twiggy.

Aside from their famous Saturday night midnight shows, the Wednesday amateur nights were an Apollo tradition, a first step up the ladder for the triumphant winners. Wilson Pickett, Pearl Bailey, Leslie Uggams, Ruth Brown, and Jimmy Charles, a 16-year-old heartbreaker from Paterson, NJ, won the competition four consecutive weeks, and at seventeen, recorded "A Million to One." his million-seller. Dionne Warwick, herself a former amateur night winner, recalled, "The theatre was drafty and dusty, but there was no place like it."

When I returned to the theatre for my second appearance, I was awarded the second floor star dressing room, which I found had been tastefully redecorated, and the backstage area had been freshly painted, with plush carpet installed from the stage right up to the second floor. My feet never had to touch the floor. "For me?" I inquired. "No. Eartha Kitt was here last week." *Whoops.*

My second week had a gimmick, "Clay Cole's All-Girl-Revue," featuring the Bobbettes, the dazzling singing star Valerie Carr and three sizeable heavyweights Big Maybelle, Tiny Topsy, and Mama Lou Parks with her Parkettes, eight amazing, fresh-looking dancers, plus newcomers, Gladys Knight & the Pips. Honi Coles had devised an opening gag; as the curtains opened to reveal the on-stage orchestra, Reuben Phillips and each member of his band were wearing glamorous blond wigs – bouffant, beehive or pig-tail. The gag worked. The audience never took us seriously for one moment. Then the eight glittering Parkettes boogied on stage for a frenetic opening production number, "*and away we go!*"

Big Maybelle was a blues shouter, big in voice and stature, tall and wide, but presented the illusion of an elegant lady, always dressed in evening gowns with long opera gloves. Big Maybelle regularly hit me up for two-dollar loans, until stage-hand Bob Hall put me wise: she was buying junk, concealing years of track-marks under her trademark elbow-length gloves. I adored Big Maybelle. I never missed her set; weeping in the wings each time she sang her only sizeable hit, "Candy" (1956). Honi Coles staged an audience-pleasing finale, the skinny white boy being squashed into the folds of two big, black mamas. With the entire cast on stage dancing, Tiny Topsy would dance towards me from the left, Big Maybelle from the right, and envelop me into their voluptuous bosoms, as the curtains slammed shut. The audience went ballistic; with a wild roar of approval!

The young Gladys Knight and her Pips, brother "Bubba" and cousins William and Edward, huddled off-stage in the wings in a silent, pre-show prayer, then exploded onto the stage with their dizzying song-and-dance act, and performing their only hit "Every Beat of My Heart." Is there anything more exciting than seeing a shooting star? Oh, so much was ahead for them.

Years later, in 1999, I visited with Gladys and brother Bubba backstage at one of her solo concert, which reaches a fever pitch with her finale, "I Heard It through the Grapevine." The sold-out house was on its feet cheering, as Gladys retreated to her off-stage dressing room to change for her encores. Close friends and VIP fans (among them Buster Lewis and his entourage) were already descending on the backstage area. But, Gladys never returned to the stage. There was grumbling all around and her backstage well-wishers, when asked to leave, seemed to turn on her.

A teary-eyed Gladys was whisked away to her waiting limousine, and a hastily arranged flight back to her home in Las Vegas. Gladys had just been given the news that her 37-year-old son was dead. Jimmy Newman was found at his Las Vegas home, dead of natural causes. On-stage, the band was still playing, the crowd was still cheering. They wanted more! They wanted more! But, there would be no encore tonight.

I had proven my acceptance to Apollo audiences, so in June, 1961, I was now offered a guarantee plus percentage. Chubby Checker was the hottest black star in America at that time, but as yet, had not appeared at the Apollo, terrified to play to an audience well-known to be tough on unproven performers. I came up with a hook, a visual crutch that would take some of the pressure off Chubby. Aside from "The Twist," Chubby's hits were all dance ditties, "Pony Time," "The Hucklebuck," and "The Fly."

I would hire Mama Lou Parks to choreograph eight dancers – this time four girls, four boys – giving Chubby on-stage support. Chubby got excited, and agreed, signing a contract for $2,000 for the week. Now feeling confident, Chubby tried something daring, and pulled it off. One of the soft ballads he sang between dance productions was "Georgia on My Mind," a recent hit of the incomparable Ray Charles. Chubby was inviting comparison, but he sang it so sweetly and sincerely that the audience exploded with approval. Chubby was a hit.

There was another memorable moment in the show involving "Alley-Oop" as sung on stage by Dante & the Evergreens. Honi Coles had a leopard-skin caveman toga made for me, complete with a gigantic green club. My appearance at the side of the stage, in just shoes, knee-length stockings with garter belt, my leopard-skin and club was too outrageous. I developed a rhythmic knee twitch to match the beat, and gave the audience my best Jack Benny gaze. If necessary, I stepped down into the audience wielding my club and, as if on cue, scores of giggling girls would scurry up the aisles, away from this crazed 'ofay' caveman. There was none better than an Apollo audience.

The week produced a box office bonanza, netting me $6,000. With an advance of $2000, Honi Coles walked me over to Western Union to wire transfer the cash as a birthday present for brother Jim, who was about to set-off to Kent State University. I was told that at the receiving office, when the Western Union clerk began pealing off, $20-$40-$60-$80, Dad almost keeled over. He took the cash back to the house and strung the 100 twenty-dollar bills across my bedroom, which brother Jim had now taken possession. When Jim returned to the house, Dad simply said, "A birthday present arrived today from Clay. I put it up in your room." As Jim scampered upstairs, Dad sat in silence awaiting the scream.

I always felt perfectly at home in Harlem, leisurely window shopping along 125th Street, dining at Frank's, or stopping enthralled at the gospel singing, ringing outward from a second-floor prayer meeting. The stage door exited out onto 126th Street, which I was told was once the most dangerous block in Harlem, but I would regularly walk out alone at the midnight hour, on my way to late-night parties at Smalls Paradise or Sugar Rays. I also believe that the Apollo audience has been given a bad-rap over the years, a notorious reputation for being brutally judgmental in their booing and cat-calls to less-talented black entertainers. This must be said: the Apollo audience was always extremely polite and respectful to any white performer who walked out onto their stage. The Apollo still stands, but no longer the legendary temple to African American culture, not even as a cultural museum. For that, one must travel to the Rock 'n' Soul Museum in Memphis, a shrine to Otis and B.B. and other Apollo greats. During my time at the Apollo, I seldom sat in my dressing room; you would find me in the wings, in the dark, learning from the pros, watching the masters mesmerize the audience, sharing a lifetime of hardship, masked in showmanship, and I would weep.

Our next Apollo show promised to be even better. Bobby Shiffman had contracted the new, blue-eyed soul duo, the Righteous Brothers as headliners for my next show. A few weeks later, an urgent call from Bobby put an end to that. The theatre was being picketed. A Black Muslim group was protesting the Shiffman family, white and Jewish, and their ownership and operation of the legendary showplace. "This is not a good time for white acts on our stage," is all the dignity Bobby Shiffman could muster. I never played the Apollo again.

1950 Memorial Day Picnic

The extended Nash family gathers in our backyard for the "first weekend of summer" holiday cookout. That's me, poised front and center as usual.

First row: Cousin Susie Nash on the lap of Aunt Gwen Nash, Cousin John Edmunds, Brother Jim Rucker, me, Al Rucker, Jr., Cousins Steve Edmunds and Mike Mahan.

Second row: Grandma Nash's sister, Annie Jewell, Grandma Helen Nash, Aunt Faye with Cousin Trevor Nash, Mom's cousin Bea with Steve Mahan, my mom Evelyn Nash Rucker cuddling baby Brother Rick; (behind Mom) are her cousins Margaret Badasky and Ruth Jewell and mom's older sister, my Aunt Louise Edmunds holding cousin Tammy Edmunds.

Back row: Uncles Arnold Edmunds and Sherman Nash, Grandpa Ralph Nash, Great (Spanish-American War) Uncle Evan Jewell, my dad Albert Rucker, Sr., Uncle "Bud" Nash and "Red" Badasky.

Notice that Grandpa Nash and Evan Jewell are sporting neckwear. The ladies are each wearing dresses, and their hubbies had discovered the trendy new "slacks," trousers in mix and match colors – all very stylish for a backyard barbeque. Neither sneakers nor flip-flops were evident at a Nash bash.

(*Photo by cousin, Lt. Commander Raymond Mahan, U.S. Navy, Photographic Unit*).

In New York, a Coke cost a dollar!
1955, Mom, Dad and me at the Copacabana in Manhattan to see the McGuire Sisters.

1953 - 1957, "Rucker's Rumpus Room".

Al Rucker, Jr. and the Baby Sitters (Janice Belleville, Jackie Ennis, Carole Dough-ton and Marilyn Smelko) launch our very first Saturday night show. In our final three years, Jackie Ennis was replaced by Jean Kerr.

My Saturday night, rock 'n' roll television odyssey began at age 15, as the host/producer of 'Rucker's Rumpus Room," a top-of-the charts, lip-synch, records show. My four "Baby Sitters" (top left, Marilyn Smelko, Jean Kerr, Carole Doughton and Janice Belleville) were joined by four squeaky-clean high-school jocks (Bob Summers, Dick Johnson, Richard Miller and Frank Pavlick). The farewell/birthday cake celebrated our year-end (and final) show on WKBN-TV. Above left, director John Yoder and Raysa Bonow offer pre-show production notes. We regrouped for the next three years, "*live* and in black-and-white," on WFMJ-TV, Youngstown, Ohio.

1958 "Al Rucker and the Seven Teens".

My new Saturday night television gang at WJAR-TV in Providence, R.I; Carey Porter-Moss, Ken Thomas, Bob DuCharme, and me, "Mr. Cool," Lynn Raymond, Tony Michaels and Elliott James.

Tony Bennett on stage with Alan Freed at the New York Paramount theatre; Columbia Records decided to promote Tony as their "teen idol".

Channel 13, WNTA-TV

"Rate the Records," my first New York television show: Jackie Wilson, Jimmy Clanton, Alan Freed, Johnny Carlton and Cash Box Editor Ira Howard; Gary Stites, Jo Ann Campbell and Teddy Randazzo launch the very first show, September 10, 1959; the Mystics, the classic Brooklyn vocal group ("Hush-A-Bye") adopted me; the Isley Brothers, Kelly, Rudy and Ronnie ("Shout") and Ben E. King ("Stand By Me"); dancing the "Bop" at Palisades Park; the Flamingos ("I Only Have Eyes For You"), with the suave, soon-to-be solo soul star, Tommy Hunt ("Human"), far left; Dion & the Belmonts ("Teenager In Love"), Carlo Mastrangelo, Freddie Milano, Dion DiMucci and Angelo D'Aleo; "the Keystone Cop and the Colorado cowboy," – the comedy begins on the very first show with Gary Stites; and with Jerry Lewis during the first of his many memorable appearances on our show; "The Jersey Boys," at work; the brilliant, creative team responsible for the Four Seasons durable, chart-topping triumphs: Joe Long, Frankie Valli, songwriter/producers, Bob Gaudio, and Bob Crewe, arranger Artie Shroek and Tommy DeVito.

1960, On Stage with Bobby Darin at Newark's Mosque Theatre, showing off my double-shuffle time-step.

"Goin' to Kansas City" with singer/ songwriter Wilbert Harrison.

Sweet 16: Marcia Habib, my fan club
president and lifelong pal, at Tavern
on the Green.

Crowning Miss Teenage America
1963, at Freedomland in the Bronx,
on WOR-TV.

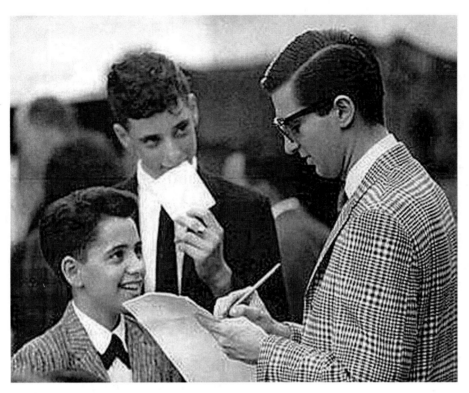

My favorite photo: Fans at Palisades Amusement Park, summer of 1960.

1959, Bronx High School of Science
I attended a full schedule of classes, expecting a scene out of *"Blackboard Jungle"*.

"Everybody's Somebody's Fool," written by Howard Greenfield and Jack Keller (above), recorded by Connie Francis in 1960, becoming her first No.1 single.

The four Stooges: Moe Howard, Larry Fine, Joe DeRita and me on our "Meet Hercules" Tour.

The Commack Arena, January 1960; my first-ever stage appearance as "Clay Cole".

The Most Beautiful Girl in the World.

Clay with Kitty Kallen (*"Little Things Mean a Lot"*); Tuesday Weld; Lillian Briggs (*"I Want You To Be My Baby"*); Connie Francis; Annette Funicello; Timi Yuro (*"Hurt"*); Chuck McCann, and our most-faithful, frequent guest star, Linda Scott (*"I Told Every Little Star"*); Jo Ann Campbell (*I'm the Girl from Wolverton Mountain"*); at the Action House, December 1966, with Nedra Talley and Ronnie Bennett of the Ronettes (*"Be My Baby"*); Tina Robin in the studio and Jo Ann Campbell on the Cyclone roller coaster.

1960. Backstage at the historic Brooklyn Paramount Theatre, during our record-breaking ten-day, all-star Christmas show.

April, 1961. Dion's dressing room at our Brooklyn Paramount Easter show with Harry Boyle of the Echoes *("Baby Blue")* and a preoccupied wanderer.

August, 1960, the "Clay Cole Summer Show," live six nights a week from Palisades Amusement Park; WABC radio disc-jockey "Cousin Bruce" Morrow arrives on the scene to introduce my very first recording *"Here, There, Everywhere"*.

Hey, Let's Twist:

Chubby Checker and Clay lead the twisters in "*e l'oro del twist*"; Shirelles on stage twisting with Billy Vera on guitar; actress Mary Mitchel and dance star Jeff Parker set the standard; Chubby and Clay twisting on stage with16-year old Vicki Spencer; "Miss Perpetual Motion," Candy Johnson, the twisting star of four beach party films and the 1964 New York World's Fair; "*The Twist,*" the record that launched a thousand hips; Clay with his unrivaled, all-time twistin' dance champs, Pat and Pete Salerno; Vicki Spencer and Clay teach the twist in a six page *Twist* magazine photo feature; Joey Dee & the Starlighters, the house-rockin' show band that ignited the twist frenzy at Manhattan's Peppermint Lounge; and Clay "*Twistin' the Night Away*" with Denise Ferri of the Delicates.

"Twist Around the Clock,"
on stage in Hollywood.

Dion, Clay and Chubby Checker,
living the dream (1961).

Clay Cole's Twist-a-rama I

The Ronettes and the Capris hit the road twistin' ("I swear we look like a bus-and-truck *West Side Story*") Ronettes from left, Sisters Estelle Bennett, Ronnie Bennett and Cousin Nedra Talley.

My full hour with just one guest:
Tony Bennett.

"Ain't that good news?"
Sam Cooke drops in.

Clay Cole's Twist-a-rama II.

The Delicates (Denise Ferri and Peg Santiglia) join me and the Capris, twistin'
to Newfoundland, and a bitter end Capris, from left: John Dante Cassese, Mike
"Mootsie" Mincieli, Vinnie Naccarato, Frank Reina.

Clay's Cole Bin

Our zany *Hellzapoppin'* segment inspired by my sidekick Chuck McCann. Our guest stars would join in the frenzy of quick-cut sight gags, pantomimes, shtick, and silly slapstick blackouts. It was great fun, a big hit and gave our show a hip New York spin, unlike any other television dance show. The fact that no videotape remains is sad; the Rascals performing *"The Night before Christmas,"* in nightshirts and caps, was a keeper

The Clay Cole Wednesday Show

The 1965 cast of talented young performers for my new mid-week show: the Del Satins (Dion's session singers), singers Tracey Dey, Angela Martin and Benny Thomas. "Do you notice a trend here; through the years I always seemed to form my own little TV gang." Tommy Ferrara (far left) later joined the Capris; Brother Freddie Ferrara and Les Cauchi formed the Brooklyn Bridge with Johnny Maestro; Tracey Dey recorded for Bob Crewe; Benny Thomas hosted a daytime talk show in Nashville and was nominated for a daytime Emmy for his role as Dr. Jack Garner in "The Doctors." Sadly, Richie Green, (far right), Benny Thomas and Angela Martin all died much too soon, much too young.

Guest Stars.

Superstar Neil Diamond was still an up-and-coming singer/songwriter when he met, and eventually married, my production assistant, the adorable Marcia Murphy; Goldie & the Gingerbreads, (Genya "Goldie" Ravan, Carol MacDonald, Margo Lewis and Ginger Bianco); Ray Reneri on the road with Eric Burdon & the Animals; with two very special guest stars, Bobby Darin and Dion; at our Rolling Stones' rehearsal, lusty little ladies from our studio audience came to the stage, flirting with the newly-arrived Brits; my infamous four-hour Beatles hair-crop from stylist, Tommy of *Rudy at the Warwick*; on Broadway at the Ambassador Theatre with the Del Satins, Tommy Ferrara, Stan Zizka and Fred Ferrara; the Vagrants, featuring Leslie West on guitar in his pre-Mountain days, checking out our go-go girls' (Marci High and Kelly Clark) disco cages.

11) Brooklyn Paramount Theatre

"Don't lie, you little tramp! You were out all night!"
To Sandra Dee, in the film, "A Summer Place," 1959

I don't remember the first time I met Sid Bernstein; he just always seemed to be there, a New York landmark like Katz's Delicatessen or Papaya King. Only the Yiddish has the proper terms of endearment to describe Sid – a *schmendrick,* a little bit *meschugana,* but a *mensch.* Sid is well-fed and speaks so softly it's almost a whisper. Sid was always broke, but he did have an "angel," a cherubic millionaire, Abe Margolies, a diamond merchant and investor in the Todd-AO process.

I have vivid memories of long, leisurely walks around midtown, Sid's arm locked into mine, whispering non-stop chatter in my right ear, while passing out flyers. Sid was the culprit; in the late Fifties every windshield, phone booth, men's room, and taxicab displayed an "I'm A Billy Fields Fan" card, carefully placed under glass, a reminder that Bernstein had struck again. Billy Fields was a singer Sid aggressively promoted, to no end. Sid's the one who took me to The Parkway, an up-the-steps restaurant in the out-of-the-way Lower East Side, for the best melt-in-your-mouth Romanian Tenderloin Steak in the city. Sid knew his food and knew where to find it – the best egg cream, franks, bialys, matzo ball soup and moo goo gai pan – and took delight in dragging me there.

On Sundays, our gang would dash over to The Stage Deli for a "salami omelet pancake-style," knowing that Sid would be there. "C'mon down to D.C.," Sid might say, "I've got Judy Garland there tonight." So off we'd go to Washington, and there would be Sid holding court in lobby. Sid invented networking. He presented everyone – Melanie at The Met ("a night of 1000 candles"), Dr. Wayne Dyer at

Carnegie Hall, the Beatles at Shea Stadium – Sid was always out-front, whispering softly into ears.

When Sid married, our little gang was abuzz, for the little Jewish nebbish was about to marry a *shiksa*, Geraldine, a drop-dead beautiful, blond cast member of Broadway's "The Sound of Music" – Gerri was one of the singing nuns. The pre-vailing joke at the time was:

Geri and a couple of cast members, still in their stage nun's habit and winged hats, dashed out between shows for a quick drink at Sardis. Two blue-haired mati-nee ladies interrupted them: "Excuse me Sisters, but you shouldn't be smoking, swearing and drinking martinis.

"Buzz-off," Geri shot back, "we're with Sound of Music!"

Sid approached me in fall of 1960 with an offer I couldn't refuse, return to The Brooklyn Paramount to continue the Alan Freed holiday tradition, a ten-day all-star rock 'n' roll extravaganza, Clay Cole's Christmas Show. The holiday season in New York is magical, its shadowed, gray avenues suddenly burst into a Disney-like Technicolor, transforming even the most belligerent into bell-ringers. It's catchy; the sparkle in the eye. To all this, add the excitement of a dazzling, ten-day Christ-mas stage spectacular and you can imagine my jubilation. I watched from across Flatbush Avenue as stagehands on scaffolds, fitted the marquee of The Paramount with foot-high letters: "Clay Cole's Christmas Show."

Eugene Pleshette, the General Manager of the legendary show palace, proudly welcomed me to his suite of offices. "The Brooklyn Paramount with 4,084 seats is New York City's second largest theatre; only Radio City Music Hall seats more," he boasted. Eugene Pleshette was a stylish showman of the old school, a tyrant to his army of dollar-an-hour ushers, revered by the moguls of the motion picture indus-try, and adored by his knockout daughter, the actress Suzanne Pleshette. Suzanne would drop by, dressed to the nines, gloves, hat and veil, languishing on daddy's desk, legs properly crossed, inhaling a fabulously long cigarette. *Pul-ease*. This was gonna be heaven.

Sid Bernstein had put together an all-star lineup of hit-makers, and knowing that he could lure audience members back for two or more shows, he signed Bobby Rydell to headline for three days, Brenda Lee for three, and Ray Charles for four. Murray the K, New York's top deejay (1010-WINS) was hired to replace me when I raced back to Channel 13 to fulfill my daily live television duties over in Newark. The supporting acts alone would cost a million dollars today, if you could even get them together:

Dion	("Lonely Teenager")
Neil Sedaka	("Calendar Girl")
The Drifters	("Save The Last Dance For Me")
The Coasters	("Searchin" / Yakety Yak")
The Shirelles	("Will You Still Love Me Tomorrow")
The Skyliners	("Since I Don't Have You")
Johnny Burnette	("You're Sixteen")
Chubby Checker	("The Twist")
Kathy Young	("A Thousand Stars")
Bobby Vee	("Rubber Ball")
Jimmy Charles	("A Million To One")
Bo Diddley	("Say Man")
Dante & the Evergreens	("Alley-Oop")
Little Anthony & the Imperials	("Shimmy, Shimmy, Ko-Ko-Bop")

Not advertised was a little-known trumpet player (with an Epic record contract, but no hits), our orchestra leader, nineteen-year-old Bobby Vinton. Bobby's dad was the leader of a well-known, big band back in Canonsburg, Pennsylvania; until his horn section formed a vocal group, the Four Coins, and recorded a huge hit "Shangri-La." Bobby pleaded with me to allow him to sing a number in the show; although we were tight, I agreed, and he sang an opening number with the band. It would be two years later that Epic would release his No. 1 classic, "Roses Are Red (My Love)".

Bobby Rydell was at his peak at that moment in time, coming off a string of energetic hits, and his upbeat "Volare" remained on the charts for 11 weeks, backing up "Wild One" and "We Got Love." At the Paramount, he introduced his sensual cha-cha- chalipso, "Sway," which would hit the national charts for ten weeks. Between shows, Bobby could be found at his drum-set, preferring the hallway "because it had the best vibrations."

"Little Miss Dynamite" Brenda Lee was hotter than a pistol in 1960, she had four Top 10 hits, two at #1, "I'm Sorry," and "Sweet Nothin's" and in December, her re-released, "Rockin' Around the Christmas Tree." Her birthday was December 11th; she had just turned 16. Brenda shared her dressing room with her mom, cousins, and gawd-knows how many hangers-on, assorted family-members and friends of friends, and I must confess her dressing room was a mess! Lordy, what a mess!

If that wasn't enough, Ray Charles rolled in with his No. 1 classic "Georgia On My Mind." One morning I was waiting for the backstage elevator to take me up to my dressing room, the doors opened, Ray Charles walked out and said, "morning Clay." Wait a minute, Ray is blind, how did he? I dunno. But it happened.

Neil Sedaka's greatest years were still ahead, but we got the benefit of "Calendar Girl," and the whole audience sang along with him. Dion, a huge star in New York, was still in his "teen tunes" period, about to leave the Belmonts. Between shows, he was methodically mastering the acoustic guitar and writing songs, a passion he shared with his new best friend, Doc Pomus (songwriter/producers Doc Pomus & Mort Shuman).

Bobby Vee and Jimmy Charles were our matinee idols, heart-throbs for the teenyboppers. I had seen Jimmy ("A Million To One") crooning his love ballad to swooning girls in the audience at The Apollo, and like Bobby Vee, he was equally charming and amiable off-stage. Bobby Vee, a cherubic little wop (Bobby Velline) from Fargo, North Dakota, was just seventeen, and introducing his new Liberty single, "Take Good Care of My Baby," (soon to become the second No. 1 hit for the songwriting team of Gerry Goffin and Carole King, knocking their Shirelles' hit, "Will You Love Me Tomorrow" off the charts.)

Most of the acts were on the charts, in the Top 10: Ray Charles' "Georgia On My Mind" was No.1, Kathy Young "A Thousand Stars," No. 3, Neil Sedaka "Calendar Girl" was at No. 4, Jimmy Charles "Million To One" No. 5, Bobby Vee "Devil or Angel" No. 6., Johnny Burnette "You're Sixteen," No. 8 and Chubby was No.10 with his first release of "The Twist."

The reaction to the show was instantaneous; there was no slow build, we sold-out the first show, with four sell-outs each day, with five on weekends, a special midnight show. The ushers could not clear the house; some audience members remained for all four shows, sitting through screenings of a gaud-awful Rory Calhoun western. The first show would hit around 10am and the last show would break about midnight. When we left the theatre at night, there would be lines around the block, waiting in the winter cold for the first morning show. With ranks of fans circling the theatre, we were basically in full lockdown for ten days. An attempt to enjoy a first-day lunch break across the street at Juniors created such tumult we were asked to leave, banned in spite of the crush of new customers our shows provided. We tacked a Juniors' menu to our backstage bulletin board with an "Off-Limits" warning to all performers; *we* boycotted Juniors! A between-shows routine quickly settled in, listening to the radio, jamming in Dion's dressing room and sending out for hot meals,

I hired Peter Salerno to be my backstage assistant, delivering chow-time grub, recycling my tuxedos in and out of the dry cleaners and keeping my dressing room bar well stocked. Peter told me "You were the only one in the theatre with a bar and you always kept a bottle of Scotch for the Drifters. The Shirelles loved Chinese food, so I was always running for take-out and hot tea, honey and lemon for Anthony Gourdine [Little Anthony] and the guys."

Christmas Eve, I took the stagehands out for a drink, and Al Saltzman, a prankster who enjoyed sparring with me backstage in the wings, threw me a sucker punch, asking me to help him pick out a Christmas tree. "A Jewish Christmas tree? – *Oy vey iz mir*! Al pulled his car onto a darkened tree lot shut down for the night, and we hauled-off a fine looking pine and raced back to the Saltzman house. We woke his wife, sat up all night, listening to carols on the radio and decorating the tree – my "tree glows in Brooklyn" Jewish Christmas.

The latest issue of *Billboard* magazine arrived announcing the new No. 1 record in the country, "Will You Love Me Tomorrow" by the Shirelles, their first at the top spot. There is no doubt, the four ladies from New Jersey were the best loved of all the Sixties girl groups, admired not only by their fans, but also by their fellow performers. Shirley, Beverly, Mickey and Doris were the house specialty, hot & spicy, sweet & sour. In their matching off-the-rack go-to-meetin' dresses, they were the perfect fresh-faced girls next door, if you happened to live in Passaic. "Scepter Records was built on the success of the Shirelles," recalls fellow Scepter star, Maxine Brown. Florence Greenberg, head honcho of Scepter Records rewarded the girls with a suite at the nearby Granada Hotel, where many of the artists lodged; the other was the St. George Hotel, bigger, but further away. I decided to throw a party for the girls in their suite and invited the cast, the musicians and the stage crew.

I sent Peter out into the street with a long list and a pocketful of cash to organize the party, and set-up a full bar, ice, mixes and music in their suite. The musicians sealed their "party animal" reputation by somehow being the last off stage and the first to arrive at the party (and the last to leave.) The merrymaking was in full swing when three stagehands decided to take a shower – together – then appeared buck-naked, drying their butts with a bath towel, a twist lesson Chubby had fabricated. In the midst of all that hysteria, I answered a knock at the door. It was Bobby Vinton, who took one long look at the debauchery inside, spun on his heels and fled the Hotel Granada.

The next morning, I found myself fully dressed in the Shirelles' guest bedroom; the sheets were still warm where the Imperials had crashed late in the night. The four ladies shared one giant-sized bed. Shirley had already called room service and ordered breakfast for five. When the waiter arrived with the cart, I buried myself under the comforter, so as not to be seen. It was our little secret; I was sharing breakfast-in-bed with the ladies with the No. 1 record in the country!

As emcee, I was on-stage for the full ninety-minute show, so I dashed back to the theatre to get into my tuxedo and onto the stage. Bobby Vinton had just concluded his opening number when I hit the wings with a buzz-saw hangover. After adjusting my starched-pleated tuxedo shirt, I was introduced, singing "Here There Everywhere." The audience was unusually zealous, roaring with approval. The screams from the audience got wilder, more intense, and I bowed, blew air-kisses to the audience and introduced the Drifters. As I raced off into the wings, the stagehands were in convulsions: "Your fly is open!" Not only was it unzipped, but the shirt-tail was peeking through the opening. I had the habit of adjusting my starched-shirt front just before going on stage by unzipping the fly and pulling down on the fabric to tweak any folds or creases. I had done that, but neglected to zip up. Normally, the Drifters called me out to join them in their encore of "There Goes My Baby." I was stalling, flushed with embarrassment, wanting to face the audience one on one. When I did appear, the hoots-and-hollers began all over again. I waited for the audience to quiet down, and in my best Jack Benny delivery, I said: "Alright. So you found out I'm not Jewish!" Well, that got such a big laugh that I wanted to keep it in for the rest of the run – or keep it out. But, I zipped-up. I behaved.

Closing day always had a sentimental edge; none of us wanted the run to end. Each of us were realizing our secret dream, performing on stage to a wildly receptive audience. I was celebrating my 23rd birthday. Backstage was jammed with well-wishers, friends and relatives. The Brill Building gang came in full-force: Carole King and Gerry Goffin; Barry Mann and Cynthia Weil; the fabulous Ellie Greenwich and her husband and writing partner, Jeff Barry; and of course, Howie Greenfield. Doc Pomus led a marathon jam-session in Dion's dressing room.

The front office staff arrived with cash, passing from dressing room to dress-ing room tallying up the draws against final payment, and suddenly everyone was flush. I was paid $10,000 for the ten days, which was usually paid in $10's and $20's, so I had quite a bankroll. It was tradition in those days to tip the stagehands, the sound and light men, the fire marshal and the four spotlight operators. There was much hugging between packing; everyone wishing to make a quick getaway after the last show. Peter returned with my souvenir program book, signed with affection by all the entertainers. Sid Bernstein came backstage, buoyant, announc-ing his Easter show plans. Abe Margolies cornered me, pumping my hand with thanks, and gifted me with a perfect blue star-sapphire ring with twin diamonds.

The Shirelles presented me a fire engine red smoking jacket with a matching ascot. All my New York fantasies were being realized. Our Christmas show proudly holds the all-time box-office record for that 4000+ seat theatre, a record that stands to this day.

> "Clay Cole's Christmas stage show at The Brooklyn Paramount broke all attendance records. He will emcee the Easter week show, headlining Jackie Wilson." – *Billboard*

Following our ten-day Easter show, the Paramount shuttered; the historic theatre became the gymnasium for Long Island University in 1962.

Spring of 1961, the bubble burst; Eli Landau called the hundreds of employees of Channel 13 to a meeting in the ballroom studios in Newark. Channel 13's license was being sold to Educational Broadcasting Corp, a commercial-free, public supported, educational station, a radical new broadcasting idea. We were closing down; I was out-of-work. All the first times were over, all the momentum my career had gathered with a hit film, and a hit record and a hit TV show came to a screeching halt.

The news of my cancellation hit me hard, but the knockout punch was about to delivered from none other than Sid Bernstein, himself. We were sharing an amicable cab ride through Central Park when he sheepishly broke the news: The Easter Show[6] at the Brooklyn Paramount was no longer mine. Without the power of my television show, he had signed radio deejay Murray the K to replace me. I was stunned. I tried to maintain my cool, but, like steam erupting in a cold-water flat, my blood was boiling. My TV show was my leverage, and I had no show. Logic prevailed – loyalty aside, this was a necessary business decision. As a consolation, Sid offered me "special guest star" billing – but it was Murray's show.

The following Christmas, Sid offer me a spot on his all-star, five-day holiday show at The Medinah Temple in Chicago (December 26-30th 1961), along with all my old pals, Dion, Frank Gari, Johnny Tillotson, Eddie Hodges, Freddie Cannon, Brenda Lee, Vicki Spencer, the Marvelettes, Solomon Burke and Clarence "Frogman" Henry – all straight off the Hot 100. Ral Donner, Chicago's own rockabilly sensation, was also featured, but in spite of that killer lineup, the house didn't rock. It was a bust that left Sid Bernstein flat broke. I purchased Sid's airline ticket home, arriving in New York on New Year's Eve – the eve of my birthday. Needing

---

6   The Easter Show headlined Ben E. King, not Jackie Wilson; also appearing were, the Isley Brothers, Dion, Del Shannon, Rosie & the Originals, Freddie Cannon, Johnny Tillotson, Frank Gari, the Echoes, Chubby Checker, and Jimmy Clanton. No records were broken.

to elevate my mood, I phoned Raysa, "put on your sparkly top, we're going out tonight!"

The classic nightspot for a New York New Year's Eve was The Stork Club, so I called on the chance we might get a last-minute reservation, and we did. This was going to be our best New Year's ever, just like in the movies. It *was* just like in the movies; Jimmy Stewart and his wife Gloria were seated at the very next table. The Stewarts were seated with the rubber baron, Harvey Firestone, and Mrs. Firestone, who was whining loudly about their high-brow television show, "The Voice of Firestone," being cancelled after twenty-five years on radio and TV. (Mrs. Firestone had composed the theme songs.) Then, Jimmy Stewart and his wife got into an escalating shouting match; champagne was stimulating their brouhaha. Raysa and I put on our little paper hats, honking into our noisemakers to lighten the mood, provoking scowls and icy stares from the stoic party-poopers at adjoining tables. At the stroke of midnight, the swells put on their little hats, honked their little horns, and then went right back to scowling, arguing, and whining into their Dom Pérignon. We cut out at five-past midnight, headed over to an Irish gin mill on Eighth Avenue, fought our way through the four-deep-at-the-bar revelers, and had a blast. The 400 blows!

As if it couldn't get any worse, Roz Ross suddenly, without notice, left GAC for a lucrative offer from The William Morris Agency, taking her entire roster of rockers, Dion, Chubby, Wayne Newton, and all the Bobby's with her. She literally did not report for work, leaving GAC scrambling.

The William Morris Agency had been brokering talent since the Ice Age, a tight ole' boy club, imbibed by ranks of Jewish octogenarians, collecting their 10% from vaudeville stars like the zaftig Sophie Tucker and the tiny Singer's Midgets – buttressing the longtime William Morris motto, "No act too big, no act to small." By 1962, the "boys" at William Morris had awakened to the realization they needed to snatch a piece of this new rock 'n' roll action. Nightclubs had been their bread and butter – Milton Berle, Danny Thomas, and Jimmy Durante – and television their gravy. So, the Morris office simply swiped the entire rock 'n' roll roster from GAC, as well as Roz's secretary Esther, Jerry Brandt and Roz Ross, herself. Overnight, William Morris was now in the business of rock 'n' roll.

MCA (Music Corporation of America), the Tiffany of talent agencies, was famous for their big band bookings and movie stars; Chairman Lew Wasserman would not acknowledge, least of all represent rock 'n' roll.

Norman Wise and Buddy Howe at GAC invited me to a breakfast meeting at the Plaza, pleading with me to remain with them. Ernie Martinelli, an independent agent recruited to salvage the crumbling GAC rock 'n' roll unit, realized that I was their last holdout. Knowing I was a Roz Ross loyalist, GAC wanted to keep me, not for my value, but as a prod to stick it to Roz Ross. GAC wooed me with promises and offers, and the infamous reminder of the William Morris legacy: "If you want to get lost, don't join the witness protection program – sign on with William Morris. No one will ever hear from you again." In spite of all the pleading and wooing from GAC, my loyalty remained with Roz Ross, and I followed her and Jerry Brandt, signing on to William Morris.

Early spring was prom time, promising fresh money for the savvy nightclub owner who booked Teen Idols to attract the Clearasil crowd. Frankie Avalon appeared at Palumbo's in Philadelphia, Dion was at the Roosevelt in New Orleans, and Brenda Lee, headlined the Latin Casino. (Brenda dislocated her neck, sending her to a Camden, N J hospital, and forcing her to cancel her last six days.) Roz booked for me for six weeks into Jack Silverman's International, a cavernous cellar club on Broadway at 53rd St, famous for their near-naked showgirls on stage and crocks of kosher pickles on the tables. Joey Adams, their mainstay headliner called it "the Jewish Copa." Neil Sedaka, Gene Pitney, Clyde McPhatter, and Paul & Paula joined me, performing to a sea of white dinner jackets, breathing in the scent of gardenias and Old Spice. Looking out from the stage at all the white dinner jackets and white tablecloths, I announced. "This looks like a meeting of the Ku Klux Klan." It was my first time working with showgirls in G-strings and pasties, girls we found to be surprisingly modest and demure backstage. When the engagement ended, Phil Black, the club's production singer, quit the show and, since I was now out of work, I took over singing the production numbers with a chorus of tap dancing girls – (they were called 'ponies,' to distinguish them from the thoroughbreds, the non-dancing topless showgirls.)

Roz Ross and I huddled to create a new television idea, a desk and couch Tonight show format with only young performers. I wanted Bobby Vinton as our band leader, (our Doc Severinson), and I called Bobby at home in Canonsburg.

"I'm defeated," Bobby told me. "I've decided to reorganize my big band and just play engagements locally, in the Pittsburgh area."

Six months later, "Roses Are Red" was the No. 1 record in the country and the singing career of the once-defeated Polish Prince was launched. ("Roses Are Red," co-written by Paul Evans and Al Byron, was released in July, 1961, and saved

Vinton from being fired from Epic Records. Epic renewed Vinton's contract but changed his artist title from bandleader to singer.)

Roz invited me up to her gloriously spacious Sixth Avenue apartment (in one of the many properties privately owned by Elizabeth, the Queen of England) for one of her famous late-night "brain-storming" sessions that required her to inhale a great amount of dope. "I can think better with a clear head," she mumbled. When the smoke cleared, the result was "Clay Cole's Twist-a-rama," a stage revue so that William Morris could capitalize on my twist record and movie. "Get your tuxedoes pressed … get some head-shots from Bruno of Hollywood … you're gonna start working the clubs."

"Twist-a-rama," – I hated the name; it sounded like an amusement park ride. Walking home along Sixth Avenue, as I passed Moondog, I'd swear I saw him cringe, which was not a good sign.

It was impossible to be an entertainer in the Sixties without becoming well acquainted with the Mafia, owners-and-operators of most all the nightclubs and alcoholic beverage establishments on the East Coast. The mob-bosses I met, as an entertainer in their clubs and bouncing to their bars, were all gentlemen, who treated me with great deference. Mobsters had an affinity for show people and relished our patronizing attention. Since prohibition, nightclubs were run by mob rumrunners who provided liquor to the speakeasies. Later they simply bankrolled the old dives, turning them into respectable supper clubs, as Frank Costello had done with The Copacabaña. Even the landmark '21' Club was a speakeasy during Prohibition, favored by Joe Kennedy, JFK's father. Sherman Billingley, the erudite proprietor of The Stork Club, once did fourteen months at Leavenworth as a bootlegger. At the Stork Club, his most visible customer was J. Edgar Hoover, the nations top G-man. So, the twains do meet.

Not only did entertainers hobnob with mobsters, it was also necessary to cozy up to the law that is if you wanted to work in establishments that served alcohol. It was mandatory for all employees to obtain a cabaret card, including musicians, chorus girls and the superstars. Performers were herded downtown to the Bureau to be photographed, fingerprinted, and interrogated for a New York City Cabaret Identification Card, and charged a fee. If you had a rap-sheet, criminal ties, or were under 18, you were rejected; Brenda Lee, at sixteen, could not work The Copa. Frank Sinatra declined all offers to appear in New York clubs, refusing to subject himself to the bureau's humiliations. Some artists' cards were revoked on deceptive grounds; the permits of Billie Holiday, Charlie Parker, and Thelonious Monk, were suspended due to drug charges, and that of Lenny Bruce for his reputed foul language. The system was politically corrupt, fraught with racial bias, favoritism and bribery.

But, trips to the Cabaret Bureau were fun for me, to catch all the visiting singing stars and comedians, the flamenco dancers for The Chateau Madrid, the hula-dancing fire eaters for The Hawaiian Room, and the cool black jazz-cats for The Embers – singers, strippers, adagio dancers, Argentine tango teams and Egyptian belly-dancers – what a magnificent mix! Then in 1960, the cabaret card of avant-garde comedian Lord Buckley was seized under mysterious circumstances, and he died soon after. The subsequent brouhaha and pressure from the press and the public embarrassed the bureau and the cabaret card was abolished, slamming the door on another bureaucratic cash cow. (There is still a two-year New York City cabaret license required for any establishment that permits dancing, which cost $600 to $1000, based on capacity.)

Roz promoted Clay Cole's Twist-a-rama as a night club tour, with my friends the Capris ("There's A Moon Out Tonight"), the Furies, a band led by drummer-showman, Lou Dana and three young dancing girls Roz had discovered twisting on the railings of the Peppermint Lounge – Sisters Veronica, 18 and Estelle Bennett, 17 and Cousin Nedra Talley, 15. The three teens came to me without an act and a refreshing "what you see is what you get" attitude. They had just signed a Colpix Record contract as the Ronettes.

The Ronettes were multiracial, which was uncommon in the '60s; the Bennett's mother was black and Native American and their father was white. The beaver-toothed Ronnie said "at one point in my childhood I was not sure if I was black or white." They were three hot-looking (Latin-looking) girls who understood their assets: they were very exotic and danced a mean shimmy. Each modeled an embellished beehive hair-do and dark Cleopatra eyeliner – little girls playing grownups. Their wardrobe was the *cheongsam*, an embroidered, tight-fitting silk dress, slit up the thigh, preferred by Hong Kong beauty queens and Imelda Marcos.

In spite of their inspiring booty, they arrived as three sweet, easy-going, eager and malleable girls. We gathered together to create an act, reaching into the Ray Charles songbook for "I Got a Woman," the Raeletts "Hit the Road Jack" and a tambourine-twirling routine to "Wha'd I Say," which became our frantic finale. I learned that Veronica, nicknamed Ronnie, could do a dead-on impression of Pearl Bailey; it was added. We assembled a medley of kooky dances and the Capris and I wrote a rock "Limbo" which became an audience-participation showstopper; it was also extremely sexy, with customers lobbing under a bamboo pole. An hour revue was shaping up. So with the blessings of William Morris and the Mafia and the abolishment of the age-restricting cabaret card, I signed a contract with The Camelot Club, at Third Avenue and 49th Street, a supper club that had been transformed to capitalize on the ongoing twist frenzy; Keely Smith and Jay & the Americans had preceded us. Any nefarious business between the William Morris agency and the show-biz wing of organized crime was conducted at The Camelot Club, fronted by Joe Cataldo (aka Joe the Wop). With the mob boys neatly ensconced in the supper club business, they needed to own a top booking agent, and that agent was Georgie Wood, a long-time trouble-shooter for William Morris. Georgie was greatly admired by the young Morris agents, as dapper and colorful as one of Damon Runyon's loveable hit men. George Raft could play Georgie Wood in the movies; he was that smooth and shifty. Georgie knew all the right people as well: Frank Costello, Meyer Lansky, "Jimmy Blue Eyes" Alo, Joey Adonis, and the mob-boss in exile Lucky Luciano.

Cabarets are either high class or low class. The Camelot Club was definitely no class – a tourist trap with a hefty cover charge, watered whiskey and a convenient midtown meeting place for the mob. It was here that Georgie Woods would be beaten to a bloody pulp.

For our Camelot Club engagement, the Ronettes, the Capris, Lou Dana and his band gathered for a long dress rehearsal on stage at the club, which was interrupted by an urgent phone call from Roz: "I'm sending you to an audition for the lead role in a new series to be shot on location at the French Riviera. You've got to get over there right now." I begged her to postpone the interview; tonight was, after all, opening night of an all-new show. She insisted, "He wants to see you now!"

I reluctantly taxied over to the Columbus Circle address to find a youthful broadcast executive alone in the offices. "The show," he outlined, "would be similar to the popular CBS hit, "Route 66" with Marty Milner and George Maharis, all about two partners on the loose along the Cote d' Azure.

"Wow, sounds wonderful," I thought.

"Of course, with the show filmed in Europe, it would be much freer, more relaxed. There will be some nudity. Do you object to being filmed naked?"

Caught off-guard, but not wanting to seem provincial, "uh, no" I boasted, "not at all."

Could you stand-up, just take off your clothes and let me see you're ...."

I bolted out of there mid-sentence, steaming mad. I called Roz Ross, furious. "I have a show to do and I am totally rattled!" Roz was never able to track down or identify the bogus creep. I almost had my first "casting couch" moment – not including my one brief haggle with Bernadette Castro over the purchase of a convertible sofa. This was my one and only casting couch encounter.

Our Camelot Club engagement went well, "playing to jammed houses throughout the run," Editor Sam Chase, reported in *Billboard*. "Cole's antics are reminiscent of Ray Bolger" and "the predominately adult audience waxed enthusiastic about the proceedings at goodly prices, the cover and minimum tariff going into effect again at each of the three nightly shows."

Wha'd I Say" was our usual finale, but with three shows a night, we sometimes alternated with "When The Saints Go Marching In," which got so spirited that often the entire band strutted off the stage, out a side door, and up Third Avenue – Lou sat alone, vamping at the drums, the Ronettes, the Capris and I banged our tambourines and the audience sat bemused, hearing the band playing like some far-off carnival – then enter the front door, through the bar, parade around the showroom and return to their places on the bandstand. It was an interminable stage wait, pending their eventual return, but exhilarating to innocent passerby's on Third Avenue. Georgie Wood walked in one night during "Saints," and seeing a vacant bandstand, whined, "We're paying for a band, where are they?" Georgie would often appear in the shadows at the back of the house, lighted only by the eerie red glow of the Exit sign, giving me the heebie-jeebies. Georgie's stone face never implied approval; his icy stares were judgmental, counting heads, taking attendance, making sure all fourteen of us were there, working. Oftentimes, at our late-late show there were more people on stage than customers in the audience.

We also had many celebrities drop in, Ann-Margret, Merv Griffin, Murray the K were among the swells dragged on stage to twist with the Ronettes or undulate under the limbo pole with the Capris. Liberace came into the Camelot Club alone and unannounced and sat through two shows, lingering on 'till six in the morning, charming us with witty stories. He generously tipped Bobby the bartender $100 when the drinks kept coming. Liberace was starring at The Latin Quarter and invited us to appear with him, along with Ethel Merman and an all-star lineup in a charity event at the legendary Broadway showroom, where as a young boy, I sat alone, bedazzled by Johnnie Ray.

We were also invited to entertain as surprise guests at a birthday bash for the film star Marilyn Maxwell at the popular in-spot, the Brasserie. Marilyn Maxwell, the last of the great platinum blonde film stars, and a Bob Hope favorite, was often compared to Marilyn Monroe: "I'm the blond with clothes on" was her snappy reply. Unlike Marilyn Monroe, who could be squirrelly and unstable, Maxwell held a long-standing reputation as being "one of the good ole' broads," steadfast like Jane Russell, Betty Grable and Vivian Blaine; "she could be trusted to keep a secret." Mingling with Maxwell and her Hollywood friends was a thrill (her publicist invited me, my friend Alan Foshko), but the evening is memorable to me as a disaster. Alan had reserved the entire Brasserie for the event, and created a make-shift stage among the tables. As we were about to perform, I passed the table of singer Fran Warren, who spoke up for all to hear, "He wouldn't know soul if he tripped over it." Can you imagine? What *chutzpah*. She obviously hadn't read the show biz rule book: "A fellow performer, a guest at a freebie birthday party, would never make such a smug remark," and just as I was about to step on stage. I was reminded later that Miss Warren's only hit record was "I Said My Pajamas and Put on My Prayers." Now *that* was a soul-stirring ditty! (Here Fran – have a Compoze!)

The Ronettes recorded five unsuccessful singles for Colpix Records and accepted an offer from Murray the K to become his "dancing girls." Later in 1963, when Phil Spector returned to New York, he struck up a friendship with Georgia Winters, and the *16* magazine editor arranged a meeting between Spector and the Ronettes – the rest is rock 'n' roll history. Phil Spector, Ellie Greenwich and Jeff Barry produced the classic, "Be My Baby," a hodgepodge of castanets, maracas, strings and Ronnie's seductive, now-legendary "who-oh-oh-oh," which drove teen boys wild. The July review in *Billboard* stated flat-out, "This is the best record the Ronettes ever made." This is also the record that defined Phil Spector's famous "wall of sound."

When we returned to The Camelot Club, two knockout seventeen-year-old singers, the Delicates (Denise Ferri and Peg Santiglia) replaced the Ronettes. Denise's mother "Mama Jo" was their chaperone, and we immediately adopted her – she was funny and gorgeous! Lou Dana snapped, "Whose gonna chaperone her?" Denise's dad owned a deli in Belleville, New Jersey; hence the name Deli-cates. (Lou's Deli itself played a role in rock 'n' roll folklore, as the neighborhood hangout to several unknown hopefuls drawn to Lou and Mama Jo – Connie Francis, Frankie Valli, Tommy DeVito, Joe Pesci and Bob Gaudio – banging out songs on their parlor piano.)

Easter weekend, we were booked into The 500 Club, Skinny D'Amato's Atlantic City hot-spot, marked by a bronze plaque announcing the dates when Martin & Lewis made their first-ever appearance as a team. Joe DiMaggio was sitting ringside and invited Denise to his table. "I was cared to death," Denise remembered. "He asked me my age – I was seventeen – and asked 'did I have a chaperone'. 'My mother' I told him. 'Good' he said 'I wouldn't want anything to happen to you cute little girls'. He was so nice. Then, I blew it. I asked him about Marilyn Monroe"

It was in that very summer of 1962 that Marilyn Monroe died, at age 36. Monroe's demise was more than the passing of a sex goddess; the event signaled the end of dangerous curves and soft-shoulders. Bottle blondes Kim Novak, Mamie Van Doren, and Jayne Mansfield were tossed into the dumpster, along with black lace negligees, garter belts and stiletto heels. The new American woman was Audrey Hepburn, a swan-necked, bag-of-bones, draped in sack dresses. The gaunt, waif-look – Twiggy, Mia Farrow, Jean 'The Shrimp' Shrimpton – became en vogue. These were hard times for Frederick's of Hollywood, flaccid for the rest of us. We were forced to retreat to the 50s Bettie Page. Our appetite for sexual fantasy was satisfied by the arrival of "I Am Curious, Yellow" and a wave of "blue films" imported from Sweden, opening the floodgates to a tsunami of porno.

Our new show at the Camelot with the Delicates was much funnier – we had several cast members who were dead-ringers for celebrities and so we staged a series of sight-gags of famous people twisting – a stone-faced Keely Smith twisting with a manic Louis Prima; Eddie Fisher strangling an Elizabeth Taylor, a three-foot-tall Joey Dee; and Laurel & Hardy twisting to their theme-song, "The Waltz of the Cuckoos." It was a riot!

Merv Griffin and his producer, Bob Shay, became regulars - Merv was a nocturnal soul and lived nearby. At the Camelot, Merv sat quietly each night at the rear of the club with our chaperone Mama Jo, Denise's mother. "He just loved the show, but we talked about a lot of things," she recalled, "He was interested in my life, impressed that I was there every night, watching over the girls. He said I was a good mom. Merv was great company, very handsome and kind. Years later, I realized who he was, the great Merv Griffin, and I couldn't get over it."

Merv would phone me at the club after our last show around 3am, to pick up a few of his favorite Danish pastries from The Brasserie and join him at the piano in his eastside townhouse, gossiping. Merv was one of the good guys. Just a year earlier, Merv hosted his own rock 'n' roll show, "NBC Saturday Prom," with big names, a big budget, and small ratings. At the time, Merv was the host of a popular daytime game show, "Play Your Hunch," broadcast live from NBC Studio 6B, which had also been converted to the new nighttime home of Jack Paar's Tonight Show. One afternoon, Paar took an unintentional shortcut through the studio right onto the stage of Merv's live broadcast. The impromptu encounter between Merv and Jack was so entertaining that Jack invited Merv into his little circle, electing him guest host, beginning what was to become Merv Griffin's long and successful legacy as a talk show host. During an appearance on "The Clay Cole Show," Merv sat in on my interview with Latin bandleader Johnny Pacheco, chatting on about his new dance hit, "The Pachanga," when suddenly in the middle of the interview, I simply went blank. Dead air. Merv jumped in and saved me. Merv was never at a loss for words, but he became a successful talk show host, not by talking, but by listening. Merv listened – another lesson learned. When Merv retired as host of "Play Your Hunch," he recommended me to producers Goodson-Todman as his replacement. Merv is also the one who introduced me to his clothier, Andrew Pallack, manufacturer of high-end haberdashery, and for the next six years at each of the four seasons, I was outfitted in the most luxurious wardrobe – sports jackets, suits, tuxedos, and topcoats embellished with Andrew Pallack's lush, paisley-patterned silk lining and matching breast-pocket handkerchief. In the grand family tradition of hand-me-downs, my elegant ensembles were passed down each season to my younger brothers Jim and Rick back home. The night before we closed at The Camelot, Bobby, the bartender, admired my blue star-sapphire ring, given to me by Abe Margolis, rewarding our success at The Brooklyn Paramount, and asked if he could wear it. The next night, when I returned to The Camelot, Bobby was gone. "Oh, Bobby left us, to work up in the Catskill Mountains for the summer. Didn't he tell you?"

Our next gig was to be an adventure – a week at Harmon Air Force Base in far-off Newfoundland, Canada. We each dashed to our Rand-McNally's in search of this 'No- Man's Land' – "oh my gawd, it's half-way to Europe." We were set for three nightly shows, first for the enlisted men, then for the non-commissioned officers and a formal event at the Officer's Club for the Commanders and their wives. Being so far away, the Department of Defense provided a roster of entertainment for the airmen – the Ink Spots were just finishing a week and the Drifters were to follow us.

We were in high spirits when we boarded our Air Canada flight; it was June 2, 1962, Denise's eighteenth birthday. By now, Mama Jo was one of the gang, so I bought her a ticket and she became our designated driver. The week that followed altered our lives forever. When the fourteen of us finally retuned home, we were traumatized by the horrific events that unfolded over that week. Each of us were so badly wounded that the scars still have not healed to this day.

We settled into our rooms in the Visiting Officer's Quarters, and all seemed to be going well, except we neglected to claim our bamboo "limbo pole" at the baggage area. "No big deal," I told them, sweeping away their anxiety, "we'll cut up a broom handle." The visiting officer's barracks was simply a long hallway of connecting single bedrooms. As we returned from our final performance (and our best show ever, with the officers and their wives), we were rousted out into the hallway by a contingent of Royal Canadian Mounted Police and Air Force Military Police. It seems a loud quarrel had erupted the day before and the subject of marijuana came up, loud enough to be overheard by two visiting Colonels in the adjoining room. Our rooms were searched and they found a small bag of a grassy substance. We were all arrested for transporting an illegal controlled substance into the boarders of Canada and onto a federal military base, a very serious offense.

We were taken to RCMP headquarters, into a cement-block cellar room in a scene from "Midnight Express" and vigorously grilled by detectives. Denise and Peggy were terrified, just eighteen, on the road, out of the country, at the end of the earth – in bleak, desolate Newfoundland of all God-forsaken places. Unbelievably, the police were particularly harsh and sarcastic to Mama Jo. Not wanting the Capris or the Delicates to be incriminated, I lied, pleading that the marijuana was mine. Meanwhile, pending an investigation, we were held under house arrest, our Air Canada flights home were cancelled.

In New York, Roz Ross reached out to the powerful New York attorney, Mort Farber, who telephoned high-ranking officials at Parliament in Ottawa, pleading in our defense. This apparently did not impress the local authorities or the Military Police – one from each of our three groups were placed under arrest pending trial. The remaining eleven of us were free to return home, vindicated, but harassed unmercifully by the Mounties and the MP's. A 'M.A.T.S.' flight home depended on availability, and days later when we finally were put on a flight, we sat on the floor, military style. At McGuire Air Force Base in New Jersey, the MP's performed another thorough search of our possessions – as if we were smuggling drugs *out* of Canada! No, this was simply to taunt us, to make us "show-people" squirm. Raysa had arranged five limousines to meet us upon arrival, a flight that was six hours late. Raysa and five chauffeurs waited patiently outside, meters ticking; the appearance of the six luxury cars seemed to make our handler's more hostile. We were just kids; and so were they. The limos weren't meant as a showy extravagance; I just wanted my humiliated troopers to return home in comfort and with some dignity.

Meanwhile, three members of our troop, one from each group, were locked up, separated, alone in cells for seventeen days. One musician lost 15 pounds. The interrogations were brutal. "They would shout at us and bang the table with a baton, purposely nearly-missing our fingers. It was so dismal. When it came time for our trial, they drove us down this long, dreary road, it was so ugly; and it was scary."

Keep in mind, this was the early 60s when the possession of marijuana was considered a very serious offense; in Canada it carried a mandatory year-and-a-half prison sentence. The Justice was unsympathetic in his denouncement of their actions, but lenient in his decision. The three were to be set free, but barred from entering Canada for two years – as if any would ever return! They were restricted to the base under house arrest until family members came to claim them.

Back home, each family dealt with this incident in different ways, but most blamed it on show business. Some parents forbid their children to continue performing; some members simply quit in disgust, defeated. Many did not speak to one another for years. I never heard from any of them for decades. This episode wiped out all my savings, the payments for the limos alone were in the thousands. I was also faced with upcoming bookings, commitments we were unable to fulfill. I was forced to make financial settlements with each of the promoters who had booked and advertised our now-cancelled shows. I was broke, in debt, off TV and out of work – but at least I didn't have to endure the humiliation that those three innocent kids had suffered. I was a free man.

It wasn't until many years later, as I was writing this book, that I learned some truths. When the tests on the marijuana came back from the labs in Ottawa, the results were negative. The bag of contraband contained oregano. None of our groups ever brought marijuana onto the military base.

Lou Dana and the Furies regrouped in 1963 with a Liberty Record deal; the Capris continued with just two original members; the Delicates, still clutching their rosary beads, were rewarded – Peg was made an Angel; she joined the group in 1963 on "My Boyfriend's Back," and Denise became a favorite session singer of producer Charles Calello with the Four Seasons, Lou Christie, Connie Francis, Al Martino and others.

And, about that hollowed-out, bamboo, limbo pole, (an ingenious hidey-hole to stash weed) forgotten at the baggage claim area at the St John's Airport – let's just hope that no one ever declared it.

I was having no luck getting back onto television. Over at the William Morris Agency, Roz Ross abruptly departed to the West Coast to head-up Dick Clark Enterprises; she simply vanished, never to resurface again. With Roz Ross gone, I was left to the mercy of agents in the television department who had no special loyalty to me. I was sent on dozens of coast-to-coast trips, dropped into the lap of West Coast agents who considered me an annoying intrusion. I sat by the phone in my room at the Beverly Hills Hotel, waiting for audition calls that never materialized. I begged for a meeting with Nat Lefkowitz, head of the New York office, whining to him that his office was not producing results. I was not getting work. "I'll get right back to you, son" was his promise. When an agent calls you "son," it's the old brush-off: "Don't call us. We'll call you." I never heard from him again. I quit William Morris.

The whole downward spiral of events quickly obliterated the momentum my career had taken. I was suddenly a man without a show. I missed the clout, the influence, the power my show had bestowed on me, and I missed the respect of my fellow performers. When I lost my show, I felt detached, with no self-worth. I avoided all my friends, not answering the phone. I lost touch with Mick & Rick, Pat & Pete, Merv Griffin, Georgia Winters and Connie De Nave; I felt irrelevant. I distanced myself from Mom and Dad, Edna and "Uncle" Clay. I discontinued my visits with Dr. Cohen. I began to drink heavily.

I commiserated with Jordan Christopher, another unhappy young man, an aspiring musician and singer who also came from Youngstown to seek his fame and fortune in Manhattan. Jordan sat on my couch, with his head in his hands, weeping over his predicament. Jordan's sexual fantasies were preoccupied by older women – *much* older women, ones you might find at The Inner Circle, an East Side hangout for single seniors. The pull was too great; he couldn't stay away from that place. Jordan's story couldn't have had a happier ending. A few years later he was booked to perform at Arthur, the discotheque owned by Sybil Burton, the woman scorned by Richard Burton for Elizabeth Taylor. Rich. Glamorous. Connected. And in her prime. Their marriage was mutually rewarding, his most-secret fantasies enriched in a most noble way. I could not see a happy ending in my future. The two hardest things to handle are success and failure.

My stature as "that sophisticated, handsome young man on TV" diminished, one day at a time. I swallowed a bottle of aspirin honestly believing it would kill me. Raysa found me unconscious, lying on my living room floor. Raysa awakened Dr. Cohen, who cautioned her not to allow me to sleep, but keep me conscious with black coffee and non-stop walking. Raysa lifted me into her arms and walked me throughout the night. The clock was not ticking in my favor. The memory of my glory days was blurring, becoming as grainy and snowy as a fading picture tube. By now the money was all gone, I was broke. I took a job behind the counter at Cobb's Corner, a twenty-four hour java joint, next to the Taft Hotel, working the night shift, serving one-dollar mugs of coffee to drooling junkies. Cobb's Corner called out to disoriented tourists trolling Times Square in search of flapjacks and a cup of coffee. But on the swing shift, at the midnight hour, the bright lights at-tracted poor lost souls, like moths to a flame. The constant buzz of the neon was maddening, but seemed to lull the all-night stoners into a comatose silence. It was the perfect hideaway for an incognito celebrity counterman. On the few occasions

I was recognized, I'd whisper, "shush, we're filming "Candid Camera." Some were fooled; others would feel so heartbroken they would leave me a 50-cent tip for a cup of coffee. That was a low point.

For a few hours each Saturday mornings, I was, at least temporarily, back in the music business. I was one of a gang of part-timers, paid $25 by *Billboard* magazine, to pull together a list of the best-selling singles from record shop owners all across America. This information was vital input to the committee of editors who assembled the all-important Billboard Hot 100, the lifeblood from which the record industry lives or dies.

I somehow pulled myself together, returning to The Gateway Playhouse, where I was paid EQUITY scale, but more importantly, provided a comfortable room and three meals a day. I was performing in "Bye, Bye Birdie" at night, while rehearsing "The Music Man" in the daytime, fueled by martinis.

I awoke from the hangover in 1963 when Mal Bailey from RKO-General, Channel 9 threw me a life raft, offering me three summertime specials, "The Teenage Fair," to be broadcast live from Freedomland, a developer's attempt to create a theme park in the Bronx. The Bronx *was* a theme park. But for me, in the summer of 1963, it was the Promised Land. "The Teenage Fair" ignited the ole' razzle-dazzle in me – another Battle of the Bands, another Miss Teen Pageant, and a fresh crop of new faces needing the big buildup, all dutifully photographed and splashed across the pages of New York's seven newspapers. I was back in action. It was reassuring to slap on my Max Factor Tan No. 2, slip into my dinner jacket, and become *Claycole* once again.

Little did I know then, my greatest success was still ahead.

Cash Box magazine, December 8, 1962

A group of 36 teen time deejays, representing a disk advisory council, had selected 30 vinyl albums for a *"Basic Pop Album Library for Teenagers."* The deejays, polled by *Ingénue,* a teen magazine, made their choices on the basis of "enduring enjoyment." Here's the total line-up of the purposely limited list of 30 LPs, with several "tied" positions:

MALE VOCALISTS
1. "Elvis's Golden Records," Elvis Presley (RCA Victor)
2. "Songs For Swingin' Lovers," Frank Sinatra (Capitol)
3. "Modern Sounds in Country & Western Music," Ray Charles (ABC Paramount)
4. "Pat's Great Hits," Pat Boone (Dot)
5. "Moon River," Andy Williams (Columbia)
5. "Roses Are Red," Bobby Vinton (Epic)
6. "Paul Anka Sings His Big 15," Paul Anka (ABC Paramount)
6. "Johnny's Greatest Hits," Johnny Mathis (Columbia)
7. "Your Twist Party," Chubby Checker (Parkway)
8. "Ramblin' Rose," Nat "King" Cole (Capitol)

FEMALE VOCALISTS
1. "Connie Francis' Greatest Hits," Connie Francis (MGM)
2. "Sincerely Brenda Lee," Brenda Lee (Decca)
2. "The Great Gershwin Song Book," Ella Fitzgerald (Verve)
3. "Judy At Carnegie Hall," Judy Garland (Capitol)

VOCAL GROUPS
1. "The Kingston Trio," The Kingston Trio (Capitol)
2. "A Song For Young Love," The Lettermen (Capitol)
3. "Something Wonderful," Ray Charles Singers (Command)
3. "Sing Along With Mitch," Mitch Miller (Columbia)
3. "Encore Of Golden Hits," The Platters (Mercury)
3. "Down By The Station," The Four Preps (Capitol)

ORCHESTRA / INSTRUMENTALS
1, "'S Continental," Ray Conniff (Columbia)
2. "Young World," Lawrence Welk (Dot)
3. "Happy Hunting," Hugo Winterhalter (RCA Victor)
3. "Goodies But Gassers," Jimmy Dorsey (Epic)
3. "If The Big Bands Were Here Today," Bernie Lowe (Cameo)
4. "Ooooo!" Jackie Gleason (Capitol)

SHOWS / FILMS / SOUNDTRACKS
1. "West Side Story," Soundtrack (Columbia)
1. "Sound Of Music," Percy Faith (Columbia)
1. "Sound Pacific," Soundtrack (RCA Victor)
2. "My Fair Lady," Original. Cast (Columbia)

12) WPIX-TV

The music business is a cruel and shallow money trench,
a long plastic hallway where thieves and pimps run free,
and good men die like dogs. There's also a negative side.
– *Hunter S. Thompson*

When the news broke that I was returning to television, I was greeted with a welcome from *NY Daily News* writer George Maksian: "Will someone please tell Clay Cole that rock 'n' roll is dead." Comatose maybe; but hardly dead. George might have been right had he predicted the end of rock 'n' roll as we *knew* it. In a single year the music world would change forever; nothing would be the same again.

What *is* rock 'n' roll? Alan Freed may have named it, but he played rhythm and blues. Early Elvis was country rockabilly. The Orioles were a cappella. Chubby was pop. The Kingston Trio was folk. By 1963, rock 'n' roll simply became any genre of music embraced by teenagers. 1963 was to be a pivotal year, the great dividing line between everything that came before, and everything that came later. In 1963, we inhaled our last breath of fresh clean air from the Age of Innocence before the napalm-soaked, ozone-layered, drug-induced, tangerine-colored, sexual Sixties came crashing down on us. Rock 'n' roll was about to become Rock! I was a witness, not a co-conspirator.

In 1963, New York was still the epicenter of the music business, but, on the heels of network television, a shift to the West Coast was imminent. Producer Phil Spector also returned to L.A. with secrets absorbed from producers Lieber & Stoller and all the Brill Building songwriters. Beach Boy Brian Wilson says that he was "inspired by Phil Spector," but greatly appalled by his so-called 'layer of sound'."

Wilson was inclined to compose more simplistic, four-part anthems to the surf and car culture, with lyrical images of California as a teenage paradise. Brian was an inspired composer, but a lousy surfer; he attempted one wave, was knocked clean and never got on a board again. But the aura was good, the harmonies were brilliant.

I had no problem playing catch up, since little had changed since I left the scene. In the early Sixties, Sh-Boomers were lulled into a retro period, rewinding old song formulas, reworking tired trends. "Answer songs" abounded: "Save The Last Dance for Me" was answered by a predictable, "I'll Save the Last Dance for You" (Damita Jo). In August, 1962, JoAnn Campbell released one of the best-selling answer records, "I'm The Girl from Wolverton Mountain," as an answer to Claude King's "Wolverton Mountain." There was also a glut of death-themed songs, involving horrific crashes with angelic images reuniting in a teenage heaven.

In 1963, we were also in the midst of yet another "folk music" revival, with countless acoustic trios blowing fresh wind into the sails of long-forgotten sea shanties. Peter, Paul & Mary, the Chad Mitchell Trio and the Limelighters gained visibility by a new television jamboree, "Hootenanny," an ABC primetime hour, broadcast each week from a different collage campus. But, on the horizon there was a modern urban folk-style, being created by the young Bleecker Street troubadours at the Gaslight, Gerde's Folk City and the Bitter End – Harry Chapin, Jim Croce, Jake Holmes, Melanie and Richie Havens. Television, my show among others, introduced them to a wider mainstream audience.

I drove up to Rhode Island for the Newport Folk Festival, a weekend dominated by predictable old-timers Woody Guthrie, Rambling Jack Elliott and Pete Seeger. The fresh new face of the folk movement was Joan Baez, a singer-songwriter with three albums on the charts and a *Time* magazine cover. That summer, Joan Baez was dragging around an awkward, intensely shy teenage hippie-boy who she'd prop up and introduce to anyone with a kind ear and a backstage pass. She even brought him onstage during her set and it was a scraggly Bob Dylan who appeared, mumbling a couple of unremarkable tunes. Dylan's appearance was uneventful; the audience was polite but unmoved.

It was also in 1963 that Sam Katzman produced Hollywood's most bizarre movie musical, "Hootenanny Hoot," a hokey folk-fest featuring boyish Johnny Cash, Sheb Wooley and the Brothers Four. It was a hoot all right and a camp classic – the film that finally put the lid on the never-ending folk revivals. It would be another two years before Bob Dylan would emerge as the leading voice of the folk-protest movement, the Byrds would introduce folk-rock, and Joan Baez would abandon traditional folk songs for "protest rock," a groove that became her rut and her ultimate demise.

1963 also produced a flurry of film stars as singers: Anthony Perkins, Sal Mineo, and Connie Stevens all had hits. "The Rifleman" Johnny Crawford and the two teen stars of "The Donna Reed Show," Shelley Fabares and Paul Petersen, appeared with hit singles. James Darren, with his movie star good looks and soothing baritone, could have been one of Dick Clark's Bandstand Boys had he not signed a Columbia Pictures contact, leaving Philadelphia for Hollywood and starring with Sandra Dee in "Gidget." "Dr Kildare" (Richard Chamberlain) and Dr "Ben Casey" (Vince Edwards), network television's dueling doctors, each recorded LP's. Vince Edwards even appeared at The Copa; his engaging bedside manner failed to transcend ringside.

WPIX-TV, Channel 11 in New York City is best known for its Christmas Yule Log,[7] a film-loop of a burning hearth, filmed at Gracie Mansion in Manhattan, designed to transform cold-water flats into Currier & Ives homesteads. The WPIX broadcasts of New York Yankee baseball were innovative and polished, yet so removed from their hackneyed studio productions that it seemed they patched into a creative unit by mistake.

Under the ubiquitous green shadow of Daily News Publisher, Capt. Joseph Patterson, Channel 11 was an Irish enclave, a satellite of Hell's Kitchen, the midtown neighborhood settled by Celtic immigrants – the strappingly longshoremen who labor the Hudson River piers, the ornery matrons who ushered the Broadway theatres and the Westies, a murderous gang of street thugs. Somehow, they also managed a hell-of-a St. Patrick's Day parade.

Channel 11 produced shows for toddlers, vintage film clip shows introduced by middle-aged Irishmen, "Captain" Jack McCarthy, the Merry Mailman, Ray Heatherton (Joey Heatherton's daddy) and Chuck McCann. Chuck hosted the most ambitious, innovative kiddies' show with puppet master Paul Ashley backstage pulling the strings. Two more Irishmen, news anchors Kevin McCarthy and John Tillman relinquished their small, tenth-floor studios to me on weekends, having determined that there was no news on Saturday or Sunday worth reporting. Channel 11 had just one studio, undersized and uninviting, with two closet-sized dressing rooms. Guests to the studio were ushered through a maze of bleak hallways lined with scuffed, yellowing linoleum, looking very much like San Quentin's

---

7   WPIX began programming the burning Yule log on Christmas Day, 1966, with a soundtrack of Christmas classics. Surprisingly, the ratings went up the chimney and through the roof. The Tribune Company syndicated the filmed clip and it has become a perennial holiday favorite.

last-mile to the gas chambers, a dreary corridor that led straight to the studio. It was here we would make magic for the next five years.

To provide a more hospitable mood for our staff, crew and guests, I borrowed an idea from Jan Murray's "Treasure Hunt" playbook and personally paid for coffee urns, bagels, donuts, and Danish; a standing order to be delivered to our studios for the next five years. To the kids in the studio audience we provided Nathan's franks or Chicken Delight dinners.

Channel 11 envisioned a teenage talk show with comedy and music, briefly calling it "The Young World of Clay Cole," with Chuck McCann as my announcer-sidekick. Chuck was an imposing 6-foot-3, 300-pound comedy whiz kid, much-loved by fans who remember him as Little Orphan Annie, in a red-dress, yellow fright wig and two white saucer eyes. Videotape was new and Chuck was perfecting amazing stunts, creating a character called Mr. Backwards who moved in rewind.

When I arrived, there was no production or programming department; Walter Engels, the news director, was in charge. Chet Dowling was to be my producer. I had known Chet at WJAR-TV in Providence, and it was he who had been instrumental in bringing me to WPIX. But first, a pilot had to be produced for the approval of Fred Thrower, Channel 11's general manager and chief leprechaun.

Chet Dowling and Chuck McCann huddled on the comedy surprises; my task was to book a guest star worthy enough not to tarnish the station brass. I called in a favor and asked Bobby Darin to appear on the pilot, a show taped for presentation purposes only, one that would never be televised. Bobby could not have been more agreeable; he appeared and based on the pilot, we got the go-ahead to begin the show in October, the start of the 1963 television season. Meanwhile, Channel 11 arranged for my return to Freedomland in the Bronx, for a late-night summer variety series, "Clay Cole at the Moon Bowl," an outdoor dance pavilion.

Our first show, July 20, 1963, featured Joey Dee, with special guest star Bobby Darin, this time *live*. The show opened with Jay & the Americans high on a rooftop, surrounded by a forest of flapping American flags, singing "Only in America." Visually, it was stunning and set the tone for more sizzling, summer Saturday nights ahead – *live* from Freedomland. Along with an all-star line-up of record stars, each Saturday show featured a big band for dancing under the stars; Count Basie ("April In Paris"); Jimmy Dorsey ("So Rare"); and Warren Covington with the Tommy Dorsey Orchestra ("Tea For Two Cha Cha"). Archie Bleyer, Bob Booker, and Earl Dowd gave us access to their hot new comedy star, Vaughn Meader (as JFK) and cast members from "The First Family," the blockbuster spoof on the Camelot presidency and the Kennedy clan. (10-million copies were sold, a milestone for a comedy album.)

It was during the summer of 1963 that I almost got hooked on amphetamines. After a routine visit to my doctor, he advised me to "lose a couple of pounds," handing me several envelops of pills, "and come back once a week for a weigh-in." The pills looked about as non-threatening as jelly-beans, a colorful assortment, green ones after breakfast, rainbow colors at lunch, pink ones at night, all carefully prescribed, but without one word of warning.

Now, it just so happened, I had a prior commitment, a week at the Steel Pier in Atlantic City, so I had arranged for Jack Jones to host the TV show in my absence. I drove down to Atlantic City in time for rehearsals and to meet Mike Clifford ("Close To Cathy"), the singing star for the week, then return to my hotel cocktail lounge for a relaxing martini. I remembered the diet pills, so I swallowed the prescribed handful, washing them down with gin and vermouth, and settled back for a quiet happy hour. I suddenly began to feel a rush of euphoria, a free and happy sensation, with unusual energy. I was unexpectedly cheerful and talkative. I was chatting away with a suddenly stimulating bartender when a sweet-looking, gray-haired old lady, who was sitting at a table with her twelve-year-old grandson, recognized me. I bought them rounds of drinks and joined them at their table. We three became instant best friends. I was unusually fascinated in all the details of their lives, I found myself exchanging phone numbers, perhaps we should all get together back in the city – a sixty-something grandmother and a twelve-year-old child? I was suddenly a witty, chatty extrovert. This was good stuff; I never missed a "weigh-in."

To manage my finances, I took on a business manager, Marty Bregman, an insurance salesman who, on the side, handled the affairs of just three other clients, actors Sandy Dennis, Elliott Gould and his new bride, Barbra Streisand. All my earnings went directly to Marty's office and his staff paid all my monthly bills. I opened a house account with "Louie" at the deli and at my drug store, dry cleaner, liquor store, and The Four Seasons restaurant. I received a $100 weekly pocket money and a Diner's Club credit card.

My move to Channel 11 also called for a change of address, a spacious apartment at 315 East 70th Street, ($200 a month), convenient to Second Avenue, within minutes of the WPIX Plaza in the art deco Daily News Building at 42nd Street. Marty Bregman had "an uncle in the carpet business," so off I went to ABC Carpet to purchase – at a deep discount – plush, Royal Blue wall-to-wall carpet, with a liner thick as a Belgian waffle. "Buy wholesale, never retail" was the Manhattan mantra. Floating on this massive sea of Royal Blue was my new king-sized bed, a TV set, and a plastic potted palm, a gift from Connie DeNave. That was it.

Walter Winchell wrote in *The N.Y. Mirror:* "Clay Cole hates cats and dogs, but has thirteen canaries in his apartment."

I neither disliked cats or dogs, nor did I own birds, but my doorman reported that he discovered a gaggle of girls on the ninth floor, listening for birdcalls, trying to locate my apartment.

"The Young World of Clay Cole" debuted at 6:30-7:30 on Saturday, October 5, 1963 with guests Steve Allen, Jane Meadows, and one of Steve's "Man On The Street" comics, Dayton Allen — as it turned out, the one Steve liked least — and two hot-looking Philadelphia ladies, Dee Dee Sharp ("Mashed Potato Time") and Diane Renay ("Navy Blue"), plus a young Texan, Jimmy Gilmer, who's "Sugar Shack" had been No.1 for five weeks. The Four Seasons, now the hottest vocal group in America, stood together up on the roof of The Daily News building, performing "Sherry" in the twilight of the Manhattan skyline. Chuck McCann was photographed upside-down in close-up, lip-synching the novelty hit, "On Top Of Spaghetti." (Tom Glazer)

The Daily News described it, "As a Steve Allen-type show — with growing pains. If youth must be served, Clay Cole is the boy to do it." It began as a talk show with an emphasis on youthful, musical guests, and young people with fresh ideas. Mod-designer Betsey Johnson introduced far-out fashions; the newly-arrived British hair stylist Vidal Sassoon reshaped heads; black-belt Aaron Banks crushed cement blocks with barehanded karate chops; and Chef Dragon demonstrated Yin Yang cooking ("His restaurant must be good; all the Chinese truck drivers stop there.") We introduced psychics, a fortuneteller, palm reader, numerologist and horoscope chart reader, (all of whom true to form, predicted a bright future for me) and an elfin singer explaining the difference between midgets and dwarfs: "We all just want to be called Little People." I sang a duet with Ron Dante, the Staten Island heartbreaker making his first television appearance, who, in 1969 would see two of his recordings reach the Top 10 on the exact same week — "Tracy" as the Cufflinks and "Sugar, Sugar" as the Archies, in the No. 1 spot. Dante sang lead and then overdubbed all the parts, but remained anonymous on both tracks. Then there was my new favorite brassy blond Lillian Briggs, a former truck driver from Pittsburgh, who played slide trombone, while singing the breathless, long-winded, "I Want You to Be My Baby." It was the appearance of my NBC Page buddy and former roommate Joey Rogers, (now as Joey Powers), singing his top of the pops "(Meet

Me At) Midnight Mary," that momentarily overshadowed a jolt of catastrophic, tragic breaking-news.

November 23, 1963, America's youngest-ever President was assassinated. We raced to the studio control room in shock, frozen in disbelief as the dozens of television monitors fed us *live* images from the streets of Dallas. First on the scene was reporter Sid Davis, my friend and former news anchor at WKBN-TV in Youngstown, unraveling the mounting, heartbreaking events. All regularly scheduled programs were cancelled.

I sat home alone on my Royal Blue carpet, watching the events unfold, *live*, on television. Skitch Henderson hastily assembled the NBC symphony orchestra in Studio 8-H to play reverential musical interludes between breaking news, counterpoint to the drumming cadence and the clomp-clomp-clomp of hoof beats, as the funeral procession passed a black veiled Jackie and a memorable salute from little John-John. On Sunday, I drove aimlessly through the deserted expressways and side streets of the Bronx, trying to blur the television images. Folks in the Bronx, like the rest of the world, were home, behind locked doors, frozen in disbelief, as events unfolded in black and white on their television screens. A shocked nation was united in mourning.

When production resumed, Chet Dowling, my link to creativity had departed, moving on to more lucrative assignments. Chet appeared one afternoon behind the counter of my neighborhood dry cleaning store, deeply engrossed with a customer.

"Chet," I interrupted, astonished, "what are you doing here?"

He gave me one of those "oh-geese, you blew-it" looks, as a clearly pissed camera crew materialized from behind the hanging laundry.

"We're filming Candid Camera!" – but, they really were.
Five years later, Chet appeared on the credit roll of "Laugh-In," as one of their inspired comedy writers.

I am not an aggressive person; I am not capable of violence. I dislike confrontations of any kind. Therefore, I never expected I'd see my picture on page 2 of *The New York Post,* under the headline:

Clay Cole Arrested In Times Square Brawl

What made it all so laughable was the picture, a boyishly innocent Bruno of Hollywood publicity shot of me in a white tennis sweater. "Tennis anyone? *Punch in the mouth?*"

Here's the story: I had been sent by William Morris to audition for an on-camera appearance in a Wrigley's commercial, singing the gum jingle ("*You'll love Doublemint Gum, Double-mint, Double-mint, Double-mint gum*"). I won the part and filmed the commercial, singing and dancing aboard a yacht with my Double-mint twin, a girl named Bonnie. My plan was to celebrate with a few drinks at the Peppermint Lounge over on 45th Street. It was a sunny, late-afternoon summer day, but the block was unusually crowded and I was suddenly mobbed by groups of fans. It was a friendly crowd; I was shaking hands, posing for pictures, signing autographs when a police officer suddenly appeared, ordering the crowd to disperse, and then whacking me on the temple with his baton. In a flash, I was lying flat on my back on the sidewalk, blood squirting profusely from a laceration over my left eye. My summer seersucker jacket was soaked in blood; the whole scene looked like the St. Valentine's Day massacre, a bloody mess.

Before I could even reconcile what had just happened, the block erupted with the honking horns and whirring sirens of emergency vehicles, ambulances, a fleet of police cars, and press photographers, flashbulbs popping. Where did they all come from? How did they respond so soon? It was chaos. I was handcuffed, arrested and hauled off to a holding cell for mug shots and fingerprints, charged with striking a police officer, at a time when violence against cops was escalating. I could never strike a police officer; this officer was black. His claim was that I had struck him, tripped over a fire stanchion and hit my head falling against a brick wall.

My friend Jay Fontana, now Murray the K's right-hand man, heard the bulletins on the radio; WINS was pumping it up as their lead story on each half-hour news break. The rock 'n' roll radio stations were relishing the news. First, Jay called the stations and begged them to lay-off the story, then rushed over to Midtown South to bail me out.

I was called on the carpet the next morning, summoned into the inner sanctum of Fred Thrower, Channel 11's general manager. Assuming I was going to receive support from my new boss, I was at a loss to understand why he presumed that I was guilty, a street-brawling thug. He put me on the defensive, reprimanding me for my bad conduct and my suspension would be based on a report from the high-powered law firm of Townley, Updike, Carter and Rogers.

Obviously, I was not guilty; several months and $10,000 later we proved it. 45th Street was mobbed that afternoon and many eyewitnesses came forward in my defense Crime scene photographs of the stanchion and brick wall were produced, illustrating that a trip and fall would have been impossible. The officer had been a rookie, his first night on congested 45th Street, so he was nervous and panicked. I testified that I did not believe the officer meant to hit me, although it happened so quickly I cannot be sure. The baton dangling from his wrist, may have struck me accidentally as he came at me. New information also came to light; the officer was once a postman fired from the postal service for destroying, rather than delivering mail, a fact that had been overlooked in the pre-screening scrutiny at the NYPD Police Academy. Not wishing to embarrass the police department and based on the evidence, the judge ordered an acquittal.

There was one moment in the three-day trial that touched me deeply. Eli Landau, the Chairman of Channel 13, my former boss, asked to testify on my behalf as a character witness. If only Fred Thrower, my new boss at Channel 11, possessed such dignity.

On Christmas weekend 1963, the WMCA Good Guys began playing "I Want to Hold Your Hand," with spirited vocals from a new British quartet called the Beatles.

The arrival of Beatlemania might have signaled a kiss of death to American pop stars, the New York, Italian-American white-boy a cappella groups and their R&B brothers. The coming blitz of Boy Bands might have put them out of business, if not for the advent of Doo Wop.

Dion defined doo wop in an *Elmore* magazine interview: "Doo wop is total street music, the original rap, the original rock 'n' roll music. We didn't have instruments on the street, we didn't even need a street; we did it anywhere."

In 1957, Dion and the Belmonts gathered in his parent's three-room Bronx apartment to sing "Teenager in Love," popularizing the form. Dion reflected, "When I look back, it was a very defining moment to do "I Wonder Why" in my house. I invited the best doo wop singers from the neighborhood – we were sixteen and seventeen years old – and we invented this thing. To be in the middle of that sound at sixteen was totally mind-blowing. I thought I was in heaven. I believe that if you make music that's undeniable, it will probably reach your heart."

But by 1963, the dominate Italian-American vocal harmony groups, the Belmonts, the Duprees, Elegants, Earls, Vito & the Salutations, Randy & the Rainbows and the rest of the so-called "old town music" boys were all losing sleep. The boys began playing musical chairs: Jay Traynor left Jay and the Americans, who then regrouped with Jay Black (David Blatt); the Tokens turned to producing and writing advertising jingles; Johnny Maestro stepped away from the Crests and joined the Del Satins. One group, consisting of the Mystics, Videls, Tradewinds, Passions and the Classics seemed to morph into one – even Paul Simon and Jay Traynor briefly sang lead with the Mystics. The new Mystics borrowed matching brown suits to perform on our show, then returned the very next week as the Videls, the same five guys, in the same brown suits. A cappella angst was setting-in. They were about to be resurrected by a simple tag – doo wop.

A white New York radio disc-jockey, Gus Gossart was the first person I ever heard use (and spell) the phrase "Doo Wopp" to describe 50s a cappella/vocal harmony groups. In the late Sixties, doo wop groups became the centerpiece of Gossart's stage shows and front and center in countless "golden oldies revival shows," most notably Richard Nader's two-decades of sold-out shows at Madison Square Garden, the first in 1969. Doo Wop today is no longer just an urban phenomenon; the genre became a nationwide sensation in – of all places – PBS, on pledge week programs produced by T. J. Lubinsky. Like pooper scoopers and bottled water, doo wop is now everywhere. It's a sound that was popular long before two-thirds of Americans were even born, but sold-out crowds of all ages turn out to hear music from this first era of rock and roll. At last vocal harmony groups were brought back to life, with a niche and their own subgenre – doo wop!

Doo Wop and Beach Music (the Shag) were career-savers, giving the pre-Beatles groups a new life and a lifetime annuity.

The Shag is a dance – laid-back Southern swing that has its roots in beach bars and spread like kudzu up and down the Southeastern coastline in the 60s. Influenced by jazz, blues and gospel music, the Shag originated in black nightclubs of the 1940s and '50s, and was danced to R&B music. Young white dancers crossed racial boundaries by going to the clubs to watch, then took the dance to the old Myrtle Beach Pavilion. The Shag was inspired by the 4/4 blues shuffle of the Coasters, Platters and Drifters ("Under the Boardwalk"), and became known as "Beach Music." Black groups suddenly found a whole new audience as well, a subculture of southern white kids at the very moment the 1964 Civil Rights Act became law. Also in 1964, popular black groups began to multiply; suddenly there were two sets of Drifters, Coasters, and Platters, second-generation members and outright imposters in matching green zoot suits, working the secondary markets of the South and Midwest. To illustrate the cross-fusion of doo wop and the shag, Kenny Vance and the Planotones' 2008 doo wop release, "There Goes My Baby" reached Number One on the Carolina Beach Music charts *and* nominated for Best National Dance/Shag Song of the Year.

Here is a sampling of "Beach Music"/"Shag" preferences, which could clearly double as a list of Doo Wop favorites, as well:

"Sixty Minute Man"	Billy Ward & the Dominos
"With This Ring"	The Platters
"Stand By Me"	Ben E. King
"Stay"	Maurice Williams & the Zodiacs
"Oh No Not My Baby"	Maxine Brown
"Hey! Baby"	Bruce Channel
"White Cliffs of Dover"	Mystics
"Higher and Higher"	Jackie Wilson
"It's All Right"	Impressions
"Mr. Postman"	Marvelettes

In the ensuing decades, specific shag groups emerged, like the Embers ("I like Beach Music"), Bill Deal & the Rhondells ("I've Been Hurt"), Chairmen of the Board ("Give Me Just A Little More Time") and the Tams ("What Kind of Fool Do You Think I Am"), exploiting Beach Music, keeping it alive through the decades. There is currently a "West Coast Swing" explosion among college kids, dancing the Shag at California beach bars and in completive dance-offs. Exhausted, as they might be after fifty years, folks still "shag" at the beach and beyond, and doo wop is the top fundraiser for PBS. There is a Shag Hall of Fame in Myrtle Beach, SC, and a Doo Wop Museum, in the Wildwoods, "down the shore" in NJ. A doo wop museum in Wildwood is redundant – the beach town itself is a museum, frozen in the Fifties with its cozy mid-Century modern motels, classic soda fountains and diners illuminated by pink and green neon and immortalized in Bobby Rydell's wistful summertime song "Wildwood Days."

My own wop-doo-wop Mafia also included two knock-around guys from Jersey City, teenage buddies whom everyone seemed to know, and love – Joe Pesci, and Frankie Vincent. Believe it or not, Joe and Frankie once formed a bar-band called the Aristocrats. (If you don't know the joke, rent the movie.) Frank was a skilled drummer and became a favored session musician, and Joe once recorded solo as Joe Ritchie and played guitar in local combos. Now, of course, Joe Pesci is the Oscar winning film star and Frank Vincent is the respected character actor from over fifty films and as "Phil Leotardo" in HBO's mob, "The Sopranos." Joe and Frank must have had a ball making all those wise guys movies together; Pesci whacked Vincent in two films, "GoodFellas" and "Raging Bull," but Vincent got revenge in "Casino," when he pounds Pesci with a baseball bat and buries him alive. Just like the old neighborhood. Hey, I've been to the Cat & the Fiddle Lounge. *Fuhgeddaboutit!*

"The Clay Cole Show" continued to sail buoyant through the rough waters of Channel 11. The show was a financial windfall, so successful that they were stuck with me. I was simply tolerated. But, the boredom factor had kicked-in again, and I was restless to kick-out with a new format. Enter, a new producer, Terry Bennett, a hyper young man who had gained success in Chicago as a ventriloquist. I was correct in my skepticism; you just can't trust a man who chats with himself – it's so schizophrenic. Terry had a discomforting dark side, capable of trickery, betrayal and down right lies, with me as the subject and victim.

Terry introduced a new feature to our show, a fast-paced Hellzapoppin' segment of skits, pantomimes, and comedy blackouts called "Clay's Cole Bin." The idea was to present a straightforward rock 'n' roll variety show for the first forty-five minutes, then a final ten minutes of non-stop comedy, with our guest stars participating in the bits. The idea worked because we had Chuck McCann as comedy actor, writer, stage director, and Paul Ashley with his troop of puppets, props and disguises. Terry, Chuck and I would create the bits and Paul and the stagehands would embellish with makeshift sets, props and special effects. It gave me the opportunity to show-off my abilities as a comedy actor.

The visiting artists loved it too; for the first time they could be seen performing, rather than the standard lip-synch, interview bit. Two performers, Merald 'Bubba' Knight, Gladys' brother from the Pips, and Earl 'Speedo' Carroll, lead singer of the Cadillacs, might have been reincarnated from a past life as vaudevillians; their strutting attitude was in their funny-bone. Johnny Tillotson had been on television for three years with his own show, juggling his studies at the University of Florida, until graduating with a Bachelor of Communications degree. Bobby Goldsboro toured the world for three years as guitar player for Roy Orbison, a seasoned veteran before ever cutting his first record. Bobby perfected a frog call, a throaty "rebut" sound that made us certain that tadpoles had infected our studio. Jose Feliciano also had a funny bone and proved to be natural comic actor; at nine-years-old, he was performing at the Puerto Rican Theater in the Bronx. Exposed to the rock 'n' roll of the 50s, Jose was inspired to sing, and taught himself to play guitar with nothing but records as his teacher, practicing for as many as 14 hours a day. If Ed Sullivan actually introduced Jose as, "He's blind and he's Puerto Rican," I'm sure no one appreciated the slight more than Jose himself, a man with a surprising gift of laughter. Showcasing Jose as a lounge singer in "Fargo" was a sardonic stroke of casting; believe it or not he began as a folk singer, down in the village at the Bitter End and Gerde's Folk City. We always looked forward to Jose's appearances on our show with mixed excitement and apprehension. Aside from his ever-present Seeing Eye dog, Jose always brought along a litany of shaggy dog stories – long, involved tales with the worst possible punch lines. Freddie "Boom Boom" Cannon was another delightful cuckoo-bird, riding high with "Palisades Park," a song written by game show producer, Chuck Barris. Freddie could never remember anyone's name, so he solved the dilemma by calling everyone "Chester."

In "Clay's Cole Bin" the hams were ripe for roasting: Maxine Brown appeared beautifully gowned, in a night club setting, lip-synching "Oh No Not My Baby" and we'd slow the record, distorting the song to a drone, then speed it up like the Chipmunks, without Maxine missing a beat. Lloyd Price, in close-up, starts to sing his recording of "Misty" – "Look at me…" – and pow! we'd hit him with a cream pie. Ben E. King lathered and shaved to the strokes of "Stand by Me" – "when the night (zap-stroke) comes in (zap-stroke) and the shadows fall (zap-stroke).

In 1964, when James Bond was all the rage and movie theatres were screening 007 'round the clock, I was among the late crowd, cueing-up for the 2am show. I created a suave, platinum-haired "James Blonde, Agent 0061/2" character for the "Cole Bin," complete with nonsensical high-tech gizmos. "Superman," the old black and white half-hour shows with George Reeves, was a big afternoon ratings winner on Channel 11, so I browsed the Third Avenue thrift shops, accumulating a wardrobe of wide lapelled, double-breasted suits and thick floral ties to become the mild-mannered reporter, Clark Kent. After a phone booth quick change, I would emerge in tights, padded muscles and a flapping blue cape, flying over the skyline of Manhattan as *Supermench*. In matching angora cardigans, white loafers and a sun-bleached wig, I appeared as both Jan & Dean, lip-synching "Surf City," satirizing the two bickering boys with no rhythm. In one skit, I sat at the piano in a well-furnished apartment, lip-synching Ray Charles' "I'm Busted," while a dozen uniformed repo men stripped bare the apartment, carting off all the furniture, finally the piano bench and piano, as I forged-on, undeterred.

It was a bold move for a teenage dance party to be doing *shtick*, but it worked for our young viewers, who enjoyed seeing performers not take themselves all that seriously. It also gave me a chance to perform, to poke fun at myself, and to prove I was more than "a young Dick Clark." It also inspired a second album "Clay's Cole Bin," a compilation produced by my buddy, Mickey Eichner (of Mick & Rick). Mickey asked Terry Bennett to write the liner notes, and the results were a collection of mean-spirited jabs at me, without revealing any hint that he might be poking fun.

"You'll like the music in this album." Terry wrote, "If you like Clay Cole you'll like *anything!*"

As it turned out, my Sh-Boomers had a sense of humor after all! The new format was a winner. Three years later, in 1968, "Laugh-In" signed on with the same silly idea.

In January of 1964, on a cold, drizzly, rainy Sunday afternoon, Steve Brandt, Georgia Winters' assistant at *16* magazine, threw a party at The Improvisation, Budd Friedman's modest but cheerful coffee bar over on West 44th Street, a showcase room for young actors to perform or sing new material, long before it became comedy central. Steve Brandt was becoming a powerful force as a freelance gossip columnist, infusing himself into the inner circle of show biz, so rain or not, an amazing array of young stars popped in: Hollywood's Andrew Prine, Sharon Farrell, Keir Dullea, Michael J. Pollard, Lyn Loring, Sal Mineo, Brandon De Wilde, singers Bruce Scott, Jack Jones and Neil Sedaka with his wife Leba and his song writing partner Howie Greenfield, Bob Crewe and from Broadway, Jill Haworth ("Cabaret"), Georgia Brown ("Oliver") and of course, Connie De Nave. My date, dancer Penny Kimmel and I were photographed chatting with a stunning, young blonde starlet named Sharon Tate.

A few years later, when I was visiting Hollywood, Steve Brandt invited me to the Fallacy, a seedy all-night dance club and juice bar, hanging off a cliff on the Sunset Strip. After paying the door fee, waiting for my eyes to adjust to dark, I spotted Steve, seated with a small party that included the actors Sal Mineo and Mia Farrow. "Don't talk to Mia," Steve whispered as I sat down, "she's on STP." I wouldn't think of talking to Mia Farrow, an ashen-looking waif in a granny dress, with spiked, sweaty hair. Sitting next to me was a handsome young man who I took to be an actor, but he corrected me: "my name is Jay Sebring, I'm a barber." *Barber?* Jay Sebring was the hottest celebrity hairstylist in Hollywood at that moment in time, 1968. By coincidence; I had a very disappointing hair cut from one of the stylists in his salon that very afternoon.

Within the year, Jay Sebring was murdered, along with that stunning, young blonde starlet Sharon Tate – slaughtered by the Charles Manson family. Sal Mineo was stabbed to death in a robbery attempt and Steve Brandt[8] committed suicide, a victim of the prevailing Hollywood paranoia. Of the party of five, only Mia and I survived.

---

8   Steve Brandt, 30, who became a Hollywood gossip columnist (*Photoplay*) and a close friend of actress Sharon Tate and her director husband Roman Polanski, was found dead on November 28, 1969, in his room at the Chelsea Hotel in Manhattan. In telephone conversations with friends shortly before he died, he said he was very depressed over the death of Sharon Tate and had taken "22 pills." The coroner said he died of a drug overdose.

13) Channel 11 – 1963

"Rock 'n' Roll is not polite. It's rude."
– *Jann Wenner, Rolling Stone Magazine*

"WPIX Rocks N. Y. Nielson Ratings with Clay Cole's Teen Beat Shows," *Variety* headlined in its November 4, 1964 issue. Ben Gross, television editor of the *New York Daily News,* wrote: WPIX programming veepee Hank Booraem reports "The Clay Cole Show" has "gone through the roof" in the Nielson ratings…and it could be that WPIX will be putting Cole up for sale [syndication] across the country soon."

"The Clay Cole Show" celebrated a first anniversary on Channel 11 by becoming their hottest property, their number one show. Rather than offer me a new contract, more money or a bonus, they renewed my old contract with the promise of syndication. As an alternative to more money, I was given a second hour show with additional duties.

I was summoned into the offices of the General Manager, an inner sanctum off-limits to most of us contract employees. He did not invite an open door policy. His suite was a plush corner workplace, tastefully furnished and with a private bathroom (so he shouldn't have to pee with us peons), and magnificent window views of the United Nations. His office was in a separate wing on the tenth floor, far away as possible from the studio and production offices; He was never seen there.

Considering the financial windfall our ratings had generated, my spirits were high, so I was totally unprepared for what was about to be revealed; it was not a congratulatory pat on the back. His agenda stunned me so gravely that his words remain embedded in my brain, word for word, to this day.

"Do you have to have all those pinheads on your show, singing 'It's all right, it's all right'…can't you get some clean-cut groups…like the Beach Boys?"

I was speechless. I stared at him in stunned silence.

Realizing the impact of what he had just said, he retreated, "Why, as a Southerner, I have done more for…." what he said next did not register. He was telling me that I had welcomed too many black artists onto the show. His "pinhead" reference was probably to Little Anthony & the Imperials' show-stopping performance of "I'm Alright," one of their best-choreographed routines. Aside from his haughty dismissal of black entertainers, he proved how little he knew about our audience. East Coast teens could care less about the Beach Boys' sun-bleached ditties – show me a kid in the Bronx who aspired to be a surfer or drive a little deuce coupe. A "woody" in the Bronx held a whole different meaning. On the other hand, Little Anthony & the Imperials were the archetypal New York group, five clean-cut, well-mannered, immaculately dressed, Brooklyn-born African-Americans, with a white fan base. On the other hand, the Beach Boys proved to be one of our most dysfunctional groups, involving drugs, bitter disputes, infighting, lawsuits and paranoid behavior. By contrast, Little Anthony & the Imperials are the East Coast opposite, and remain one of our best-loved groups, performing still. At long last, fifty-one years after recording their first charted hit, "Tears On My Pillow" (1958), Little Anthony & the Imperials were inducted into the Rock and Roll Hall of Fame (2009).

This was not a whimsical Bill O'Reilly 'pin-head' slur; this was niggardly and disturbing. "Pinhead" seared in my gut, vibrated in my brain. I was seething. On my show, I embraced the Shirelles, just as I hugged the Shangri-Las! I kissed Dionne Warwick! I kissed Sammy Davis Jr. for chris-sake! I hailed Apollo stars with the same gusto as the Boys from Bandstand. I had built my reputation on a welcoming show with an integrated studio audience, dancing cheek-to-cheek with black teenagers, singing alongside the Drifters, Coasters and the Isley Brothers, welcoming Bo Diddley, Percy Sledge, Rufus Thomas, and a toothless, former Bed-Sty gang member, Richie Havens. I slammed a whipped cream pie in the face of Lloyd Price – oh, how Mr. President must have relished that moment

The Motown cannon was poised to set off a new musical explosion, and in the coming years, all the greats would walk down our hallway – Stevie Wonder, Mary Wells, the Marvelettes, Martha, Tammi Terrell and Marvin Gaye and their incomparable, groups – the Temps, the Tops and Gladys Knight & the Pips. In the coming year, I would present televisions first all-black hour, an all-star "Salute to Motown."

There was no soul-searching necessary for me. It was going to be business as usual at "The Clay Cole Show." I would not be bullied by this ignorant bigot; and besides, who would believe me? The President and General Manager of the most important independent station in the nation and in liberal New York City of all places!

A few months later, I arrived at the office to find my staff huddled over a copy of *Variety*. In a front-page story, Channel 11 announced with great pride they had been at the forefront of the Civil Rights Movement with their long history of presenting black artists on their station. Then they proceeded to list the dozens of black artists who had appeared on my show, with the President of the station taking full credit. By 1964, it had become fashionable ("politically correct") to feature black entertainers on television, and he was ready to take the bows.

There is one lingering myth that continues to dog me, branding me a racist. Judy Clay was much too spiritual to have had so much bad luck, both in her personal life and in her recording career. Judy had been adopted by Lee Drinkard, of the famous gospel group, the Drinkard Singers. (Lee was Cissy Houston's sister and Dionne Warwick's mother). Judy's God-gifted voice first soared as an early member of the Sweet Inspirations, performing with Cissy, Dee Dee and Dionne Warwick. In 1968, Judy teamed up with Billy Vera, in what Vera considered "the first inter-racial soul duo in record history." They recorded a duet, "Storybook Children," and appeared together on-stage at the Apollo Theatre. In 1979 Judy was diagnosed with a brain tumor, but died in a tragic automobile accident in 2001 at age 63. Upon her death, Billy Vera wrote: "The Clay Cole Show" taped us but, once they knew our racial makeup, our segment was never aired."

I do not remember their appearance, nor do I recall the duo taping my show. It is possible that their tape had technical glitches (which often happened), or they taped their appearance after I left the show – it was a minor hit in early 1968. Of this I am certain: the incident did not happen on my watch. Check my record.

(Billy Vera's giant 1986 solo hit, "At This Moment," became a Johnny Carson favorite and an AC-radio classic.)

It was not until forty-five years later, in 2008, that the following story was revealed to me in amazing detail. I had finally found an ally to support, confirm and corroborate my 'pinhead' episode.

Ken Johnson, a 22-year-old comic book aficionado, fresh off the campus of Carnegie Technical Institute, with a bride and a newborn baby, burst through our revolving door marked 'producer' Ken was hired as a producer/director, assigned to my Saturday hour and to develop my new Sunday show. For the first time, WPIX set in place a "programming department," managed by a natty, old-time radio man, Hank Booraem, and Lloyd Gaynes, as Executive Producer of all live shows. The Channel 11 news division could breathe a sigh of relief; rock 'n' roll and the Merry Mailman were no longer their responsibility.

Kenny was a spitfire, full of oomph and fresh ideas. I was no longer the youngest member of the team. Kenny gave the shows a refreshing energy and a modern look, elevating the ridiculous to the sublime.

The tone for our Sunday show was set by Kenny's choice of theme music, the Swingle Singer's[9] vocal orchestrations of the Rondo from Mozart's *Eine Kleine Nachtmusi* – hardly a choice for a rock 'n' roll show. Our new theme song was played over the opening titles, inner-cut with me on a motorcycle zooming around town, up and down ramps, in and out of tunnels with Kenny capturing every speed bump, tightly clutching his hand-held camera. I remember it was an early Sunday morning in October, and Pope Pius VI was on his first papal visit to Manhattan, so the streets were eerily empty around the U.N., allowing us to violate speed restrictions. I was totally invigorated by the rush of speed, power, freedom and the prospect of danger. I was hooked; I purchased the Honda 90. Kenny then edited a quick-cut montage to visualize the dizzying tempo of the Swingle Singers frantic doodling. Kenny was a one-man wunderkind.

So, with the production staff in place for our second season, rules had to be set. This is the story I never knew, until Ken Johnson revealed it to me forty-four years later:

"I was surprised when I was told by my boss Lloyd Gaynes and his superior, Hank Booraem that, as producer, I was required to submit photos of any potential black performers for the approval of the station's General Manager, Fred Thrower. He did not need to review the white performers.

---

9   The Swingle Singers are a classical-jazz vocal ensemble founded by Ward Swingle in France in the early 60s, of session backup singers for Charles Aznavour and Edith Piaf. In their off-time, they began rehearsing a cappella Bach in be-bop terms, riffing and scatting like jazz musicians. In 1962, they approached Philips about making a recording, thinking they might sell a few copies to families and friends. As a matter of fact, in France that's about what happened. Kenny's instincts were exactly right; when the album was released in the States, it began climbing the charts, eventually making the top 10, then staying in the top 100 for almost a year and a half. That first recording, and the two that followed it, won Grammies for "Best Performance by a Chorus". The first "Bach's Greatest Hits" also won a Grammy for "Best New Artist". (The other albums were *Going Baroque* and *Anyone for Mozart*.)

Why just the black acts?, I asked. I was told by both Lloyd and Hank that Mr. Thrower wanted to make certain they were "presentable" and not what Mr. Thrower referred to as "pinheads." This was very offensive to me, but as the youngest, newest and least-experienced person on the station's staff, I decided that I had to go along to get along. It was also clear to me that this process was equally offensive to Lloyd, Hank and certainly to Clay as well. I don't recall any specific people that Mr. Thrower directed me not to hire, but the pressure was constant and may well have caused me and others to make preemptory judgment calls on who would be acceptable to Mr. Thrower."

Ken Johnson was born in the South of the 1940s to parents born and raised in Arkansas. "All my relatives were in the South," he told me. "I was raised by my mother in Maryland near Washington, D.C. in a virulently bigoted and anti-Semitic household. I had always heard such racial slurs and prejudice from her and my Irish Catholic Yankee stepfather, but somehow I had never bought into that kind of intolerance. Nonetheless, I expected to hear it from them on a daily basis or from some of my relatives in the South during my visits."

Ken continued:
"After working at WPIX for nearly a year, I was summoned to Mr. Thrower's office. It was the first and only time I met the man – until we later faced each other in federal court. Mr. Thrower said he was very pleased with how well my shows were going (they were two of the station's biggest drawing hits). But, he continued, 'I don't want to see you get too many niggers on them'."

"I remember staring at him slack-jawed."

But sitting in the office of a TV station's General Manager on the upper floor of the N.Y. Daily News building at 42nd Street & Second Avenue in mid-town Manhattan – the most liberal city in America – I was stupefied at what I heard come out of Mr. Thrower's mouth. I was literally speechless. I sat there dumbfounded while he went on a bit. Then the meeting was over and I walked back to the elevator in a daze. When I got back to our offices, I went to Lloyd Gaynes and told him that he had my notice. He was surprised, and asked if I had another job. I said no, but I couldn't work for Mr. Thrower. I left the station within a month to become a producer on "The Mike Douglas Show," where I was privileged to work with many of the same black performers I had at WPIX."

I was never aware of Kenny's meeting with Fred Thrower or the real reason he abruptly resigned. Nor was I aware that photos of black artists required the personal approval of our General Manager. After great success as producer of the Mike

Douglas Show, Kenny relocated to Los Angeles in the early 70s, and told his 'Fred Thrower bigotry story' to a number of people in the industry. "One night I got a call from Harry Belafonte's people," Kenny told me. "They had heard the rumor and asked if it was true. When I confirmed it, they asked if I would be willing to testify at an FCC hearing in Washington. I agreed immediately, though many people tried to dissuade me, including Lloyd Gaynes, who cautioned that some people might not take kindly to me blowing the whistle on a former boss. But I was determined to go."

Forum Communications Inc., a consortium of New Yorkers led by future PBS and NBC News president Lawrence Grossman, "Wonderama" kiddie show host/producer Sonny Fox, Harry Belafonte and others, petitioned the FCC to challenge WPIX Inc.'s license to operate on channel 11. Most notably, their news operation was accused of falsifying news reports broadcasts in the late 1960s, such as labeling stock footage as 'via satellite', and saying a voice report was 'live from Prague' when, in actuality, it was made from a pay telephone in Manhattan. The litigation stretched on for years, beginning in 1968, the year I departed Channel 11 in disgust.

During the Soviet invasion of Czechoslovakia in 1968, WPIX-TV carried what seemed like an enterprising special report for a non-network local channel. WPIX News, as it proclaimed on the air at the time, presented its "Russian authority," Dr. Max J. Putzel, in "an eyewitness account from Moscow." Fact of the matter, Max Putzel was a professor of German literature who happened to be a cousin of a WPIX news producer and who at the time of the broadcast, was not in Moscow but back home in Gary, Indiana. That incident is the basis for one of many allegations brought against WPIX. Several days before the Putzel caper, the FCC says, WPIX ran a scene identified as Prague with the subtitle "via satellite" when in fact it was not a satellite transmission but a dusty old film. Another night, a voice report out of Vienna was labeled as Prague, and they passed off canned footage of a Boston high school disturbance as a local ghetto riot. Besides the FCC, other complainants allege that 1) WPIX has discriminated against blacks and other New York minorities in hiring, 2) it has made no effort to program for such groups, and 3) from 1963 to 1967 it demanded kick backs or "payola" from some singers it put on the air. (The check-swapping arrangement established and sanctioned by AFTRA years earlier.) Kenny continued his story:

"They flew me to Washington. It took me about twenty minutes to tell my story in court for the Forum lawyers. Then, the WPIX lawyers kept me on the stand for eight hours, trying to punch holes in my story. They were unable to. Throughout, Fred Thrower was sitting not fifteen feet in front of me. I was pleased to be able to look right in his eyes and repeat his hateful words. I was also able to make it clear that Lloyd Gaynes and Hank Booraem were not parties to Mr. Thrower's prejudice. I later heard that, although Forum was unable to get the broadcast license away from WPIX, Mr. Thrower was fired."

Against the advice of *my* friends, I too stepped forward to tell my 'pinhead' story to a gathering of Forum attorneys and WPIX lawyers in Manhattan. I just had the feeling that no one in the room believed my story, especially after the Ch 11 lawyers reeled off a seemingly endless list of black performers who had appeared on my show. I was too humble to take the credit, too angry to play the martyr. I just let it be.

After ten years of costly litigation, WPIX prevailed. In 1979, Forum received a $9-million dollar settlement and WPIX retained their broadcast license. Even though Forum failed, their challenge became a wake-up call for independent television stations across the nation. Many upgraded their local news and public service, a victory to minority viewers all across the country. Grossman said, "For the first time in over 20 years, we have the promise of seeing important improvements in the quality of local television."

Since the Forum challenge, WPIX doubled its news staff and air time and rushed to schedule community shows like "Black Pride," "Puerto Rican New Yorker," "Jewish Dimension" and "Aprenda Ingles" (Learn English). Over the years, channel 11 has won many awards for news, and was the first independent station to win a New York-area Emmy Award for outstanding newscast in 1979 and again in 1983. It was a significant comeback for a news operation that had no newscasts on Saturday and Sunday and was accused of falsifying news broadcasts.

Ken Johnson became the multi-award winning über-producer/writer/director of "The Incredible Hulk," "Bionic Woman," "Alien Nation" and NBC's science-fiction miniseries masterpiece, "V" – so much for comic book geek!

Our control room director, the easy-going, low-key Ivy Leaguer, Barry Glazer, had absolutely no rhythm, and couldn't cut cameras on the beat. But, with the arrival of MTV and music videos, no one cuts on the beat anymore. Barry Glazer went off to Hollywood to direct the final decades of Dick Clark's "American Bandstand" at ABC.

Channel 11 had renegotiated my contract with a promise to syndicate my show coast-to-coast, which never happened. They did, however, purchase the syndicated Lloyd Thaxton show, the very first station in the country to sign-up.

When producer Gary Smith asked me to be the permanent announcer on his forthcoming NBC "Hullabaloo" show, Channel 11 refused flat-out, "it will interfere with our syndication plans," they reasoned.

Most celebrity-driven television shows rate a professional photographer on the set to capture the moment; not so at Channel 11. We neither had a makeup man nor hair person; visiting artists were on their own, borrowing my Max Factor Tan No. 2 and grooming products from my Videl Sassoon gift-basket.

I was expected to reciprocate the entertainers who had "swapped checks" to be on our show, by attending their performances, club dates or opening nights at The Copacabaña. The station refused to reimburse my expenses, even though I was essentially booking the show.

I requested an office. The station arranged for an unfurnished room in a remote wing of the Daily News Building, so far removed from our studios and production office that it required two elevators to get there.

When London became the hot-spot of the Sixties mod scene, they refused my request to visit the UK with, or without, a camera crew.

I pleaded with the station to allow me to do a late night New Year's Eve rock 'n' roll special, the hook being my January 1st birthday. Channel 11 didn't recognize the opportunity and refused. In 1972, ABC launched their annual midnight event, "Dick Clark's Rockin' New Year."

Months before Tiny Tim became a national television favorite, I spotted him at Page Three, a dim, dank downstairs club in the Village where Tiny was performing for free meals and tips. I was overjoyed at discovering such a wildly unique performer, a perfect send-up for the pretentiousness of Sixties entertainment, perfect for our show. I was turned down flat. The station only permitted him to appear on our show once he had a hit album, and had been embraced by Johnny Carson and the entire nation

I was a team player; they just did not want me on their team. I was never invited to the station's annual Christmas party. Like it or not, "The Clay Cole Show" defined Channel 11 as their signature success. Instead, they chose to treat me just like another vendor. So much for loyalty – my one solid virtue and they just refused to tap into it.

My five seasons at Ch 11 proved to be triumphant years, and should have been my most rewarding, memorable time. Talent doesn't need to be coddled, but a small nod of appreciation would be nice. When I look back on my career, my three years at Ch 13 were the happiest time of my life. Although our Ch 13 bosses weren't capable of rewarding me financially, they awarded me with support, encouragement, and gave me opportunities with challenges. Ch 13 was operated by a pioneering, inventive manager, Eli Landau. Ch 11 was administered by a bigoted hypocrite. But hey; $500 a week was a decent paycheck back in the mid-60s and I was still seated at the best table in all the best restaurants and all the 45 singles and LPs I could carry home.

Little Anthony & the Imperials continued to appear on my show, without so much as a squawk from the front office. It was during a return appearance that our Cuban-born cameraman Dulio zoomed in on the group and whispered to director Barry Glazer:

"They were white the last time they were here."

"They were what?" a flustered Barry shouted back, over the music.

"I said, the last time they were here they wore white."

That cleared that up.

14) Family Matters

"Music hath charm to soothe a savage beast,
to soften rocks, or bend a knotted oak."

– English playwright and poet, William Congreve

Although $500 a show was a lot of money in the mid-Sixties, it was not com-
miserate with my stature as the host of a wildly successful show. So, in order to
maintain something resembling a celebrity lifestyle, I had to crank-up the personal
appearances and nightclubs.

I appeared at an Eastside supper club, The Living Room, a dark and intimate
room with a reputation as a cheater's rendezvous. I regularly joked from the stage,
"It's so nice to see so many fathers sitting here with their sixteen-year-old daughters," which generally got a big laugh. One night I spotted Hank Booraem, our new
Channel 11's program manager, sitting cozily with a young lady, and I directed the
joke at him. Turns out, she was with his *real* sixteen-year-old daughter.

Murray Grand wrote and produced my Living Room appearances, an hour
of special material, comedy and songs, attended by an audience of notables, from
Rocky Marciano, Vivian Blaine, Martha Raye, Roddy McDowell to the legendary
queen of burlesque, Ann Corio (who was starring on Broadway in her hit show,
"This Was Burlesque"). Many young colleagues from the music-biz – Tina Robin,
Dick Roman, Diane Renay, Michael Allen, Leslie Uggums – dropped in. Murray
called them my "Trail-Mix," a mixed bag of fruits and nuts.

Roddy McDowell stopped backstage, greeting me, "Hello Al Rucker." I was
flabbergasted. Turns out, Roddy was pals with Sharon Farrell and Andrew Prine,
two stars from my Providence days, before I became Clay Cole. Roddy told me

that when he was appearing on Broadway in "Camelot" the cast would remain in the theatre between shows on Saturday matinee days, order up a food delivery and gather in his dressing room to watch "The Clay Cole Show." Can you imagine – Richard Burton, Julie Andrews, and Robert Goulet? You just never know who's out there.

My contract with the Living Room allowed me one night-off each week to tape my TV show, with my spot filled by Marty Richards, a very social and ambitious young singer, who later became the multi-millionaire, Oscar-winning producer of "Chicago." Marty once asked if he could bring a friend, "a big fan," back to meet me. The fan was Truman Capote! Two teenaged girls let out a piercing screech, and leaped wildly into the air when we met. They were Walter Cronkite's daughters, Nancy and Kathy Cronkite.

The Living Room invited me back for two weeks during spring prom time of year and again for a Christmas - New Year's engagement; this time, we broke the all-time house record. The Living Room's manager and talent booker was Jerry Weintraub, a young man with higher ambitions. Jerry approached me about personal management. I had turned down a similar offer from Dion's manager, Sal Bonafede, as well as an offer from the music magnate Don Kirchner, the man responsible for the Monkees. Kirchner was the impresario hired by ABC to oversee its late-night "In Concert" series, but quickly quit, saying: "ABC executives didn't know the difference between the Allman Brothers and the Osmond Brothers." *I could relate to that.*

I said no to Jerry Weintraub as well; I would never allow anyone to get too close. This was a very bad move on my part. I needed guidance, a manager to negotiate my deals and advance my career. I had no business sense or the concept of "saving for a rainy day." "Uncle" Clay Cole, a financial wiz and multimillionaire, taught me how to make a martini, but not how to make money.

Jerry Weintraub[10] became the entrepreneur who delivered one million dollars in cash to Colonel Tom Parker for the rights to produce an Elvis Presley tour. Jerry

---

10   Ironically, in the early 1970s, Sal Bonafede joined Jerry Weintraub's Management III where he was involved in the careers of John Denver, Elvis Presley, Bob Dylan, Frank Sinatra and others. Prior to that, Bonafede managed Rod McKuen, the Doors and Dion. In the business, he was best-known as Neil Diamond's tour director for more than 30 years. Diamond says, "He organized the tours, he planned the dates, he worked with the promoters and venues, not only in the States, but all over the world." Diamond says he was lucky and proud to call Bonafede "my manager, my consigliore and, most of all, my friend." In addition to Diamond, Bonafede played a key role in producing Michael Jackson's international "Bad" tour. Sal Bonafede passed away in February 2007 at his home in Los Angeles. He was 74. (Source: *Billboard* magazine)

was the first to bring Elvis to a Manhattan venue – other than the Ed Sullivan Theatre – Madison Square Garden. Jerry produced all the major stage and arena appearances of Neil Diamond and Frank Sinatra, as well as scores of major motion pictures and television events.

On the red-eye from L.A. to N. Y. Jerry invited me to be his guest at his Elvis concert at the Garden, and I was seated with his stunning wife, (and my longtime secret crush), singer Jane Morgan, looking fabulous, covered in fur. After the show, she offered me a lift uptown in her limousine. It was another "Fascination" realized.

Oh. Elvis was good too.

"I've just come from two luncheons," I told Broadway columnist Earl Wilson at our interview at The Spindletop restaurant: "After this I'm going to a birthday party for Claire Hogan, then we're going to The Copa to see Marilyn Maye." Claire was a fellow Ohioan and girl Friday to composer, Cy Coleman. ("Witchcraft") Claire was once a big band singer with the Jimmy Dorsey Orchestra, now a four-pack a day smoker with a whiskey voice. Claire had the look of the Irish, a big full-moon face, round and flat as a pancake, with the skin texture of a waffle, imposing legs and abundant breasts – she scrubbed-up swell. Claire turned me on to The Tibetan Book of The Dead, B-12 shots, Edgar Cayce, The Aristocrats joke, and the music business hangout, Al & Dick's Steakhouse. She would phone me up, imitating a drunk, slurring, "Let's go to Al & Drinks for a dick!" One afternoon over cocktails at Al & Dick's, discussing my unhappiness with my career; I confessed to Claire, "I'm my own worst enemy."

"Not as long as I'm alive," she snapped.

Claire and I became drinking buddies, joined at the hip for the next ten years.

Life is what happens while you're making other plans. In 1965, Mom died. When I received an emergency middle-of-the-night phone call from a hospital, Dad was on the phone: "It's your mother. She's had a stroke. You'd better come home."

I arrived at the hospital the next afternoon in time to hear Mom take her final breath; the nurse touched her pulse, pronounced her dead. I am sure she held on, waiting for my arrival, before she passed on. She was 52. Brother Jim arrived, on emergency leave from Marine boot camp at Parris Island, Rick was sixteen, and Tama was seven. Dad was totally unprepared, physically unable to care for youngsters. Tama tells me she was sent off to school in the morning, disheveled, in mismatched clothes.

Things had not been going well on the home front for some time. The G-F had offered Dad a promotion as Plant Supervisor of his own chair division, in a factory to be built in North Carolina. This of course meant that the family would have to relocate, and move south from Ohio. Mom was overjoyed at the idea, a fresh start, a new home and refuge from Ohio's brutal, cold winters. On Dad's 54th Birthday, June 13, 1963, the Rucker station wagon rolled into Forest City, a small, historic Southern town at the foothills of the Appalachian Mountains, with then-14-year-old Rick about to be a high school freshman and Tama, 5, ready for kindergarten. Brother Jim had enrolled at Kent State University, at the time, a junior. Dad bought property and built their dream house, a three-bedroom ranch with a rumpus room in the basement, on a quiet cul-de-sac, overlooking the mountains. One year later, Grandma and Grandpa Nash joined them, selling the homestead in Hubbard, and welcomed by Mom, who became their nurse and caregiver.

Dad was able to bring a lifetime of knowledge to his new responsibilities, having come up through the ranks at The G-F, his sole, lifelong employer. His cost-cutting innovations saved the company millions of dollars in the unique manner by which he arranged the assembly lines, from aluminum sheets, cold-rolled steel and cowhide bolts into a finely crafted upholstered chairs. The G-F brought in an outsider to act as Plant Manager, a school teacher and someone's brother-in-law, a man who knew nothing about the furniture industry. Dad was duty-bound to report to this newcomer. Over time it became evident to Dad that the new man and his cronies were underhandedly stealing from the company, selling scrap aluminum, clandestinely pocketing personal riches. Dad was honest beyond reproach, a loyal company man, and became so pained by the events that he had a complete physical and mental breakdown. Dad was in and out of the hospital, forced by his doctors to retire at age 56. Mom was left to run the household, look after Rick and Tama, care for Grandpa Nash, then make twice daily trips to a near-by nursing home to visit her mother and to the hospital to visit Dad. The stress simply killed her.

Dad hadn't known there were other forces at work behind the scenes at The G-F. Stock profiteers snapped-up the company, then sold it in a manipulation to rob The G-F of its assets and pension fund, gutting the company. A onetime leader in the manufacture of metal office furniture, the company was now bankrupt. After 38-years of loyal service, Dad lost his pension. The CARE packages were now sent home *from* me.

As to Mom, I could never understand the depths of her unhappiness. Years later, I stumbled across the answer in an old nursery rhyme, ironically "Old Mother Hubbard" (Ohio), with a simplistic metaphor that held the key:

"Old Mother Hubbard went to the cupboard,
to give her poor dog a bone;
But when she got there the cupboard was bare,
and so the poor dog hand none."

Mom was capable of love; she had just temporarily run out. The cupboard was bare.

Two months after we buried Mom, I married a young girl I hardly knew. We both quickly realized our mistake. I could cope with my own demons, but I was totally unprepared to share them with another person. Mom's death plunged me into deep soul searching. I married because I knew it would have made Mom happy, but it brought great unhappiness to my young bride and me. Marriage was my final effort to please my mother. Psychoanalysis, hypnotherapy, spiritual healing, acupuncture – even a botched suicide – had not provided a remedy, and marriage certainly wasn't the answer. Add marriage counselors to the list.

I was too independent to be married, too irresponsible to raise children. I could barely manage my own affairs. I lived the gypsy life, impulsive, able to pick up and go on a moments notice. Living on a whim is the one luxury of living alone. I lost all interest in a career. Fame seemed no longer important; in fact it was a distraction. In the big picture, my television show and my role in it seemed trivial. My heart was broken. My spirit was broken. With Mom gone, I had nothing left to prove.

"Youth fades, love droops, the leaves of friendship fall; a mother's secret hope outlives them all" – *Oliver Wendell Holmes*

15) Girl Groups

"Girl Groups are strictly an American phenomenon:
We like our four-part harmony in three-inch heels."

Rock writer Lillian Roxon defined girl singers of the Sixties: "The rule for female singers was for the voice to be insistently high, penetrating and shrewish." Leslie Gore comes to mind. "In her day she was the reigning queen of teen-suffering, musically fashionable [and commercially successful]. Sixteen-year-old Leslie Gore came onto the scene in the summer of 1963 bleating, "It's My Party," and a million or so teen buyers emphasized with the plight of being dumped on." In real life, Leslie had hardly been forsaken; her father was the well-to-do manufacturer of Peter Pan Bras. Leslie was an early feminist, ("You Don't Own Me"), and I have often wondered if she ever set fire to her own daddy's bras.

I thought highly of her mom and dad, proud parents who were thrilled for her unexpected fame and I tolerated her annoying little brother Michael, a piano-pounding nuisance who later became the Oscar-winning composer of "Fame" (lyrics by Dean Pitchford).

Connie Francis and Brenda Lee, who had dominated the pop charts for five years, would, after 1963, never appear on the Billboard Top 10 again, and by the end of the decade they were off the Hot 100 completely. Connie Francis wisely advanced her international stardom by recording pop doggerel in every imaginable language, and Brenda Lee cultivated her country roots. Each carved out a niche that would keep them in pantyhose for a lifetime.

Connie had a rough row to hoe; her brilliant talent and superstar career was far overshadowed by her tragic personal life. She was never able to escape her hot-tempered, controlling father George and his humiliating rejection of Bobby Darin, the love of her life. Connie and her third husband adopted a son, Joseph Garzilli, Jr., but her four attempts at a happy marriage became a mélange of physical and mental abuse, haunted by memories of her much-publicized rape incident.

That violent, destructive, abusive rape occurred in 1974 at a Howard Johnson's Motel, following a performance at the Westbury Music Fair on Long Island. Connie subsequently sued the motel chain for failing to provide adequate security and reportedly won a $3 million judgment, at the time one of the largest such judgments in history. She did not perform again for seven years. Connie was later diagnosed with bipolar disorder. She had long suffered from ongoing mental impairments that developed as a result of her rape, including drug dependencies and suicide attempts. She used lithium to treat the illnesses. Physically she's diabetic and suffers high blood pressure. My dear Connie has endured more than her share of adversity.

It's paradoxical that Connie's signature song (and biggest hit) "Who's Sorry Now" was recorded at the suggestion of her father, who convinced her it stood a chance of becoming a hit because it was an established song, known by adults, but new and fresh to teenage ears. His logic was valid and paid-off big-time for Connie – it sold over a million copies. In 1958, "Who's Sorry Now" reached No. 1 and Connie Francis became one of the most popular vocalists in the world.

I have one enduring image of Brenda Lee that will remain with me for the remainder of my life: "Little Miss Dynamite," standing on an open stage in a torrential rainstorm, an umbrella in one hand, a microphone in the other, delivering a full ninety-minute set – as long as the audience remained hunkered under tarpons and umbrellas, she sang. After the performance, with her tour bus idling nearby, awaiting the overnight trip back to Nashville, Miss Lee stood in the downpour signing autographs late into the night.

By 1963, Connie and Brenda were replaced on the charts by fourteen-year-old, 4' 10" Little" Peggy March. Her single "I Will Follow Him" soared to No. 1 on the *Billboard* charts, the youngest female artist ever to score a number one. Her March, 1964 appearance on our show became a milestone event – it was Peggy's sixteenth birthday, and we ceremoniously removed the "Little" from her billing. Peggy recalls, "I remember my mother came on-stage with a surprise birthday cake with my name on top; the 'Little' was crossed out in the frosting. We celebrated the end of my moniker."

March's success also came with financial failure. She was a minor and the Coogan Act[11] prevented her parents from managing her money. The responsibility was placed on her personal manager. It was discovered in 1966 that he had squandered the fortune away, leaving her with a mere $500. When Peggy graduated from high school in 1966, she started all over again with a new manager, Arnie Harris, who stole her heart. They married and have one daughter, "little" Sande, born in 1974.

Annette Funicello's last charted song was in 1961, but her career was salvaged by television specials, Skippy Peanut Butter commercials and eighteen feature films, most notably her bikini beach film partnership with Frankie Avalon. (Walt Disney himself, for the sake of her virginal image, asked her not to wear any attire that showed her navel; thankfully she did not comply.) I recently received a note from Annette, carefully written with a shaky hand, as Annette suffers from multiple sclerosis. Annette had kept her condition a secret for many years, but in 1992 felt it necessary to go public to combat vicious tabloid snipes that her impaired carriage was the result of alcoholism. In 1993, she opened the Annette Funicello Fund for Neurological Disorders. She now lives quietly in California as Mrs. Glen Holt.

Finally, my closest buddy among all the singing ladies, was the wholesome, wacky, Linda Scott ("I Told Every Little Star"), who seems to have fallen off the radar. Linda was a radio star with Arthur Godfrey and the television co-host of ABC's afternoon beach party, "Where the Action Is" with Steve Alaimo and Paul Revere & the Raiders. Linda recorded one of the first collaborations of the legendary writing team of Hal David and Burt Bacharach ("Who's Been Sleeping In My Bed"). After years of searching, I found Linda in a small country village in upstate New York, caregiver to her then-89 year old mother, with no computer, website, or Email address. She's a polyester babe, happily frozen in the Sixties. Linda dropped out of show-biz in the early 1970s to become an Army medical technician, stationed in Fort Sam Houston, Texas, where she met and married a fellow serviceman. The marriage produced a son, Steve (a graphics artist, now married); Linda's ended in divorce. She later taught music at the Christian Academy in New York. In the Seventies, Linda lived in Cocoa Beach, Florida and performed in a night club revue, before settling upstate New York, "my roots." "I get the biggest kick out of watching us on cable," she wrote, "Turner Classic Movies and PBS specials. Saw you just last month. My movies, "Teenage Millionaire" and "Don't Knock the Twist" are on occasionally – cracks me up!" Oh, how I miss my visits with the dry, rye, devilish Linda Scott.

---

11   The California Child Actor's Bill (also known as Coogan Act) is a law applicable to child performers, designed to safeguard a portion of their earnings for when they enter adulthood. The original Bill was passed in 1939 by the State of California in response to the plight of Jackie Coogan, who earned millions of dollars as a child actor only to reach adulthood and discover that his parents had spent almost all of his money. Since then, it has been revised a few times, most recently in 2004, stating that 100% of the money earned by the child actor is solely theirs, and unauthorized use by the parents is considered, by law, stealing.

By 1963, we were a full decade away from the epic explosion of the solo diva Cher, seven years to the creation and self-destruction of Janice Joplin, and about four years away from Aretha. Oh, Aretha was recording all right. At just twenty, she signed on to Columbia Records, where she recorded old school minstrel show ditties like "Rock-A-Bye Your Baby with a Dixie Melody." According to Pete Hamill at the time, "Aretha came on like a road-company Nancy Wilson." Columbia had no idea how to record her, but to be fair; there never had been a woman with Aretha's vocal power and divine inspiration. She spent six years roasting chestnuts over at Columbia until, in 1968; she broke loose, turning to Atlantic Records and into the hands of producer Jerry Wexler, who once guided the early Ray Charles and Wilson Pickett. When the Natural Woman was unleashed, Aretha demanded Respect – and got it. From 1968 and throughout the rest of my life, I spent more time alone with Aretha than with any other woman. Aretha has been in heavy rotation on my stereo throughout all those long, lonely nights, both at home and in hotel rooms around the world.

1963 was the year of Barbra Streisand, discovered at The Bon Soir, a down-the-steps cellar club in Greenwich Village. Columbia Records was at first unsure on how to showcase the "new" sound that Barbra represented, so they turned to Mike Berniker, a young jazz producer at their Epic subsidiary, and asked if he might be able to successfully translate Barbra's unique vocal qualities into a successful studio album. Berniker leapt at the chance to work with someone whose voice was strong, profound, and perhaps most importantly, different. "I could not believe that this wasn't terrifically important to record," Berniker recalled. As producer, he treated Barbra's voice as a jazz instrument, carefully mixing her vocals with arrangements that would blend together perfectly. With the success of Barbra's first three albums to his credit, Mike Berniker set an industry standard that was emulated by many record producers throughout the sixties. Berniker began producing for such notable artists as Connie Francis, Perry Como, Johnny Mathis and Eydie Gorme. With Berniker at the helm in 1966, Eydie Gorme received a Grammy as Female Vocalist for her now classic rendition of "If He Walked Into My Life." In all, Mike Berniker's projects were awarded nine Grammys, including "Album of the Year" for "The Barbra Streisand Album." Berniker knew what to do with Streisand all right, but it made Barbra nuts that she wasn't on *Billboard's* singles charts. Barbra was *that* singer who comes along once in a lifetime, blessed with God-given talent, but, Barbra wanted to be a pop star, recording second-rate songs like "Stoney End." Mercifully, she snapped out of it. That leaves us with the ultimate popular singer of the Sixties, an artist who has been venerated by all generations over the past forty-plus years.

I fell in love with this delicate, young singer from East Orange, New Jersey, with a pure soulful sound, an intoxicating vocal range, and a powerful, yet effortless delivery. Dionne Warwick emerged from an extended family of vocal divas, all members of the celebrated gospel group, the Drinkard Singers (her mother Lee's maiden name was Drinkard), with her sister Dee Dee Warwick, her aunt Cissy Houston, and then, of course, cousin Whitney Houston. Dee Dee, Cissy and Judy Clay also were among the vocal ensemble the Sweet Inspirations, most notably in the studio with Aretha, on stage with Elvis, and on the charts with their one hit, "Sweet Inspiration."

Burt Bacharach, a little-known songwriter had just teamed up with lyricist Hal David when he first heard Dionne, one of the backup singers hired for a Drifters recording session. Burt described her as "the girl in pigtails and white sneakers, with a voice as high as her cheekbones." Burt took a demo record of "Make It Easy on You" over to Florence Greenberg at Scepter Record, hoping to interest her in the song.

"Forget the song! Who's the singer?" Florence demanded.

It was Dionne. Florence quickly signed a contract with the unknown singer and her two unproven producers, a package deal that was to become the launch of the Warwick-Bacharach-David dynasty. ("Make It Easy on Yourself" was passed on to Jerry Butler and became a Top 20 hit for him in 1962).

Dionne bided her time for over a year, toiling as a studio backup singer, cutting demos and filling-in at stage shows as one of the Shirelles, awaiting a Bacharach-David inspiration. Dionne's solo career was finally launched in 1963 with the release of "Don't Make Me Over," and, due to a misprint on the label, Warrick became Warwick. In 1964 alone, Dionne charted five times, amazing stats for a newcomer, in a landscape littered with girl singers and girl groups.

The little girl in tennis sneakers with the high cheek bones was transformed into the most breathtaking, elegant diva in New York. Her debut concert at Philharmonic Hall in Lincoln Center brought out the limousine crowd, a star-studded audience of Broadway and music-biz royalty. Dionne was plugged-in that night; she was electric. Sparks were flying! The after-show buzz in the foyer was euphoric. Noone wanted to leave, to break the spell.

As a side note to the event, Dionne had the foresight to present Little Anthony and the Imperials as her opening act. I witnessed something I have never seen before or since. The audience gave the group a standing ovation on their very first number. It was a night I will remember forever.

As her fame skyrocketed, Dionne never once refused my many request for an appearance on my show. With a bottle of Smirnoff's under her arm, Dionne paid a surprise visit to our studio one Saturday afternoon, to the delight and surprise of our crew and her pals, the Shirelles. The rehearsals turned into a convivial party, and as the hour approached show time, feeling no pain, I asked Dionne to stick around, sing a couple of hits. "Give me a minute," she said, and disappeared, across 42nd Street to The Plymouth Shop, bought herself a dress, slapped on some make-up and hit her mark, singing "Walk on By."

The early Sixties was the Golden Age of the Girl Group, and "The Clay Cole Show" became defined by our inexhaustible lineup of effervescent trios and quartets in perky party dresses. Fred Schneider of The B-52's told *Rolling Stone* magazine, "I was fascinated by the early-Sixties girl groups, they were always so mysterious. You'd see 'em on Clay Cole and they'd just be sitting there on those stools singing. You could hardly see their eyes because of their hair. It seemed real erotic." The Internet lists over 750 all-girl groups on the charts in the early Sixties alone, from the Chicklettes to the Revlons.

The giants among girl groups are the Andrews Sisters, Patti, Maxine and La Verne, "the GI-jive bombshells of World War II," who sold over 80-million records. The Andrews Sisters enjoyed a brief revival in the 1970s after Bette Midler re-corded a note-for-note cover of "Boogie Woogie Bugle Boy," and Patti and Maxine returned to Broadway for a two year run at The Schubert Theatre in a wartime mu-sical "Over Here," featuring three young unknown actors, Treat Williams, Marilu Henner and a klutzy, rubber-legged, soldier boy John Travolta. The renewed inter-est in the Andrews Sisters inspired imitators; trios of girls in WAC uniforms and sensible shoes sprang up all across America. "Sitting through these tribute shows were painful to watch," Patti told me. "My husband [Wally Weschler] dragged me to a club out in the San Fernando Valley to watch a tribute show and they sat us ringside, with no chance of escape. It was endless. These girls sang every song we ever recorded, and we made 1800 f--- records!"

The McGuire Sisters, Phyllis, Dotty and Chris, three fresh-faced milk-maidens from Middleton, Ohio ruled the early 1950's with pleasantly palatable pop hits, along with the Chordettes and the Fontane Sisters. We also had the five De Marco Sisters, the four Lennon Sisters, the three De Castro Sisters, the two De John Sisters, and Patty Page, who overdubbed her own three-part harmonies, creating the first one-woman girl group. Page recorded her first single in the midst of a strike at her record label, so background singers were not available to provide vocal harmonies. Instead, Page and Mitch Miller, who produced for Mercury Records, decided to overdub her vocals on the song, which made it seem as if Page was harmonizing with herself. ("Confess" 1947) Patti Page became the first pop artist to overdub her own vocals. This idea would later be used on Page's biggest 1950s hits "Tennessee Waltz," (13 weeks at No.1 between 1950 and 1951) and "(How Much Is That) Doggie In the Window," a 1953 novelty tune, selling over a million copies, and staying on the best-sellers chart for five months.

The "overdubbing" technique was tuned to perfection by Les Paul in the early 1950s for recordings with his wife, Mary Ford, harmonizing with herself, giving the vocals a very novel sound. Their sessions were recorded to disc, bouncing from one disc to the other. The couple's early 50s mega-hits included "How High the Moon," "The World Is Waiting for the Sunrise," and "Vaya Con Dios."

In the modern era, the first all-girl groups came to us from Los Angeles. Shirley Gunter and the Queens were the first recorded rock 'n' roll girl group, formed in 1954 by the sister of Cornell Gunther, a future member of the Coasters. Shirley began her singing career as a solo artist in 1953 when Cornell, then a member of the Flairs, took her to Flair Records. Shirley put together her own group the Four Queens in 1954 and they appeared, billed as "the first all-girl group." Etta James called them "the first female group, where all the girls could sing." The four girls were fooling around on the piano and came up with a Sh-Boom-like ditty with nonsense lyrics called "Oop Shoop." Flair released "Oop Shoop" in August 1954, and within two months it entered the R&B charts and rose to number eight. In New York, Alan Freed began spinning the 45, but before the record had a chance to cross over into pop territory, the Crew-Cuts, who had a major hit covering "Sh-Boom" (by the Chords), quickly covered "Oop Shoop" as well. After four more singles and a couple of tours with the Queens, Shirley Gunter joined her brother's group, the Flairs in order to make way for Flair Record's newest hit-makers, the Teen Queens.

In 1956, sisters Betty and Rosie Collins, as the Teen Queens, recording of "Eddie My Love" reached No. 14 on the *Billboard* charts. Although the Teen Queens are forerunners of the girl group sound, they also fall into the one-hit wonder category. They never had a charted song after the success of "Eddie My Love," written by their brother, Aaron Collins, a singer with the Cadets. Two other sisters, Patience (age 14) and Prudence (11) hit the charts twice in 1956, sweetly harmonizing old-fashioned shuffle songs, "Tonight You Belong to Me," and "Gonna Get Along Without You Now," popular for sure, but hardly rock 'n' roll. Their father Mark McIntyre was a West Coast bandleader who launched their career with Liberty Records, then took it away from them. He was very strict with the girls and wanted them to get an education, so he refused to allow them to tour or appear on the Ed Sullivan Show. It's been reported that "once they were old enough, they left home and would have nothing to do with their father."[12]

The Golden Age of the "girl group era" began in 1957, with two teen groups from the Bronx – the Chantels and the Bobettes. The first to break onto the pop charts were the six Bobbettes, eleven to fifteen years old, who wrote and recorded "Mr. Lee," a rhythmic novelty tune with a catchy hiccup gimmick, all about a Bronx schoolteacher they disliked. In 1957, Mr. Lee became the most famous high school teacher in America.

Right on their heels were five students trained in the intricate, demanding harmonies of Gregorian Chants, an unlikely, yet perfect stepping stone to the pure-sounding, inspirational laments preferred by teenage record consumers. The Chantels perfected their sound through seven years of choir training in the glee club at their Bronx Catholic high school, which gifted them with a clear natural projection, and an instinctual ability to harmonize. Their first recording, "He's Gone" in 1958, with fifteen-year old Arlene Smith on lead vocals, is a classic, establishing them as the first pop-rock girl group to chart. Their second single, "Maybe" hit the charts, No. 15 on *Billboard's* Hot 100. Also in 1958, three school girls out of Cleveland, Ohio, the Poni-Tails recorded "Born too Late," arriving at No. 7 on *Billboard's* Hot 100.

Girl Groups from the Bronx seemed to be abundant as four-leaf clovers on St Patrick's Day. When the Tokens presented the Chiffons in 1961, the four Bronx ladies' first recording, "He's So Fine" remained No. 1 on the charts for four weeks. (The last I heard, the Chiffons were still performing eight shows a week in Branson, Missouri, in the clover fields of America's heartland.)

---

12   Where they are today: <u>Queens:</u> Shirley Gunter left the music business in 1958 and, now blind, lives in Las Vegas singing gospel. Brother Cornell was murdered in a Las Vegas parking lot. Lula Kenney also moved to Vegas, working as a showgirl and briefly sang with The Platters. Blondene Taylor recorded with Junior Ryder under the name Sugar & Spice. <u>Teen Queens</u>, sisters Betty and Rosie never surfaced again. It has been reported that drugs took their toll, and both died 30 years ago. <u>Patience and Prudence</u> seemed to just vanish. An Internet blogger recalls an interview in which the sisters said, "Once they were old enough they moved away and would have nothing to do with their strict, controlling dad." No word if they ever did go off to college. <u>The Bobbettes</u> broke up in 1974; different members continued to perform. Jannie Pought died at the age of 34, stabbed to death while walking down a street in Jersey City, New Jersey. Laura Webb died at the age of 59 from complications of colon cancer. <u>Chantels:</u> Arlene Smith fronted a new Chantels in the 1970s which featured disco diva Carol Douglas ("Doctor's Orders" 1974) and continues to perform. The remaining original Chantels regrouped as well and hired Noemi (Ami) Ortiz as their new lead singer. Jackie Landry died in 1997. The Chantels were inducted into The Vocal Group Hall of Fame in 2002. <u>The Poni-Tails:</u> went off to college and withdrew from the music biz.

It was the much-loved Shirelles who all other girl groups emulated and revered. The four ladies from Passaic, New Jersey (Shirley Reeves, Beverly Lee, Doris Jackson and Micki Harris, along with their road manager and stage emcee, Ronnie Evans), became the archetypal Sixties girl group, with an unprecedented string of Hot 100 Hits. There was a brief flurry of girl groups in the disco decade – Sister Sledge, LaBelle, and the Pointer Sisters – but not until the arrival of Destiny's Child has their been singing ladies as well-liked as the Shirelles.

Phil Spector, that eccentric producer from the Bronx, was also keen on girlie groups. Spector moved to Los Angeles as a teenager and at seventeen became a singing member of the Teddy Bears, recording "To Know Him Is to Love Him," a song he had written in memory of his father (who had committed suicide in 1949). Spector then guided San Francisco's Paris Sisters ("I Love How You Love Me" 1961) onto the Top 10, and recruited the Blossoms, a Los Angeles trio featuring Darlene Love, to record as the Crystals ("He's A Rebel" 1962), and as Bob B. Soxx & the Bluejeans ("Zip-A-Dee Doo-Dah" 1962). Phil Spector's manipulative use of Darlene Love has caused her great pain. Darlene has unfortunately carried her grudge with Phil Spector onto the stage in her club concerts, casting a negative pall over her performances. You don't drag dated vendettas onto the stage as talking points for an otherwise upbeat show. Spector's final girl group effort was with the New Orleans' Dixie Cups, "Chapel of Love," a song he had originally written for the Ronettes.

The Shangri-Las ("Leader of the Pack") were the white bitch goddesses that stirred up pubertal fantasies. I'm sure teenage boys imagined the Shangri-Las arriving at our studio on thundering Harley-Davison's – actually they traveled like average shop girls on the subway from Queens. Lead singer Mary Weiss recalled: "We were on Clay Cole all the time, we sure were. WPIX, and his show, was my second home when I was a kid. Clay had us on so often, I knew the guards by name. I felt safe; I really felt at home there."

By the mid-Sixties, the Golden Age of Girl Groups would end with three New York trios, Raparata & the Delrons, ("Whenever A Teenager Cries,") the Angels ("My Boyfriends Back") and the Toys ("A Lover's Concerto") The very next year, in 1964, the Supremes' exploded, annihilating not only their Motown sisters, the Marvelettes and Martha & the Vandellas, but all girl groups. For the remainder of the decade, the Sixties belonged to the Supremes.

Girl Groups, like Teen Idols, twisters, rockabilly guitarists, and singing deejays were out of step with the marshalling new counter culture. Hippies were now dancing to a different drummer. Traditional American vocal groups, (the Four Aces) also vanished; their memory preserved at the Vocal Group Hall of Fame (founded by the Lettermen) in Sharon, PA, just a few miles east from my hometown, Hubbard, Ohio.

Like canaries in a Cole mine, Girl Groups were chirping a warning of things to come.

16) British Invasion

"The British Are Coming! The British Are Coming!"
– *Paul Revere, 1775, late-night news broadcaster*

Carmella Sgalambro, a schoolgirl from Brooklyn's Our Lady of Guadalupe remembers: "In 1964, my friends and classmates went to see the Dave Clark Five, but a bunch of pseudo-Beatlemaniacs were screaming, not allowing Clay Cole to get a word in."

Up in the Bronx, a pre-teen named Terry Adamo could see Dave Clark at the RKO Fordham "only if my older brother went with me. She remembered, "After the show I left the theater and followed you onto the bus, screaming "Clay" and "Mike" – Mike Smith was my favorite. A police officer came up behind me and pulled me off the bus, and my brother came up and rescued me. It was my very first brush with celebrity."

It was my very first brush with "Beatlemania," that wave of hysteria that accompanied the arrival of the Brit-Boy-Bands during the so-called British Invasion. I had been engaged by the RKO Theatre circuit to accompany the Dave Clark Five on another three-day, thirty-theatre tour, to promote their film "Having A Wild Weekend" (Called "Catch Us If You Can" in the rest of the word, the title of their No. 1 hit and the first film of director John Boorman, who later created the 1971 film classic, "Deliverance," with the unforgettable dueling banjos.) Needless to say, with Dave Clark and more specifically Mike Smith, his handsome lead singer on board, screeching females, wailing like police sirens, escorted our caravan throughout the five boroughs.

It may appear glamorous, stepping off a bus into a sea of pre-menopausal pubescent nymphets; rather it's more like piercing root canal with thirty dentists, repeated hourly over a three-day period. Seeking solitude from Carmella and the Ladies of Guadalupe, sanctuary was provided within strategically placed rest stops. RKO carefully planned our itinerary and after our appearance at the RKO 86th Street in Manhattan, our busses were shuttled over to The Jaeger House, a popular dining room in the heart of Germantown. As I was addressing my platter of Jägerschnitzel (veal cutlet smothered in brown gravy with sautéed mushrooms), an impeccably dressed, quite formal London Records executive approached me. "Would you," …choosing his words carefully, "consider…having the Rolling Stones on your program?"

To catch my breath, to allow his words to resonate in my brain, I wiped my lips and took a hearty swig from my stein.

"Would I," I thought. "Is he kidding? *The* Rolling Stones?"

"Absolutely," I confirmed, but "London Records will have to pay for their appearance, the AFTRA minimum scale for a group of five was approximately $600." Channel 11 would pay the appropriate pension and welfare payments, then AFTRA would mail checks to Mick, Keith, Bill, Charlie and Brian. No problem. The Clay Cole Show was to be the first television show in America to present the Rolling Stones, and they paid *us* to appear.

The British Invasion began for me with a group, Billy J. Kramer and the Dakotas, performing "Little Children," a recording produced by George Martin. The record broke big, on the charts for twelve weeks and into the Top 10. Billy J. Kramer's manager was so thrilled with the results of his appearance that he channeled all his Brits to my show. The manager's name was Brian Epstein. Peter Noone, the ever-youthful lead singer of Herman's Hermits, confessed to me recently, "When we were sent to America for the first time, we were told, you must do Ed Sullivan and Clay Cole. Trouble is…we didn't know which was which."

Luckily, I was on the dance card of all the Brits, and they waltzed into our dingy, little studio – far from the comfortable accommodations of the Ed Sullivan Theatre on Broadway – and gave our show a much-needed jolt.

British rock bands arrived like invading aliens, bizarre creatures, speaking a strange language, impish in manner, and – ouch – that hair. The Beatles arrived as cuddly, mop-topped teddy bears, neatly dressed in tidy, matching mohair suits with velvet lapels, neckties, and pointy little boots, quite non-threatening. The

Rolling Stones on the other hand, were rumpled roughnecks; the rock 'n' roll bad-boys. The rock journalist Lillian Roxon was famously quoted, "The 1964 Beatles looked as if they had been personally scrubbed down by Brian Epstein himself and the 1964 Rolling Stones looked as if they had been sent to bed every night for a week with the same clothes on and no supper. The Beatles' songs had been rinsed and hung out to dry. The Stones had never seen soap and water."

There was an on-going debate among fans: who is better, the cuddy Beatles or the raunchy Stones? The Beatles just want to hold your hand, the Stones demanded "Satisfaction." In an interview with Bob Lardine, in the *Daily News,* (December 27, 1964) I was asked to predict which of the two groups would endure. The odds on a correct answer were 50-50, but I correctly predicted the eventual outcome, pronouncing in favor of the Rolling Stones, not a popular sentiment in 1964.

"I believe the Rolling Stones are a better musical group than the Beatles," I said in the interview. Even the Beatles admitted they weren't great musicians, just clever songwriters. Lardine's story continued: "Memphis-born [deejay] Lloyd Thaxton disagrees with Clay's opinion of the Rolling Stones, "To me they're just a fad," says the thirty-seven-year-old TV host. The Beatles are really talented...and I believe they will last for quite some time."

The ultimate Clay Cole Show was the appearance of the Rolling Stones on a program with only one other group – the Beatles. As we were preparing for the Rolling Stones appearance, Channel 11's sister station WGN in Chicago wired us to announce they had gained permission to videotape the Beatles at a local arena and "could they test our all-new satellite, by feeding us concert footage?" This was too good to be true. To capitalize on the on-going rivalry amongst fans, I advanced the controversy by calling our show, "The Beatles vs. The Rolling Stones," a pre-sumption to be sure, for it was never intended to be a battle of the bands, but a highly promotable hook for the show.

The Rolling Stones touched down at the newly-named JFK International Air-port on June 1, 1964 for their first-ever American tour. Connie De Nave had care-fully choreographed an airport press conference with an equal mix of accredited journalists, freelance photographers and screaming teenage nymphs. The Stones began to roll.

The Stones arrived at WPIX, lumbering down our San Quentin hallway look-ing dazed and confused, with no groupies, roadies, or hangers-on, no matching suits or make up; they carried their own grips. Their tall, thin manager/sidekick, Andrew Loog Oldham reached out, grabbed a few of my fingers in a limp handshake, and mumbled "hello, mate." Oldham has equally fond memories of me as well. In his 2003 memoirs, "2-Stoned" Oldham wrote, "Clay Cole looked like an electro-shock Anthony Perkins on steroids."

Bill Wyman arrived late, huffing and puffing that he "had been on the wrong side of a police barricade." Keith, at a time when he could utter a complete sentence without becoming distracted, commented: "Nobody realizes how America blew our minds – and the Beatles' too. I can't even describe what America meant to us. We first started to listen to Otis Redding when we got to the States, and picked up our first Stax singles – and Wilson Pickett....and, er..." – (*Yes, and then?*)

Mick sang, "It's All Over Now," "Around and Around," and "Confessin' the Blues," to screams of approval from our studio audience, mostly teenage girls. The interviews went well, although it was difficult to stand too close. Mick and the boys had not yet learned about personal hygiene, the American custom of daily showers or deodorant – engendering a lingering, intoxicating memory. Mick was the most animated; one photograph shows him in a moment of garrulous laughter. When we brought girls to the stage for some one-on-one questioning, the segment fell apart – the girls were dumbstruck and giddy, and the Stones were preoccupied bird watching, soaking up their first whiff of teenage America. Actually, it's the girls who inhaled the memorable whiff, launching the gag, "never trust anyone over dirty."

The Stones then taped "Little Red Rooster," an old black man's blues standard, once recorded by Sam Cooke, "Carol" a Chuck Berry tune, and their latest single, "Tell Me" (to be broadcast on future shows.) The Beatles' video from Chicago was so thrilling that the hairs on my neck were fighting the goose-bumps on my arms for attention. It was the crowd reaction that was so rousing – thousands of Instamatics popping simultaneously creating fireworks combined with the roar of recognition and the massive gasp of breath at the Beatles entrance.

Such events are best remembered by impressionable young viewers and Paul Slansky later described his reaction to the Stones is in an article published in the September 30, 2002, edition of *The New York Observer*.

"The bands all wore jackets and ties on stage, and though everybody's hair was a little long, no one - not even, at this point, John Lennon - was looking for trouble. The Stones' first American television appearances slyly subverted these tidy notions. They appeared twice on The Hollywood Palace, where stupid jokes were made at their expense by host Dean Martin, and once on the Clay Cole Show. I saw them all, but it's the Clay Cole appearance that I won't forget. Mr. Jagger performed in jeans and a pullover - it could have been a sweatshirt or a sweater, but whatever it was, it looked even grubbier on my small black-and-white set. His outfit screamed "F--- you!" to everyone who thought a proper gent got dressed up to perform.

And then there was the music. Unless you came of age in this period, chances are you're unaware of the pre-"Satisfaction" Stones era, during which they covered everything from R&B to soul to hard-core Chicago blues, Marvin Gaye to Solomon Burke to Willie Dixon. No white guys ever played black music better, and no matter what artist's lyrics Mr. Jagger was singing, he always put his own undeniable imprint on them.

At a time when the Beatles were riding the charts with "P.S. I Love You," the Stones' sound was anti-pop: aggressive, intense and nasty - a rawer version of Phil Spector's Wall of Sound, with the relentless beat driven home by raging guitars, wailing harmonica and, most of all, Mr. Jagger's cocky , arrogant, lewd voice.

As I watched Mick Jagger leering into Clay Cole's camera, flapping his huge wet lips and singing "I Just Want to Make Love to You," my mother stood in the bedroom doorway watching me watching the Stones. Eventually, she called out for my father to join her. I was thrilled. Teenagers-particularly teenage boys-are an angry lot. They're confused and embarrassed by the chemical changes their bodies are going through. They're increasingly aware of how imperfect the world is, and how harshly the world can judge their own imperfections. In short, they're pissed off. And it's not enough to tell their parents about it. They need to make them feel the way they do, experience their rage and revulsion, and the time-honored way to do this is to embrace that which their parents fear and hate. There was nothing about the Rolling Stones that said "Love me," and for that - and for the looks of horror that these surly hooligans put on my parents' faces - I instantly and passionately loved them."

Clay Cole presents "The Beatles vs. The Rolling Stones" pulled the highest rating in our history ("the ratings went through the roof," reported *Variety*), prompting the station to repeat the hour on three different nights, with equally high numbers. I was told later that Stones taped a Hollywood Palace and a Dean Martin Show, but were unhappy with the ridicule leveled at them by the show's writers. Dean and Milton Berle made them the butt of "longhaired" jokes, and Mick was clearly pissed. By the time the Rolling Stones returned for their second appearance in May of 1965, they were clearly on their way to being considered "the greatest rock and roll band of all-time." With sold-out concert events, albums and singles flying off the shelves, they were now as self-confident as their new No. 1 signature song, "(I Can't Get No) Satisfaction."

When I was a teenager, "longhair" was a put-down, meaning "not with-it," like dead poets or classical musicians – oddballs like Einstein. Now, ten years later "longhair" was the in-thing. My singular nod to the caveman look was my own Beatle haircut. My best physical asset had always been my hair, thick and black, severely parted to the left in the style of Cary Grant, although it was commonly called the "Peter Gunn," inspired by the popular TV crime drama starring Craig Stevens. My hair was razor-cut by Rudy of the Warwick, Perry Como's stylist, and given that Perry was once a barber himself, Perry's choice made Rudy the premier cutter of show-biz men. Paul Anka, Sid Caesar, Douglas Edwards, Colonel Tom Parker – even Elvis, himself lumbered up the steps to the Warwick Hotel mezzanine to pay the staggering $15 for a Rudy cut. On camera, my long, shaggy "Beatle cut" now cascaded over my forehead like Mamie Eisenhower bangs; off-camera, I was not bold enough to appear in public making such a radical statement; I combed it back. After several months of brushing my hairs forward for the cameras, I simply had my bushy Beatle cut exorcized on the show, on-camera for the full hour by my stylist Tommy from Rudy's Warwick salon. (Since we taped the show, it became a four-hour haircut.) Producers of a new rock musical, wishing to invoke images of a Sixties hippie tribe, simply marketed their show as "Hair." Long hair had become the iconic symbol of the times. In the film "A Hard Day's Night," a reporter asks George Harrison, "What do you call your haircut?" To which George responded, "Arthur." That bit of trivia seemed insignificant until film director Mike Nichols suggested to Sybil Burton that "Arthur" might be the perfect name for her club. In 1965, "Arthur" became the hippest dance club in New York.

Not all young people embraced long hair; in the beginning it was a big city statement for Greenwich Village types and musicians. The sissy-looking locks repelled our country cousins. Backwoods deer hunters would've liked nothing better than to return home with a dead hippie strapped to their hood. John Wayne summed it up for Middle America when he pronounced: "If a guy wants to wear his hair down to his ass, I'm not revolted by it. But I don't look at him and say, "Now there's a fella I'd like to spend the winter with.""

Nowadays, $15 is an average price for a haircut and it seems that rural rednecks, country singers and garage mechanics are the gentlemen who now prefer long hair, while big city boys favor the trendy buzz-cut, or the "bald is beautiful" look – cue balls like Daughtry.

When Beatles' records were initially released in America, most deejays tossed them in the trash bin; many thought the Beatle was a German car. Capitol Records, their USA distributor refused to release their singles, and the rights were licensed to Vee Jay, a company that failed to pay royalties. DJ Dick Biondi on Chicago's powerhouse WLS placed "Please Please Me" into rotation in late February 1963, to no reaction. In August 1963, the Philadelphia-based Swan label tried again with the Beatles' "She Loves You," tested on Dick Clark's "American Bandstand," resulting in laughter and scorn. Murray the K featured the song on his 1010-WINS show in October to an under-whelming response.

Beatlemania began with Sid Bernstein. Eager to sign the Beatles to his American agency, Sid brought a publicity photo, pitching the untried group to GAC (General Artists Corporation), but was turned down flat. Jack Paar, who had been in London filming some "Tonight" show segments, was the first American to report on Beatlemania, and Ed Sullivan, on a stopover in England, also got caught-up in the frenzy. The accumulating buzz accelerated rapidly throughout the industry grapevine, and Norman Wise, vice president in the GAC variety department, flew to the UK to sign the group to an exclusive agency contract. GAC rewarded Sid Bernstein with the rights to promote Beatles' concerts in America.

Capitol Records planned to hold the release of "I Wanna Hold Your Hand" until after the '63 Christmas holidays, but then, out of left field, Walter Cronkite, "The Most Trusted Man in America" broadcast a short quirky clip December 10th on the CBS Evening News (no doubt prompted by his two teenage daughters). Brian Epstein came to town to solidify a three-show television deal with Ed Sullivan and personal appearances in New York and Washington, DC with Sid Bernstein. Based on the Cronkite reaction and the Sullivan booking, Capitol Records rush-released "I Want To Hold Your Hand" the day after Christmas and shelled out $50,000 to plaster New York City with five-million posters, bumper stickers and radio ads, announcing, "The Beatles Are Coming!" When the hype began – via Jack Paar, Ed Sullivan, and Walter Cronkite – deejays jumped on the bandwagon. Capitol Records encouraged the New York deejays to broadcast their actual arrival time: "The Beatles will be arriving February 7, 1964, at 1:20pm."Cut school, show up, and see the Beatles." Ray Reneri recalled, "Radio deejays once accustomed to promoting hype suddenly fell victim to the build up."

The Beatles touched down at JFK in a Pan Am Clipper (paid for by CBS), with "Defiance" emblazoned on the fuselage. They were greeted by Murray the "K," who had already dubbed himself "the fifth Beatle," and three thousand screaming fans. A reporter for the *Saturday Evening Post* noted: "Anyone listening to a pop radio station in New York would hear a Beatle record every four minutes." "I Want to Hold Your Hand" was No. 1 on the *Billboard* charts, selling 2-million units, rolling over Bobby Vinton, Bobby Rydell and the Singing Nun. Their first U.S. album was just hitting the stores.

"So this is America," mused Ringo, "they all seem out of their minds."

"What an ugly race," said John.

George immediately came down sick.

Every deejay in town was up their ass. Murray "The K" took John, Paul and Ringo out on the town, leaving George at the Plaza in his sick bed. They hit the Playboy Club, where Paul found himself a Bunny and to the Peppermint Lounge, with John accompanied by his wife Cynthia, and where Ringo disappeared for hours.

(My hunch is this was the night Ringo met the youngest of the Ronettes, Cousin Nedra Talley, beginning an ongoing, hush-hush romance.)

Radio bulletins updated an anxious nation on George's condition. Ed Sullivan announced he would stand in for George if needed. George managed to stagger out of bed in time for the broadcast, and their Ed Sullivan appearance attracted 70-million people, 60% of America's television viewers.

At first The Beatles were indistinguishable, but *The Daily News* sorted things out:

> *"Four slender young men, in four black suits and four knit ties, with four Prince Valiant haircuts and four bemused expressions. The oldest, 23-year old Ringo Starr attacked the drums, John Lennon was the chief Beatle, who is married and has a son, a third one, Paul McCartney with Lennon writes Beatle songs, and the last one, George Harrison, was the lead guitar."*

The Rolling Stones, prompted by an intervention from Alan Klein signed on with Jerry Brandt at The William Morris Agency. Klein was the American accounting wizard who first renegotiated a million dollar deal for Sam Cooke with RCA, then lost Sam Cooke to a bullet fired in a seedy Los Angeles motel. Alan Klein continued to break all the existing rules, renegotiating contracts, resulting in lucrative financial rewards of unpaid royalties and performance fees for Bobby Vinton, Bobby Darin, and the Brit boy bands, the Dave Clark Five, Herman's Hermits and the Animals. He forced British Decca to tear-up the Rolling Stones old contract and renegotiated a $1.25 million advance. Alan Klein also negotiated a Stones deal with Jerry Brandt at William Morris that was unprecedented; a 7% agency commission (rather than the standard 10%), a guarantee of $25,000 against percentage of the gate, and a similar fee for each Ed Sullivan appearance. Brian Epstein had settled for a $10,000 offer for three Sullivan appearances of the Beatles, Colonel Parker had settled for $50,000 for three Sullivan appearances for Elvis, but Alan Klein demanded and received $25,000 for *each* Rolling Stone appearance. Ed Sullivan's ceiling price of $7,000 applied to his biggest guest stars – Martin & Lewis, Ethel Merman, and Senor Wences – now went through the roof! I still believe I cut the best deal of all; three appearances of the Rolling Stones, and they paid us to appear.

The Dave Clark Five signed with Associated Booking, a talent agency headed by the colorful Joe Glazer, the lifelong promoter of Louis Armstrong and Little Richard. (Glazer once mistakenly ordered Little Richard out of his Park Avenue reception room: "get that sissy messenger-boy out of here.") With the power of Louis Armstrong as leverage, Glazer successfully booked the Dave Clark Five on the Ed Sullivan Show a record number of times, more than any other rock group. During that period, the "DC5," placed 15 consecutive singles in the U.S. Top Forty. It is one of the most impressive statistical feats of the British Invasion.

The Dave Clark Five, powered by Mike Smith's vocals, made the DC-5 recordings explosive, on hits such as "Glad All Over," "Bits and Pieces" and "Catch Us If You Can." Mike had a formidable growl, unleashed on soul songs like "I Like it Like That," and on the Contours' "Do You Love Me," the latter being three minutes of all-out shouting. "A huge voice, with unmatched power and depth," said Bob Berry, former CKLW (Detroit-Windsor) disc jockey. "He needed every ounce of it to cut through the compression Dave Clark put on those recordings. Sometimes the reverb was so thick on DC5 records; it sounded like Smith was shouting his songs from an underground tunnel."

The remainder of the first-wave groups like Herman's Hermits, the Animals, Gerry & the Pacemakers and Manfred Mann signed on with the relatively new Premier Talent, an agency managed by Frank Barcelona. Frank started in the mail room at GAC at the time when Roz Ross up and left and, desperate for agents in their rock 'n' roll division, he was elevated as assistant to Ernie Martinelli, with a warning: "Don't get too comfortable in that desk." He was a $75 a week junior agent, but learned well, eventually forming his own small agency at 200 West 57th St. Connie De Nave's PR division was one floor down, so Connie and Frank formed an alliance, to promote and sell The British Invasion. Connie put a romantic spin on these boys from the back streets of Manchester, Liverpool and London, and like Dickens's Fagin, she adopted these poor little urchins and groomed them to hit the road and collect gold coins. Ray Reneri, fresh off the road from another now-archaic Dick Clark Cavalcade of Stars tour, was recruited to lead the British Invasion as Tour Manager, introducing the boy-bands to the hinterlands of America. Now all the elements were in place – the American promoters, the booking agencies, the public relations machine, the fan club organizations, the disc jockeys, and the tour manager. The British Invasion was underway – staged by Americans.

Music critic Robert Christgau reminded us: "Don't forget, the Beatles started off by turning on little twelve-year-olds too." In the early stages, a pretty face, and a chart position took precedence over quality and excellence. These were topsy-turvy years, with groups jockeying for position. The Dave Clark Five were favorably compared to the Beatles; and the Who was opening for Herman's Hermits. In those days, the Who were too poor to destroy their instruments at the end of every set – the outrage was all about Roger Daltry's shirt, a British flag, long before the Queen began collecting royalties on shot glasses, shopping bags, gewgaws and souvenirs emblazoned with the Union Jack. There was a huge national flap when CBS forced Merv Griffin to censor an American flag shirt worn by the radical Yuppie, Abby Hoffman. A few weeks later, all was forgiven when Roy Rogers & Dale Evans appeared in stars-and-stripes shirts, tailored by Nudie, the designer of Elvis Presley's $10,000 gold lamé suit, which the singer wore on the cover of his *50,000,000 Elvis Fans Can't Be Wrong* album. A flag shirt today is not seen as a protest, rather a statement of patriotic pride.

Three of the best Brit groups got lost in the shuffle, pushed aside in the rush of second-rate, Mickey Mouse pop groups (i.e. Manfred Mann's "Do Wah Diddy Diddy"). The Kinks, one group most admired by other musicians, were banned in the USA by the AFM (musician's union) during the four decisive years in the mid-60s, and fell by the wayside, as did the Zombies, another highly-regarded group, unable to tour because of immigration problems. The Yardbirds, great musicians, ho-hum performers, lacked a charismatic frontman like a Mick Jagger, Gerry Marsden or Peter Noone.

At the outset, the Beatles appeal was grossly miscalculated; they played the undersized 2,800-seat Carnegie Hall. "We could have sold 50 days worth of shows at two shows a day," the box-office manager groaned to a dumbfounded Sid Bernstein. "He'd never seen anything like it." He told me, "Kids were sleeping in the street last night in the wintertime! Their mothers were bringing them blankets!'"

As Tour Manager, big-brother and mother confessor to the British Invaders, it took Ray Reneri only a few one-niters to recognize a problem: Security! Uncontrollable fans mobbed Herman's Hermits in a limo trying to exit an arena tunnel, and their car was nearly upended. Ray pleaded with Frank Barcelona back in New York, "We need more security!" "But, I gave you twenty men," Barcelona reasoned.

"20? We need 200!"

Ray devised distractions: "Groups arrived in Brink's armored cars or dropped in by helicopter. Another diversion was to force groups to lie on the floor of departing sound trucks, while the sound crew, acting as decoys, exited in limousines. Groups trapped at the far end of Atlantic City's Steel Pier were rescued by the Coast Guard and returned to their hotel by sea. We arrived in town in every conceivable way, except by parachute – but don't think it wasn't considered."

Rifle-toting vigilantes fired on tour buses. Renegade county sheriffs harassed the busses, pulling them over for middle-of-the-night searches. Much like the fear and loathing many black entertainers encountered while touring throughout the South, the new British groups experienced America's newest twisted bias – long hair. A busload of longhaired freaks, strolling into an all-night Midwestern diner, became the subjects of ridicule and revulsion. They were refused service. "No Long Hairs Served" signs sprung up. This was the America of 1964. It was all about the hair.

Tour buses were abandoned in favor of air travel; at the very least on a plane they could be served a meal. On commercial prop planes arriving at mid-sized airports, fans would run amuck out onto the tarmac, energized by the local radio guys. Finally private jets, with unannounced arrival times, were taken into service. To break the monotony of touring, Peter Noone once performed the entire set-list of the Dave Clark Five. Not to outdone, Dave Clark and Mike Smith, sustaining the pretense, took to the stage performing all the hits of Herman's Hermits. Once, when band equipment got lost in transit, the groups performed the entire show a cappella.

George Harrison once made an innocent remark about jellybeans as his favorite snack food. In response, his mostly teenage, mostly female concertgoers began showering him with jellybeans. Soon, every group was plummeted by jellybeans. Often, Reneri was faced with an impossibly tight schedule, two shows a day, in two different cities. To adhere to the schedule, Ray devised a plan, based on a "security clause" in the performance contract. If one of the musicians was injured because of lack crowd control, the performance could be halted. So, on cue, halfway through a set, one of the band boys would fall victim to a fake jellybean abrasion. The show was stopped and moved on to the next city with plenty of time to spare – saved by the jellybean.

The place to play in Ottawa was Lu Lu's, a notorious rock 'n' roll club with "the world's longest bar." Attempting to cross over into Canada with the Yardbirds (the

Jeff Beck-Jimmy Page unit after Eric Clapton departed) presented a problem at the custom's checkpoint. Jimmy Page always tightly guarded a black satchel, which he was now asked to open for inspection. Panic set in; Reneri was bewildered, but curious. The agent opened the contents to find whips, chains, garrotes, and hand-cuffs – a bag of tricks. Page, totally embarrassed, unable to provide an explanation, turned to Ray Reneri for help. Ray jumped in, "Entertainers," pointing to the work papers. "The circus!" The agent stamped the papers and passed them through, no problem. "Welcome to Canada."

Back in New York, at 200 West 57th Street, the familiar whirr of Connie De-Nave's clumsy old mimeograph machine gave way to the clankety-clank of new-fangled Xerox copiers, spitting out press releases, this time for her Boy Bands. Their fan club division was now generating millions of dollars, one dirty little dollar at a time. Connie once turned down a *Life* magazine editor's request to interview and photograph Mick Jagger, knowing that the more she dissuaded, his level of interest would escalate. Connie was holding out for *Life*'s coveted cover. Finally, she relented, and Mick did not disappoint, arriving at the photo shoot in full drag. Mick eventually did appear on a *Life* cover, photographed in a pro football jersey, with those famous pouting lips glossy red, his face powdered and rouged, done up in Max Factor and Maybelline. Georgia Winters' comic book-style *16* magazine covers now displayed the *new* teenage dreamboats; cutouts of Peter Noone replaced Paul Petersen, Ringo replaced Fabian.

Meanwhile, while we were caught up in the Mersey-beat, dancing "The Fred-die," the Beatles were quietly writing and releasing distinctive, innovative singles, consistently maintaining their stranglehold on all the pop charts. On August 15, 1965, Sid Bernstein presented his career-defining event; the Beatles at Shea Stadium, a milestone moment in rock 'n' roll history.

Having learned his lesson at Carnegie Hall by booking the Beatles into an auditorium with a mere 2800 seats, Bernstein was thinking bigger-than-life. He envisioned a massive arena; even Madison Square Garden would be too small. The newly-built Shea Stadium might be perfect; it was a venue that had never hosted a concert before. But first he had to convince Brian Epstein.

"Brian at first said no," Bernstein recalls. "He didn't want his boys playing to empty seats." Bernstein finally convinced him to take a chance, and then pleaded with Mayor Wagner into letting him promote a spectacular Shea Stadium event with its 55,000 seats. The mayor forced Sid to pay for a host of extra cops, and wouldn't allow Beatlemaniacs to sit on the field. The mayor assigned his intern, a teenaged Jeffrey Katzenberg (yes, *that* Jeffrey Katzenberg) to be his eyes and ears, to report back, to make sure things went according to plan – and did it ever! Rock 'n' Roll was no longer a passing fad if over 55,000 fans would shell out the $5 to fill the seats of a stadium. Years later, Bernstein says, John Lennon turned to him and said, "Sid, at Shea Stadium, I saw the top of the mountain." There was mistiness in his eyes.

When Walter Winchell first coined the phrase "disc jockey," he was referring to Martin Block, a dapper old-time radioman; but – have you ever noticed how unattractive most radio disc jockeys appear? I remember my disillusionment seeing my favorite radio deejay in person for the very first time. The voice and the face didn't match; it was not a pleasant sight. Radio is show business for ugly people. An ugly puss is nature's way of saying, "go into radio." Ugly behavior is another matter; it's just bad manners. During the British Invasion, disc jockeys really got ugly.

Radio stations became Beatle Central, Official Beatles Station, Beatle Headquarters, W-A-Beatle-C, "all Beatles all the time," turning their backs on American groups and record stars. Count the number of careers that were crushed, not by the British invasion, but by disc jockeys. By totally abandoning American groups, the deejays forgot all those American artists who had been their ticket to ride. How could America's disc jockeys forget all the freebee appearances at their lucrative record hops, all the in-studio interviews and "phoners" that gave them clout and stature in their markets? In a snap, they bought into Beatlemania. I became heartbroken over all the popular American recording stars that had a quick taste of fame, approval from their families, adoration from fans, stage and radio and television bookers begging for their attention, only to fall out of favor into oblivion. No airplay – no hits!

Nowhere was this behavior more squalid than in New York City. Deejays from the three major Top 40 stations, 77-WABC, 1010-WINS and "The WMCA Good Guys" were falling all over themselves, cueing up in the hallways of the Warwick or Plaza Hotel, to get an exclusive, a sound bite, a picture, anything to get close to the Fab Four. The Beatles, strangers in a strange land, were accommodating, obliged to win the favor of the powerful men of the airways.

"The idea of just coming to America was the mind-blower," Ringo recalled. "No one can imagine these days what an incredible feat it was to conquer America. No British act had done it before. We were just coming over to do our stuff, hopefully get recognized and to sell some records. But it turned into something huge."

Out-of-town radio stations added to the frenzy with on-the-spot live radio reports from airports, motorcades, hotels and arenas across America: "The Stones private jet will touch down at 10:12... Herman's Hermits motorcade is approaching the Logan Tunnel ... Dave Clark was spotted at Union Station...This is 'Beatle' Mitchell Reed backstage at the arena..." This is Dick Biondi / Gary Stevens / Joey Reynolds ... we estimate The Yardbirds /Zombies/ Animals arrival at the Hyatt / Hilton / Holiday Inn will be 11:07 ... on and on. All this made it impossible to secure and properly protect the artists.

While arriving in Chicago during the Beatles' 1964 world tour, a decision was made by someone outside of the Beatle camp to change the landing site of their airplane to a more secretive spot on the airfield. This last-minute change would end up disappointing the large crowd of devoted fans who had waited many hours for a chance to see the Beatles at the airport. The next morning there was a major brouhaha in the media, blaming the Beatles for rudely snubbing their fans. The Beatles were incorrectly blamed for the incident and sought to set the record straight. Paul explained to the press, "I was watching the TV last night, and on the news they showed all the fans ... sort of disappointed, and they didn't actually say anything about whose fault it was. They just said, 'Police commissioner so-and-so said the Beatles *wanted* to land there.' and they said no more. That really sounded as though we'd said, 'Please don't let us land amongst all those fans. We hate them,' which is completely untrue, you know. We definitely asked to meet them or at least drive past 'em, and they told us, 'No'. Thousands of fans also waited to greet the Beatles at the Washington, D.C. National Airport, while the Beatles quietly snuck into town by train, arriving without fuss at Union Station.

No disc jockey displayed more chutzpa than the audacious antics of Tom Clay in Detroit. Clay, an earlier target of the payola purge, found his popularity soar again through his meetings and on-air interviews with the Beatles. Once again, he became the victim of his own greed. This time, he was fired over a scheme in which he collected one dollar from each listener for membership in a "Beatles Booster Club," a non-existent organization which had no benefits beyond a membership card. According to fellow DJ Dave Shafer, Clay promised each listener who sent in a dollar a personal item used by one of the Beatles; these "personal items" turned out to be disgusting items like cigarette butts and used tissues. However, since over 80,000 fans responded, he was able to live comfortably on the cash that appeared in his personal post office box (the equivalent of about half a million dollars today). Dave Shafer told David Carson in "Rockin' Down the Dial" that Clay skipped town in the wake of the Beatles Booster fiasco, leading to Shafer's being briefly jailed on charges of international fraud.

In 1964, before the Beatles and the Boy Bands of the British Invasion, there were no singer/musician quartets on American music charts, you were either defined as an instrumental group, like Johnny & the Hurricanes, the Bill Black Combo, Booker T. & the MG's or as a vocal group, likes the Platters, the Miracles, or Danny & the Juniors. Since the collapse of the swing bands, Americans partied to polka bands, country/western bands, or wedding bands, combos with a saxophone, drums, stand-up bass and keyboard (often an accordion). Well-known bands were simply there to support the lead singer, the Comets for Bill Haley, the Crickets for Buddy Holly or the Hawks for Ronnie Hawkins. (The Hawks, in actual fact, resurfaced appropriately as The Band.) The Beatles themselves began as a back up band; John, Paul, George, with drummer Pete Best and Stu Sutcliffe on guitar, were booked as the backup band for a singer named Tony Sheridan.

The Beatles and all the subsequent Brit bands freely admit that they were influenced by American artists and recordings – the blues, rhythm and blues, gospel, rockabilly, and the rock 'n' roll of Bill Haley, Buddy Holly, Charlie Gracie, the Everly Brothers, Chuck Berry, Bo Diddley and Elvis. This may explain why the Beatles spoke with an English accent, but sang with a clear Southern twang. John and Paul sounded just like Don and Phil Everly. Keith Richards told *Rolling Stone* magazine that he credits Bo Diddley for teaching him how to be wild and professional at the same time.

"Touring in the early 60s, I became Bo's groupie: "The Duchess was there [on guitar] and Jerome Green with maracas in each hand. I was minding Jerome. It was my job to fetch him from the pub, 'You're on, mate!' We were opening for Bo Diddley, Little Richard and the Everly Brothers [in 1963] and I learned more in those six weeks than I would have learned from listening to a million records."

As if returning the favor, the Beatles and the Brits gave us American Boy Bands, as we know them today – KISS, the Eagles and Grand Funk Railroad. Would there be a Monkees, Earth, Wind & Fire, or a Crosby, Stills, Nash & Young without a John, Paul, Ringo and George? I don't think so. Since 1964, singing musicians have been the dominant force of American popular music. Without delay, vocal groups like the Tokens, the Beach Boys and the Four Seasons scrambled to tune-up their instrumental skills, becoming "self-contained groups."

Like the Brits, American Boy Bands could now demand a proper sound system, stage lighting, sound checks, backline equipment and a custom-made contract rider. Personal appearances were now called "concerts." America's Boy Bands were rewarded financially as well, finally earning top dollar and claiming a percentage of the gross, winning parity with the Brits. "It was crazy," Tommy DeVito of the Four Season says. "We went from making $1,000 a week to $1,000 a day."

Charlie Calello, the well-respected arranger and producer, briefly sang with the Four Seasons, replacing Nick Massi, before Joe Long became a permanent member in 1965. Charlie recalled a remarkable incident: "In 1963, Frankie Valli went to England with the Four Seasons and came back with about a dozen records. I went over to his house and he played me "I Want to Hold Your Hand," "Please Please Me," the first five Beatles' hits over in England. We brought them to Bob Crewe and Bob Gaudio and played the records for Bob Crewe and Frankie says, "We should cut these songs now. These are smashes. They were hits in England, and we should cut these songs." And Bob Crewe says, "I think we write better songs" and we never cut them. Now we were big enough at that particular time to where we could have cut those songs, covered them. We may not have done them as well, but we would have cut those songs and we would have released them, and some of those songs could have been hits and that would have been the end of the Beatles." The point is, "Frankie was aware that this was the new hot stuff, and he said, "This is where we should be".

Many American groups took the British Invasion literally, dressing in combat gear for the ultimate "battle of the bands." Gary Puckett & the Union Gap chose Confederate gray Civil War gear, strange considering that Puckett is from Minnesota and formed his bar band in San Diego. Gary Puckett's yearning vocals needed no gimmick, and after a few hits, they abandoned the uniforms. Paul Revere & the Raiders, a group formed in Idaho, dressed as 18th Century Colonial Boston Red Coats. (*16* magazine editor Georgia Winters confided in me that Paul Revere's birth name was Paul Dick – and she would know.) The Doughboys, a bar band from New Jersey, dressed in full WWI military gear, and Emitt Rhodes' L.A. group, The Palace Guard dressed in the royal red kits of London's rigid Buckingham Palace Guards; turncoats, nonetheless, but a good Kodak moment.

The first East Coast group to successfully challenge the Beatles was a zany bunch of local boys who needed no uniforms and produced astonishingly original hits, combining good-time rock 'n' roll, folk-rock and traditional blues, with hard-driving riffs, a mouth-harp and a jug-band feel. Sounds kookie? – Who'd have thought! The Lovin' Spoonful were four of the funniest guys who ever waltzed into our studios, and for the first time I was able to relate one-on-one with a "tie-dyed group." Our common ground was that they were street-smart New Yorkers with good-natured humor. Just a year earlier, in 1964, John Sebastian and Zal Yanovsky were already veterans of the Greenwich Village folk scene, singing at The Café Wha' with the Mugwumps along with Cass Elliott and Denny Doherty, who later joined the Mamas & The Papas. John and Zal could be spotted singin' 'n' strummin' in Washington Square Park where they hooked up with "one of the few drummers in the Village," Joe Butler (from Long Island), and rhythm guitarist, Steve Boone (from North Carolina) who played bass. With John Sebastian as principle songwriter, they rehearsed (famously, endlessly) in the old Albert Hotel in the Village and with their first, "Do You Believe In Magic" (1965) to "Nashville Cats" (1967), the Lovin' Spoonful appeared on our show multiple times, introducing each of their seven singles, all of which scored in the Top Ten on the national charts, a phenomenal achievement in the midst of Beatlemania. To me they were simply my all-time favorites; four-wild-and-crazy guys! If you want to see the proof of their power and appeal, rent the wacky 1966 Woody Allen film, "What's Up, Tiger Lilly?" and check out the Lovin' Spoonful on stage, in full force, preserved on celluloid as young and spunky as we want to remember them.

Following the Beatles, the first British band to have a No.1 song on the American charts was the raspy-voiced Eric Burdon and the Animals, with Alan Price on his bluesy Hammond-organ performing "House of the Rising Sun." Their appearance was a wakeup call – "Watch out America, there are plenty more bad-assed bands back home where we come from, not just the Beatles and the Stones!" It was in 1965 that Eric Burdon introduced me to the new wave of girl groups. Eric and his producer/sidekick Mickey Most asked me for some pub-crawling tips for a night on the town and I gave them directions to several Time Square clubs. Passing by The Wagon Wheel, Eric and Mickey were attracted to a "kick-ass sound" blasting out onto 45th Street. Once inside, expecting a black man blues band, it was four girls on stage. Eric called me, enthusiastic about a new girl group he and Mickey had discovered, "four birds that blew us away…perfect for your show."

Goldie and the Gingerbreads is a name suggesting pigtails, pinafore dresses and peasant blouses. So it was a jolt when Goldie and the Gingerbreads arrived at our studios packing guitars, a drum kit and a humongous Hammond-B3 organ – an all-girl rock band. It was startling, the guitar, that macho phallic symbol of sexual domination, strapped to a woman! Carol MacDonald strapped it on, and with Ginger Bianco on drums, Margo Lewis pumpin' the pedals of her Hammond B-3, and "Goldie" (real name Genya Ravan) singing lead, I introduced the first self-contained all-female band.

Goldie & the Gingerbreads were more than a novelty attraction; they were an incredibly hip black-sounding blues band. In England, the Stones were their warm-up band. In one really unusual instance of reversal, Goldie and the Gingerbreads had a huge hit record in England, "Can't You Hear My Heartbeat," the very same song that was a hit for Peter Noone and Herman's Hermits here in the states.

It was equally jolting to witness the upstart black rock 'n' roll bands. Guitar-based Boy Band had always been the domain of white boys; black entertainers found their niche as rhythm and blues or soul singers. "Funk is just the blues speeded up," says George Clinton, the kid from Plainfield, NJ, who formed the Funkadelics as a guitar-based rock band. Two West Coast rock bands also surfaced in New York in 1965, Sly & the Family Stone and the Chamber Brothers, who added drummer Brian Keenan, affecting the guitar-bass-drum set-up. In spite of the later appearance of the Brothers Johnson, Jimi Hendrix, Earth, Wind and Fire and Prince, the rock 'n' roll band has remained white boy territory.

Much to my benefit, television producers had no idea what to do with the procession of scruffy boy bands that began to appear in 1963. The standard variety show formula still worked for sparkly-dressed girls, like the Supremes, and the black-tie boys like the Four Seasons, but the new boy bands had abandoned matching suits, in favor of jeans and tee-shirt or the trendy gypsy look, like the Stones or the Lovin' Spoonful. The staging of their songs made them look uncomfortable and out of place. On the big-budget network shows, the musicians would be immobile, each stranded on a little platform, brightly lighted on a deep stage, set against a stark, white cyclorama and then crazed choreographers would surround them with flocks of jiggly go-go girls, bouncing to the boogaloo. It was madness: "…and now, here on our stage, Eric Burdon and 'War!'"

The well-worn, cramped Clay Cole studios offered a shabby comfort zone, surroundings reminiscent of a sleazy club; they were right at home.

The Beatles arrival in 1964 signaled the ascent of the singer/songwriter/musician, the Boy Band, the concept album, and elevated rock 'n' roll as the singular popular music preference of America – and so the world. Now into its third generation, rock 'n' roll is so imprinted into our psyche that's it's become America's Muzak, in Wal-Mart, Stop-n-Shop, on elevators, on hold, on ring-tones and on the moon – mood music for rocket scientists. Oh, and yes, the hair; that much-maligned mark of our halcyon days still grows.

17) Clay Cole's Happening Place

"When I read about the evils of drinking,
I gave up reading."
– Henny Youngman

"To drink is a Christian diversion, unknown to the Persian – beware of the man who does not drink." Our generation was drinkers, at a time when Ike and Mamie knocked back a few each night watching Walter Cronkite. After work cocktails were a New York ritual the cocktail dress, cocktail party, and the cherry-topped Manhattan all made it so civil, so acceptable. Commuter trains added bar-cars. Young ladies aspired to be "Miss Rheingold;" young men slugged down boilermakers. Frank Sinatra said, "I feel sorry for people who don't drink. When they wake up in the morning, that's as good as they're going to feel all day."

Peggy Lee's biographer Peter Richmond put it all into perspective: "To judge the drinking habits of the early Eisenhower years from the perch of the clean, sober, righteously judgmental twenty-first century make no sense."

Never mind that we were now in the throws of a post-Kennedy hangover, we partied on. I had an unusual high capacity for alcohol; Raysa said I had a hollow leg.

The saloon might be a playground for the workingman, but it's a workplace for the entertainer. Playing clubs, between-show snorts, hanging out at the bar, buying a round of drinks, after-hours clubs, was all part of the ritual. I developed the ability to drink large amounts and still maintain a celebrity persona. Approach me in a bar room, engage me in conversation, take a picture, and scribble an autograph; no problem. If I were "three sheets to the wind," no one could tell.

"Wine for my men; we ride tonight!" I wasn't a trendy weed smoker; marijuana turned me into Gumby. Like most of my crowd, I just popped a diet pill, washed it down with a martini, and waited for the "bottoms up" to kick in. Of course, we were indulging ourselves with "uppers" – amphetamines – the most noxious and addictive of all recreational drugs. "Speed" wrecks havoc with the brain and the chemical balance of the body. It's lethal! But, *who knew?*

The best that could be said of Channel 11 was its proximity to Louie's East, a tavern at the backdoor of the Daily News building, a few feet from the loading docks, where News delivery trucks sat idling like quivering green elephants at a watering hole, awaiting bundles of the early edition to come rolling down the chute from the pressroom. The drivers did their idling inside Louie's, alongside a most colorful collection of newspapermen: loud-mouthed sportswriters, loutish proof-readers, crime scene photographers, statisticians, tittle-tattle gossip mongers, mild-mannered reporters, Linotype operators, and ink-stained pressmen in white paper hats, all there to throw back a few with sob-sister Kitty Hanson, the last of the great courtroom reporters, and the tough-as-nails television critic, Kay Gardella, got up in knee-length mink. Louie's really got hummin' around three in the morning.

The Daily News paid me a token-dollar to endorse the paper, and for months my picture went up on the side of the fleet trucks, out and about the five boroughs, cross-promoting Clay Cole's Disk-O-Tek. The discotheque phenomenon gave us our best-ever television format. Actually, the French created the discotheque as a prudent way to amuse the trendy jet set; we simply made disco palatable and easier to spell, twelve years before "Saturday Night Fever."

In the studio, we set-up a club atmosphere, tables around a dance floor, and a corner booth for me and my guests, (borrowed from Sherman Billingsley's Table #1 at The Cub Room of The Stork Club). I hired two hot-looking dancers, Marci High and Kelly Clark and perched them in cages, dressed in Betsey Johnson's mod-miniskirts and shiny white go-go boots, their hair styled in the angular, razor-sharp cut of Vidal Sassoon, himself. I was told when auditioning dancers, I rejected both Geri Miller and Goldie Hawn. Geri was now a go-go girl at The Rolling Stone club, the girl with her legs in the air on their famous swing. Geri was overly ripe at a time when the Twiggy-look was all the rage. If only her brain were as big as her bosom. As Dominique, Geri became one of Andy Warhol's underground film stars, then a super-groupie, a topless dancer and finally a porn star. Goldie Hawn was a skilled dancer and camped out daily in my office with her scrappy little puppy, pressing me for the job. In exasperation, it was the mutt I ejected, not the nut. Goldie moved west as a showgirl in Las Vegas, then onto "Laugh-In" in Hollywood and an Academy Award for "Cactus Flower." Goldie neglected to thank me in her 1969 Oscar acceptance speech. "Sock it to *me*, Goldie!" If I had hired Goldie, interrupting that sequence of events, she might still be dancing in a cage somewhere over on Forty-Fifth Street.

By 1965, half the population was under 25 years old; the first wave of the 1947 baby boom was now turning eighteen. On "Clay Cole's Disk-O-Tek," our studio audience was no longer high school teenyboppers, but an older gathering of discophiles, dancers from the hip clubs and trendy discos around the east coast. The demographics of our home viewer shifted as well, to include 18 -35 year old adults, who at that hour were showering, shaving and dressing for a Saturday night date. "We have the largest naked audience in the United States," reported *Record World* magazine. The joke was: "Nielson simply tallied our ratings by counting belly buttons." Since the show now skewed to young adults, we relaxed our audience dress code, and the program began to make a fashion statement; the trendy outfits of our in-studio audience dancers became a show unto itself. Sh-Boomers in New Jersey, Long Island and Atlantic City actually tuned-in to see what was trendy in Staten Island, Harlem or Bed-Sty. It didn't escape the attention of Seventh Avenue either; "garment district" designers were turned-on to the edgy new styles created on the streets, in the bodegas and bedrooms of the far-flung boroughs. Art does imitate life and street fashion became all the rage. I too ditched my tuxedo in favor of the lush, seasonal wardrobe provided to me by Andrew Pallack. Our show was layered with a distinct New York perspective, a point-of-view that set us apart from all other television rock 'n' roll shows – wit, style and sophistication.

Our guest stars also responded positively to the change, the new atmosphere was familiar territory, a small club stage, a hip audience, a good vibe. For the first time, rock 'n' roll groups seemed at home in a television studio, it was all very natural. To accommodate the trendy folk-rock singers – hippies with guitars, sandals and love beads – we created a Folk-Lounge, very Greenwich Village with red brick walls, checkered tablecloths and candles for the likes of Cree-Indian Buffy Sainte-Marie, Gale Garnett, Donovan, Judy Collins, the Serendipity Singers. Peter, Paul & Mary, and the television debut of Richie Havens. All in all, it worked beautifully; our format for the next three years.

The big-budget network shows that had dogged us, ABC's "Shindig," NBC's "Hullabaloo" and "Hootenanny" were all cancelled, and we were, once again, the only game in town. Channel 11 brought us our own competition, the hour-long "Lloyd Thaxton Show," positioned M-F at 7:30, a west coast production totally out of synch with our New York sensibility. The Thaxton show became a component in Channel 11's sales strategy: If a sponsor wanted to buy into Clay Cole, they had to take on a run of spots on Lloyd Thaxton as part of the package. Not only was our show used as a sales leverage, but also Thaxton's ho-hum ratings reflected my longtime belief that he was put there to keep me in line.

Clay Cole's Disk-O-Tek became known in the music business as a launching pad for the new, young stars we introduced; among our home viewers were the all-important television producers and talent bookers. Aside from Merv Griffin and his talk show producer Bob Shanks, there were Nick Vanoff, Gary Smith, and Bob Precht and Vince Colandra, talent bookers for Ed Sullivan. Our show became a stepping-stone to the networks.

Booking comics on a rock 'n' roll show was a novel idea at the time, but we weren't your average everyday rock 'n' roll show. There was a sudden rush of brilliant young comedians that demanded to be showcased. The notion was a winner not only for our show, but also for the comics. They were each given a seven-minute, no-holds-barred segment, and a sit-down interview, the perfect platform for a network audition. The check-swapping rule did not apply to comics since they had nothing to promote; each received scale, about $125. Richard Pryor would appear, not for the laughs, but for the much-need $125, and our Chicken Delight dinners. Richard Pryor was a scrawny twenty-three-year old, the most original of all the young comics, filling his segment with sidesplitting improvisations – like his fish under water pantomime.

George Carlin ("the hippy-dippy weather man") was a regular favorite, as well as John Byner (the first to impersonate Ed Sullivan's *"really-big-shew"*), Fannie Flagg, Godfrey Cambridge, Norm Crosby, Dennis Wholey, Pat McCormack, Rip Taylor, David Frye, London Lee, Jackie Mason, Dick Shawn, Bernie Allen, Marty Ingles, Soupy Sales, "Professor" Irwin Corey and dozens more appeared.

The Firesign Theatre, a four-man troop, each born under a "fire" sign and called the "Beatles of Comedy," were regular contributors. The Ace Trucking Company and the Uncalled For Three, comedy troops from The Bitter End, were regulars, along with double acts, Tony Hendra and Nic Ullett, Marty Allen & Steve Rossi, and Joe Balogna and Renee' Taylor. Renee' ("The Nanny") and I did a series of improvisations based on spontaneous suggestions from our studio audience. One wiseguy called out "a waitress and a sailor!" Renee' and I huddled for a second and surprise: Renee' played the sailor, I played the waitress." Dick Shawn walked away with more than just $125; he walked away with my lady friend as well. I had been dating Penny Kimmel, one of the "pony" dancers from Jack Silverman's International, who was sitting backstage for the taping. After the show, making excuses, she abruptly left. The next day in *The New York Post* in his column "It Happened

Last Night," Earl Wilson reported that "shapely dancer Penny Kimmel and Dick Shawn were canoodling, close and cozy at a Manhattan night spot." Shawn got caught with his pants down; as for Penny, *that's Earl brother.*

Our most outrageous comedy guest had to be Mrs. Miller, a song-stylist in the tradition of Tiny Tim and William Hung, often out of tune, off the beat and wobbly. Her rendition of "Downtown" includes an instance where she briefly breaks into giggling and forgets the lyrics. Despite this, her "Downtown" single barely missed the *Billboard* Top 40 in 1966.

Mrs. Miller is not to be confused with Miss. Miller, the persistent TV audience member, Lillian Miller, who never missed a Steve Allen or Merv Griffin talk show and would often chat with the hosts on camera. Lillian Miller was actually christened "Miss Miller" by Jack Paar. As an NBC page on the Jack Paar show, I used to chat with the scatter-brained, middle-aged Miss Miller nightly as she waited, quietly and patiently in front of the line at the old Hudson Theatre on West 44th Street. By the time Johnny Carson moved the "Tonight" show to the West Coast in 1972, Miss Miller was already enjoying minor notoriety, so she packed her bags and moved west as well; the original groupie.

Ever since I first stepped in front of a television camera in 1953, I ad-libbed every single word; I never had the luxury of a writing staff. After all these years, I yearned for some help, some clever new way just to say "hello, welcome to the show."

Kenny Solms and Gail Parent had been newly-signed to William Morris, based on their Epic comedy album, "I Were a High School Graduate," and after an appearance on our show in April 1967, it was clear to me that their skills as writers did not extend to performing. Off stage, Kenny and Gail were at their best improvising off the cuff. I took these two whiz kids under my wing, briefly putting them on the payroll to write for our show – but they never wrote a single word, but contributed in a most unusual way. Kenny and Gail sat on stools outside of camera range, ad-libbing comments, which I would repeat.

For example, when I was about to introduce Simon and Garfunkel, Kenny whispered, "Sounds like a law firm…"

"Sounds like a law firm," I would announce, which would then send me off, riffing in the voice of a telephone operator:

"Good morning, Simon and Garfunkle. May I direct your call?" (Cupping the phone, talking to camera) *"Did you ever hear the sound of silence? Try asking lawyers for free advice – that's the sound of silence!"*

For a very brief moment in time, I was the fastest ad-libber on television.

Shortly thereafter, Kenny and Gail went off to Hollywood to become the brilliant writers of the long-running Carol Burnett Show on CBS. "Sheila Levine Is Dead and Living in New York" was Gail's book-length suicide note, an elusive look at the Swinging Sixties singles scene, and a classic best seller. Gail also wrote for "Maude," "Golden Girls" and Tracy Ullman; Kenny produced countless television specials for Ann-Margret, Bill Cosby, Neil Diamond, and was awarded a Peabody for "Sills and Burnett at the Met." Like a proud uncle, I closely followed their careers, happy to say that I gave them their first job on television.

Roz Ross had created Dick Clark's Cavalcade of Stars with Ray Reneri as Tour Manager – busloads of record artists barnstorming the hinterlands, performing endless one-nighters in arenas, armories and auditoriums, staged by regional boxing and wrestling promoters. That may explain why vintage rock 'n' roll show posters look exactly like those one-color showcards promoting fight nights.

Ray Reneri recalls the bargain basement practice Roz perfected in booking the Dick Clark bus tours: "The Supremes were grateful to receive $600 a week as a supporting act on the bill, but as the tour progressed, so did their latest record, "Where Did Our Love Go." As their song moved up the charts, so did their position on stage. Soon, with the No.1 record in the country, the Supremes got star-billing, and closed the show, but still earning $600 a week. Roz, and Jerry Brandt had the knack of smelling a hit, an inclination that allowed them to buy cheap, with Dick Clark reaping the rewards." Dick Clark soon became enthralled with Roz's frugal spending methods and whisked her away to L.A. Jerry Brandt became head of the William Morris music division.

It was Jerry who, in spite of objections from elder agents, flew to London and signed the Rolling Stones to the agency. Jerry was a brash, energetic Sephardic Jew from Brooklyn, a born hustler, trained as a pitchman by one of the best, Roz Ross. Jerry was tall, strikingly good-looking, and cut quite a sartorial figure. On his trip to London, to meet with Alan Klein, Jerry acquired a taste for Savile Row tailored suits, and the boutique-styles of "happening" Carnaby Street and Kings Road. William Morris agents had always distinguished themselves by their somber, business-like black mohair suits and polished black shoes – there was a shoeshine attendant on staff – but Jerry's new mod-music division set a modern tone, and a new motto:

"Think Yiddish, Dress British." Jerry brought style, youthful energy and tons of money into the agency, to the bewilderment of older agents who had no idea what he was doing. Jerry simply started breaking all the rules.

David Geffen, a college dropout from the working-class neighborhood of Borough Park, Brooklyn, fresh out of the William Morris mailroom, was over-anxious to make it in the motion picture department, but was drawn to the golden glow radiating from Jerry's quarters. "*Schmuck,*" Jerry wailed, "forget motion pictures. Get into the music business. Down here nobody knows what we're doing, and nobody knows how to do it."

Wally Amos, Jerry's assistant, brought in a new unknown act he wanted to sign, two boys with a name that produced snickers of disbelief from the other agents – Simon and Garfunkel. Jerry and Wally knew that rock 'n' roll was their bailiwick; the other agents didn't have a clue. Simon and Garfunkel sailed to No. 1 with "Sounds of Silence," just as Jerry was organizing the Stones first USA tour. In addition, they represented the Beach Boys, Sonny & Cher, the Smothers Brothers and Elvis. Jerry's music department was now generating the highest commissions of the entire agency, which should mean lavish cash bonuses in their year-end, Christmas envelopes.

At the end of 1967, expecting a $25,000 bonus, Jerry's envelope contained a mere $6,000. Jerry left the music department, took a settlement check for $14,000 and opened one of the first mega-discos The Electric Circus at St. Mark's Place, on the lower east side. In his book, "Radical Rags, the Fashions of the Sixties," Joel Lobenthal wrote: "The Electric Circus became New York's ultimate mixed-media pleasure dome. Its hallucinogenic light baths enthralled every sector of New York society."

Opening night, in the scorching heat of summer 1967, I huddled with the uptown crowd gathering on the long, winding stairway up from the street – dazzling stars, producers and the glitterati, all standing elbow-to-elbow with the East Village Others, Andy Warhol superstars and the paparazzi, with invitations in hand awaiting Jerry's opening nod. Inside, trapeze artists performed during musical sets, strobe lights flashed over a huge dance floor and multiple projectors unreeled film clips. Jerry had officially launched the psychedelic disco. We had never seen anything like it

William Morris would not elevate Wally Amos, a black man, to a power position, so Wally departed as well and became the cookie mogul, 'Famous Amos'. Wally had the good fortune of marketing his cookies at the precise moment Flower

Children were getting "the munchies." Hippies everywhere were suddenly ravenous for Macadamia Nut Chocolate Chip cookies! It was Famous Amos to the rescue – a joint alliance, to be sure.

It was about this time that I was called to a Top-Secret meeting at The William Morris Agency, down a long hallway to a locked, windowless room, and in the center shrouded beneath a canvas tarpaulin, was the secret weapon. I pledged confidentiality. I was about to witness the unveiling of the French-made Scopitone (pronounced, Scope-a-Tone), a regulation coin-operated jukebox with one variation; mounted on top was a large framed screen, much like a television set. Scopitone was going to revolution the vending business, playing 16mm color-film clips with a magnetic soundtrack of artists performing their hits. William Morris and their "associates" in the jukebox distribution business – the "boys" who supply America's bars, bowling alleys and cocktail lounges with vending machines – would be the exclusive marketers of this new-fangled novelty. Georgie Wood had secured the U.S. and Latin American distribution rights for William Morris, and had orchestrated the financing from his underworld friends from as faraway as Las Vegas, a deal that would be worth over a million dollars to William Morris, plus 10% of the production costs of each film clip.

What William Morris wanted from me, aside from the promise of silence, was a sample film clip for demonstration purposes, to facilitate the marketing of their innovative new idea. They arranged for a studio and a crew and I filmed a clip, lip-synching my latest record. That's the last I heard of Scopitone. It wasn't until much later I learned that *all* my friends made a free, promotional clip – Dionne Warwick, Dion, Neil Sedaka, Bobby Vee, Bobby Rydell, Timi Yuro, *everybody*. Little-known Robert Altman directed a clip for Herb Alpert & the Tijuana Brass, but most of the clips were cheesy, quickie productions of pop songs, adorned with an abundance of tits-and-ass. Hard rock groups were shelved; the prevailing notion was that longhaired rockers were a passing fad, even at the height of the current British Invasion. "Musical tastes and trends changed too quickly," Scopitone producer Irving Briskin noted to *Variety* in the February 23, 1966 issue. Safer artists like Jane Morgan, Johnny Mathis, Kay Starr, Vicki Carr and Nancy Sinatra were offered contracts. The heavily endowed B-movie starlet, Joi Lansing, dubbed "The Queen of Scopitone" performed numerous topless, stripper-themed clips.

The bare-breasted Les Ballet Africans were filmed on stage in a racy, rambunctious National Geographic-style clip. These titillations were produced and shipped off to Europe, where Scopitone was all the rage. Shillings, denaro, francs, lire, marks and assorted currency were deposited into these musical money machines across the Continents, winding up in unknown pockets, certainly not the artists.

Scopitone had been plugged-into most of Europe since 1960, especially in France, England and West Germany. In America, Scopitone was a bust. The machines required too much maintenance and the clips were crude and silly – boy singers promenading exotic beaches, crooning to hordes of well-oiled, bosomy bikini bunnies. In addition, there was the stigma affixed to the nefarious entanglements of Georgie Wood and his shady partners, the jukebox distributors.

The final nail in Scopitone's coffin came with the sudden death of Georgie Wood, himself. As I heard the story, Georgie was brutally beaten by the mob-boys in a scuffle at The Camelot Club and, battered and bloody, he checked himself into the safety of Mount Sinai Hospital, where he died the next morning of a massive coronary. Georgie had been William Morris' chief troubleshooter since 1940, and as Abe Lastfogel's right hand man was one of the family. The family all turned out for his funeral at Campbells – Ed Sullivan, Frank Costello, "Jimmy Blue-Eyes" Alo, Joe "Socks" Lanza, and the plainclothes boys from the Central Investigation Bureau, across the street, jotting down license plates.

An interesting relic remained from Scopitone – the clips themselves. Today, these film strips offer a visual legacy of early rock 'n' roll artists, filmed in vibrant color, rather than the black and white standard of 60s television and B-movies. More significantly, Scopitone film-clips unwittingly gave birth to music videos, a new form of record promotion that would transform the music industry and rouse the creation of MTV, launched in 1981.

A new British group, Procol Harum had released "A Whiter Shade of Pale" in the spring of 1967, and instantly sold two and a half million singles the first few weeks. It became the biggest record of the year. I had to have Procol Harum on my show. Trouble is, there was no Procol Harum, just a bunch of studio musicians. Organizing a hastily arranged promotional tour of the states – work permits, passports, personnel, management changes and a new US distributor – proved traumatic. Instead, in the mail I received a small box marked with a Scopitone label, containing a film-clip of "Whiter Shade of Page." Infused with cash and creativity, the producers, inspired by the free-form style of Richard Lester's Beatles films and Keith Reid's surrealistic lyrics of "vestal virgins, flying ceilings and fandangos," patched together a three minute montage, with images borrowed from underground films that were beginning to surface, – stop-motion sunsets, slow-motion horses galloping through the surf, hippies dancing in Trafalgar Square – visual images set to "Whiter Shade of Pale," minus the performing musicians. Scopitone clips had now become a marketing device, a less-costly tool to promote the sale of recordings. To accommodate this additional musical source, I announced a new, weekly segment called "Clay Cole's Cinematheque." We simply lowered a screen, dimmed the lights, and projected the very first music video.

The Doors had a strong interest in film as well, since both lead-singer Jim Morrison and keyboard player Ray Manzarek had met while studying film at UCLA.

A clip was produced for the Doors debut single "Break on Through," a filmed performance, but notable for its atmospheric lighting, camera work and editing. Soon, the Moody Blues released a clip of "Go Now," followed by the Who, the Byrds, and the Beach Boys. The Beatles took the genre to new heights with their groundbreaking clips for "Penny Lane" and "Strawberry Fields Forever" made in early 1967 which used many techniques borrowed from avant-garde films – dramatic lighting, unusual camera angles and rhythmic editing. These two landmark films are among the very first purpose-made concept videos that attempt to "illustrate" the song in an artful manner, rather than just creating a film of an idealized performance.

For the record, Tony Bennett can take credited for having made the first music video. Tony was filmed while walking down Serpentine Lane in Hyde Park, London, as his recording of "Stranger in Paradise" played. The clip was then distributed to television stations across America in 1956.

Danny's Hideaway was a restaurant for stand-up guys: boxing champs, saloon singers, character actors, teamster bosses, well-heeled merchants and well-mannered mobsters. Presided over by Danny Stradella, Danny's Hideaway at 151 East 45th St. was a clubby Italian Steakhouse with no menu. Regulars ordered the Caesar salad, prepared at your table in massive wooden bowls, and the New York strip steak with a side of Fettuccini Alfredo. The small stand-up bar at the entranceway was generally where you'd find Johnny Carson, absolutely alone, propped against the bar like a ladder against a barn, feeling no pain, while Ed Mc Mahon, perfectly sober, held court at an upstairs table.

I watched with great fascination as Tony Bennett, seated alone, got up to leave and dropped by the table of Henry Fonda to pay respect. He then turned on his heels and making steely-eyed contact with me, approached my table. "Clay Cole," he said placing one hand on my shoulder and vigorously shaking my hand with the other, "I'm Tony Bennett. When are you going to invite me to be on your show?" As simple as that, another historic Clay Cole Show was consummated. Tony was hotter than a pistol at that point in his career, having charted with "I Left My Heart in San Francisco" a year earlier and was now getting $25,000 a week in Las Vegas, a record fee. Even then, Tony Bennett was attentive to teenage record buyers, keen to win them over. That explains his unparalleled longevity. Tony knew how to beguile an audience, as he proved forty years later with the MTV generation. I decided that his star status demanded a full-hour and with Tony's quintet backing him, it would be a "live" set. Tony's point man Joey Petralia handled all the details. It was a very informal hour, Tony and I sat on stools surrounded by his musicians, chatting small talk between his all-time greatest hits.

After the show, Channel 11 executives jumped all over him, pushing me aside, in an effort to make Tony agree to a television special. Tony, the gentleman that he is agreed on the conditions that I introduce him and only if they pay me for the appearance. Tony videotaped his nightclub act from The Empire Room of The Waldorf-Astoria, with me introducing him, and predictably, once it aired, they erased the tape.

During my Christmas holidays engagement at The Living Room, I was approached by the Pasquel family, operators of a failing Italian restaurant, on 45th Street at Second Avenue, just a few doors east of Danny's Hideaway and just around the corner from another successful dance club, The Rolling Stone.. They had a long lease, no customers and were eager to involve me in the creation of a nightclub. One look at the space and I became wildly enthusiastic, the perfect layout for a dance club. Our deal was simple. I would have complete creative control; the Pasquel's patriarch and his two sons would operate the business aspects, splitting the profits. I set about to minimally redecorate the room, add a bandstand, sound, lights and dance floor in the backroom, install small cocktail tables, and in the front room, canopied the spectacular stand-up bar with an upside-down, green felt crap table, a unique touch. Against the red felt walls, I hung a few dozen, massive, black-and-white blowups of pop icons, Sonny & Cher, Bo Diddley, the Vagrants, plus our centerpiece photo, the Rolling Stones and me. I hired eight eye-catching, young go-go girls and Betsey Johnson agreed to dress them head to toe in an assortment of ultra-mod miniskirts. We printed up 200 invitations for a press preview, canapés and cocktails at the five-o'clock hour. The invitations held a photo of me with the Rolling Stones laughing with the caption: "They all laughed when I told them I was opening another dance club," then on the inside, "but I did anyway, and you are invited. RSVP."

No one responded. No calls. No RSVP's. Our two bands were warming up on the bandstand. Betsey Johnson's wardrobe arrived last minute by messenger; I dug in my pocket for the $800. The hors d'oeuvres were hot and the champagne was cold. We were ready to rock 'n' roll. But, not one phone call. Then suddenly, at 5:25, Earl Wilson of *The New York Post* arrived with an entourage. Tony Bennett pulled up. Soupy Sales dropped in. By 6:00 the house was jammed; lines formed around the block. We had called it "Clay Cole's Happening Place," and it became *the* happening place in Manhattan. I hired my friend Scott Ross, who was laboring in the record library of radio station 1010-WINS, to moonlight as our house MC, presiding over our Sunday night dance contest, handing off a $100 cash prize. Scott Ross was an appealing, young singer/songwriter with aspirations of becoming a radio disc jockey. Scott was also involved in a tug-of-war with Ringo Starr over the affections of Nedra Talley, the youngest of the Ronettes. Every evening, at the stroke of midnight, Monte Rock III, dressed in black, descended onto the stage like Count Dracula, casting a hypnotic spell over the pulsating dance floor. Our two continuous live bands were top-notch, and our hot-looking go-go girls were like a dollop of whipped cream on Irish coffee, sweet, smooth and unexpected. Our bar was elbow to elbow, the dance floor toe to toe. The cash registers were ringing. The "happening" was taking place every night 'till four in the morning. We were a hit.

A few weeks after our opening night, following a leisurely Sunday night dinner at Danny's Hideaway, I strolled over to the club, just in time for the explosion. I was handing my overcoat to the hatcheck attendant when an eruption suddenly detonated from the back room. One of our bouncers shoved me to the floor of the coatroom, threw my topcoat over my head and hollered, "Cover up, lie still, and don't get up!" There were violent crashes, screaming, and the sounds of shattering glass vibrating over the din. The boys on the bandstand stopped playing. I could hear the muffled voice of Scott Ross, a frantic outcry from the stage mike, followed by that intolerable piercing screech of audio feedback. Someone was having a violent fistfight, and it was moving closer and closer. I buried my head deeper into the blanket of overcoats and tried not to breathe. The grunts and blows seemed to be right on top of us. Then just as suddenly as it erupted, all was still.

The racket boys had moved in, making more than just a racket. They made a mess. Every columned mirror was broken, bottles and glasses were smashed, and shards littered the floor. Women and men were crying, bleeding. Police cars arrived, with the house lights on and up full; the room was a sea of blue uniforms, squawk boxes, sputtering static. We attended the wounded, picked up the pieces and patched together a scenario. Against his better judgment, our front-door host had admitted a large party of men, eight or twelve of them, violating our normal policy of couples only. Greed had got the better of him when he admitted a dozen big spenders. They were low-level wise guys sent to deliver a message. They wanted a piece of the action.

We opened as usual the next night to a packed room, visited by several plain clothed detectives from the New York City's bureau of investigation. "Holy, shit," one detective whispered to me after surveying the room. "This place is about to explode. Over there, the Brooklyn contingent, over there, the guys from Queens, you got the uptown guys, the downtown guys, and the whole shooting match." Sure enough, I was visited by a stream of "sympathetic friends," who heard about my "little problem and would be willing to help me fix it." "Just let me put my kid on the door; you won't have no more trouble." Everyone wanted me to put his kid on the door. A foot in the door is a wiseguy way of saying, "I'm gonna be your partner." The Pasquel family suffered the most. One son had a bottle of liquor broken over his head, requiring many stitches. The father was followed home. Threats were ongoing, but the Pasquels, a stubborn, proud Italian family, soldiered on, refusing to give in or give it up to the Mafia.

The emblematic banner that fluttered over 45th Street with my name and likeness was dismantled. I could not maintain a television persona and be married to the mob. I walked away from The Happening Place, and with dwindling interest, so did the Pasquel family. They put up a good fight, but they were no match to the slings and arrows of the mob. The last I looked, it was a Thai restaurant catering to the tastes and whims of that other Mafia, at the nearby United Nations.

Years later, appearing at a night club in Brooklyn, making my way through the tables to the stage, I was stopped by a table of men. One grabbed my arm holding me back, saying "don't you remember us? We wrecked your joint on 48th Street." His companions were all grinning proudly, like Eagle Scouts about to receive a Merit Badge. My blood suddenly turned hot; a dozen Fran Warren's sitting ringside.

"Yes, I remember you; but first, I have a show to do."

18) Motown

"Soul is like electricity. I don't know how
it works, but it sure lights up a room."

By 1965, as Ray Charles persisted in successfully recording country blues bal-lads with violins and choir, Memphis introduced us to Wilson Pickett, Sam & Dave and Otis Redding, megawatts of soul-power to illuminate every home in America. Sam Cooke was gone (shot dead the previous December in a sleazy L.A. motel room), Aretha had not yet been unleashed (her Atlantic classics hit the air-waves in 1967) and Motown continued to record sugar-coated rhythm and blues, with bouncy arrangements and that prominent, danceable backbeat – pop tunes with a "hook."

Motown began for me in 1959, with my can of "Slop Powder" and Barrett Strong's "Money," a truly funky recording, the first written, produced, distributed and financed by Berry Gordy. In his ensuing recordings, rather than seeking nir-vana in pure rhythm and blues, Gordy manufactured chocolate-marshmallows. "It raised a few eyebrows among traditional black musicians; who called it "black Muzak." But to teenagers, it was a revelation – any jelly-legged slug could dance to the pulse of Motown. A Motown single played at a record hop was a surefire icebreaker, guaranteed to jam an empty dance floor. Sh-Boomers were getting their first taste of soul – or at least what they *thought* was soul. It was jam for white bread; the best of Motown was yet to come.

I began to assemble the biggest television show of my career, a full hour "Salute to Motown," with an all-black cast of singing stars. The folks back at Hitsville-USA in Detroit were delighted, and invited me to Motown for a first-hand look. Chorographer Cholly Atkins and music director Maurice King, legendary music

243

men greeted me at 2648 West Grand Boulevard, and gave me the grand tour of the row-houses now converted to studios and offices occupied by Berry Gordy & Company. We toured the famous first floor recording studios where the mythic Funk Brothers created Motown magic, visited the rehearsal studios where dance routines were choreographed, and the wardrobe room, watching neat-as-a-pin grannies tediously hand-sew sequins onto feather boas. What struck me was the Quality Control department, an idea borrowed from Gordy's days on the Lincoln-Mercury assembly-line.

Before Motown eclipsed everything before it, Detroit had a rich musical history: Jack Scott. Del Shannon. John Lee Hooker. Little Willie John. Jackie Wilson. Della Reese and of course Aretha Franklin. As a child, Aretha sang in the choir at her father, the Reverend C. L. Franklin's New Bethel Baptist Church, one of the first ministries to have a nationally-broadcast radio show. The fiery reverend was a well-regarded celebrity in the black community, and Sam Cooke, Clara Ward, Mahalia Jackson, Jackie Wilson, and other famous black musicians often visited the Franklin home to pay their respects to the powerful preacher. At this place and time, Aretha had a recording contract with Columbia Records, signed by the illustrious John Hammond, who declared that "Aretha Franklin was the greatest voice since Billie Holiday." Unfortunately, he had different ideas about the direction of her career, and at Columbia she could not find her voice; her Atlanta years were yet to come

Marvin Gaye invited us to dinner and a night on the town, a whirlwind tour of Detroit's musical nightlife, winding down at the late-show for an Adam Wade set at the Playboy Club. Marvin was the perfect host, soft-spoken, extremely polite, but intense, taller than I imagined, trim and exceptionally handsome. Marvin invited me back to Studio A, where he sat at the piano, singing late into the night. It was a memorable, enchanted evening.

Our "Salute to Motown" went on the air with Stevie Wonder, the Four Tops, the Temptations, Mary Wells, Martha & the Vandellas, the Marvelettes, Gladys Knight & the Pips, Tammi Terrell & Marvin Gaye, and comic Willie Tyler with "Lester," the greatest hour of all-black artists assembled up to that time.

Mary Wells ("My Guy"), like Diana Ross, had an indefinable "sound," a thin voice, but one that recorded well. The Marvelettes gave Motown their first million-selling pop hit, "Please Mr. Postman" and Martha & the Vandellas became Motown's first crossover girl group, amassing important hits and becoming headliners. Meanwhile, the Supremes were still languishing in the back of the bus, with six unremarkable flops. But, in 1964, with Holland-Dozier-Holland producing, they charted an impressive five back-to-back No. 1 mega-hits; the first, "Where Did Our Love Go." The Supremes were never idolized as a traditional three-part harmony girl group; they were clearly manufactured by Berry Gordy, choreographed by Cholly Atkins, gowned by Bob Mackie, and then sprayed with lacquer. They were endearing campy kewpie dolls; the fuss was all about the glitter, and the cat-like purr of Miss Ross. The three Cinderella-girls from the Brewster Housing Projects shaped a modern-day storybook fairy tale. They were lovely, but not loveable. It became apparent they didn't love one another either. Florence Ballard died of a broken heart with a welfare check in her mailbox, Mary Wilson emerged a martyr and Diana Ross became the super diva, Miss Ross.

Berry Gordy's Motown was propelled by his fixation on The Copacabaña – the plastic-palmed, sequined-feathered, pink-spotlighted supper club in the cellar of Manhattan's Hotel Fourteen. "You hadn't made it 'till you played the Copa," Martha Reeves remembers; The Copa was *the* benchmark of success among Motown stars. The Motown machine was set in motion for the purpose of transforming these street kids into Copa stars; their motto: "dressed for success." The slickly-produced Motown acts should have been perfect for The Copa, but you cannot fool that sophisticated, sometime jaded, audience; this was, after all, not Las Vegas.

Martha & the Vandellas and Gladys Knight & the Pips were among the first to succeed, with their razzle-dazzle hits, heavy on the horns, and spot-on choreography. The Temptations were also a perfect Copa attraction, sparked by both David Ruffin and Eddie Hendricks' contagious energy, and, for the first time, their specially built microphone stand, with five mics on one stanchion, liberating the five Temptations to dance unencumbered.

For the debut of the Supremes, I invited their promotions director and his wife to be my guest opening night, as a token of appreciation for my visit to Hitsville in Detroit. I gave them the deluxe New York treatment, sent a limo to their hotel, took them for pre-show cocktails, and then supper at The Copa. While I was wining and dining them, the room began to fill, elbow-to-elbow with the city's top disc jockeys and their wives, all guests of Motown. Mary Wilson reported that the tab for the first show was $10,000, plus $4,000 in liquor. The Supremes were paid $2,700 a week. The tab for me: priceless.

The hip, well-oiled audience, that included Sammy Davis Jr. and Ed Sullivan, was ready to be jolted by Diana, Flo and Mary, the three hippest chicks on the planet, and by that celebrated Motown backbeat. What they delivered was a crazy quilt – yards and yards of special material, patched together by the" Singer Sewing Machine Company" – Motown. All their greatest hits were tossed away in a medley, to make room for gems like "The Girl from Ipanema" and "You're Nobody Till Somebody Loves You." Berry Gordy was grinning from ear-to ear. Unlike the musical direction he envisioned for Marvin Gaye, Berry Gordy's mission with the Supremes was to transform his three pop stars into a polished adult attraction, singing show tunes and standards, acceptable to a sophisticated white audience. But to me, this was a major let-down, especially on their first Copa appearance. Here was the hottest pop music group in the world in straw-hats and canes, strutting to "Rock-a-bye You're Baby with a Dixie Melody," recalling the McGuire Sisters.

"Thin is in," Diane announced.

"But fat is where it's at," Flo shouted from upstage.

The audience roared, but to me it was a self-denigrating swipe, to the benefit of Diana.

After the first show, the promotions man agreed with me that the Supremes were off-target, and he insisted on going straight up to their dressing room to set them straight. We begged him to stay put, wait until morning, but nothing could dissuade him; he was adamant, and also drunk as a skunk. He was fired the very next morning.

It was the "little" Stevie Wonder who first appeared at The Copa, as yet to blossom into the gifted singer/songwriter he was to become. What are memorable to me about his performance were his vocal runs, the technique of vacillating up and down the scale. To my ear it was irritating. I didn't like it. Ray Charles hit the notes, dead on; no fussy embellishments. Unfortunately, less talented singers have adopted this gimmick as an attempt to sound soulful. I call it "yodeling" – with apologies to Swiss Alps mountaineers and Appalachian hog-callers.

Marvin Gaye was the last of the Motown stable to appear at the Copa, still in his suave, Nat "King" Cole mode, crooning show tunes and standards, driving Berry Gordy nuts. At the Copa, Gordy would gnash his teeth and blurt out "Sing your hits! Sing your hits!" Gordy recalls, "We released an album of standards on him, "The Soulful Sounds of Marvin Gaye." It contained some beautiful, classy vocals, but it didn't do well. He was determined to be a crooner like Frank Sinatra. Whenever we approached Marvin to record more commercial stuff, he stubbornly refused. Marvin was the most stubborn guy around." Gordy finally turned him around with "Stubborn Kind of Fellow," which catapulted him back onto the singles charts. (Marvin Gaye's "live" Copa performance was recorded, but the album was never released – that is, until 2005. "Marvin Gaye at the Copa" is now available.)

The Four Tops did not roll off the factory assembly lines of Motor City; they are the Lamborghini of vocal groups –"energetic velocity set against a framework of unrestrained elegance." Accelerated by Levi Stubbs power-vocals, "Duke" Fakir, "Obie" Benson and Lawrence Payton were Motown's class act. Unlike many of the label's own hand-groomed and manufactured bands, the quartet was around long before Motown started, and its original lineup continued decades after most Motown bands had become tribute acts filled with ringers. Watching their smooth, seamless performances, I came to understand that puzzling expression, "*I slept like a top.*" Their panache was further advanced by their choice of venue: the Four Tops preferred to showcase their talents at the bourbon-soaked Basin Street East, rather than the champagne-bubbly Copa.

It wasn't until 1971 that Motown got funky. Marvin Gaye discarded his tuxedo, writing and producing his legendary, highly personal album, "What's Going On." Motown renegotiated a new contract with Marvin that allowed him complete creative control; a deal worth $1 million, making Marvin Gaye the highest-earning black artist in music history at the time.

With Marvin's "Mercy, Mercy, Me" and Sexual Healing," and the Temptation's "Pappa Was a Rolling Stone," Motown was becoming more brooding and introspective. It was Harlem-born songwriter Norman Whitfield who became Motown's architect of psychedelic soul. With collaborator, lyricist Barrett Strong, their social commentary and psychedelic arrangements connected with the counter culture in the era of Vietnam, Nixon and the Black Panthers. Despite Berry Gordy's reservations over a perceived pro-drug message, they delivered "Cloud Nine," "Ball of Confusion," "Smilin' Faces;" War" and changed Motown overnight. During that period Berry Gordy was preoccupied with Diana Ross and focused all his attention on her Hollywood screen career. When Gordy loosened the reins, the thoroughbreds in the Motown stable galloped; but – back in the Sixties – Motown was all about The Copa.

I will confess a confidence here: Once, on live television, I interviewed a mother whose young son was in need of a life-saving operation, a costly procedure that the mother could not afford. Within minutes, Diana Ross called our control room and, on the promise we would never reveal her gesture, pledged all the financing necessary to facilitate the operation and save the boys life. Years later, Cher came to the rescue, under similar conditions of anonymity during a heartbreaking interview. Cher called the control room, volunteering to underwrite all the legal costs. We were sworn to secrecy.

Our Executive Producer at Channel 11, assigned to oversee the Clay Cole Show was Lloyd Gaynes, an impeccably-groomed Hollywood wheeler-dealer, with a permanent tanning-parlor glow. Lloyd acted as a buffer between management and me – a little late, but welcome just the same. To maneuver around our slim production budget, Lloyd outwitted the penny-pinching tightwads in the front office, by arranging access to all-expenses-paid press junkets, which provided access to Hollywood stars. Over time, Lloyd became my sidekick, companion, producer, tour guide and de facto manager.

Lloyd arranged a 20th Century Fox press junket, a weekend in Puerto Rico, including a deluxe cabaña at the El San Juan Hotel to film interviews with a gathering of stars. Betty Grable was stretched out on the beach towel next to mine; her million-dollar legs tanned a dark chocolate, her platinum hair flecked with silver gray. Ms. Grable had recently divorced husband, bandleader Harry James and retired from film. In her final picture, "How to Marry a Millionaire" (1953), Ms. Grable graciously surrendered the picture to Marilyn Monroe, acknowledging a new generation's screen queen.

While cameras were rolling, Art Linkletter sat cross-legged with fingers intertwined, proper as a Presbyterian preacher. As soon as the cameras shut down, he unraveled a string of the raunchiest zingers imaginable, punctuated with four-letter words. Sammy Davis Jr., after two years starring on Broadway in "Golden Boy" (1964) with Billy Daniels, was premiering his new nightclub act at the El San Juan showroom. Diana Ross, Mary Wilson and Florence Ballard sat ringside, dressed to the nines, sparkling, dazzling, and smiling from earring to earring. Sammy's one-man, tour de force performance soared through the ceiling. I had seen Sammy perform many times, first as a boy when Sammy came to Youngstown, featured with his Dad and Uncle in the Will Mastin Trio, again in the late Fifties on Broadway in "Mr. Wonderful" (1956), with Jack Carter, and in the intimate setting of the Copacabana. But here, in the cavernous El San Juan showroom, Sammy's performance was epic.

Sammy had agreed to meet us at noon to film his interview by the pool, but, as the crew was setting up, Sammy strutted out, on time, dressed and ready; we were not. Unfazed, Sammy took me by the arm and marched me over to the Tiki Bar for breakfast. Pina Coladas! This was my first time for the sweet rum, coconut, and pineapple blend, and the first twelve went down as smooth as milkshakes. Sammy kept-'em coming.

The noonday sun baked us. The Pina Coladas fried us. Our interview was well done – loose and funny, so they tell me. I was in my room, on me knees, praying to Thomas Crapper.

That evening, I was entertaining a couple I had met earlier at the beach, cocktails and shrimp on the open patio of my cabaña cottage, when Sammy Davis appeared, ambling along the cobblestone walkway." "Hi-ya Clay," he waved, as he sauntered on alone, to his first show of the evening. .Well, my guests were certainly impressed: "you *know* Sammy Davis Jr.?" The husband turned out to be Bill Lear, inventor of the personal Lear Jet. *I was impressed!* Lear had also just developed the Stereo 8-track cartridge to solve the problem of music on his new business jets. (A consumer version of Bill Lear's 8-track player was introduced in 1965 in new Fords.) Bill Lear offered me a personal jet for the day, "just pick a destination," he laughed.

I chose lunch in Old Quebec, Canada.

This was a day that cried-out to be filmed, and with Ken Johnson off to the Mike Douglas show, Lloyd struck a deal with a one-man film unit, an aspiring film director Vernon Zimmerman, who owned a camera, could film 16mm and edit segments for our show. Camcorders or hand-held videotape playback units had not yet been perfected, so with Vernon as our personal cinematographer, we were free to explore the world outside the studio. With Vernon and his trusty camera filming every breathtaking minute, we took off – literally – to Old Quebec, Spring Break in Ft Lauderdale, Christmas in North Carolina, the New York Giants training camp, a dude ranch, a ski lodge, on the beach and out to sea on the QE-2. When Sonny Bono called to say he and Cher were caught between flights at the airport, we packed our gear and we were rolling film faster than you can say "I Got You Babe."

By 1965, the New York recording industry had shifted to Los Angeles. At the height of the British Invasion, singles from Los Angeles occupied the No. 1 spot for 20 weeks, compared to just one for New York. We became regulars on the Red Eye and in Hollywood, Lloyd, Vernon and I stayed at the Continental Hyatt House on the Sunset Strip. "The Riot House," was the rock 'n' roll hotel preferred by the touring Brits with their teenage groupies camped outside. James Brown's tour bus was usually parked in the circular driveway and Little Richard maintained a permanent residence. (He'd answer his phone disguised as his maid.) The Hyatt coffee shop was also the hangout of west coast music men, song-pluggers, radio deejays and musicians.

When "Batman" exploded on ABC – POW! Bam! Ugh! – we interviewed Adam West and Burt Ward, (Batman & Robin), and back at our studios, Bob Kane, the creator and illustrator of Batman comics drew his superhero on a large pad, which he presented to me. We traveled upward on a dusty, dangerous mountain road to interview the macho cowboy star Stuart Whitman, who had invited us into his unpretentious rustic cabin at the top of a canyon, then modestly pointed out that all the real estate below, as far as the eye could see, was his property.

In the mansion of Zsa Zsa Gabor, priceless artwork from all the great 20th Century masters were displayed in her massive living room – all portraits of Zsa Zsa herself! Zsa Zsa made a delayed entrance down a grand staircase, so dramatic I was expecting to hear Max Steiner soundtrack music. Zsa Zsa, of course, had no memory of our adventures in the cellar of Jack Paar's Hudson Theatre. She was more interested in hooking me up with Francesca Hilton, her daughter with former husband, Conrad Hilton. Francesca was in need of an escort to a black-tie birthday bash that very night for Conrad at his Beverly Hilton Hotel.

Zsa Zsa, Ann Miller, Debbie Reynolds, all the glamorous Hollywood broads turned out, décolletage dripping diamonds, bouncing to the twist. Florabel Muir, the flamboyant Hollywood crime correspondent sat nearby with her reporter's notepad poised. The very next morning, I was mentioned in her *N Y Daily News* gossip column "as Francesca Hilton's new beau." Francesca was a really lovely person, not at all like that other Hilton, Paris the airhead-heiress.

Over at Mitzi Gaynor's house, she also had other plans for me. Mitzi needed a gorilla and I fit perfectly into the ape costume she had borrowed, worn by David Niven in "The Pink Panther." Mitzi was soon to open in Las Vegas and needed a dancing King Kong as part of a film montage to be projected on stage. With me as King Kong deposited on a hill in Griffith Park, and Vernon behind the camera, out-of-sight, on a faraway bluff, I was to emerge from the bushes and terrorize imaginary bi-planes. From the eyeholes of the gorilla mask I spotted a lone motorcyclist stop to observe from the street below. As I emerged from the shrubs, menacing, he shouted up at me: "F--- you! You ain't no bear!"

On the island of Jamaica, where Johnny Nash had befriended a resident reggae musician named Bob Marley, I was driven out to the beach shack of an aging Rastafarian hermit to partake in the local ritual of smoking homegrown weed. I was clearly out of my league, an amateur among hard-core dopers. I did my best impression of a "dude," partaking of long, deeply-held drags and nodding agreeably. "Good chit, mon."

I became riveted into a squat position, bolted to the earth, grinning like a boggle-head doll, melting into the most spectacular sunset I have ever witnessed.

We were in Jamaica to report on the filming of James Coburn's Double-O-Seven spoof, "In Like Flint." Later, back in our New York studios, Coburn nonchalantly admitted that he was a devotee of the new mind-altering LSD. His confession passed without a single raised eyebrow. On another occasion, Arthur Fiedler, of all people, the grand-fatherly maestro of the Boston Pops Orchestra, owned up to smoking marijuana before conducting his symphonic medley of Beatle hits. Neither of these confessions caused bells to go off over at the Associated Press; simply a sign of the times.

My Channel 11 years peeled away like the calendar pages in a Frank Capra movie, best marked by my absurd assortment of personal appearances. Lloyd Gaines negotiated a new agreement for me to appear at Palisades Amusement Park to host the Sunday afternoon Free-Act Stage and emcee the Miss American Teen-ager pageants, culminating each September in the one-hour TV special. My image not only appeared on Daily News trucks, but once again on three-sheet Palisades Park posters plastered on signboards all over town. As a perk, Irving Rosenthal gave me a state of the art Dodge Charger to drive for the summer; not only did it have two bucket seats in the front, but went the next step with two more in the back!

It was at Al & Dick's I met Art Trefferson, a producer at Scepter Records, where he was having a very public, hush-hush affair with Florence Greenberg, the New Jersey housewife turned music mogul. Art Trefferson had a vision of turning the tiny Carnegie Hall Cinema, the movie theatre in the basement of the great concert hall, into a midtown Apollo Theatre. His idea was to run continuous weeklong rock 'n' roll shows, with me as the presenter. Somehow Carnegie Hall agreed and we opened our first week with an all-star line-up headlining the Platters and Bobby Lewis. The afternoon matinee went smoothly. During the first evening show, security guards from Carnegie Hall raced downstairs to halt our show. The soft romantic ballads of the Platters were fine, but the rousing thumping of Bobby Lewis' "Tossing and Turning" vibrated throughout the rafters into the great hall above. The next morning, Beverly Johnson, the classical music reviewer for *The New York Post*, wrote about the horrific interruptions to the Hungarian Symphony Orchestra. Our shows were cancelled.

I also spent two sweltering summers entertaining at the New York World's Fair, performing for tourists, happy to pay a dollar for a place to sit, rest their feet and eat their Belgian waffles. Jay Fontana handled all the business and production chores at the Bourbon Street pavilion, a jazz joint with Gene Krupa's quintet at the bar. As an extra added attraction, Jay found Candy Johnson, a knockout blond, billed as "Miss Perpetual Motion," who twisted so fast and furious that she claimed to lose ten-pounds during each performance. We did four shows a day, and scales were dragged out onto the stage for a pre-show weigh-in. It was all too wacky. The scales didn't lie; she dropped ten pounds four times a day. Candy enjoyed brief, but memorable appearances in four "Beach Party" movies with Annette and Frankie,[13] and then worked the lounges at the Thunderbird in Las Vegas, and the El Mirador in Palm Springs. By the time "Miss Perpetual Motion" arrived at Flushing Meadows, she had amassed a colossal collection of tight-fitting, fringed shimmy dresses in every imaginable color. This whole summer was so bizarre.

Robert Moses had very conservative mainstream taste when it came to entertainment. His three grand spectacles, "To Broadway with Love" in the Texas Pavilion; Dick Button's "Ice-travaganza" in the New York City Pavilion and "Wonderworld," a two-million dollar production at the Meadow Lake Amphitheatre, all quickly closed, suffering heavy losses. Clearly, fairgoers didn't journey to Flushing Meadows for the entertainment. Just fifteen minutes away in Manhattan, one could choose among "Hello Dolly," "My Fair Lady," "Funny Girl," "Barefoot in the Park," and the Radio City Music Hall.

When "Wonderworld" shutdown, our little twenty-member troupe was invited to appear at the 11,000 seat arena, based on the approval of fair officials. We were required to audition for the ubiquitous Robert Moses, the sourpuss, self-proclaimed arbiter of taste to the cultured masses who shuffled aimlessly around Flushing Meadows each day. Robert Moses sat way back there, alone in the bleachers, and we danced our way through our hour of mashed potatoes, slop, Popeye, pony, monkey, mouse, jerk, fly, swim, stroll, cha cha, chalypso, funky-chicken, boogaloo, limbo, hully-gully, hucklebuck, hand-jive, and twist. The next day, in a page one story in *The New York Times*, Mr. Moses declared "Clay Cole's Twist-a-rama is a dirty, filthy, rotten show." Thanks to Mr. Moses' front-page review, we played four shows a day for much of the summer. We were not paid by the theatre; we were working off the $1.00 admission. We folded because a 200-member audience was lost in an 11,000 seat arena. Often there were more people on stage than in the grandstand. We boogied on home.

Jay Fontana took the show to Broadway as a stage revue, "The Big Beat on Broadway" at The Ambassador Theatre, with Lloyd Price and his Orchestra, Freddie Cannon, Linda Scott, the Duprees, the Orlons, April Stevens & Nino Tempo

---

13   Candy Johnson's four AIP pictures were "Beach Party" (1963), and "Pajama Party," "Bikini Beach," and "Muscle Beach Party," all in 1964. She also recorded an LP, which features "Candy Johnson and her Exciters" (Canjo Records)

("When The Deep Purple Falls"), and the Del Satins, who had sung unaccredited backup vocals on Dion's early solo hits. I staged the brilliant comedy routine "Officer Krupke," just as I remembered from sneaking into "West Side Story" years before. The number was so successful that we built an entire "West Side Story" medley around it, concluding with the stirring, "The Jets Song" as a finale. We previewed the show at The 5000 Club in Brooklyn to a standing ovation and shouts of "encore!" It was electric. Now, I had finally made it to Broadway, through the back door.

Jay Fontana also presented an all-star show with me at the Walker Theatre in Brooklyn, and when I arrived at the afternoon rehearsal, he announced that he had added another act to the already fully stacked lineup of artists. The Righteous Brothers, needing cash to get back to Los Angeles, had agreed to perform the two nights for $175.

It was in several appearances at The Steak Pit in Paramus, that I uncovered an entirely new audience – toddlers. Owner Leo Pincus created a series of Sunday Family Nights, at $5 a head, an all-you-can-eat buffet, dancing and a show. *The Bergen Record* reported: "The Pied Pieper of the disco-set came to town last night and more than 400 mamas and papas and their offspring [came to] a merry romp in electric sound…parents, teen-agers, preteens and preschoolers crowded the floor at every opportunity to do versions of the jerk, the monkey, the ching-a-ling… Cole was surprised by the number of young children who sat in an adoring circle around the dance floor."

"Sandy and the Sandpipers started out the evening in bright green satin cavalier shirts and later switched to World War II army jackets dyed maroon. There was Your Father's Moustache, a group with a Roaring Twenties beat. Also on the bill were The Angels, dressed in black-and-white floral culottes, followed by a brief Mod fashion show, the latest from a Paramus boutique." Marci and Kelly, freed from their disco-cages, invited fathers up on the floor for go-go lessons, which was funny, and Kenny Solms and Gail Parent were on hand with some comedy relief, which was not.

The Record reported: "The show was an enormous success if comments from the paying customers were any indication." For me it was a totally satisfying series, seeing the dance floor crowded with toddlers and teens, hair neatly combed, in Mary Jane's and saddle shoes, their parents sitting back, proudly beaming. My next generation was warming up, on the dance floor of The Steak Pit. Is it possible that these sweet, innocent Baby Boomers will soon be the ones vomiting into the mud at Woodstock, tripping on angel dust, hustling for smack? *Unthinkable!*

It was Peter Salerno, my sidekick/assistant, who gave me my most memorable personal appearance. Peter had become a corrections officer, assigned to Riker's Island and had persuaded the warden to allow me to being my troop of musicians to entertain the inmates at this fortress-like prison out in Queens. Warden Castro gave me the grand tour, showing me an impressive cache of shives, makeshift knives, ice picks and weapons they had confiscated on a pre-show lock-down. Hundreds of inmates quietly entered the large auditorium, orderly, in single file, but the best seats, about one hundred seats front and center on both sides, remained strangely empty. It was only when a parade of sissy Mary's sashayed into the room, to wolf-whistles, woof-woof's and whoops of delight; it became clear who was sitting in the privileged front-row VIP seats. The show was going so well, I got caught up in the excitement and whispered to the band to play "Kansas City," I wanted to sing. I was into the second chorus when one skinny, little Puerto Rican queen in the front row, stood up and shouted at me: "You sing one more verse; I'm going back to my cell!"

19) American Boy Bands

"Let's hear it for the boys ..."

Bobby Rydell's final chart hit "Forget Him" was prophetic, signaling an end to the "Teen Idol." By 1963, pop stars of the late Fifties now stood like vintage Chevy's on a used car lot – out of fashion, not yet collectable. Ducktails, like tail-fins, were outdated. The Brylcreem Boys of Bandstand were permanently airbrushed from the cover of *16* magazine, replaced by cuddly, shaggy-haired hippie boys. Teen Idols fulfilled their promise – purchase a house for mom and pop, released a greatest hits album, marry a beauty queen and settle into a modest ranch house in the San Fernando Valley.

Pat Boone and Elvis had lead the way West, finding a successful second career in Technicolor Hollywood, starring in a series of regrettable wide-screen, stereophonic musicals. Ricky Nelson, a veteran child actor was a natural for the big screen and Fabian proved to be a formidable sidekick to John Wayne and Jimmy Stewart. Producers turned to young men with name recognition – "marquee value" – to entice their alienated youth audience back into the new suburban multiplex. Most successful was Bobby Darin, who escaped a disastrous interlude as a folk singer by proving to be a first-rate dramatic actor and marrying the reigning teen queen of the silver screen, Sandra Dee. Fabian, with the help of Tommy Sands and Paul Anka invaded the beaches of Normandy to recreate "The Longest Day" and Frankie Avalon scored with Annette in their series of highly-popular, low-budget bikini beach comedies, twisting in the sand.

So, with the era of the Teen Idol diminishing, it was a 25-year old Neil Diamond, a soft-spoken nebbish with a guitar, who walked into our studios, May 7, 1966, for his first television appearance. Although Diamond structured his songs on the guitar, his hero was the piano-composer Neil Sedaka, revered by his class-mates at Brooklyn's Lincoln High School. Diamond transferred from Erasmus Hall (where he sang in the glee club with Barbra Streisand) to Lincoln High, the "Rock 'n' Roll High School" of Mort Shuman, Howard Greenfield, the Tokens and Neil Sedaka. Neil Diamond realized at an early age that fame is sweet but fleeting; it's the songwriter who reaps the greatest rewards, with record sales, jukebox, airplay and publishing, accumulating a song catalogue that generates royalties far into the future. He was to become the last of the Brill Building Brooklyn dynasty.

As an entertainer, Neil was a stiff. Like Ricky Nelson, Roy Orbison and Del Shannon, Neil shielded himself from his audience, hiding behind his guitar, unable to project anything resembling charisma. Neil was so wooden you wanted to spray him with Liquid Pledge. Other than as an acoustic troubadour strumming tunes at Gerde's Folk City, any future opportunities for Neil Diamond escaped me.

The first record he introduced on "The Clay Cole Show" was "Solitary Man," a moody soliloquy Neil had originally composed with Bobby Darin in mind. As produced by his partners, Jeff Barry and Ellie Greenwich, the effort was a solitary flop, barely making a dent in the charts. (Bang Records later re-released "Solitary Man" in 1970; it became a huge worldwide hit, remaining on the charts for seven weeks.)

Neil Diamond returned in the fall of 1966, holding a fresh copy of "Cherry, Cherry" tightly in his grip. Dad, sitting backstage with Neil during rehearsals, offered to help promote the record, taking it back to North Carolina to the local 50-watt station. Unfortunately, it was Neil's only copy. In spite of Dad's best effort to help an aspiring singer, "Cherry, Cherry" became Neil's first breakout hit. Neil's original title was "Money, Money," but "love is more important than money," reasoned Jeff Barry and Ellie Greenwich; "kids want *love* and kids buy records." It soon became a Top 10 hit, on the charts for nine weeks. (Neil's *live* version of "Cherry, Cherry," from his "Hot August Night" album was re-released in 1973 and became a national chart hit once again.)

About that time, we hired a low-level production assistant who's main duties were to order the hot-dogs, fries and soft drinks to reward our studio audience for the dreary delays of assembling a taped show. Aside from her terrific sense of humor, Marcia Murphy was a rather mousy, terrified little creature, with one slight crossed eye, but loveable and loyal, dedicated to her duties. She once forgot to place an order of refreshments for our studio audience and became an emotional wreck, fearing she would be fired. Nathan's Famous came to her rescue, delivering franks and fries. But, no way would we sack our Marcia; we'd rather allow our malnourished studio audience to simply waste away.

I asked Neil to guest-host my show, sitting in for me while I attended to family business back in North Carolina, and it was during that period that Neil and Marcia's orbits collided. Neil and Marcia began seeing each other secretly, meeting at Marcia's modest little West Village apartment, a hush-hush arrangement that required clever juggling of roommates. We all pledged to secrecy as Neil was married to a Brooklyn school teacher (1963) and they had two young children. When Neil eventually moved to California, they divorced (1969) and a few months later Neil and Marcia married.

In the early Seventies on my trips west, I visited Marcia in the Diamond's unpretentious, but cozy "hippie pad" in the canyons above the Hollywood Hills. Neil was never home, always on the road, but Marcia was an agreeable host, breaking-out Neil's "secret stash" for nostalgic reminiscences by their roaring fireplace.

In 1972, Marcia offered me VIP seats, front row center at the Greek Theatre in Los Angeles for the debut of the *new* Neil Diamond. I agreed to go, but with low expectations. Although by now, Neil's eighteen charted hits had elevated him to superstar status, in my mind he was still that nebbish from Brooklyn. "Song Sung Blue" was number one on the national charts that weekend, but is that enough to fill the 6,100 seats of the Greek?

The formidable stage at the Greek was cluttered with kettledrums, tympani, harps, chimes, all the bells and whistles, a symphony orchestra and a choir. His stage lighting cues were so precise that they could have been designed by Peggy Lee herself. Neil appeared in his now-trademarked sparkling, bloused shirt and simply blew me away. The whole effect was so over the top that that earth rumbled, like a Cape Canaveral space launch – proof that the meek shall inherit the earth. Neil's show was thrilling.

At the finale, I was on my feet, cheering, and crying and weak from clapping at his "Coming to America" finale, with the thundering appearance of an American flag blanketing the stage. Backstage, Marcia greeted me grinning ear-to-ear, with, "I told you so," sparkling in her eyes. But, "See?" was all she said.

When Marcia and Neil split, Marcia received $150-million, plus vacation homes in Aspen and their Beverly Hills estate. Compared to Paul McCartney's $102-million settlement with Heather Mills in 2007 and Steven Spielberg's $100-million settlement with Amy Irving in 1989, Marcia received the single largest divorce settlement in show-biz history. Married for twenty-five years, with two sons, Jesse and Micah, Neil said, "She's been with me through thick and thin. She deserves half of my fortune." Marcia filed for "irreconcilable differences" after throwing Neil out of the house during a reported affair with a rodeo cowgirl. Neil's parting remarks: "I wish her all the happiness $150-million can bring." And to think, he found his million-dollar baby in my five-and-ten cent store.

Clay Cole's Disk-O-Tek began to attract many mainstream movie stars; everyone from Omar Sharif "Lawrence of Arabia" to Michael J. Pollard "Bonnie & Clyde" to Hermione Gingold "Gigi." Tony Randall loved to perform hokey old Music Hall songs on our show, but insisted that no one in the studio smoke. Well we all smoked. Finally, after several appearances, the stagehands offered a seemingly agreeable solution to Tony: "We won't smoke, if you won't sing!" No one laughed harder than Tony Randall. George Segal was another actor who loved to appear, strumming cornball tunes on his banjo.

It was a visit from Jerry Lewis that made an immense impact on me, and my eventual decision to leave the show. Before Jerry arrived, his PR advance team warned us that Mr. Lewis was on a tight schedule, with a full day of interviews, and instructed us to have the videotape machines cued-up and ready for his arrival. They would allow us just ten minutes with the star. Jerry arrived, handed off his trench coat, sat down and talked for an hour and a half. His PR men were pacing behind the cameras, tapping their wrist watches, shaking their heads in disbelief. Jerry was unmovable. Although I greeted Jerry with a cheerful façade, Jerry somehow sensed my melancholy.

Jerry had produced, directed, written and starred in over fifty motion pictures, every one a highly-profitable moneymaker. He was a well-loved fan-favorite, a superstar who personally delivered hundreds of millions of dollars to the studios, but was never fully appreciated by the Hollywood establishment. Believe it or not, Jerry claimed to be a Hollywood outsider.

"All those wonderful Hollywood parties you hear about...I'm not on the guest list. I'm never invited. But I can't let that bother me. I have to sort out what is important in my life. I have to just believe in myself and do what I think is best for my life. You must do the same."

In 2009, an 82 year old Jerry Lewis stepped onto the Academy awards stage for the first timer in 50 years, to receive an Oscar – and wouldn't you know, it's the wrong one. *Time* magazine's Richard Corliss reported, "He surely merits one of those Lifetime Achievement Awards the Academy passes out to distinguished film folk who never won a competitive Oscar and might die soon." In an interview with *Entertainment Weekly*, Lewis explained the hurt: "Because they didn't think enough of my work. Because what I did didn't command consideration because it's slapstick, because it's lowbrow, because the Academy's always been cautious about comedy." It's a measure of his lingering impact that Hollywood is still embarrassed by the very idea of Jerry Lewis, let alone his presence." (One producer cruelly called Martin and Lewis 'the organ grinder and the monkey').

The tape was rolling, the conversation was getting very personal and I was aware, out of the corner of my eyes that the PR natives were getting restless. So, I wrapped up the interview, thanked Jerry, and stopped tape. But, Jerry didn't budge, he sat determined not to leave until I got the message, which was, quite simply: "This above all, to thine own self be true."

In spite of my TV-Q popular appeal score and my soaring Nielson ratings, Jerry was trying to make me aware of one simple truth. I was the host of a rock 'n' roll show, not the stuff that engenders Emmy nominations, Friars Club roasts or an audience with the Pope. The old-boy network did not embrace rockers; to most, rock 'n' roll was the modern day equivalent of burlesque – highly popular, titillating and fun – but damned as low-class, sleazy and undesirable. "Don't expect to get no respect."

After about ten minutes, when his entourage finally gave up, I suggested that we might as well continue to roll tape. Jerry agreed and we taped another half-hour. To Jerry, reaching out to a fellow performer was simply more important than his pending schedule. I will neither forget Jerry's kindness, nor the way our eyes locked when he said, "If you're deprived of love when you're young, you can never have it given back to you."

At once, I understood everything. I certainly understood Jerry. Most of my private conversation with the engaging, sensitive Jerry Lewis never aired, it was much too personal, but it still plays over and over in the tape recorder in my head.

When Jerry left, I couldn't move. The staff, the crew and I just sat there dumb-struck at what had just occurred. We were snapped out of our trance about ten minutes later when Jerry Lewis came bounding back into the studio, alone. He had gone downstairs to his limousine and returned with a beautifully inscribed autograph. Over his photograph, Jerry had written: "Clay. Think and walk tall. You are. Love. Jerry."

By the mid-Sixties, British and American Boy Bands, Folk-Rock artists and Motown legends stood side-by-side on the play lists of Top 40 AM Radio. Motown was now getting grittier and much more soulful in their treatment of R&B, and the folk-rock movement was droning-on, spearheaded by Bob Dylan, fueling the anti-war fire. I did not acquire a taste for Dylan; his genius escaped me. I was more tuned-in to the folk-rock of the Byrds, Judy Collins and the First Edition (with unknown lead-singer, Kenny Rogers).

In 1966, when the second wave of British Boy Bands arrived in America, the Beatles were now at the pinnacle of the entertainment establishment – the biggest musical attraction to ever hit the planet. The faces of John, Paul, Ringo and George were etched into the hard rock Mount Rushmore of Tin Pan Alley. There were a few American groups still standing, most notably the East Coast Four Seasons ("Dawn"), and the West Coast Beach Boys ("I Get Around."). The important new American groups were the Association ("Cherish"), Fifth Dimension ("Up-Up and Away"), Mamas & The Papas ("California Dreamin'") and Tommy James & the Shondells ("Hanky Panky"), each unique and impressive.

Channel 11 expanded our show to a full ninety minutes, which meant we were opposite the first half-hour of Jackie Gleason's show on CBS and we often gave the Great One a run for his money, winning our timeslot in the ratings. Two new pop music shows were launched directly opposite us on Saturday night, a big-budget, full-color Bruce Morrow show on WABC and a no-budget, black-and-white UHF dance party "Disc-O-Teen," hosted by John Zacherley in full monster make-up. "Budget alone does not make good television," Lloyd Gaines assured me, "nobody tunes in to see the sets." Lloyd was right; 'Cousin' Brucie's show soon bit the dust. As for Zach, low ratings meant nothing. "That was three of the happiest years of my life," the 'cool ghoul' told me. I could relate to that.

The extra half-hour also meant booking more Boy Bands! There were so many bands in and out of our little studio that Executive Producer Lloyd Gaines cleared a second full day of studio time for us to videotape the sheer volume arriving each week. Out of the corner of my eye, I was vaguely aware of the intrigue and drama being played out in our infamous San Quentin hallway. Our guest stars and groups were often visited by process servers, immigration and naturalization field officers, U.S. Marshals, divorce attorneys, DEA agents and AFTRA / AFM union reps. For most groups, this was their first visit to New York City and for many, their first television appearance. In all cases, they seemed awed and overwhelmed. Visiting performers would often pull me aside, asking me to recommend clubs or disco-theques, where they might jam, hear some live music or pick up chicks.

Performing a *live* television show is like working a well-oiled assembly line; various parts come together and accelerate toward a finish line, the final product accomplished by adrenalin and ability. But a show taped in haphazard segments is like doing piecework in a sweatshop, with no end in sight and no joy in the final product.

In my memory, tape days were a whirlwind, producing a blur; sadly, there are no videotape reminders to jog the memory, not even a snapshot. Taping the artists destroyed any interaction between the artists, a live studio audience and me. In years to come, I would receive inquiries from groups, television producers and documentary film directors seeking clips or videotape from my show. I had to admit, not only was there no videotape, but I had no memory of the group ever having being there. The Yardbirds, the Who, the Doors were all there, but I have no remembrance, no anecdote, not even a photo to mark their appearance. It works both ways. The west coast Fifth Dimension performed on my show on a dozen or more occasions, but when I introduced myself to the original members backstage in the late 1990s, they had absolutely no recollection of ever having appeared. They simply became a slug in the listings of *TV Guide*:

> [11] 6:00 CLAY COLE – Music
> Clay welcomes the Turtles ("Happy Together"),
> Critters ("Younger Girl") We Five ("You Were on My Mind"),
> Gary Lewis & the Playboys ("This Diamond Ring"),
> Happenings ("See You In September"), singers, Laura Nyro, Bobby
> Hebb and comedian Sandy Baron. (90 Minutes)

Color cameras arrived at Channel 11 on June 27, 1967. Soupy Sales ribbed me: "You look great in color. Your eyes have that patriotic look – blue with red whites!" (*Rim-shot*) Nevertheless, I still believe I will always be remembered in black and white.

Beatle-wannabes, like June-bugs, were bustin' out all over. Suddenly, a boy with a guitar became a chick magnet – the football hero, prom king and Valedictorian rolled into one; the boy most likely to succeed with the ladies; E-G-B-D-F. Guitar teachers quit their day jobs; "Guitar Lessons Given" signs went up all over the country and boys lined up to plug in.

I like the way Peck's Bad Boys, a popular local boy-band, describe the scene in 1966: "New York bands were not garage bands…we didn't have garages. We were more like basement bands; if you were lucky enough to have a band member whose father was a Superintendent of a large building, you could rehearse in those big, echoing boiler rooms."

Back in the doo wop days, a Brooklyn trio, the Echoes, had a Top 10 vocal harmony hit, "Baby Blue," but each were accomplished musicians as well. We invited the Echoes to appear on our 1961 Easter Parade of Stars at the Brooklyn Paramount Theatre and Murray the K pulled them aside to give them some advice: "Lose the instruments, that is, if you wanna be successful." In 1964, after the Beatles made Boy Bands cool, the Echoes jibed; "Hey, Murray. Are you gonna tell Paul McCartney to lose his guitar?" After the British Invasion, the Echoes polished up their kits and maintained a lifetime of employment as the Scoundrels – a Brooklyn Boy Band.

What is it that drives these guys? What inspires these kids to study, practice, rehearse and make endless sacrifices? Is it just the need to be heard? Or are they driven by the legend of the Beatles, Brian Epstein and the Cavern club? Every Boy Band who ever played a motel lounge, Moose Lodge, barroom or bowling alley will secretly admit to the Brian Epstein fantasy – one night, the right person might walk in, whisk them away from their mundane nine-to-five jobs and deposit them into a world of never-ending possibilities. It's the dream…the secret dream.

A back-alley cellar club in Atlantic City is about as far removed from "The Big Time" as a group could get. In the summer of 1964, while bouncing around the bars at the Shore, I stumbled into the Alibi Lounge and encountered the Rhondells, a frat-band on summer break from Lafayette College in Pennsylvania, fronted by Tom Dowes, an ex-folkie from Brooklyn. Their tight vocals set them a cut above the average club band, and offstage they were bright and funny, perfect gentlemen. I dropped in regularly, chatting between sets, offering encouragement. But, when Nat Weiss dropped in, he offered them an opportunity.

Nat Weiss at thirty-five was already well known, a well-established music business attorney with connections to Brian Epstein. "Opportunity comes when talent and luck collide." Weiss initiated a series of events that propelled the Rhondells beyond their wildest dreams. First, a management contract with Brian Epstein, *the* manger of the Beatles, and a name change ("Rhondells" resonated of the Fifties). It was John Lennon who suggested the Cyrkle, borrowing the spelling from the Byrds. A recording contract from Columbia Records followed, and then Paul Simon offered up a song, "Red Rubber Ball." Amazing! Their recording went on the charts, up to No. 2, rewarding them a spot on the Beatle's 1966 summer tour; the clean-cut Cyrkle in their snazzy, striped blazers with the bad-assed Ronettes in their sequined shifts.

Brian Epstein was now surefooted enough to begin managing American groups, and he invited me to attend a press conference to introduce the Cyrke, his first American group. In the summer of 1966, the press came out in full force, but it was really Brian Epstein they wanted to meet. It was on that occasion that the Australian journalist Lillian Roxon famously questioned Brian: "Mr. Epstein, are you a millionaire?"

The subtext of her question was really: "So … rock 'n' roll is big-business now, isn't that so Brian?" (1966 was the first year that rock 'n' roll became a billion-dollar industry.)

Time, Newsweek, The Village Voice, were there, Ellen Willis from *The New Yorker* and Ellen Sander who wrote for *Life,* all the A-List press. It was here that I first perceived the power and privilege granted to Georgia Winters, my *16* magazine pal. Just as the party seemed to be winding down, the seas parted, as Georgia Winters, fashionably late, swept in for a private, one-on-one introduction to the band. Her *16* magazine now boasted a circulation of 1.2 million subscribers, which translated into about five million pass-around monthly readers. Georgia was now the preeminent arbiter of pop culture. In addition, she was in the midst of a secret affair with one of *16* magazine's archetypal shirtless pinup boys, Jim Morrison of the Doors. Their drama had a long run, but was hardly poetic, with Georgia falling victim to Jimmy's sadistic mind games, her one and only passionate conquest in which she did not maintain the upper hand.

Brian Epstein himself was rather shy; he would only appear on my show via a telephone interview. One summer Sunday I sat with Brian and his guests, including Peter Noone, on his yacht docked at the Fire Island Pines and found him relaxed and unassuming, not at all like a driven man in the midst of building an billion dollar empire. Brian was a proper English gentleman who would rather defer to the whimsy of Peter Noone than to be the center of attention himself. But don't be fooled, the Beatles declared that his faith, persistence and level-headedness prevailed. He discovered them. He made them! Proof is, when Brian died, the Beatles managed themselves. But, can you imagine the migraines he must have suffered trying to manage the Beatles in their heyday?

Brian Epstein died in the summer of 1967 from an overdose of sleeping pills at age thirty-two and the Cyrkle expired as well. Their second release, "Turn Down Day" was visionary. Their success may have been brief, but for one shining moment four fresh-faced kids were *there,* in the Big Time: Marty Fried became an attorney; Earl Pickens a doctor; Tom Dawes found a new, lucrative career as a commercial jingle writer; and Don Danneman became musical director of children's television shows, then formed a company specializing in music and audio for the ad industry.

The Ronettes were soon to be history as well; Ronnie, Sister Estelle and Cousin Nedra split up in 1965. Nedra Talley, after a longtime on-again, off-again romance with Ringo Starr, married my Happening Place dance club MC, Scott Ross and maintained a highly-visible lifestyle. Scott enjoyed great success as a television talk show host and a contributor to Pat Robertson's Christian Ministries, appearing as an on-camera interviewer on the 700 Club television shows.

Estelle Bennett, on the other hand, simply drifted into the shadows. Estelle lived for many years in Brooklyn with Ronettes' former road manager Joey Dong and they had a daughter Toyin, who friends say, might have been raised by record producer Teddy Vann and his wife Rita. Estelle made several failed attempts at a solo career with Teddy, but she struggled with anorexia and schizophrenia and at times had been homeless, wandering the streets of New York.

"Estelle had such an extraordinary life," Nedra Talley Ross told *The New York Times*. "To have the fame and all she had at an early age and for it all to come to an end abruptly. Not everybody can let that go and then go on with life."

Kevin Dilworth, at the time a Newark Star-Ledger reporter, befriended Estelle and told me, "Rather than stay in her modest one-bedroom apartment in Englewood, NJ (her daughter Toyin Hunter found her the place and paid the monthly rent), she would travel to Harlem to attend St. Mary's Episcopal Church where she sang in the choir and volunteered to work in the soup kitchen."

In the winter of 2009, it was a concerned Dilworth who visited Estelle's apartment and found her dead. "It was not until she died that her daughter told me that her mother suffered from mental illness for years. I just accepted her for the way she was, soft-spoken, kind-hearted and someone who needed a friend."

Finally married in 1968, Ronnie and Phil Spector had a stormy relationship; Spector forced her into retirement, forbidding her to tour with the Beatles, replacing her with yet another Bennett cousin. After their widely reported, high profile divorce, and the publication of her heartbreaking tell-all book, Ronnie remarried, and as Mrs. **Jonathan Greenfield**, lives quietly and comfortably in Connecticut, simply becoming a rock 'n' roll legend. At long last, the Ronettes[14] were inducted into The Rock and Roll Hall of Fame in 2007.

In 1966, Bob Crewe brought to our show his latest discovery, a blue-eyed soul phenomenon, Mitch Ryder and his Detroit Wheels. Mitch was to the Sixties what KC (Of The Sunshine Band) was to the Seventies – a wildly handsome, funky-sexy, electrifying performer. Bob created unique hard-driving medleys, ("Devil with the Blue Dress On," "Good Golly Miss Molly") songs that sent Mitch to the national charts five times in succession. Then a most damaging change occurred, launched for the first time on our show. The Detroit Wheels, his funky Detroit band members were replaced by a full-orchestra, dressed in white dinner jackets, with specially-made white Lucite music stands, with Mitch as the front man. This is the same regrettable transformation I had witnessed five years earlier with Ray Charles at the Apollo. Mitch barely made the Top 30 with this effort, and never climbed the charts again.

Another of Bob Crewe's new Boy Bands, Richard & the Young Lions broke-up just hours before a scheduled *live* appearance on our show. By chance, the frantic lead-singer, Richard Tepp stumbled upon a drummer and guitar player at an ice cream parlor in South Orange, NJ and hijacked them over to our New York studios. Their performance was flawless and no one knew the difference, including Bob Crewe.

On the surface, the Cowsills appeared to be the typical American family, surprisingly popular at a time when pop music was becoming grungy, anti-social and psychedelic; their music made flower-power palatable to mid-America's mamas and papas. Here was a family band, seemingly perfect in every way, brothers Bill, Bob, Barry, Paul and John, sister Susan, mother Barbara, and dad as their manager, backstage pulling the strings. Dad was an ex-Navy man with the perfect 'Joe-six-pack' name – "Bud."

The group started as a Boy Band, the four brothers inspired by the Beatles, playing at school socials in their hometown of Newport, RI. When they came to the attention of record producer Artie Kornfeld, it was he who conceived the concept of a family collaboration, adding mom and the rest of the siblings to the group. MGM Records, thrilled at the marketing possibilities, released "The Rain, The Park & Other Things," which became a million-seller. Aside from the cozy-family gimmick, it didn't hurt that Barry was a heartthrob, a perfect fantasy poster

---

14   To set the record straight: the Ronettes did not appear in "Twist Around the Clock" as has been noted in most every rock encyclopedia and Internet biography and erroneously repeated in the pages of *People* magazine. It was following the release of the film, on my subsequent 1962 Twist-a-rama tour that our lives became irrevocably linked.

boy and an ideal cover cut-out for *16* magazine. The Cowsills charted a handful of hits in the mid-Sixties, which led to multiple appearances on our stage, on Ed Sullivan and on their own wholesome television special, sponsored by the American Dairy Association.

As sweet and sunny as The Cowsills appeared, rumors abounded about the darker side of the family, particularly in the maniacal management style of daddy "Bud," said to be a hard-driving tyrant. There was still another son Richard, who, it was believed, "Bud" cruelly pushed aside. When Columbia Pictures approached "Bud" about developing a Cowsill Family series for ABC, "Bud" refused. He didn't like the idea of Shirley Jones playing mother Barbara, not exactly a rational business decision.

Their final and biggest hit, "Hair" was released in 1967, and when "The Partridge Family" hit the airwaves in 1970 without them, the band disbanded, each moving on to assorted musical pursuits. Mother Barbara died in 1985. Brother Barry, chasing a solo career, was living in New Orleans when Hurricane Katrina arrived. Four days after Katrina struck, a telephone message from Barry to his sister Susan was recorded: "I don't know how to get out of town except wait for a bus. I've been so lonely; I hope I get in touch with you." Four months passed without a word, his frantic family begging for information, plastering the town with posters, eager for some sign of hope. Then the decomposing body of a male was found floating in the muddy waters near downtown New Orleans. Dental records confirmed, Barry Cowsill, 51, musician, cause of death: unknown.

Sid Bernstein waltzed into our studios with his latest Boy Band, four young men in Little Lord Fauntleroy outfits, the first television appearance of the Young Rascals. Felix Cavaliere (on a Hammond-B3), Gene Cornish, and Eddie Brigati left Joey Dee's Starlighters, and teamed up with drummer Dino Danelli, producing hard rock 'n' roll and funky R&B, in what became known as 'The New York Sound'. "When we were with Joey Dee on tour in Europe," Felix remembered, "the first thing I saw was a Hammond B-3 organ. I had seen one, but I never touched one in my life." It provided him with the concept for the Rascals' sound – "the rich-sounding organ as a blanket, while keeping the guitar and drums for essential rhythm." The Rascal's breakthrough came with "Good Lovin;" and "Groovin' (On A Sunday Afternoon)," two pop-classics that sailed straight to No. 1, and still define summertime to this day.

"The group built its sound around Felix Cavaliere's Hammond-B3 organ and the soulful lead vocals of Cavaliere and Eddie Brigati. In Cavaliere's words, "Marvin Gaye's voice, Ray Charles' piano, Jimmy Smith's organ, Phil Spector's production and the Beatles' writing — put them all together and you've got what I wanted to do." The Rascals were masters of the three-minute single: sustained bursts of energized pop-soul made to be blasted over transistor radios or danced to at parties and discotheques."

On our Christmas show, I persuaded the portly Sid to dress as Santa Claus – the ultimate Jewish joke - and his Lord Fauntleroy boys dutifully sat on his lap, delivering their wish list. Their wish to "get rid of these stupid plus-fours and foppish cravats" was granted in 1967. They also dropped the "Young," becoming, simply, the Rascals.

The funky R&B pop sound of the Rascals was a perfect fit for Atlantic Records and its jet-setting co-founder Ahmet Ertegun, who took the boys under his wing and onto the international party circuit. They became the house band to the Hamptons, playing a summer-long gig at the Barge. They jammed with James Brown, Jimi Hendrix and an unknown Bette Midler and then dazzled all of Europe, revered as rock royalty by musicians and fans alike. In spite of a swelling bank account, they remained four loveable little rascals from the Choo Choo Club in Garfield, New Jersey, just lookin'to meet chicks.

Just as the Rascals had successfully emerged from Joey Dee's Starlighters, the Four Seasons and Blood, Sweat & Tears evolved right before our cameras, as well.

It began in the late Fifties with a one-shot group, the Royal Teens and their summertime novelty hit "(Who Wears) Short-Shorts" with group members Al Kooper and Bob Gaudio. Al Kooper created the Blues Project, which led to Blood Sweat & Tears, and Bob Gaudio became the musical backbone of the Four Season. By the mid-Sixties, the Four Seasons were so popular that they were now demanding personal appearance fees comparable to the biggest British groups. In 1965 the quartet released a recording of "Don't Think Twice" as the Wonder Who, simply to prove they could score a hit without the charmed Four Seasons name on the label. In 1967, Frankie Valli, with one of the most distinctive voices in pop music, introduced his now-classic soundtrack staple "Can't Take My Eyes off of You," as a solo single, while still continuing to work and record with the Four Seasons. Frankie Valli and the Four Seasons have sold more records than any other American group, so their 1980 induction into the Rock and Roll Hall of Fame was inevitable. Frankie is now one of the highest-paid entertainers on the road today, but – can you imagine being on the road for over fifty years?

The last time I saw Frankie Valli was in 1999, a chance meeting in the lobby of a mid-western hotel. Frankie was alone at the reception desk when I stepped off the elevators close to midnight. "Nothing like the old days," he repeated over and over as we bear-hugged. "I've thought about giving it all up, but…" his voice trailed off, with a shrug. When he pulled out the wallet photos of his six-year-old twins and a handsome twelve-year-old, I understood why the thought had crossed his mind. Frankie had just landed on a flight from his home in Los Angeles, arriving alone at the Hotel-Casino in a white, stretch limousine, although he had requested a less-fussy Town Car. No posse, hangers-on or bodyguards. He dragged his own little bag-on-wheels up to the Presidential Suite with its sumptuous living room, two master bedrooms with marble baths and Jacuzzi whirlpools plus a formal dining room, seating twelve. He called down to the front desk, politely requesting a single room with an outside view.

There is an unmistakable masculine force behind Frankie's falsetto, which make it acceptable to a mass audience – boys in the pool room sing-along shamelessly. His influence has been felt through three generations of natural falsetto hit-makers, from Lou Christie, Eddie Kendricks (the Temptations), Barry Gibb (the Bee Gees) to Chris Martin (Coldplay) among many others. Aside from thirties bluesman Robert Johnson, who also sang falsetto, Frankie is the original.

Al Kooper's musical innovations evolved in front of our cameras, first in the late 50s as a member of the Royal Teens, ("Short, Shorts"), then in the mid-Sixties, on his "incandescent" electric organ, fronting the Blues Project with guitarist Danny Kalb. The group cut three albums, and settled into the Café a Go Go on Bleecker Street, playing an electric-folk, bluesy-jazz synthesis. Out of the Blues Project grew Blood, Sweat and Tears, (with Steve Katz and Bobby Colomby), augmenting a traditional rock quartet with a horn section, fusing rock and jazz. After signing to Columbia Records, the group released one of the most critically acclaimed albums of the late 1960s, "Child Is Father to the Man," that featured the Harry Nilsson song, "Without Her" and Kooper's most memorable blues number, "I Love You More Than You'll Ever Know." Kooper then left the group to become a record producer at Columbia.

It was the addition of vocalist/frontman David Clayton-Thomas that sent Blood, Sweat & Tears to the charts, creating a fresh, new sound. Reportedly, Judy Collins had seen the Canadian blues singer perform at a New York City club and was so moved by his performance, she introduced him to her old her friends Bobby Colomby and Steve Katz. Blood Sweat and Tears second album with Clayton-Thomas singing his own composition "Spinning Wheel," became a worldwide hit, producing three gold singles and three Grammy Awards, including Album of the Year.

Kooper also played keyboards on "Like A Rolling Stone" with Bob Dylan," You Can't Always Get What You Want" with the Rolling Stones and "All Those Years Ago" with George Harrison, and played on sessions with Jimi Hendrix, B. B. King, Gene Pitney and the first rock jam album with Mike Bloomfield, Stephen Stills and Johnny Winter. His production credits include "Free Bird" & "Sweet Home Alabama" by Lynyrd Skynyrd, Bob Dylan's "New Morning" album, and if that's not enough, he wrote "This Diamond Ring" for Gary Lewis & the Playboys. Any one of these amazing credits would be enough to grant celebrity status, yet surprisingly, Al Kooper is not a household name – revered mostly in the inner-circle of the music biz.

Two musical instruments, once considered "old school" square, also gained newfound popularity – the organ and the harmonica. In the 1940s, Larry Adler had elevated the harmonica to virtuoso status on the concert stage, only to have it bulldozed by the vaudeville slapstick of the Harmonica Rascals and the cartoon cliché of jailhouse blues men. Harmonica virtuoso "Little Walter" (born Walter Jacobs in 1930; died in 1968, at age 37), was one of the last links to the classic Chicago blues men Muddy Waters and Jimmy Rogers in the first half of the fifties. Both as a sideman and bandleader, "Little Walter" revolutionized the sound of blues harmonica through amplification, clasping a mike to the harp as he played, now the widely-accepted norm among modern-day players. Posthumously, "Little Walter" became the first musician, primarily known for playing harmonica, to enter the Rock and Roll Hall of Fame, Class of 2008.

The blues harmonica tradition has been passed down through the decades by illustrious bluesmen like, "Sonny Boy" Williamson, "the father of modern blues harp" and George "Harmonica" Smith, "the master of the chromatic blues harmonica." The best of our current disciples are two youthful, white virtuosos, Dennis Gruenling and Steve Guyger, who have recorded a CD, "I Just Keep Lovin' Him," a tribute to "Little Walter" (Back Bender Records).

Now, a generation later, artists as diverse as Stevie Wonder, Bob Dylan, Neil Young, and Mickey Raphael (with Willie Nelson), have made the mouth organ a widely-accepted musical gift. The harmonica was the attention-grabber that elevated Taylor Hicks to "American Idol" winner in 2006. Bob Dylan takes full credit. He simply says, "The Harmonica is the world's best-selling musical instrument," then adds, "You're welcome."

The harmonica could be slipped into your hip pocket; the Hammond-B3 organ, on the other hand, required a U-Haul and four Teamsters. By the mid-Sixties, one could not diminish the importance of the Hammond Organ to pop rock and funky R&B. But before rock 'n' roll, the organ resonated of roller rinks, ballparks and Radio City Music Hall, and in the first half of the Twentieth Century, two wildly disparate performers popularized organ music – both named Smith. Ethel Smith appeared in splashy 40's Hollywood musicals with her stylish ankle-strapped shoes, dancing across the foot pedals to "Tico, Tico" and Jimmy Smith, (no relation), a jazz musician who achieved prominence in the 50s creating a style known as 'funk' or 'soul jazz' on the organ. Ethel and Jimmy Smith legitimized the Hammond Organ as a pop music force.

But in the 60s there is no doubt that Felix Cavaliere's Hammond-B3 ignited a fire under other pop-rock bands: the Vagrants (with Leslie West), the Hassles (with Billy Joel), Vanilla Fudge (with Carmine Appice) and Goldie & the Gingerbreads (with Margo Lewis tapping the bass foot pedals.) A local vocal group, the Dedications, (Brothers Richie and Charlie Ingui) was going nowhere until they added a Hammond-B3 – as the Soul Survivors their recording of "Expressway to Your Heart" went straight to No. 1. Junior Walker & the All-Stars' "Shotgun" and Booker T & the MG's "Green Onions" are just two more organ-driven instrumental dance classics. When a teenage film actor named Billy Preston ("Birth of the Blues") rolled his 'B3' into an Apple recording session, he became the official Fifth Beatle, the only musician to be included in the label credits of the "Let It Be" and "Abbey Road" albums, as well as the landmark "White Album." Billy also appeared with them in the films, "The Complete Beatles" and "Let It Be," as well as performing with them during their historic final rooftop concert. The Beatles embracing the 'B3' made it official. The organ became an integral component of mid-Sixties pop, defining the sound that became known as New York rock 'n' roll.

Bruce Milner's organ sequences were the key hooks to Every Mother's Son 1967 hit,
> *"Come on Down To My Boat (Baby)"*
> *The Animals with Alan Price on "House of the Rising Sun"*
> *The Spencer Davis Group with Steve Winwood on "Gimme Some Lovin'"*
> *The Doors' Ray Manzarak, "Light My Fire"*
> *and Procol Harum's Mathew Fisher on "Whiter Shade of Pale."*

To illustrate the power of a key musical hook, a British Court awarded Procol Harum's Mathew Fisher a forty-percent share of the copyright, saying his organ solo was "a distinctive and significant contribution to the overall composition" of "Whiter Shade of Pale."

Al Kooper played the organ behind Bob Dylan at the 1965 Newport Folk Festival, the historic night Dylan officially plugged in to an amp, "resulting in a response of cheers and boos. Dylan left the stage after only three songs, but re-emerged and sang two acoustic numbers. This shift marked his changing artistic direction as he moved from leading contemporary songwriter of the folk scene to rock 'n' roll star." From the moment Dylan plugged in, the electric bill at Gerde's Folk City soared. The Bitter End, the Café Wha?, the Café A-Go-Go, the Village Gate and all the folk clubs across Bleecker Street now had a new partner – ConEd.

20) The Party's Over

"In 1967, America didn't just turn on and tune in –
it also began hurtling towards a nervous breakdown."
– *Rolling Stone* magazine

The Age of Aquarius was upon us. The seeds of the baby boom were blossoming into twenty-something hippies. The Sixties have been endlessly analyzed, scrutinized, and dissected in the recorded history of the 20th Century – political assassinations, the backlash to the Vietnam War, the civil rights movement, cities demolished, looted, and reduced to ash. But that's for someone else's book. Our 10th Floor studios did not dispense the news on Saturday night; our news was delivered in "concept albums," on vinyl LP's played on that new freeform FM radio. We had walked down the well-worn path of folk, folk-rock and protest songs and bridged the British Invasion, but by 1967 we were entering unfamiliar territory, the quicksand of psychedelic "acid-rock." This is where they began to lose me. I was a black-tie, tuxedo guy adrift in a tie-dyed, tee-shirt world.

Out in San Francisco, young people were embracing LSD, a trippy new way to listen to the cryptic innuendo buried within layers of recorded music. "Turn on, tune in, drop out" was the message that barefooted, beaded, bell-bottomed flower children would chant for the next ten years. "Don't Drop Bombs, Drop Acid" was the mantra. "Legalize Marijuana" was the bumper sticker. Head shops dotted the city, with flower-power paraphernalia, pipes and bowls and the fiddlers three – Chairman Mao, Che Guevara and Lenny Bruce pictured on giant black and white posters. The "Peace and Love" generation were fingering a peace sign with one hand, and torching a bong with the other. "Praise the Lord and Pass the Ammunition." The rush into a purple haze accelerated in the Seventies, a decade journalist Tom Wolfe famously labeled "The Me Generation."

The rhythm of Manhattan nightlife shifted as well. Rumba bands folded, finding new careers "parking cars and pumping gas" The new late-night "In Crowd" were the 'stoners', who found hipper, happening places like Max's Kansas City and Steve Paul's The Scene or the garish discotheques, Cheetah, Ondine and the Electric Circus, which offered live bands.

I read the news today, oh boy.

Murry Frymer, a reporter from *Newsday* wrote a brutally honest feature story, the most accurate ever written about the show and of my state of mind at that time. Murry began visiting the set, observing unobtrusively in the background, taking notes. His article appeared on September 25, 1967:

"The 10th Floor of the Daily News building, the home of Ch. 11: It's a little grim. The walls are yellowing. A long corridor leads to the studio. People are standing around, including a bunch of teenagers, most of them who are roughly dressed – boys with long hair, skinny tall girls in tight little miniskirts. Everybody looks tired. Clay Cole, a shiny young man with a loud tie, sits in a corner and he looks tired. 'I hate doing the show the way I have to do it,' said Cole. 'Tape has destroyed my enthusiasm for TV. It takes all the fun out of it.' The night's taping is over and the group lines up for their free records and jokes about its Chicken Delight dinner. Cole, who has heard the gags before, jokes back mildly. The set sits there looking silly and, like everything else, tired. There are colored cages for the thin little girls to dance in. The girls, puffing languidly on their cigarettes and looking as fatigued as everyone else, leave as soon as their bit is taped." So now here is Cole, the biggest attraction at Ch. 11, a star at 29. He says he's ready to quit."

It was a long time coming, but I decided to quit – walk away from it all. I no longer related to my audience, or the shift in pop music to psychedelic rock and heavy metal. I felt like a lava lamp in a lighthouse, without purpose and out-of-place.

I had been invited to perform for a week at the legendary New York Paramount Theatre, the mystical stage with its spectacular orchestra pit that rises up on hydraulic lifts. I had seen the newsreels, Martin & Lewis hurling autographed photos from their dressing room window to the uproarious fans below, and Frank Sinatra and his squealing bobbysoxers, when Benny Goodman, reacting to the screeching girls, muttered, "What the f--- was that!" It was a historic theatre, but a lackluster week for me. Motown star Mary Wells ("My Guy") was our headliner with the Marvelettes, Ronnie Dove and Charlie & Inez Fox, whom I mistakenly introduced as Ike & Tina Turner one blurry-eyed matinee and neither the audience nor Charlie and Inez seemed to notice. My only backstage visitor was Frankie Lymon, wishing to borrow fifteen dollars, "train fare to a gig in Hartford," he said, but in reality it was money to score smack. There was no crush of well-wishers, telegrams or flowers; no celebrity drop-ins; no "center-of-the-universe" event like my Brooklyn Paramount shows. We would simply grind-out four shows a day, collected our pay and slip away, unnoticed. The thrill was gone. Murray the K was now staging holiday shows at the Brooklyn Fox theatre with groups like Cream, not my cup of tea.

I attempted to open another dance club in the pre-war, basement ballroom of the Essex House Hotel in downtown Newark, a space we called "Clay Cole's Land of 1000 Dances." Jay Fontana managed the room; I lived in a suite upstairs. We featured two live bands on stage and on weekends added two big-name attractions, always one white, one black, maybe the Duprees ("Have You Heard") at the early show and Ben E. King ("Stand by Me") for the late show. At first only sporadic fistfights erupted, but as the weeks wore on, slugfests escalated into dangerous brawls. Responding to the mêlées were two Newark cops, Carmine and Al, ironically one white, one black, who answered our call so often we became friends. The racial tension escalated to the point we were forced to close down the club. That signaled the end for me.

I informed Channel 11 that I would leave the program in January 1968, giving them eight weeks notice. "Clay Cole's Disk-O-Tek" was more popular than ever, so I was not deserting a sinking ship. Miraculously, they quickly found a replacement for me, a movie-star handsome, twenty-four year old Peter Martin from Canada. From *Canada!* "A snowball's chance in hell!" Knowing Channel 11's track record, I could have predicted they would hire the wrong person. They just didn't know – or understand – my audience. I was happy they had chosen a young man to replace me; I believed a youngster should take over for me. I was, after all, an old man, turning thirty. To my audience, he couldn't cut the mustard.

As a final indignity, Channel 11 management decreed that he sit next to me on my remaining four shows, as co-host. This was a clever maneuver on their part, meant to imply my personal endorsement of my new replacement and I did my best to make him comfortable. But even Peter Martin could sense that he was being manipulated at my expense. He requested that he not sit with me on my last show, a request that Channel 11 honored.

WPIX-TV also implied that I had discovered Martin, that he was my protégé and my choice as replacement. Matt Massina wrote in his *N. Y. Daily News* television column: "Cole spotted Martin last summer at Montreal's Expo 67, performing under the Gallic name Pierre Lalonde, appearing on a French-language Canadian TV show." This is all untrue. I have never been to Montreal, nor visited the Expo. The first time I laid eyes on Peter Martin was the night he sat next to me as co-host of my own show I was never aware of this deception until forty-years later while exploring news archives for this book. I also learned that Pierre's father, Jean Lalonde, was a popular singer, known as the "Bing Crosby of Canada" before World War II.

The special guest on my final show was Paul Anka, now the stage savvy 'superstar,' as generous as when appearing on my shows nine years earlier. The Cowsills appeared one last time, as a reminder that Sh-Boomers may be squeaky-clean and still achieve success in the music-biz. But, it was a remarkably uneventful hour until a surprise phone call from Jerry Lewis threw me. Barry Glazer simply placed a telephone on my table and said "pick it up."

On the other end was the manic-hyper Jerry Lewis, the wild and crazy one, babbling away. My first thought was that Jerry had pre-taped a greeting, so I sat quietly startled, letting him babble-on. After a long silence, Jerry said: "What's the matter, you never talked to a big star before?" He was *live*. I learned later that he arranged with Barry Glazer to phone me at a precise time, then went to his dressing room at NBC-Burbank and phoned as promised. Once again, I was humbled by his gesture. Then… it was over: "This is Clay Cole, thanking you very much and saying, *good-bye*."

Like many other Sixties signposts – drive-in movies, drug store soda fountains and *The Saturday Evening Post* – I simply vanished. Everything I accomplished beyond 1968 is irrelevant, not worthy of a footnote. No other period in my life brought me more joy than being front and center during the explosion and acceptance of rock 'n' roll. My fifteen years of fame filled me with a lifetime of memories, but it was time to move on. *"There is no better time than the first time, because you'll never have the first time again."*

My contract with Channel 11 dictated that I could not appear on any other New York station, so I left town, distancing myself from the long good-bye. A few months later, the *Daily News* announced, "Peter Martin has asked for and received permission to be released from his WPIX contract." Martin was now hosting a similar show, "Music Hop" in Montreal, Saturday night at 6:00.

As I had predicted, Peter Martin was overwhelmed, soon to be replaced by a series of guest hosts, finally settling on a permanent choice, the popular (and handsome) disc jockey Frankie Crocker. The final irony is, of course, Frankie Crocker is black. Channel 11 pulled out all the stops to book big-name artists onto the show, calling on Frankie Crocker's extensive Rolodex. In spite of Crocker's star power, the ratings fizzled; the show faded and within eight months, the show, now called "The Electric Village," was off the air. I took some selfish satisfaction hearing the news. It was an astonishing revelation. For the first time, it occurred to me that my audience tuned in to watch *me*. They liked me.

In the protective darkness of my bedroom, wrapped in my 400-thread-count comforter, I listened in horror to late-night radio bulletins, with tears on my pillow. Detroit in flames; Newark destroyed; Asbury Park in ruins; Riots. Arson. Looting! "Hark, Hark, What's that sound, everybody look what's going down." Life's wrecking ball then demolished the remaining symbols of my good times: the Apollo, the Brooklyn Paramount, Palisades Amusement Park, Reuben's, Ratner's and Rapoport's. The Copacabaña, Latin Quarter and Basin Street East were unable to compete with the cash pay-outs offered by Las Vegas casino showrooms and lost Peggy Lee and Trini Lopez, to be replaced by less illustrious attractions like Roberta Sherwood and Jimmy Roselli. The Stork Club shuttered amid the clamor of racial bias and union pickets. The jet set abandoned El Morocco for the sequestered safety of the ultra-exclusive discotheque, Le Club, operated by the Cassini Brothers, Igor and Oleg.

I had grumbled for years over the fact that not one second of videotape remains from my remarkable and historic shows – the Motown Show, the Rolling Stones, Tony Bennett and all those Brill Building songwriters. In the Sixties, videotape was on bulky, two-inch reels costing about $200, so tapes were erased or recorded over as a cost-cutting directive from Channel 11 managers. The front office penny-pinchers could not imagine the future significance of those archives. Forget about the fiscal value; what about the historical importance. With forethought or direction, I could have purchased the tapes and owned the material; a personal manager would have negotiated that into my contract. Life is full of obstacles; in my case, I was the chief obstacle.

Years later, David Hinckley reflected in the *NY Daily News*, "Clay Cole launched one of New York's most famous rock-'n'-roll TV shows, and while no video survives, "The Clay Cole Show" imprinted on a few million teenagers. Cole's show was more than just another local knockoff because he had the whole New York music industry to draw on, and to watch him."

Today, I find it providential that no video remains; memories are much more indelible, a more powerful image. In the imagination, it's always summertime, we are forever young and the world is filled with possibilities. Weren't we something?

Remarkably, I never had another stretch of depression, no more blue funks. A stress-induced stiff-neck I had suffered throughout the Sixties, to which I tended by crazily rotating my head, diminished, and then disappeared. I finally got my head together; now my body is falling apart. I was left with one occupational hazard from those days, Tinnitus, a piercing, high-pitch ringing in my ears. Specialists at The Eye, Ear, Nose and Throat Hospital diagnosed the probable cause as the high-decibel volume emitted by rock bands.

Truthfully, I never imagined I would make it to this age. Rock stars, notorious for their "crash and burn" lifestyles really are more likely than other people to die before reaching old age. A recent study of more than a thousand British and American artists, spanning the era from Elvis Presley to rapper Eminem, found they were two to three times more likely to suffer a premature death than the general population. Then there's the aging rockers credo: "Old rockers never die ... they just tour Australia."

Relinquishing my former big-shot celebrity status did have its downside. I was no longer ushered to the front of the line at government bureaus, Radio City Music Hall or urinals. I can now enjoy the privacy of a public toilet without peeping pen pals. I'm off the A-list, RSVP events and VIP seating; I see movies with the masses, not in private screening rooms. I no longer get the best table in restaurants, but I can dine without ear-bending intruders who disrupt dinner mid-bite, chatting away, snapping Instamatics, while my linguini cools.

In 1975, HBO invited me to host a two hour concert, "Clay Cole's 20 Year of Rock 'n' Roll," their first-ever special event, from the stage of Rockland Community College in upstate New York. Great performers from my earlier years, the Drifters, Coasters, Platters, Skyliners, the Five Satins and the Brooklyn Bridge, appeared in what was to be my last grand hurrah. Naturally, *that* videotape remains to haunt me forever, and it was an embarrassing performance. I arrived in the early morning feeling disoriented, unable to focus, clearly disconnected. "Probably a seasonal allergy," was the diagnosis of an obliging production assistant, who handed me some sort of medication. As the day wore on, the pill just seemed to make matters worse. I was out-of-focus, as if under water.

My backstage interviews with the groups (which were taped and edited into the concert later on) were slapdash and amateurish. Johnny Maestro, who had merged with the Del Satins to form the Brooklyn Bridge ("Worst That Could Happen"), gave me the best laugh of the day, albeit a disturbing moment of truth: I asked him to recall the worst moment of his career. He snapped back, "this interview!" To compound the fracture, on stage I introduced his hit "Sixteen Candles" as "Happy Birthday Sweet Sixteen." So, my single remaining legacy is a two-hour video, repeated endlessly on HBO, then syndicated to broadcast television stations and then made available to collectors on VHS cassettes, and now on DVD. You are only as good as your last show.

I learned late in life that "no good deed goes unpunished" and in fact, may come back to bite you. Jay Fontana was no Boy Scout, but he loved to "do good deeds." In the late 60s, while managing the Del Satins, he came to the aid of several successful New York musicians – including Hank Mendress of the Tokens and Les Cauchi and Tommy Ferrara of the Del Satins – who had received their draft notices. Serving in the military would severely impact their rising careers, much like Clyde McPhatter, Jack Scott, and Jimmy Clanton who served honorably, but lost momentum. It wasn't until 1973, at the end of the Vietnam War, that Congress abolished the draft in favor of an all-volunteer Army.

Jay became an intermediary, attempting to impede their deferment; money exchanged hands and Jay was caught, and indicted. Hank, Tommy, Les and the others packed off to basic training.

In 1974, Jay pleaded with me to join him in managing the Mambo-Hy Agency, a service for nightclubs who featured an ever-changing line-up of 'go-go girls'. Mambo-Hy (Hyman Balick, a former dancer at the bungalow colonies of the old Jewish Catskills) had died suddenly and club owners demanded an uninterrupted flow of fresh faces – and we had hundreds of fresh faces. But the 'go-go girl' dance scene was getting bolder and the dancers, eager for larger tips, began flashing more than smiles. We were on the cusp of the topless era, but *our* girls were required to wear pasties, g-strings and net stocking. Wait, it gets better.

In the middle of all this madness, scheduling hundreds of girls in multiple shifts in dozens of clubs, I was targeted as a sexual predator. One by one, our "dancers" were receiving confidential phone calls from "Clay Cole" offering $1000 one night stands with a wealthy client. Several girls met this "customer" at a designated motel, where they were severely denigrated, assaulted and robbed.

It was happening almost daily; each morning Jay Fontana would receive a phone message from a distraught, abandoned girl, in some far-off motel, accusing me of being in cahoots with this deranged deviant. The girls assured Jay that the voice on the phone was mine, coercing them into prostitution. As the days progressed, it became even more terrifying for me. Many of the girl's husbands and boyfriends were now after me and not to share lunch. I was going to be lunch!

All the hundreds of ladies on our roster were alerted, and sure enough, "Peaches" – my favorite of all the girls – got the call. She agreed to meet the man at his white Cadillac parked outside a Queens' subway stop. Jay rallied the troops and bashed him in the head with a telephone receiver ripped from a near-by phone booth. Jay was arrested and the perp was rushed to the hospital.

I arrived at the police station with a taxi cab overflowing with tits and ass, ladies fuming with anger, cursing like sailors and threatening vengeance. Lucky us! Our cab arrived at the exact moment that the cops were returning the "victim" from the hospital, his head swathed in turban-like bandages. What a riot! The precinct boys were giddy with delight, licking their chops over the half-dozen clams on the half-shell who suddenly descended into their headquarters, squealing profanities at the terrified captive. The cops were equally baffled – a Catch-22 – who was the victim here? The ladies claimed to have been the victims, but they *had* accepted the offer to engage in prostitution, and Jay *had* committed assault and battery with a deadly weapon – a telephone – and the perpetrator *was* a dangerous sex maniac, a real creep. The cops simply locked-up everyone until this madness could be sorted out. The only truly innocent player was me.

We later determined that this sicko obtained the ladies personal phone numbers from our answering service. He would call the service early in the morning before office hours pretending to be me and the operator would give him all the messages with phone numbers. He'd then tell the operator to "hold the messages and repeat them to Jay when he checks in."

In 1979, I created the "People" show on CBS, with Raysa Bonow and David Susskind, based on the popular magazine. Phyllis George was signed-on to host, but David was having problems finding a male co-host, and asked me to do a screen test. I quickly forgot all about it and was in Baltimore taping a segment with teen-idol David Cassidy, when I got an urgent phone call: "Return to Manhattan immediately. Susskind wants to see you!"

David loved my test and offered me $5000 a week to co-host with Phyllis George. Zowie! CBS primetime with Miss America! David presented me to CBS for approval, and in the time it takes to drink a celebratory martini, I was rejected. CBS ran a background check and my association with the operator of a topless go-go agency sent up a red flag. If the show were a success, the press would surely expose me; much too risky for the conservative purists at CBS.

There is a topper to this story. Jay had allowed two young, would-be filmmakers Nicholas St John and Abel Ferrara to use one of our unused offices to write screenplays. They quietly witnessed the tension of this ongoing daily drama. In July of 1984, I was invited to the film premier of "Fear City," written by Nicholas St John and directed by Abel Ferrara, based on the episode, but with the drama heightened to include murder. Jay and I were played by Tom Berenger and Jack Scalia, with a cast that included Billy Dee Williams, Melanie Griffith and Rossano Brazzi.

I spent the next thirty-five years living the gypsy life, a solitary nomad. Unencumbered, with no ties or attachments, I became a freelance television producer, loyal only to the one who signed the checks. Like a private eye, I took on the case and solved the crime. I worked when I pleased, always available, packed and ready to go. Its feast or famine for a freelancer – broke most of the time, then short bursts of the high-life. The perks are first-rate: four-star hotels with room service, first-class air travel, and an expense account. I was able to travel America, not as a tourist, but living for extended periods in all our great cities, Hollywood, Philadelphia, Boston, Tampa, Dallas, Cleveland, Indianapolis and D.C., always returning home to Manhattan to resume my life as a New Yorker.

I explored Europe royally; first class to Monaco with Gloria Gaynor, during the Monte Carlo Grand Prix, performing for the royal family, as well as France, Sweden, Germany, the Netherlands and, finally, to England, then roughing it through Asia, six days in Turkey with a busload of celebrity look-a-like drag queens, then an oppressive six-months in communist China, jazzing-up a dismal $40-million amusement park.

There was a welcome irony in my very last job. When I first arrived in Manhattan in the summer of 1957, "Volare," written and recorded by Domenico Modugno, was the big hit song, the grand prizewinner at the very first San Remo Song Festival in Italy and "record of the year" at the very first Grammy Awards in America. So now, I was invited to write and produce a two-hour television special, based on the 2002 San Remo Song Festival, which would mean three months work in Italy – Rome, Milan and San Remo. The annual San Remo Festival is like a full-season of "American Idol" condensed into five nightly, primetime broadcasts, a most impressive way to bookend my television career.

Italy was unforgettable, to the credit of the youthful, all-girl production staff assembled by a princely-handsome television entrepreneur, Filippo Chiusano. Unlike most of the eager, young production assistants who came in and out of my life in America, Italian young people are rooted in deep respect of the wisdom acquired by old folks – it's in their genes. In spite of the devotion of my Italian staff, being young and spirited, they had lovers and friends to fill their nights. Rome is such a romantic city, meant to be shared with a lover. But love is for a very lucky few. For me, dinner for two was me and a damn good waiter. I dined each night in a cozy thirty-table trattoria, just around the corner from my hotel, in the heart of the Piazza Navona, with my waiter Franco.

San Remo 2002 featured the hottest international pop stars and, with the exception of Michael Bolton, it was an all-girl show:

Britney Spears	USA
Destiny's Child	USA
Alicia Keys	USA
Alanis Morissette	Canada
Anastasia	UK
Gabrielle	UK
Kylie Minogue	Australia
Shakira	Columbia
Paulina Rubio	Mexico
The Corrs	Ireland
The Cranberries	Ireland

Surrounded by all that pop diva Teen Spirit, surprisingly it was the arrival of our Latin-American host, Luciano Morad that set the Italian paparazzi spinning on their Vespas. Luciano, a towering Amazon beauty, is the infamous mother of Mick Jagger's love child, Lucas. Apparently, on a 1998 tour of Brazil, during a one-nighter in Sao Paulo, the Mick *schtupped* Ms. Morad. This made Luciano Morad very "preggie." This made Jerry Hall very grumpy. This made Mick write checks. Each got Satisfaction.

As a boy, sitting in the darkness of the Palace Theatre in Hubbard, Ohio, I never imagined I would someday be attaching Hong Kong, Istanbul, Rome, and Monte Carlo stickers to my steamer trunk. I never thought I'd own a steamer trunk! All these exotic places seemed so remote and unreachable to me. My rewards have been beyond my wildest dreams. Along the way, I also won two Emmy Awards as "producer of outstanding entertainment programming" (NARAS), topped only by my induction into the NYPD Honor Legion, my proudest distinction. Pardon me, if I take a step back and say "Wow! What a wonderful life I've had."

As I look back, I realize I was born at the perfect place and time; I was allowed to savor the cool, romanticism of Glenn Miller, Louis Armstrong, Nat "King" Cole, Perry Como, Peggy Lee, and Count Basie, before the heat of rock 'n' roll overtook me. I still tear-up each time I hear Paul McCartney sing "Baby I'm Amazed." Sadly, only a dwindling number of Sh-Boomers remember these milestones in modern music.

Tony Bennett had not meant to be pessimistic when he told Esquire in 2003, "History always tells us what the future holds." But, he raises an interesting hypothesis; since young people today have no memory of Irving Berlin, Cole Porter, or the Gershwin's, it begs the question: "Is there some mighty force of music, unknown to us, waiting out there to erase the memories of Lennon & McCartney, Bacharach & David, Leiber & Stoller, Pomus & Shuman and Ashford & Simpson?" *You, betcha!*

Today's music can be so irritating, it is played as "torture music" to prisoners in Iraq, Afghanistan, at Abu Ghraib and Guantanamo Bay, where terrorist are treated to the full non-stop blast of Britney Spears, Metallica. AC/DC, Aerosmith, Dr Dre and Eminem's Slim Shady.

It was the Gershwin's who wrote the song that has haunted me since I was a teenager:

> *"Where is the shepherd for this lost lamb?"*
> *"I'm a little lamb who's lost in the wood*
> *I know I could, Always be good*
> *To one who'll watch over me."*

I like the words. I like the beat. Save the last dance …for me.

Coda

"Old age is no place for sissies."
– *Bette Davis*

I left Manhattan on September 1, 2001. As a farewell, my "Claymates" fan club founder Marcia Habib rounded up some new recruits for a night on the town, winding down at a laid-back little piano bar in the Village. Maxine Brown sang my Gershwin song.

The next afternoon, as Marcia and I shared a champagne Sunday brunch at the Water Club, she quietly pressed into my hand the keys to a Cadillac Deville. Marcia does not take pleasure in splashy displays of affection; her gestures are muted, but generous beyond imagining. My pet name for Marcia is "*Marciabird*," so I christened my big, blue Cadillac, "the Bluebird."

A few days later, the World Trade Center became ground zero.

I now live at the beach, "a quaint little drinking village with a fishing problem" – an island off North Carolina, where the Cape Fear River flows into the Atlantic Ocean. I quickly discovered "this idyllic paradise" does have its downside; a few distractions the real estate lady forgot to mention. We are situated directly in the path of seasonal hurricanes, (which, in itself, is ok by me; I am happily invigorated by thunderstorms and torrential rain.) But, we are also just three miles downwind of a nuclear power plant that shares riverside acreage with the largest military ammunition port in the nation, the Army's warehouse for bullets and bombs, sent by barge down the Cape Fear River, out to sea and off to the warfront. Hurricanes, a nuclear power plant and a munitions warehouse confirm that, no matter where you choose to settle down, all men are cremated equal.

285

Oak Island is not a resort destination, rather a family community that happens to sit between the Intercostals and the Atlantic Ocean, with its exceptional South-facing beaches. It is a village of summer homes handed down from generation to generation. In the summertime, tourists appear in store-creased Big Kahuna shirts and Tommy Bahama straw hats, looking very much like those fruity rum concoctions with the paper umbrellas. In the winter hunting season, the locals pack away their shorts and sandals, favoring camouflage, arriving for their morning coffee dressed as shrubbery. I have very little in common with the locals. I do not fish, hunt, kayak, play golf or bridge, collect seashells or harvest azaleas. I have no grandchildren. I am not into long, moonlit walks, beach blanket bingo or shag dancing, which immediately disqualifies me from computer dating. I am perhaps the only local who owns the "Cooking for One" recipe book.

Nowadays, to me, 'happy hour' is a nap. (Chika-boom!)

Old Age, I decided, is a gift. I am now, probably for the first time in my life, the person I have always wanted to be. Retirement suits me; I feel like a kid again. I live on a five-dollar allowance, bologna sandwiches and Popsicles. Nevertheless, the days, weeks and months pass quickly. I'm kept busy searching for misplaced essentials, like car keys, bifocals or my remote control. This is where a wife would come in handy – women always know where things are.

Our island is a fisherman's paradise, with the ocean, rivers, canals, Intercostals, and two piers for casting a line. The Midway Trading Co. over on the mainland proudly displays a giant neon sign in their window announcing "Worms and Coffee." Bloodworms are sold everywhere, in the cooler right next to the Popsicles. Sushi is called bait. Our medium-sized, salty-fresh local oysters are succulent and peal-and-eat shrimp is available straight off the boat. Watching shrimp boats gather offshore at sunset is a wistful reminder of why I'm here, drawn to the mystery and majesty of the ocean.

Down here, seafood restaurants offer the local favorites, hush puppies, shrimp with grits and Calabash-style spicy, lightly fried seafood. Years ago, when Jimmy Durante performed in Myrtle Beach, he would bring his troupers up to Calabash, NC for a seafood feast at Lucy Coleman's little sea shack. Jimmy called her "Mrs. Calabash."

It's impossible to find a Kosher Corned Beef sandwich on sesame-seed rye with spicy mustard, a half-and-half pickle and a Dr. Brown's Cream Soda. O, how I miss the Carnegie Deli.

This is also NASCAR country. Before Marcia gifted me with a car as big as a Chris Craft, I never owned a vehicle. That generated lots of laughs from the boys down at the DMV. Lady drivers here are amazing; they can smoke a Camel, drink a Dr. Pepper and chat on the cell phone, simultaneously honking and waving at the neighbors. Men have not yet learned that motor vehicles come with a turn signal; they are never used. Western Auto will never run out of replacement bulbs. A popular Tarheel bumper sticker pretty much sums-up the local sentiment: "We don't care *how* you did it up North."

Music is still my major passion. Radio is my daytime companion; I prefer the "Beach, Boogie, and Blues" stations that play Dionne and Dion and the rest of my old gang. Down here country music is the big-thing. It's catchy. I got caught hummin' it just the other day:

"I ain't good as I once was,
My how the years have flown,
But there was a time back in my prime,
When I could really hold my own.

Toby Keith. I can dance with that.

Country music radio is like mosquitoes – in the air, buzzin' around, gettin' under your skin, takin' bloody bites. The tradeoff is, I no longer have to suffer Mariah, Celine or Whitney. When they start to yodel, it's time to roll out the weed-whacker. I prefer my yodelers in Resistol hats, Justin boots and Wrangler jeans.

I am also surrounded by my lifetime collection of LP's, thousands of neatly stacked vinyl, marking the days, weeks, months and decades of my life. Tony Bennett. Dinah Washington. The Beatles. Saturday Night Fever. Johnny Mathis. Magic moments in life are measured by music and music triggers memories. Was there no greater joy than removing the cellophane from a new album, the smell of factory-fresh vinyl, the smooth, unblemished surface, the cover art and graphics, reading, then re-reading the liner notes looking for clues? The album cover was also the perfect surface for extracting seeds and stems from a nickel bag of Panama Red. And music, it's a miracle – a tone that floats through the air and strikes an emotional chord in your soul. How could that be?

Crying is another good thing. It's affirmation that we are still alive and can still feel something – *anything*! I cried when Ernie Kovacs died. I cried when Johnny bid farewell to the "Tonight" show. I cry watching Jerry's kids or Bob Hope's USO shows. Returning troops embracing wives and babies, hero firemen and cops, school kids making sacrifices, kind-hearted nobodies doing good deeds, all make me weepy. I cry watching "American Idol," for gawd sake!

Sometimes, I set myself up for a good tearjerker. For instance, every Christmas, I light-up a few candles, snuggle up under blankets and watch "Umbrellas of Cherbourg." Before the final fadeout, when the snow falls on that Esso Station and Michel Legrand's music swells up, so do my tears. This one motion picture has been my perennial manifestation of lost youth, broken promises, shattered dreams and unrequited love – a weeper to be sure.

Show me a man who doesn't sits back to watch "Field of Dreams," knowing full well he'll be bawling by the final credits. Same goes for "Forrest Gump" and "Saving Private Ryan." Bob Dylan says, "I don't trust a man who doesn't tear up a little watching Old Yeller." I was totally blind-sighted by "Brokeback Mountain;" like a kick in the gut. A fence needs two posts was the message; it's as simple as that. I grieved for Ennis del Mar like a best friend. It's such a secret place, the land of tears.

I now live my life like a character in my own TV show. In *my* show, I am the star – there are no co-stars, sidekicks, feature players, guest stars or ensemble cast. Friends come and go; enemies accumulate – a person who knows no one has no enemies. There is no script, I make it up as I go along, keeping it fresh, keeping it interesting. Cancellation is an imminent threat. I live every day as if it were my last, because one of these days I'll be right. In my show, I'm not a hero. I have not acted bravely under fire, saved lives or changed the world. So, I live my life in the pursuit of one simple virtue, that one day, I might merely be remembered as a good person. Sh-Boom!

Here, There and Everywhere

Dad – Eight months after Mom died in 1965, Dad married the widow next door, Virginia Biggerstaff, a by-the-book, proper Southern lady, who raised Brother Rick and Sister Tama, while continuing a sixty-year career as Managing Editor of the local newspaper. Each night, dinner was served on fine china, with fresh flowers, soft music and candlelight. Neighborhood boys would kneel at their window in the dark, dumbstruck by such a civilized scene. (Photo above, dad and me in the dining room, the candles lighted.) Dad died in 1995, at age 86, but his demise came years earlier as he slowly fell into the shrouded arms of Alzheimer's.

Edna and Clay Cole – "Uncle Clay" Cole retired to Ft. Lauderdale, Florida, amassing a second fortune developing several profitable publishing ventures. Working in his home-library late one night, he swiveled in his desk chair, fell and snapped his neck, killing himself instantly. His million-dollar insurance policy generated a double indemnity payout to his widow. "Uncle Clay" left a six million-dollar estate and a living will to provide for Edna's well being. Their paintings, antiques, object d'art were all photographed, tagged and catalogued, and his brand-new Cadillac rested on deflated tires in the basement garage under a blanket of dust.

I visited Edna in her Galt Ocean Drive condominium and was greeted by a fragile recluse, terrified she might displease the bankers and lawyers placed in her charge, fearful her assigned caretakers would withhold her weekly stipend. Edna lived on a $125 allowance and dined at Denny's. Paranoia drove her batty. She died a decade later of natural causes.

Brother Jim: First Lieutenant **Jim Rucker**, USMC came home from service in Vietnam, (1965-1969) physically powerful, but mentally wounded, with the echo of "incoming" still resonating in his subconscious. Jim was looking forward to returning to the tranquility of college, the solidarity of Fraternity and he resumed studies at Kent State University, May 1, 1970. Noontime on May 4th, as he was shuttling between classes, gunfire erupted on campus. Ohio National Guardsmen had opened fire on a group of students, killing four. Others lay bleeding. With the nightmare killing fields of Vietnam still fresh in his head, he was now witnessing blood spilled on American soil. These were troubling times for him, but Jim's salvation was Jesus Christ, and with spiritual guidance, he now lives the Christian life with his wife Sherry and three grown sons. Jim became a graphic artist, recognized in his field as one of our country's top designers of environmental graphics; among his projects were Disney's Animal Kingdom Lodge, Mandalay Bay Casino Hotel, Sea Pines at Hilton Head and The Palace of the Lost City in Johannesburg.

Brother Rick aspired to be a baseball player, but his sports career was cut short at age 18 by a brutal automobile accident. Being part Cherokee, little brother Rick is a life-long, devoted fan of the Cleveland Indians. Rick is our family historian; his steel-trap mind can call up minute details, times and places, what we wore and what we ate. Rick is also a movie buff and a few summers past, while attending a family reunion in Newport Beach, California, Rick asked me to join him on a pilgrimage to John Wayne's gravesite. The headstone was etched with a rendering of John Ford's Monument Valley, with the inscription:

> *"Tomorrow is the most important thing in life,*
> *Comes into us at midnight very clean.*
> *It's perfect when it arrives and puts itself in our hands.*
> *It hopes that we've learned something from yesterday."*

Rick has found a peaceful life with his wife, Dinah, just down the road from me on the ocean. When the mood strikes him, he cooks Grandpa Nash's secret-recipe meatballs and spaghetti, and we dine and reminisce about where we've been, what we wore and what we ate.

Sister Tama (Vallarino), the wilderness child, retreated, with her master's degree, to Alaska, as a marine biologist. Many years ago, Tama and her future-husband Mark journeyed 'cross country, camping out in our national parks, arriving at my doorstep in Manhattan looking disheveled, with backpacks and bedrolls, intending to sleep the night in Central Park. Today, they are devotees of four-star hotels with amenities, traveling the world with a Michelin Guide and their smarter-than-a-whip son Trevor, who can say "please" and "thank you" in seven languages.

My New York friends **Peter Salerno, Murray Grand** and **Jay Fontana** moved, as most natives do, to Florida. **Raysa Bonow**, after hop-scotching all over the east coast with her beloved beagles, eventually returned home to Youngstown, Ohio. **Marcia Habib**, born in New York, remains, dedicated to her Sutton Dog Parlour, successfully entering it's forth decade, grooming the puppies of the yuppies of the Upper East Side.

Ray Reneri is still 'king of the rock 'n' roll road," but when he gets off the tour bus, it's New Jersey he calls home, just a stones throw to the GW Bridge. His road show stars, Jerry Lee Lewis, Chuck Berry and Little Richard have become the three old lions of rock 'n' roll, cranky and ornery; Ray is the only one I know who can enter their cage without a chair or a whip and make these old cats roll over and purr. Ray has staged over fifty rock 'n' roll shows at Madison Square Garden, finally finding his arena as "the Günther Gebel-Williams of Rock 'n' Roll."

Georgia Winters, Editor-in-Chief of *16* magazine (1958-1975) left the magazine after seventeen years, following a dispute with her publisher. At the time *16* had more than five-million readers. In 1983, Georgia, a long term smoker, died of lung cancer at Presbyterian Hospital in New York. She was 56 years old.

Roz Ross, my GAC / William Morris agent, moved to the west coast to work with Dick Clark and – like many of her big-name clients – was never heard from again.

Connie De Nave, the maharishna of pop-rock babble-on, retired in the 70s, married a photographer and opened an upper Eastside pizzeria; the "crust" is extra-thin, but they lay on the "cheese" real thick.

Lillian Roxon, the Australian journalist, died in the early seventies from an acute asthma attack, shortly after completing her monumental Roxon's Rock Encyclopedia.

Jules Podell's Copacabana, (10 West 60th St) closed down in the early seventies after 40 years; for a brief period it operated as a disco. The Apollo, like Radio City Music Hall, abandoned its stage show policy; these legendary showplaces are now venues for concerts and special events.

Demolished as well were the Brooklyn Paramount, the New York Paramount and Ben Maksik's Town and Country in Brooklyn (at 3000 seats, the world's largest night club, and for a short-lived dance club, Clay Cole's Action City in 1967.) Reuben's, Ratner's and Rapoport's – Gone!

Also gone are the Peppermint Lounge, the Wagon Wheel, Headliner, Barney Googles, Rascals, Rolling Stone, Trude Heller's, Town Hill, Elegante' on Ocean Parkway, 5000 Club, Johnny M's Safari Club, Long Island's Action House and New Jersey's Rag Doll, Cat & the Fiddle lounge, Luciano's, Smart Set, Rahway Rec, Choo Choo Club and Crocitto's on Staten Island; the Rainbow Club (Wildwood). Still rocking after all these years is Martell's Sea Breeze Club (Point Pleasant Beach), Surf Club (Orley Beach), and the Beach Club (Seaside Hts.)

Index

303

316

About the Author

Clay Cole is one of *live* television's true pioneers, beginning in 1953 at age 15, as host and producer of his own Saturday night teenage music show. By the time he was 21, he was the wildly-popular singing-dancing star of New York's top-rated *Clay Cole Show* from 1959 to 1968.

Clay has written and produced over 3500 broadcast television shows, winning two Emmy Awards, and induction into the NYPD Honor Legion, his proudest moment.

After forty-four years as a New Yorker, Clay now lives on a remote island in North Carolina, where the Cape Fear River flows into the Atlantic, "a quaint little drinking village with a fishing problem."

www.claycoleshow.com

David Hinckley joined the *New York Daily News* in 1980 and has spent most of his years there writing about music, radio and television. He has also served as critic-at-large, from which perch he has tried to frame a context for modern American popular culture while often settling for a reference to Chuck Berry or the Brooklyn Dodgers. He lives in New Jersey with his wife and more recordings than he'll ever be able to listen to.

BUY A SHARE OF THE FUTURE IN YOUR COMMUNITY

These certificates make great holiday, graduation and birthday gifts that can be personalized with the recipient's name. The cost of one S.H.A.R.E. or one square foot is $54.17. The personalized certificate is suitable for framing and will state the number of shares purchased and the amount of each share, as well as the recipient's name. The home that you participate in "building" will last for many years and will continue to grow in value.

Here is a sample SHARE certificate:

HABITAT FOR HUMANITY

THIS CERTIFIES THAT

__YOUR NAME HERE__

HAS INVESTED IN A HOME FOR A DESERVING FAMILY

1985-2005

TWENTY YEARS OF BUILDING FUTURES IN OUR COMMUNITY ONE HOME AT A TIME

1200 SQUARE FOOT HOUSE @ $65,000 = $54.17 PER SQUARE FOOT
This certificate represents a tax deductible donation. It has no cash value.

YES, I WOULD LIKE TO HELP!

I support the work that Habitat for Humanity does and I want to be part of the excitement! As a donor, I will receive periodic updates on your construction activities but, more importantly, I know my gift will help a family in our community realize the dream of homeownership. I would like to SHARE in your efforts against substandard housing in my community! (Please print below)

PLEASE SEND ME _____ SHARES at $54.17 EACH = $ $_____

In Honor Of: _____

Occasion: (Circle One) HOLIDAY BIRTHDAY ANNIVERSARY

OTHER: _____

Address of Recipient: _____

Gift From: _____ *Donor Address:* _____

Donor Email: _____

I AM ENCLOSING A CHECK FOR $ $_____ PAYABLE TO HABITAT FOR HUMANITY **OR** PLEASE CHARGE MY VISA OR MASTERCARD *(CIRCLE ONE)*

Card Number _____ Expiration Date: _____

Name as it appears on Credit Card _____ Charge Amount $ _____

Signature _____

Billing Address _____

Telephone # Day _____ Eve _____

PLEASE NOTE: Your contribution is tax-deductible to the fullest extent allowed by law.
Habitat for Humanity • P.O. Box 1443 • Newport News, VA 23601 • 757-596-5553
www.HelpHabitatforHumanity.org

LaVergne, TN USA
08 October 2009

160246LV00003B/6/P